Third
Edition

UNDERSTANDING AND MANAGING DIVERSITY

Readings, Cases, and Exercises

Carol P. Harvey

Assumption College

M. June Allard

Worcester State College

PEARSON
Prentice
Hall

PEARSON EDUCATION INTERNATIONAL

Project Manager: Ashley Keim
Senior Acquisitions Editor: Jennifer Simon
Editor-in-Chief: Jeff Shelstad
Media Project Manager: Jessica Sabloff
Marketing Manager: Anke Braun
Marketing Assistant: Patrick Dansuzo
Managing Editor: John Roberts
Permissions Supervisor: Charles Morris
Manufacturing Buyer: Michelle Klein
Production Manager: Arnold Vila
Cover Design: Bruce Kenselaar
Cover Photo: Todd Davidson/Illustration Works, Inc./Getty Images, Inc.
Composition: Integra
Full-Service Project Management: Pine Tree Composition, Inc.
Printer/Binder: Phoenix

Pearson Education LTD.
Pearson Education Singapore, Pte. Ltd
Pearson Education, Canada, Ltd
Pearson Education–Japan

Pearson Education Australia PTY, Limited
Pearson Education North Asia Ltd
Pearson Educación de Mexico, S.A. de C.V.
Pearson Education Malaysia, Pte. Ltd
Pearson Education, Upper Saddle River, New Jersey

10 9 8 7 6 5 4 3 2 1
ISBN 0-13-129391-5

From June: Dedicated to family and friends
without whose support this book would not be possible.

From Carol: Dedicated to Steve, Kevin, and David Harvey whose
support and love makes this work possible.

Contents

Preface—For the Instructor

Diversity is a more controversial topic today than it was when the second edition of this book was published four years ago. Due to immigration patterns, changing demographics, increasing global business, and technological innovation, there is no question that the composition of today's workforce is more diverse. However, recent high-profile lawsuits, such as Texaco, Denny's, and Coca-Cola, showcase the human, public relations, and financial costs of failing to understand and effectively manage this new workforce.

Consequently, learning how to motivate, communicate, and work productively with coworkers, subordinates, managers, and customers who may differ in significant ways is a necessary workplace skill. A recent survey of American colleges and universities found that 63 percent of them currently have or are planning to add a diversity course requirement to their curriculum. Organizations, too, recognize this need. Millions of dollars are spent every year on diversity training efforts.

Effective diversity management is a complex issue. We believe that both individuals and organizations need to begin the process by becoming more knowledgeable about their values and beliefs as well as those of people who may be different in their salient social identities. Increased awareness and heightened understanding become the foundation on which individual and organizational changes can build. Superficial diversity efforts, like unexamined thinking, often produce superficial results. Diversity efforts involve both individual and organizational development.

OBJECTIVES FOR THIS EDITION

Two goals motivated us to produce the third edition: first, to make teaching diversity-related courses easier for the instructor by providing a wide range of classroom material and instructor support material, and second, to make learning about diversity interesting, timely, and thought provoking for the students.

Teaching about diversity is more complex than teaching other courses. Clearly diversity is an interdisciplinary field. Much of its theoretical framework originates in the social sciences. Adapting and applying this material to organizational diversity issues can be a challenge. Because of the rapid increase in college-level diversity courses over the past ten years, many of those who teach in this field are struggling to find appropriate classroom materials that balance the theoretical with practical applications to meet the learning needs of their students. Although we teach in business and psychology, our contributors represent a wide range of additional disciplines such as sociology, history, and English. Teaching diversity-related courses can be draining for the instructor because these topics often challenge students' core beliefs, generate conflict, and require a high level of student involvement in the learning process.

There is little agreement among scholars on the definition of diversity, much less what should be included in a diversity textbook. Many books and courses focus only on some or all of the so-called primary dimensions of individual difference such as race, gender, ethnicity, age, sexual orientation, and physical/mental challenges, which was how we organized the first edition. Others extend the definition to include secondary dimensions, such as religion, social class, communication style, and family status, and this was one of the changes that we added in our second edition. Both the first and the second editions were organized by separating the readings, cases, and exercises into separate sections.

CHANGES IN THE THIRD EDITION

To meet these challenges, we gathered a wealth of information from those who best understand these issues: faculty and trainers who teach courses involving diversity. As part of the process, we compiled data from over 50 syllabi both from instructors who used our previous editions and from those who used other texts. In addition, our second edition was thoroughly reviewed by professors who used that book over several semesters and who told us frankly what worked in their classes, what didn't, and what they thought should be included in the third edition.

This wealth of information resulted in an extensive revision with many changes in terms of organization, content, and approach. In this edition, we divided the material into three logical sections working from the micro to the macro level. In the Instructor's Manual, available online and in print to adopters, these sections are all integrated into an analytical framework that incorporates the development of critical thinking skills.

- **Section I—Individual Perspectives** serves as a foundation to the study of diversity by increasing students' personal awareness in terms of ethnocentrism, values, stereotypes, conflict, and communication.
- **Section II—Group Identity Perspectives** provides a foundation of understanding for some of the complexities and issues of many different and multiple group identities.
- **Section III—Organizational Perspectives** examines diversity issues put into action within organizational contexts.

Reviewers told us that one of the strengths of the second edition of the book was the experiential material, and they asked us for additional exercises. As a result, we have added fifteen totally new exercises and revised and updated four from the previous edition.

Our analysis of adopters' (and nonadopters') syllabi for required readings revealed that there is no one authority in this field, and this is as it should be. By its nature, the study of diversity requires multiple perspectives. We have reprinted classic essays by major authors such as Milton Bennett, Peggy McIntosh, Thomas Sowell, Deborah Tannen, David Thomas, and Robin Ely. We added new material on ethics (McNett), the business case for diversity (Robison and Dechant), intercultural communication (Bennett), media (Allard #36), first-person accounts of experiencing diversity (Baldino, Diodati, Ross and Whitty), several Web-based exercises (Sherer #22 & #33, Harvey #48), and material on diversity in the NAFTA countries (Muller on Mexico, Hunt #3, and Mentzer on Canada). In addition, each of the three sections now begins with learning outcomes and ends with a capstone reading, assignment, or exercise designed to assess student achievement in terms of the material.

INSTRUCTOR'S MANUAL

In keeping with our belief that diversity is a complex subject to teach, we have prepared a comprehensive instructor's manual available through your Prentice Hall sales representative to simplify your class preparation work. The material includes sample syllabi; matrices for incorporating the readings, cases, and exercises text into Human Resources, Organizational Behavior, Diversity with a social science approach, and Management courses; teaching tips; website resources; suggestions for related assignments; answers to discussion questions; a list of suggested video resources; and PowerPoint slides. Adopters should contact their Prentice Hall sales representative for a user name and password for access to this site, which is located at www.prenhall.com/Harvey.

ACKNOWLEDGMENTS

In terms of this text, the sum is far greater than its individual parts. We wish to thank the contributing authors whose work reflects their expertise in terms of teaching and learning about diversity. They are the core of this text. We are grateful to our reviewers for their honesty and constructive suggestions. We have incorporated many of your ideas into this edition. Our thanks go to Joyce McNichols, Anna Maria College; Dr. Helen J. Muller, University of New Mexico; and Marge Zuba, Capalla University.

Thank you to Julie Kieck and Larry Spongberg of Assumption College, and Pamela McKay, Linda Ellis, and Sharon Corey of Worcester State College. We couldn't have done this without your efforts. We appreciate the assistance from the staff at Prentice Hall, particularly Jennifer Simon, Acquisitions Editor, Ashley Keim, our much appreciated and ever so efficient Project Manager, Jessica Sabloff, Media Project Manager, Anke Braun, Marketing Manager, and John Roberts, Managing Editor. Special thanks also go to John Shannon and the staff at Pine Tree Composition, Inc., for their meticulous and timely copyediting.

We welcome comments and suggestions from instructors who use this text. Please send us your syllabi so that we can make future editions even more relevant to your classroom needs. Do not hesitate to contact us if we can help you in any way.

Carol P. Harvey, Ed.D.
Assumption College
Department of Business Studies
500 Salisbury Street
Worcester, MA 01609

M. June Allard, Ph.D.
Worcester State College
Department of Psychology
486 Chandler Street
Worcester, MA 01602

ABOUT THE AUTHORS

Carol P. Harvey (Ed.D., University of Massachusetts at Amherst) is associate professor and former Chair of Business Studies at Assumption College. She holds an MBA and a Certificate of Advanced Studies from Northeastern University and an MA in Psychology from Assumption Colleges. She is a site visitor for NEASC (New England Association of Schools and Colleges) for college accreditation and consultant to businesses, particularly in the areas of mentoring and organizational development. Formerly employed as a manager at the Xerox Corporation, her research interests include implementing diversity initiatives in organizations and improving critical thinking skills in the college classroom. She is the co-recipient of the 2004 Roethlisberger Memorial Award from the Organizational Behavior Teaching Society for the best article from the Journal of Management Education for "Critical Thinking in the Management Classroom: Bloom's Taxonomy as a Learning Tool."

M. June Allard (Ph.D., Michigan State University) is professor and Chair of Psychology at Worcester State College. She is a social and experimental psychologist with research and teaching interests in international and cross-cultural psychology and in assessment and evaluation. A site visitor for NEASC (New England Association of Schools and Colleges) for college accreditation, she consults to colleges on assessment and conducts undergraduate program evaluations. A lifelong world traveler, she lectures on research and evaluation internationally in countries such as Morocco, Costa Rica, Poland, Mexico, Turkey, Nicaragua, Bolivia, Brazil, and Italy and has conducted research projects for the U.S. Peace Corps, UNESCO, and USAID and educational evaluation for the International Baccalaureate Organization (Cardiff, Wales).

INTRODUCTION TO *UNDERSTANDING AND MANAGING DIVERSITY—* FOR THE STUDENT

Carol P. Harvey
Assumption College

- When was the last time that you heard the word *qualified* used in reference to a white job applicant?
- How could a global company like Coca-Cola wind up paying out over $195 million to settle a diversity lawsuit?
- Forty years after the passage of Title VII of the Civil Rights Act, why are 95% of the top corporate managers in the United States still white males?
- Why are only 32% of the working-age disabled people employed either full or part time?
- Why do women earn 73 cents for every dollar that men earn?

Obviously, if you have the correct answers to these questions, you may not need to take a course in diversity. Conversely, when was the last time that you heard or said, "I'm open-minded," "I treat everyone as I would like to be treated," "I don't see you as. . . . (Asian, Jewish, etc.)," "We're really all alike inside," "I bet he got the job because of affirmative action," "I am not prejudiced," "In this country, everyone has the same opportunities, some just work harder than others," or "This country is a melting pot." If you can identify with any of these statements, this course will help you understand the complexities of 21st-century workplace diversity.

Although there has been much progress in the workforce in terms of differences, these questions and often-heard comments illustrate that there is still a long way to go before individuals and organizations recognize how to implement the changes that are necessary to unleash the productivity of a more diverse workforce. Today 26.6% of the United States population is African American or Latino, (Lopez, 2003–4, p. 81), and 11.5% was born in another country (Zeilberger, 2003, p. 71). (See Hunt and Mentzer articles in this text for similar data on Canada.)

Globalization, technology, and legislation are driving these changes. However, just because workers differ in terms of their demography (age, race, gender, etc.), the heterogeneous workforce represents much more than a simple demographic shift. These workers bring a wider range of values, needs, communication styles, and experiences to their jobs. Although this can be advantageous to an organization in terms of a better understanding of the needs of a diverse customer base, creative problem solving, and increased productivity (Orlando, 2000, p. 164), these changes, if not understood or well managed, can result in poor hires, decreased motivation, increased conflict, absenteeism, turnover, harassment, costly lawsuits, and decreased productivity. As Cox and Beale write, "The challenge is to manage in such a way as to maximize the potential benefits of diversity and minimize its potential disadvantages" (1997, p. 42).

The bottom line is that learning how to deal effectively with a more heterogeneous workforce is a business imperative requiring an understanding of the new workers as people. Then organizations can begin to make the most effective systemic changes in terms of leadership, motivation, policies, and procedures.

The purpose of this introduction is to provide an understanding of the basic terms used by authors throughout the text and a brief historical and theoretical context for exploring issues of workplace diversity.

DEFINING DIVERSITY AS A BASIC ISSUE

There is little agreement about the definition of diversity among those who train, teach, research, and are responsible for implementing diversity policies and procedures in organizations. One of the most commonly used ways to define diversity is through demographic and/or psychographic variables. This is the basis for legal definitions in the United States (Title VII of the Civil Rights Act, The Americans with Disabilities Act, etc.) and in Canadian (see Mentzer) employment statutes.

Loden's (1996) wheel of primary and secondary dimensions of diversity provides an example of this approach. Loden defines the dimensions of diversity in terms of core characteristics or primary dimensions (such as race, age, gender, ethnicity, sexual orientation, mental/physical abilities) that we cannot change and are more important to our construct of self and secondary dimensions (such as, religion, communication style, education, income, geographical location) that are usually viewed as more changeable and less influential to our self-identity.

Others think of diversity in a broader context. Cox and Beale (1997) write that diversity is "a mix of people in one social system who have distinctly different socially relevant group affiliations" (p. 1). The Pillsbury Company, well known for its workplace diversity initiatives, describes diversity simply as "all the ways in which we differ" (Hayles & Russell, 1997,

p. 11). However, Thomas, moves diversity away from an us versus them issue by incorporating similarities as well as differences into his definition: "individuals who are different in some ways and similar in others" (1999, p. 5).

Because this text is focused on diversity strictly as an organizational issue, we have chosen to define workplace **diversity** within that context as social identities that can affect workplace interactions and require new ways of interacting among individuals and groups and systemic changes in the ways that organizations function. This is a more inclusive definition that allows diversity to include individuals who are often excluded. For example, white males may have diversity issues in terms of their gender identity when they choose to work in predominately female occupations such as nursing or in predominately female functional departments such as human resources.

UNDERSTANDING CULTURAL HISTORICAL AND WORKPLACE CONTEXT

North American culture is built on the myth that we are all immigrants and that everyone has equal opportunities to succeed if he/she just works hard enough. Although this may be true for some, for many others this belief ignores the reality of being born into poverty, not being white, and having roots that trace back to slavery or the situation of the indigenous peoples in Canada, Mexico, and the United States. Today workers want to be seen as individuals and to maintain their identities as Cubans, males, and so on. Assimilation into the dominant culture (i.e., the "melting pot") is no longer as valued and for most people always was a myth. Today's workforce is very different from the workers of just a generation ago. Today's workforce is older, more nonwhite, more female, more likely to be immigrants from a non-Western country, more open about their sexual orientation, and more likely to speak a second language at home. They are less likely to be Christian, have a stay-at-home spouse, and be willing to conceal who they are. All these changes call for adaptations in the ways that we manage people and in the ways that organizations operate.

UNDERSTANDING INDIVIDUAL AND GROUP IDENTITIES: PRIVILEGE AND OPPRESSION

To successfully change the ways that diversity is managed in the workplace, individuals must build on a base of awareness and knowledge that comes primarily from the social sciences. **Social identity theory,** based on the work of Tajfel (1981) and Tajfel and Turner (1986), is a term used to describe how people define themselves in terms of the individual importance of their sociocultural categories. For example, a white male with the best of intentions is trying to communicate his lack of prejudice to a black female coworker. He is puzzled when she reacts negatively to his saying, " I don't see you as a black woman." If being black and being female (i.e., in this example multiple group identities) are important to her self-esteem and if she closely identifies with these groups, such a statement can negate the importance of who she is and can impact her self-esteem.

Throughout her life, she may have experienced very different reactions to her race and gender than those of her white male colleague. **Oppression theory** holds that in every society there are constraints, often unconscious, in terms of social inequality and group memberships that shape a person's life choices. As members of society, people internalize these power relationships into "isms" like racism. Although these "isms" are often unrecognized, they can impact other people's attitudes in terms of internal prejudices and/or external discriminatory behaviors.

One can be considered as having **privilege,** an assumption that everyone experiences the world with the same, often unearned advantages that we do or as oppressed on the basis of membership in social groups. Those in the so-called **dominant** or **agent groups,** in this example the white male colleague, are the ones with the most power and privilege and have the luxury of seeing themselves as individuals. However, those in **subordinate or target groups,** in this case the black female, is the one that is more often defined by others in terms of group memberships (Bell, 1997, p. 9). Although we don't hear people say, "I don't see you as a white male," in dominant groups, we may often hear coworkers defined in terms of their membership in subordinate groups. In this example, it is in terms of race and gender, both subordinate groups.

What a particular society holds as more valuable is often a social construction based on time and place that gives individuals who belong to those groups more status. In some Asian and Native cultures, older people belong to the dominant group because they are seen as holding the power of wisdom. In contrast, in North American businesses, older workers often are devalued because youth and attractive physical appearance are stronger values.

History is full of examples of efforts used to make subordinate groups blend into dominant norms and language. For example, Native American children were forced to move away from their families, give up their tribe's dress and language, and attend special boarding schools to acculturate them into Anglo-European ways. In the 1970s John Malloy's *Dress for Success* was a best-selling book that urged women to dress more like men to get ahead in the business world. Recently, in France there has been discussion about wearing yarmulkes, head covering for women, and large jewelry crosses in the workplace.

UNDERSTANDING PREJUDICE AND STEREOTYPES

Prejudice is an attitude, usually with negative feelings, that involves a pre-judgment about the members of a group (Plous, 2003, p. 3). Even if we know little about a group and have had limited experience with its members, we may prejudge an individual based on his/her membership in that group. Although rationally we realize that not all Muslims are terrorists, we may be less likely to trust Muslim coworkers since 9/11. Plous wrote, "No one capable of human thought and speech is immune from harboring prejudice; it often takes deliberate effort and awareness to reduce prejudice; with sufficient motivation, it can be done." (2003, p. 38).

Stereotypes are formed when we ascribe generalizations to people based on their group identities and the tendencies of the whole group rather than seeing a person as an individual who may or may not have these tendencies. The term *stereotype* was originally coined in 1798 by a French printer, Didot, who used it to refer to a printing process for reproductions (Ashmore & Del Boca, 1981). For example, as a whole group, it is a well-established fact that Asian students tend to be stronger in math performance than American students. If a teacher has internalized this as a stereotype for all Asians, she may consciously or unconsciously, hold an Asian student to a higher performance standard in math than a non-Asian student.

UNDERSTANDING WORKPLACE DIVERSITY: THREE APPROACHES

Because organizations operate within this sociocultural framework, integrating the new workforce into existing organizations has proved to be challenging. The major approaches to this process can be divided into three categories: **affirmative action, valuing diversity,** and **diversity management.**

The first, affirmative action, takes its name from the legislation beginning with the passage of Title VII of the Civil Rights Act of 1964. This law and subsequent statutes such as the Americans with Disability Act were attempts to "correct" past workplace injustices. Although this approach did result in opening doors for many women and minorities, it often suffered in its execution. Some managers, misunderstanding the intent of the legislation, hired "by the numbers," assuming that these workers would assimilate into the predominately white male organizational cultures. This caused backlash for individuals and conflict within the organizations. Affirmative action, however, continues to be a controversial topic. A recent survey revealed that 51% of the general population and 89% of African Americans think that it needs to be continued (Diversity Factoids, 2003, p. 16).

The second approach, valuing diversity, focuses on making individuals more aware that a wider range of behaviors and styles can add value to the quality of the work. When this is done well, the intent is to change the organizational culture, often by training, so that the diverse workforce is valued for its ability to see problems from a range of perspectives. Much of the focus is on creating awareness of the worth of different styles to build a more inclusive work environment (SHRM, 2003). This approach has sometimes been criticized as trivializing diversity when organizations showcase their diversity efforts through ethnic food celebrations, diversity T-shirts, and playing diversity games and for limiting the career progress of diverse individuals into jobs that relate mostly to their particular social identities, such as working as an affirmative action officer.

The third approach, managing diversity, requires that diversity efforts link to the strategic mission and goals of the organization and maximize the contributions of individual workers. In this case managing diversity means that diversity is a process requiring changes in the organizational culture to enable all workers to achieve their full potential. Consequently, workers and managers both need to develop a wider range of communication and leadership skills, which is why this is a major focus of this book.

Today there is an added emphasis on linking these managing diversity efforts to "the business case for diversity." This means that diversity efforts contribute in a measurable way to the productivity of the organization. Efforts to quantify the contribution of diversity to an organization's bottom line have proven very complex to evaluate (Bean, 2003–2004). In the meantime, other measures of the worth of diversity such as reduced employee turnover are being used to make the business case (see Robertson & Dechant article in this text). We challenge you to learn as much as you can about the new workforce and to develop the knowledge and skills needed for productive management in the 21st century.

Bibliography

Ashmore, R.D., & Del Boca, F.K. (1981). Conceptual approaches to stereotypes and stereotyping. In D. L. Hamilton (Ed.), *Cognitive processes in stereotyping and intergroup behavior* (pp. 1–35). Hillsdale, NJ: Erlbaum.

Bean, L. (2003–2004 December–January). What went wrong with the MIT led diversity study? *DiversityInc.,* 38–40, 2, 6.

Bell, L.A. (1997). Theoretical foundations for social justice. In M. Adams, L.A. Bell & P. Griffin (Eds.), *Teaching for diversity and social justice: A sourcebook* (pp. 3–15). New York: Routledge.

Cox, T., Jr. & Beale, R.L. (1997). *Developing the competency to manage diversity.* San Francisco: Berrett-Koehler.

Diversity Factoids. (2003). Racial divide. *DiversityInc.,* 2, 4, p. 16.

Hayles, V.R., & Russell, A.M. (1997). *The diversity directive.* Chicago: Irwin.

Loden, M. (1996). *Implementing diversity.* Chicago: Business One: Irwin, p. 16.

Lopez, E.M. (2003–2004, December–January). We can't find any black accountants. *DiversityInc.,* 81–82, 2, 6.

Orlando, R. (2000). Racial diversity, business strategy and firm performance: A resource based view. *Academy of Management Journal, 43* (2), 164–77.

Plous, S. (2003). The psychology of prejudice, stereotyping, and discrimination: An overview. In S. Plous (Ed.), *Understanding prejudice and discrimination* (pp. 3–48). Boston: McGraw-Hill.

SHRM. (2003, December 15). *How is a diversity initiative different from my organization's affirmative action plan?* Retrieved December 15, 2003, from http://www.shrm.org/diversityvaffirmativeaction.asp

Tajfel, H. (1981). *Human groups and social categories: Studies in social psychology.* Cambridge: Cambridge University Press.

Tajfel, H, & Turner, J.C. (1986). The social identity theory of intergroup behavior. In S. Worchel & W. Austin (Eds.), *The psychology of intergroup relations* (2nd ed., pp. 7–24). Chicago, Il: Nelson-Hall.

Thomas, R.R., Jr. (with Woodruff, M.I. (1999). *Building a house for diversity.* New York: AMACOM.

Zeilberger, R. (2003, October–November). Changing faces: How immigrants impact U.S. businesses. *DiversityInc.,* 71–74, 2, 5.

PART

I

INDIVIDUAL PERSPECTIVES ON DIVERSITY

The first section of this book is designed to provide a foundation for the study of differences and diversity management. To help the student become more aware of where he/she is in terms of understanding some of the underlying issues of diversity, these readings and exercises are on introductory topics such as values (Allard #1), demographic changes in the workforce of the United States (Gorski) and/or Canada (Hunt #3), ethnocentricity (Miner, Allard #5, Sowell, Allard & Harvey #10), stereotypes (Bowen, Allard #7), conflict (Parker #11, Parker & Klein #12), and a theoretical perspective on intercultural communication (Bennett).

Learning Outcomes for Section I

- Students should understand why the demographic changes in the workforce require additional management, leadership, and communication skills.
- Students will learn how values, ethnocentricity, and stereotypes can alter their perceptions of coworkers, customers, clients, managers, and subordinates.
- Students will learn that increased workforce diversity may provide new perspectives but can also lead to conflict that needs to be managed in a positive way.
- Students will learn the importance of understanding the roles of culture, subcultures, and the importance of effective intercultural communication in the new workplace.

Notice that all material is numbered in the Table of Contents but we will use the number in the introductory sections only when the author has written multiple entries.

I AM . . .

M. June Allard
Worcester State College

Goals

- To help you learn about yourself by examining your group member-ships (i.e., dimensions of culture by which you define yourself)
- To further examine your self-descriptors for indications of your most important group memberships

Instructions

1. Think about how you would describe yourself to someone you have never met. On each line that follows, write a single-word description.

I AM a(an)

_____	_____
_____	_____
_____	_____
_____	_____
_____	_____
_____	_____
_____	_____
_____	_____

2. Place a star by the three most important descriptors.

MULTICULTURAL EDUCATION AND EQUITY AWARENESS QUIZ (ARE YOU BEING MISLED?)

abridged version

Paul C. Gorski

Hamline University

Please circle the correct answer for each question.

1. According to the U.S. Census Bureau, the majority of poor children live in:
   a) Urban areas
   b) Suburban areas
   c) Rural areas

2. Which of the following variables most closely predicts how high someone will score on the SAT test?
   a) Race
   b) Region of residence
   c) Family income
   d) Parents' academic achievement

3. The U.S. military budget is by far the highest of any country in the world. By 2003, the U.S. military budget was roughly equal to that of:
   a) The next 5 countries combined
   b) The next 10 countries combined
   c) The next 15 countries combined
   d) The next 20 countries combined

4. How many of every thousand senior-level male managers of *Fortune* 1000 companies are Asian or Asian American?
   a) 3
   b) 47
   c) 99
   d) 153

5. According to a *Business Week* study of 3,664 business school graduates, how much more, on average, does a man with an MBA from one of the top 20 business schools in the United States make during the first year after graduation than a woman in the same situation?
   a) About $1,500 more
   b) About $3,000 more
   c) About $6,500 more
   d) About $10,000 more

6. Compared with schools in which 5% or less of the students are people of color, how likely are schools in which 50% or more of the students are people of color to be overcrowded (25% or more beyond capacity)?
   a) Equally as likely
   b) Twice as likely
   c) Four times as likely
   d) Six times as likely

7. Ninty-seven percent of all students in public high schools regularly hear homophobic comments from peers. What percentage report hearing homophobic remarks from school staff or faculty?
   a) 5%
   b) 27%
   c) 53%
   d) 74%

8. What percentage of the world population regularly accesses the Internet?
   a) 2%
   b) 15%
   c) 29%
   d) 51%

9. In 1999 the average U.S. worker earned $26,105. This represents what percentage of the average CEO salary that year?
   a) 0.21%
   b) 1%
   c) 6%
   d) 17%

10. According to the U.S. Department of Education, about 61% of public school students in the United States are white. What percentage of public school teachers is white?
    a) 61%
    b) 73%
    c) 87%
    d) 99%

Sources

Center for the American Woman and Politics

Chideya, F. (1995). *Don't believe the hype: Fighting cultural misinformation about African Americans.* New York: Plume.

Gay Lesbian Straight Education Network

National Council on Education Statistics

Public Citizens Health Research Group

U.S. Census Bureau

U.S. Department of Education

U.S. Department of Justice

WHAT IS YOUR WORKFORCE I.Q.? CANADIAN VERSION

Gerald Hunt

Ryerson University

Read each of the following statements and mark them **T** for True or **F** for False.

_____ 1.   Over 50% of students entering Canadian universities are female.

_____ 2.   About 5% of the Canadian population is estimated to be gay or lesbian, and this figure rises to around 10% when bisexuals and transgendered people are included.

_____ 3.   Eighty percent of Canadian women between the ages of 25 and 44 work outside the home.

_____ 4.   Visible minorities will make up close to half the population of Canada by 2005.

_____ 5.   Same-sex couples can now get married in Canada.

_____ 6.   Disabled people are the most likely group to be unemployed.

_____ 7.   It is estimated that only 2% of directors of corporate boards in Canada are female.

_____ 8.   Study after study has found that immigrants are less likely than Canadian-born workers to end up on welfare.

_____ 9.   Canadian unions have become strong supporters of gay, lesbian, bisexual, and transgender issues.

_____ 10. Canada is home to at least 4.3 million first-generation immigrants.

Total number of true answers _____
Total number of false answers _____

BODY RITUAL AMONG THE NACIREMA

Horace Miner

The anthropologist has become so familiar with the diversity of ways in which different peoples behave in similar situations that he is not apt to be surprised by even the most exotic customs. In fact, if all of the logically possible combinations of behavior have not been found somewhere in the world, he is apt to suspect that they must be present in some yet undescribed tribe. This point has, in fact, been expressed with respect to clan organization by Murdock (1949:71). In this light, the magical beliefs and practices of the Nacirema present such unusual aspects that it seems desirable to describe them as an example of the extremes to which human behavior can go.

Professor Linton first brought the ritual of the Nacirema to the attention of anthropologists twenty years ago (1936:326), but the culture of this people is still very poorly understood. They are a North American group living in the territory between the Canadian Cree, the Yaqui and Tarahumare of Mexico, and the Carib and Arawak of the Antilles. Little is known of their origin, although tradition states that they came from the east. According to Nacirema mythology, their nation was originated by a culture hero, Notgnihsaw, who is otherwise known for two great feats of strength—the throwing of a piece of wampum across the river Pa-To-Mac and the chopping down of a cherry tree in which the Spirit of Truth resided.

Nacirema culture is characterized by a highly developed market economy which has evolved in a rich natural habitat. While much of the people's time is devoted to economic pursuits, a large part of the fruits of these labors and a considerable portion of the day are spent in ritual activity. The focus of this activity is the human body, the appearance and health of which loom as a dominant concern in the ethos of the people. While such concern is certainly not unusual, its ceremonial aspects and associated philosophy are unique.

The fundamental belief underlying the whole system appears to be that the human body is ugly and that its natural tendency is to debility and disease. Incarcerated in such a body, man's only hope is to avert these characteristics through the use of the powerful influences of ritual and ceremony. Every

13

household has one or more shrines devoted to this purpose. The more powerful individuals in the society have several shrines in their houses and, in fact, the opulence of a house is often referred to in terms of the number of such ritual centers it possesses. Most houses are of wattle and daub construction, but the shrine rooms of the wealthy are walled with stone. Poorer families imitate the rich by applying pottery plaques to their shrine walls.

While each family has at least one shrine, the rituals associated with it are not family ceremonies but are private and secret. The rites are normally only discussed with children, and then only during the period when they are being initiated into these mysteries. I was able, however, to establish sufficient rapport with the natives to examine these shrines and to have the rituals described to me.

The focal point of the shrine is a box or chest, which is built into the wall. In this chest are kept the many charms and magical potions without which no native believes he could live.

These preparations are secured from a variety of specialized practitioners. The most powerful of these are the medicine men, whose assistance must be rewarded with substantial gifts. However, the medicine men do not provide the curative potions for their clients, but decide what the ingredients should be and then write them down in an ancient and secret language. This writing is understood only by the medicine men and by the herbalists who, for another gift, provide the required charm.

The charm is not disposed of after it has served its purpose, but is placed in the charm-box of the household shrine. As these magical materials are specific for certain ills, and the real or imagined maladies of the people are many, the charm-box is usually full to overflowing. The magical packets are so numerous that the people forget what their purposes were and fear to use them again. While the natives are very vague on this point, we can only assume that the idea in retaining all the old magical materials is that their presence in the charm-box, before which the body rituals are conducted, will in some way protect the worshipper.

Beneath the charm-box is a small font. Each day every member of the family, in succession, enters the shrine room, bows his head before the charm-box, mingles different sorts of holy waters in the font, and proceeds with a brief ritual of ablution. The holy waters are secured from the Water Temple of the community, where the priests conduct elaborate ceremonies to make the liquid ritually pure.

In the hierarchy of magical practitioners, and below the medicine men in prestige, are specialists whose designation is best translated "holy-mouth-men." The Nacirema have an almost pathological horror of and fascination with the mouth, the condition of which is believed to have a supernatural influence on all social relationships. Were it not for the rituals of the mouth, they believe that their teeth would fall out, their gums bleed, their jaws shrink, their friends desert them, and their lovers reject them. They also believe that a strong relationship exists between oral and moral characteristics. For example, there is a ritual ablution of the mouth for children which is supposed to improve their moral fiber.

The daily body ritual performed by everyone includes a mouth-rite. Despite the fact that these people are so punctilious about care of the mouth, this rite involves a practice which strikes the uninitiated stranger as revolting. It was reported to me that the ritual consists of inserting a magic bundle of hog hairs into the mouth, along with certain magical powder, and then moving the bundle in a highly formalized series of gestures.

In addition to the private mouth-rite, the people seek out the holy-mouth-man once or twice a year. These practitioners have an impressive set of paraphernalia, consisting of a variety of augers, awls, probes, and prods. The use of these objects in the exorcism of the evils of the mouth involves almost unbelievable ritual torture of the client. The holy-mouth-man opens the client's mouth and, using the above mentioned tools, enlarges any holes, which may have been created in the teeth. Magical materials are put into these holes. If there are no naturally occurring holes in the teeth, large sections of one or more teeth are gouged out so that the supernatural substance can be applied. In the client's view, the purpose of the ministrations is to arrest decay and to draw friends. The extremely sacred and traditional character of the rite is evident in the fact that the natives return to the holy-mouth-man, despite the fact that their teeth continue to decay.

It is to be hoped that, when a thorough study of the Nacirema is made, there will be careful inquiry into the personality structure of these people. One has but to watch the gleam in the eye of a holy-mouth-man, as he jabs an awl into an exposed nerve, to suspect that a certain amount of sadism is involved. If this can be established, a very interesting pattern emerges, for most of the population shows definite masochistic tendencies. It was to these that Professor Linton referred in discussing a distinctive part of the daily body ritual which was performed only by men. This part of the rite involves scraping and lacerating the surface of the face with a sharp instrument. Special women's rites are performed only four times during each lunar month, but what they lack in frequency is made up for in barbarity. As part of this ceremony, women bake their heads in small ovens for about an hour. The theoretically interesting point is that what seems to be a preponderantly masochistic people have developed sadistic specialists.

The medicine men have an imposing temple, or latipso, in every community of any size. The more elaborate ceremonies required to treat very sick patients can only be performed at this temple. These ceremonies involve not only the thaumaturge but a permanent group of vestal maidens who move sedately about the temple chambers in distinctive costume and headdress.

The latipso ceremonies are so harsh that it is phenomenal that a fair proportion of the really sick natives who enter the temple ever recover. Small children whose indoctrination is still incomplete have been known to resist attempts to take them to the temple because "that is where you go to die." Despite this fact, sick adults are not only willing but eager to undergo the protracted ritual purification, if they can afford to do so. No matter how ill the supplicant or how grave the emergency, the guardians of many temples will not admit a client if he cannot give a rich gift to the custodian. Even after one has gained admission and survived the ceremonies, the guardians will not permit the neophyte to leave until he makes still another gift.

The supplicant entering the temple is first stripped of all his or her clothes. In everyday life the Nacirema avoids exposure of his body and its natural functions. Bathing and excretory acts are performed only in the secrecy of the household shrine, where they are ritualized as part of the body-rites. Psychological shock results from the fact that body secrecy is suddenly lost upon entry into the latipso. This sort of ceremonial treatment is necessitated by the fact that the excreta are used by a diviner to ascertain the course and nature of the client's sickness. Female clients, on the other hand, find their naked bodies are subjected to the scrutiny, manipulation, and prodding of the medicine men.

Few supplicants in the temple are well enough to do anything but lie on their hard beds. The daily ceremonies, like the rites of the holy-mouth-men, involve discomfort and torture. With ritual precision, the vestals awaken their miserable charges each dawn and roll them about on their beds of pain while performing ablutions, in the formal movements of which the maidens are highly trained. At other times they insert magic wands in the supplicant's mouth or force him to eat substances which are supposed to be healing. From time to time the medicine men come to their clients and jab magically treated needles into their flesh. The fact that these ceremonies may not cure, and may even kill the neophyte, in no way decreases the people's faith in the medicine men.

There remains one other kind of practitioner, known as a "listener." This witch-doctor has the power to exorcise the devils that lodge in the heads of people who have been bewitched. The Nacirema believe that parents bewitched their own children. Mothers are particularly suspected of putting a curse on children while teaching them the secret body rituals. The counter-magic of the witch-doctor is unusual in its lack of ritual. The patient simply tells the "listener" all his troubles and fears, beginning with the earliest difficulties he can remember. The memory displayed by the Nacirema in these exorcism sessions is truly remarkable. It is not uncommon for the patient to bemoan the rejection he felt upon being weaned as a babe, and a few individuals even see their troubles going back to the traumatic effects of their own birth.

In conclusion, mention must be made of certain practices which have their base in native esthetics but which depend upon the pervasive aversion to the natural body and its functions. There are ritual fasts to make fat people thin and ceremonial feasts to make thin people fat. Still other rites are used to make women's breasts larger if they are small, and smaller if they are large. General dissatisfaction with breast shape is symbolized in the fact that the ideal form is virtually outside the range of human variation. A few women afflicted with almost inhuman hypermammary development are so idolized that they make a handsome living by simply going from village to village and permitting the natives to stare at them for a fee.

Reference has already been made to the fact that excretory functions are ritualized, routinized, and relegated to secrecy. Natural reproduction functions are similarly distorted. Intercourse is taboo as a topic and scheduled as an act. Efforts are made to avoid pregnancy by the use of magical materials or by limiting intercourse to certain phases of the moon. Conception is actually very infrequent. When pregnant, women dress so as to hide their condition. Parturition takes place in secret, without friends or relatives to assist, and the majority of women do not nurse their infants.

Our review of the ritual life of the Nacirema has certainly shown them to be a magic-ridden people. It is hard to understand how they have managed to exist so long under the burdens which they have imposed upon themselves. But even such exotic customs as these take on real meaning when they are viewed with the insight provided by Malinowski when he wrote (1948:70).

> Looking from far and above, from our high places of safety in developed civilization, it is easy to see all the crudity and irrelevance of magic. But without its power and guidance, early man could not have advanced to the higher stages of civilization.

Discussion Questions

1. What general message do you think the author was trying to convey in this description of one aspect of American culture?
2. Why are some behaviors described as "magic"?
3. Why are some behaviors described as "rituals"? Do you think this is a fair label?
4. Does the humorous approach to our culture bother you? Do you feel that the description is belittling or sarcastic in tone?
5. Imagine that you are a member of the author's culture. What kinds of sterotypes could you have of the American culture and its people if this reading is your only source of information?

References

Linton, Ralph. (1936). *The Study of Man.* New York: D. Appleton-Century Co.

Malinowski, Bronislaw. (1948). *Magic, Science and Religion.* Glencoe: The Free Press.

Murdock, George P. (1949). *Social Structure.* New York: The MacMillan Co.

NACIREMA EXTENDED

M. June Allard
Worcester State College

Goals

- To develop awareness of how the U.S. culture may appear to people from other cultures
- To demonstrate how distorted impressions and stereotypes can arise from incomplete information
- To extend the lessons of the Miner "Body Ritual among the Nacirema" reading to modern-day America

Instructions

1. Read the "Body Ritual among the Nacirema" article by Miner.
2. Moderate to large classes: form groups of 3 to 5 members each; small classes or online courses can work individually.
3. Read the following to yourself:

   You have come to investigate American civilization by observing cultural activities. Using a writing style similar to Miner's, describe your observations of one of the following

   - College graduation ceremonies
   - Football, soccer, or hockey games
   - A national political convention
   - A wedding
   - Parades
   - Rock concerts or symphonies
   - New Year's Eve
   - A blind date
   - A spring break trip
   - Online auctions: buying and/or selling
   - A job fair
   - Teeth whitening
   *•
   - •

*Space intentionally left blank for other events and rituals.

SAMPLE DESCRIPTION–OBSERVATION OF CULTURAL EVENT CALLED HALLOWEEN

Halloween is a very strange custom. It doesn't appear to be a holiday; it is more like an event—an event characterized by at least two rituals and many symbols.

The chief rituals appear to be the (1) Ritual of the Pumpkins and (2) the Ritual of the Begging.

Ritual of the Pumpkins. The pumpkin vegetable, which apparently is eaten at other times of the year, is not eaten at this event. Instead, the people paint strange faces on pumpkins or carve faces on empty pumpkin shells. Lighted candles are placed inside the carved pumpkins. Decorated pumpkins appear in windows facing outdoors or on displays outside of homes.

Ritual of the Begging. On Halloween night, children dress up in costumes that frequently represent mythical characters—ghosts, witches, monsters, ghouls, cartoon characters. They wear masks to hide their identities.

After dark the children go begging from house to house, calling out "Trick or treat." People then open their doors and give candy to the children. Sometimes the children play pranks on the people.

Symbols. Among the prominent symbols of Halloween are ghosts, skeletons, spiders, witches, black cats, graveyards, and monsters, all of which seem to be very frightening, gory, ugly, or sinister in character. Not only are these symbols displayed in the costumes the children wear, but many houses are adorned on the outside with displays of them, particularly witches and ghosts.

Sometimes people visit "haunted houses" (eerie houses where frightening creatures lurk in dark corners to scare people). Sometimes, too, people attend Halloween parties and play strange games, such as dunking their heads in buckets of water trying to catch an apple in their mouthes.

4. All class members take notes as each group or individual report is presented.
5. Compile notes from the reports into a "picture of the American culture" *based solely* on the information in the reports. What kinds of stereotypes of American culture could result from these observations?
6. Relate the stereotypes of American culture to those that class members hold of other cultures.

---

*Your instructor may direct you to write the description as a journal entry, out-of-class writing assignment, online assignment, or in class.

INCREASING MULTICULTURAL UNDERSTANDING: UNCOVERING STEREOTYPES

John R. Bowman
University of North Carolina at Pembroke

Goals

1. To help individuals become aware of their own values
2. To show individuals how their culture programs them to react to and judge others in automatic and stereotypic ways
3. To discover the types and sources of stereotypes about others
4. To provide an opportunity for participants to see how their stereotypes create barriers to appreciating individual differences

Instructions Before Class

1. Turn to the Uncovering Stereotypes Worksheet.
2. Follow your instructor's directions for completing the blank category boxes to reflect different special populations.
3. Working individually:
   - Complete the First Thought/Judgment column by writing your first thought about or judgment of each category. Refer to the example given on the worksheet.
   - Rate each thought/judgment as positive (+), negative (−), or neutral (0).
   - Complete the Sources column by indicating the source of your judgment for each category.
4. As a group in class:
   - Turn to the Uncovering Stereotypes Group Summary Sheet.
   - Five categories (family, media, experience, work experience, friends) have already been listed on the summary sheet. Add

additional categories (derived from your group discussions) to the sheet.
- Take a quick count of the number of positive, negative, and neutral thoughts/judgments made by your group for each of the Source Categories and enter totals on the last line.

5. As a class:
- Discuss which sources lead to positive, which to negative, and which to neutral judgments.
- Discuss the implications of having negative or positive stereotypes/ judgments from different perspectives; for example, among workers, between managers and workers, and at the corporate level.

Uncovering Stereotypes Worksheet			
Category	First Thought/ Judgment	Rating*	Sources
Working Mother	Neglects children, busy, tired		Own experience, movies
Southerner			
AIDS Carrier			
Smoker			
Hispanic			
African-American Male			
Female President of the United States			

*(+) = positive
 (−) = negative
 (0) = neutral

Uncovering Stereotypes Group Summary Sheet			
Source Categories	Positive (+) Thoughts/ Judgments	Negative (−) Thoughts/ Judgments	Neutral (0) Thoughts/ Judgments
Family			
Media			
Experience			
Work Experience			
Friends			
Total			

CHOOSING THE BOARD

M. June Allard
Worcester State College

This exercise is based on the author's experiences serving on governing boards and board development committees. It is fictitious, but representative of situations faced by boards of profit and nonprofit organizations.

Heritage Medical Center is a moderately sized suburban hospital currently plagued with financial and management problems so severe they are reaching the crisis stage. A Board of Directors comprised of 12 members governs the hospital. At the moment there are four empty seats on the board.

The eight remaining board members are fiscally conservative, well-to-do industrialists who have known each other for years and who frequently see each other socially and at community affairs. Many of these men belong to an exclusive country club, a few to a very exclusive yacht club. Board members are expected and do donate generously to the hospital fund-raising campaigns.

There is friction among these board members who are very concerned about the future of the hospital, but who cannot agree on what course of action to take in the face of its mounting problems.

You serve on the Board Development Committee, which must now fill the four empty seats. Eight people have been nominated for the four seats. Brief biographies of the nominees are provided here. Read the biographies carefully to help you select the best candidates.

NOMINEES

Drake Covington II is a very bright 23-year-old computer systems analyst. He marches to a different drummer and is considered "far out." He is the nephew of an influential board member and owes his nomination to his uncle.

Layla Amini is a successful 27-year-old financial analyst. She is very quiet and very conservative, a traditionalist with a solid reputation. She was nominated by her cousin, a state senator.

Carmen Diaz is a 33-year-old highly respected medical doctor. She is very innovative and a self-starter who has already set up a clinic. She has never met anyone on the board, but does know the hospital CEO. She was nominated by a group of doctors practicing at the hospital.

Charles Wong is a 35-year-old management systems analyst. He lives near the hospital and works out of his home. He is reputed to be a team player and supportive person. He was nominated by the union representing the hospital staff.

Peter Skylar is a 46-year-old CEO of an Health Maintenance Organization (HMO) who by nature of his position is very familiar with hospital operations. He is brilliant, a loner, and connected to the state regulatory agency. He is considered to be in the "out-group" by those members of the board that he knows.

Sue Novenski is a 42-year-old social worker who works in a battered women's shelter. She works well with groups, is low key, and is extremely collaborative. She knows no one on the board; she was nominated by the hospital's Patients Advisory Committee.

Katherine Dobbs Courtney is a 55-year-old widow of a very wealthy industrialist who served on the board. She has served on community boards. She is an idea person, an individualist, and outspoken. She plays golf with the mayor, who nominated her.

Lamar Leroy Woods is a 56-year-old retired owner of a profitable manufacturing company. He is very wealthy and has donated large sums of money to the hospital. He is conservative, easygoing, intelligent, and comfortable to be with. He was nominated by the hospital CEO.

1. Which four of the nominees would be your choices? Please list them in order of preference and explain why you chose them.

    A. _____
    Why?

    B. _____
    Why?

    C. _____
    Why?

    D. _____
    Why?

2. Replacing one third of the board members all at once will mean a radial change for this board. This is a source of concern for the board members and a serious concern of the hospital CEO, who deals frequently with the board. What will you do to ease the transition for the board members and for the CEO?

REINCARNATION

M. June Allard
Worcester State College

If you believed in reincarnation, how would you choose to come back in your next life?

Age:

Gender:

Occupation:

Ethnic heritage:

Race:

Other (religion, social class, roles, etc.):

Mental/Physical Abilities and Characteristics:

Gender: **M** **F**   *Age:* *under 23* *23–43* *44–60* *61+*

A WORLD VIEW OF CULTURAL DIVERSITY

Thomas Sowell

Diversity has become one of the most often used words of our time—and a word almost never defined. Diversity is invoked in discussions of everything from employment policy to curriculum reform and from entertainment to politics. Nor is the word merely a description of the long-known fact that the American population is made up of people from many countries, many races, and many cultural backgrounds. All this was well known long before the word *diversity* became an insistent part of our vocabulary, an invocation, an imperative, or a bludgeon in ideological conflicts.

The very motto of the country, *E. Pluribus Unum,* recognizes the diversity of the American people. For generations, this diversity has been celebrated, whether in comedies like *Abie's Irish Rose* (the famous play featuring a Jewish boy and an Irish girl) or in patriotic speeches on the Fourth of July. Yet one senses something very different in today's crusades for "diversity"; certainly not a patriotic celebration of America and often a sweeping criticism of the United States, or even a condemnation of Western civilization as a whole.

At the very least, we need to separate the issue of the general importance of cultural diversity—not only in the United States but in the world at large—from the more specific, more parochial, and more ideological agendas that have become associated with this word in recent years. I would like to talk about the worldwide importance of cultural diversity over centuries of human history before returning to the narrower issues of our time.

The entire history of the human race, the rise of man from the caves, has been marked by transfers of cultural advances from one group to another and from one civilization to another. Paper and printing, for example, are today vital parts of Western civilization, but they originated in China centuries before they made their way to Europe. So did the magnetic compass, which made possible the great ages of exploration that put the Western hemisphere in touch with the rest of mankind. Mathematical concepts likewise migrated from one culture to another: Trigonometry from ancient Egypt, and the whole numbering system now used throughout the world originated among the Hindus of India, though Europeans called this system *Arabic numerals* because it was the Arabs who were the intermediaries through which these numbers reached medieval Europe. Indeed, much of the philosophy of ancient Greece first reached Western Europe in Arabic translations, which were then retranslated into Latin or into the vernacular languages of the West Europeans.

Much that became part of the culture of Western civilization originated outside that civilization, often in the Middle East or Asia. The game of chess came from India, gunpowder from China, and various mathematical concepts from the Islamic world, for example. The conquest of Spain by Moslems in the eighth century A.D. made Spain a center for the diffusion into Western Europe of the more advanced knowledge of the Mediterranean world and of the Orient in astronomy, medicine, optics, and geometry.

The later rise of Western Europe to world preeminence in science and technology built upon these foundations, and then the science and technology of European civilization began to spread around the world, not only to European offshoot societies such as the United States or Australia, but also to non-European cultures, of which Japan is perhaps the most striking example.

The historic sharing of cultural advances, until they became the common inheritance of the human race, implied much more than cultural diversity. It implied that some cultural features were not only different from others but better than others. The very fact that people—all people, whether Europeans, Africans, Asians, or others—have repeatedly chosen to abandon some feature of their own culture in order to replace it with something from another culture implies that the replacement served their purposes more effectively. Arabic numerals are not simply different from Roman numerals, they are better than Roman numerals. This is shown by their replacing Roman numerals in many countries whose own cultures derived from Rome, as well as in other countries whose respective numbering systems were likewise superseded by so-called Arabic numerals.

It is virtually inconceivable today that the distances in astronomy or the complexities of higher mathematics should be expressed in Roman numerals. Merely to express the year of the declaration of American independence as MDCCLXXVI requires more than twice as many Roman numerals as Arabic numerals. Moreover, Roman numerals offer more opportunities for errors, as the same digit may be either added or substracted, depending on its place in sequence. Roman numerals are good for numbering kings or Super Bowls, but they cannot match the efficiency of Arabic numerals in most mathematical operations—and that is, after all, why we have numbers at all. Cultural features do not exist merely as badges of identity to which we have some emotional attachment. They exist to meet the necessities and to forward the purposes of human life. When they are surpassed by features of other cultures, they tend to fall by the wayside or to survive only as marginal curiosities like Roman numerals today.

Not only concepts, information, products, and technologies transfer from one culture to another. The natural produce of the earth does the same. Malaysia is the world's leading grower of rubber trees—but those trees are indigenous to Brazil. Most of rice grown in Africa today originated in Asia, and its tobacco originated in the Western hemisphere. Even a great wheat-exporting nation like Argentina once imported wheat, which was not an indigenous crop to that country. Cultural diversity, viewed internationally and historically, is not a static picture of differentness but a dynamic picture of competition in which what serves human purposes more effectively survives while what does not tends to decline or disappear.

Manuscript scrolls once preserved the precious records, knowledge, and thought of European or Middle Eastern cultures. But once paper and printing from China became known in these cultures, books were clearly far faster and cheaper to produce and drove scrolls virtually into extinction. Books were not simply different from scrolls; they were better than scrolls. The point that some cultural features are better than others must be insisted on today because so many among the intelligentsia either evade or deny this plain reality. The intelligentsia often use words like *perceptions* and *values* as they argue in effect that it is all a matter of how you choose to look at it.

They may have a point in such things as music, art, and literature from different cultures, but there are many human purposes common to peoples of all cultures. They want to live rather than die, for example. When Europeans first ventured into the arid interior of Australia, they often died of thirst or hunger in a land where the Australian aborigines had no trouble finding food or water, within that particular setting, at least, the aboriginal culture enabled people to do what both the aborigines and Europeans wanted to do—survive. A given culture may not be superior for all things in all settings, much less remain superior over time, but particular cultural features may nevertheless be clearly better for some purposes—not just different.

Why is there any such argument in the first place? Perhaps it is because we are still living in the long, grim shadow of the Nazi Holocaust and are, therefore, understandably reluctant to label anything or anyone "superior" or "inferior." But we do not need to. We need only recognize that particular products, skills, technologies, agricultural crops, or intellectual concepts accomplish particular purposes better than their alternatives. It is not necessary to rank one whole culture over another in all things, much less to claim that they remain in that same ranking throughout history. They do not.

Clearly, cultural leadership in various fields has changed hands many times. China was far in advance of any country in Europe in a large number of fields for at least a thousand years and, as late as the sixteenth century, had the highest standard of living in the world. Equally clearly, China today is one of the poorer nations of the world and is having great difficulty trying to catch up to the technological level of Japan and the West, with no real hope of regaining its former world preeminence in the foreseeable future.

Similar rises and falls of nations and empires have been common over long stretches of human history—for example, the rise and fall of the Roman Empire, the "golden age" of medieval Spain and its decline to the level of one of the poorest nations in Europe today, the centuries-long triumphs of the Ottoman Empire intellectually as well as on the battlefields of Europe and the Middle East, and then its long decline to become known as "the sick man of Europe." Yet, while cultural leadership has changed hands many times, that leadership had been real at given times, and much of what was achieved in the process has contributed enormously to our well-being and opportunities today. Cultural competition is not a zero-sum game. It is what advances the human race.

If nations and civilizations differ in their effectiveness in different fields of endeavor, so do social groups. Here is especially strong resistance to accepting the reality of different levels and kinds of skills, interests, habits, and orientations among different groups of people. One academic writer, for example, said that nineteenth-century Jewish immigrants to the United States were fortunate to arrive just as the garment industry in New York began to develop. I could not help thinking that Hank Aaron was similarly fortunate that he often came to bat just as a home run was due to be hit. It might be possible to believe that these Jewish immigrants just happened to be in the right place at the right time if you restricted yourself to their history in the United States. But, again taking a world view, we find Jews prominent, often predominant, and usually prospering, in the apparel industry in medieval Spain, in the Ottoman Empire, in the Russian Empire, in Argentina, in Australia, and in Brazil. How surprised should we be to find them predominant in the same industry in America?

Other groups have excelled in other special occupations and industries. Indeed, virtually every group excels at something. Germans, for example, have been prominent as pioneers in the piano industry. American piano brands like Steinway and Knabe, not to mention the Wurlitzer organ, are signs of the long prominence of Germans in this industry, where they produced the first pianos in Colonial America. Germans also pioneered in piano-building in Czarist Russia, Australia, France, and England. Chinese immigrants have, at one period of history or another, run more than half the grocery stores in Kingston, Jamaica, and Panama City and conducted more than half of all retail trade in Malaysia, the Philippines, Vietnam, and Cambodia. Other groups have dominated the retail trade in other parts of the world—the Gujaratis from India in East Africa and in Fiji or the Lebanese in parts of West Africa, for example.

Nothing has been more common than for particular groups—often a minority—to dominate particular occupations or industries. Seldom do they have any ability to keep out others and certainly not to keep out the majority population. They are simply better at the particular skills required in that occupation or industry. Sometimes we can see why. When Italians have made wine in Italy for centuries, it is hardly surprising that they should become prominent among winemakers in Argentina and in California's Napa Valley. Similarly, when Germans in Germany have been for centuries renowned for their beermaking, how surprised should we be that in Argentina they became as prominent among brewers as Italians among winemakers? How surprised should we be that beermaking, in the United States arose where there were concentrations of German immigrants in Milwaukee and St. Louis, for example? Or that the leading beer producers to this day have German names like Anheuser-Busch or Coors, among many other German names?

Just as cultural leadership in a particular field is not permanent for nations or civilizations, neither is it permanent for given racial, ethnic, or religious groups. By the time the Jews were expelled from Spain in 1492, Europe had overtaken the Islamic world in medical science, so that Jewish physicians who sought refuge in the Ottoman Empire found themselves in great demand in that Moslem country. By the early sixteenth century, the sultan of the Ottoman Empire had on his palace medical staff 42 Jewish physicians and 21 Moslem physicians.

With the passage of time, however, the source of the Jews' advantage — their knowledge of Western medicine — eroded as successive generations of Ottoman Jews lost contact with the West and its further progress. Christian minorities within the Ottoman Empire began to replace the Jews, not only in medicine but also in international trade and even in the theater, once dominated by Jews. The difference was that these Christian minorities — notably Greeks and Armenians — maintained their ties in Christian Europe and often sent their sons there to be educated. It was not race or ethnicity as such that was crucial but maintaining contacts with the ongoing progress of Western civilization. By contrast, the Ottoman Jews became a declining people in a declining empire. Many, if not most, were Sephardic Jews from Spain, once the elite of the world Jewry. But by the time the state of Israel was formed in the twentieth century, those Sephardic Jews who had settled for centuries in the Islamic world now lagged painfully behind the Ashkenazic Jews of the Western world — notably in income and education. To get some idea what a historic reversal that has been in the relative positions of Sephardic Jews and Ashkenazic Jews, one need only note that Sephardic Jews in colonial America sometimes disinherited their own children for marrying Ashkenazic Jews.

Why do some groups, subgroups, nations, or whole civilizations excel in some particular fields rather than others? All too often, the answer to this question must be: Nobody really knows. It is an unanswered question largely because it is an unasked question. There is an uphill struggle merely to get acceptance of the fact that large differences exist among peoples, not just in specific skills in the narrow sense (computer science, basketball, or brewing beer) but more fundamentally in different interests, orientations, and values that determine which particular skills they seek to develop and with what degree of success. Merely to suggest that these internal cultural factors play a significant role in various economic, educational, or social outcomes is to invite charges of "blaming the victim." It is much more widely acceptable to blame surrounding social conditions or institutional policies.

But if we look at cultural diversity internationally and historically, there is a more basic question than whether blame is the real issue. Surely, no human being should be blamed for the way his culture evolved for centuries before he was born. Blame has nothing to do with it. Another explanation that has had varying amounts of acceptance at different times and places is the biological or genetic theory of differences among peoples. I have argued against this theory in many places but will not take the time to go into these lengthy arguments here. A world view of cultural differences over the centuries undermines the genetic theory as well. Europeans and Chinese, for example, are clearly genetically different. Equally clearly, China was a more advanced civilization than Europe in many ways, scientific, technological, and organizational, for at least a thousand years. Yet over the past few centuries, Europe has moved ahead of China in many of these same ways. If those cultural differences were due to genes, how could these two races have changed positions so radically from one epoch in history to another?

All explanations of differences between groups can be broken down into heredity and environment. Yet a world view of the history of cultural diversity seems, on the surface at least, to deny both. One reason for this is that we have thought of environment too narrowly, as the immediate surrounding circumstances or differing institutional policies toward different groups. Environment in that narrow sense may explain some group differences, but the histories of many groups completely contradict that particular version of environment as an explanation. Let us take just two examples out of many that are available.

Jewish immigrants from Eastern Europe and Italian immigrants from southern Italy began arriving in the United States in large numbers at about the same time in the late nineteenth century, and their large-scale immigration also ended at the same time, when restrictive immigration laws were passed in the 1920s. The two groups arrived here in virtually the same economic condition—namely, destitute. They often lived in the same neighborhoods and their children attended the same schools, sitting side by side in the same classrooms. Their environments, in the narrow sense in which the term is commonly used, were virtually identical. Yet their social histories in the United States have been very different.

Over the generations, both groups rose, but they rose at different rates, through different means, and in a very different mixture of occupations and industries. Even wealthy Jews and wealthy Italians tended to become rich in different sectors of the economy. The California wine industry, for example, is full of Italian names like Mondavi, Gallo, and Rossi but the only prominent Jewish winemaker, Manishewitz, makes an entirely different kind of wine, and no one would compare Jewish winemakers with Italian winemakers in the United States. When we look at Jews and Italians in the very different environmental setting of Argentina, we see the same general pattern of differences between them. The same is true if we look at the differences between Jews and Italians in Australia, or Canada, or Western Europe.

Jews are not Italians and Italians are not Jews. Anyone familiar with their very different histories over many centuries should not be surprised. Their fate in America was not determined solely by their surrounding social conditions in America or by how they were treated by American society. They were different before they got on the boats to cross the ocean, and those differences crossed the ocean with them.

We can take it a step further. Even Ashkenazic Jews, those originating in Eastern Europe, have had significantly different economic and social histories from those originating in Germanic Central Europe, including Austria as well as Germany itself. These differences have persisted among their descendents not only in New York and Chicago but as far away as Melbourne and Sydney. In Australia, Jews from Eastern Europe have tended to cluster in and around Melbourne, while Germanic Jews have settled in and around Sydney.

They even have a saying among themselves that Melbourne is a cold city with warm Jews while Sydney is a warm city with cold Jews.

A second and very different example of persistent cultural differences involves immigrants from Japan. As everyone knows, many Japanese-Americans were interned during the Second World War. What is less well known is that there is and has been an even larger Japanese population in Brazil than in the United States. These Japanese, incidentally, own approximately three-quarters as much land in Brazil as there is in Japan. (The Japanese almost certainly own more agricultural land in Brazil than in Japan.) In any event, very few Japanese in Brazil were interned during the Second World War. Moreover, the Japanese in Brazil were never subjected to the discrimination suffered by Japanese-Americans in the decades before the Second World War.

Yet, during the war, Japanese-Americans overwhelmingly remained loyal to the United States and Japanese-American soldiers won more than their share of medals in combat. But in Brazil, the Japanese were overwhelmingly and even fanatically loyal to Japan. You cannot explain the difference by anything in the environment of the United States or the environment of Brazil. But if you know something about the history of those Japanese who settled in these two countries, you know that they were culturally different in Japan before they ever got on the boats to take them across the Pacific Ocean and they were still different decades later. These two groups of immigrants left Japan during very different periods in the cultural evolution of Japan itself. A modern Japanese scholar has said: "If you want to see Japan of the Meiji era, go to the United States. If you want to see Japan of the Taisho era, go to Brazil." The Meiji era was a more cosmopolitan, pro-American era; the Taisho era was one of fanatical Japanese nationalism.

If the narrow concept of environment fails to explain many profound differences between groups and subgroups, it likewise fails to explain many very large differences in the economic and social performances of nations and civilizations. An eighteenth-century writer in Chile described that country's many natural advantages in climate, soil, and natural resources and then asked in complete bewilderment why it was such a poverty-stricken country. The same question could be asked of many countries today.

Conversely, we could ask why Japan and Switzerland are so prosperous when they are both almost totally lacking in natural resources. Both are rich in what economists call "human capital"—the skills of their people. No doubt there is a long and complicated history behind the different skill levels of different peoples and nations. The point here is that the immediate environment—whether social or geographic—is only part of the story.

Geography may well have a significant role in the history of peoples, but perhaps not simply by presenting them with more or less natural resources. Geography shapes or limits peoples' opportunities for cultural interaction and the mutual development that comes out of this. Small, isolated islands in the sea have seldom been sources of new scientific advances of technological breakthroughs, regardless of where such islands were located and regardless of the race of people on these islands. There are islands on land as well. Where soil, fertile enough to support human life, exists only in isolated patches, widely separated, there tend to be isolate cultures (often with different languages or dialects) in a culturally fragmented region. Isolated highlands often produce insular cultures, lagging in many ways behind the cultures of the lowlanders of the same race—whether we are talking about medieval Scotland, colonial Ceylon, or the contemporary montagnards of Vietnam.

With geographical environments as with social environments, we are talking about long-run effects not simply the effects, of immediate surroundings. When Scottish highlanders, for example, immigrated to North Carolina in colonial times, they had a very different history from that of Scottish lowlanders who settled in North Carolina. For one thing, the lowlanders spoke English while the highlanders spoke Gaelic on into the nineteenth century. Obviously, speaking only Gaelic in an English-speaking country affects a group's whole economic and social progress.

Geographical conditions vary as radically in terms of how well they facilitate or impede large-scale cultural interactions as they do in their distribution of natural resources. We are not even close to being able to explain how all these geographical influences have operated throughout history. This too is an unanswered question largely because it is an unasked question, and it is an unasked question because many are seeking answers in terms of immediate social environment or are vehemently insistent that they have already found the answer in those terms.

How radically do geographic environments differ, not just in terms of tropical versus arctic climates, but also in the very configuration of the land and how this helps or hinders large-scale interactions among peoples? Consider one statistic: Africa is more than twice the size of Europe, and yet Africa has a shorter coastline than Europe. This seems almost impossible. But the reason is that Europe's coastline is far more convoluted, with many harbors and inlets being formed all around the continent. Much of the coastline of Africa is smooth, which is to say, lacking in the harbors that make large-scale maritime trade possible by sheltering the ships at anchor from the rough waters of the open sea.

Waterways of all sorts have played a major role in the evolution of cultures and nations around the world. Harbors on the sea are not the only waterways. Rivers are also very important. Virtually every major city on earth is located either on a river or a harbor. Whether it is such great harbors as those in Sydney, Singapore, or San Francisco; or London on the Thames, Paris on the Seine, or numerous other European cities on the Danube—waterways have been the lifeblood of urban centers for centuries. Only very recently has man-made, self-powered transportation, like automobiles and airplanes, made it possible to produce an exception to the rule like Los Angeles. (There is a Los Angeles River, but you do not have to be Moses to walk across it in the summertime.) New York has both a long and deep river and a huge sheltered harbor.

None of these geographical features in themselves create a great city or develop an urban culture. Human beings do that. But geography sets the limits within which people can operate and in some places it sets those limits much wider than in others. Returning to our comparison of the continents of Europe and Africa, we find that they differ as radically in rivers as they do in harbors. There are entire nations in Africa without a single navigable river—Libya and South Africa, for example.

"Navigable" is the crucial word. Some African rivers are navigable only during the rainy season. Some are navigable only between numerous cataracts and waterfalls. Even the Zaire River, which is longer than any river in North America and carries a larger volume of water, has too many water-falls too close to the ocean for it to become a major artery of international commerce. Such commerce is facilitated in Europe not only by numerous navigable rivers but also by the fact that no spot on the continent, outside of Russia, is more than 500 miles from the sea. Many places in Africa are more than 500 miles from the sea, including the entire nation of Uganda.

Against this background, how surprised should we be to find that Europe is the most urbanized of all inhabited continents and Africa the least urban-ized? Urbanization is not the be-all and end-all of life, but certainly an urban culture is bound to differ substantially from non-urban cultures, and the skills peculiar to an urban culture are far more likely to be found among groups from an urban civilization. Conversely, an interesting history could be written about the failures of urbanized groups in agricultural settlements.

Looking within Africa, the influence of geography seems equally clear. The most famous ancient civilization on the continent arose within a few miles on either side of Africa's longest navigable river, the Nile, and even today the two largest cities on the continent, Cairo and Alexandria, are on that river. The great West African kingdoms in the region served by the Niger River and the long-flourishing East African economy based around the great natural harbor on the island of Zanzibar are further evidences of the role of geography. Again, geography is not all-determining—the economy of Zanzibar has been ruined by government policy in recent decades—but nevertheless, geography is an important long-run influence on the shaping of cultures as well as in narrow economic terms.

What are the implications of a world view of cultural diversity on the nar-rower issues being debated under that label in the United States today? Although "diversity" is used in so many different ways in so many different contexts that it seems to mean all things to all people, there are a few themes that appear again and again. One of these broad themes is that diversity implies organized efforts at the preservation of cultural differences, perhaps governmental efforts, perhaps government subsidies to various programs run by the advocates of diversity.

This approach raises questions as to what the purpose of culture is. If what is important about cultures is that they are emotionally symbolic, and if differentness is cherished for the sake of differentness, then this particular version of cultural diversity might make some sense. But cultures exist even in isolated societies where there are no other cultures around—where there is no one else and nothing else from which to be different. Cultures exist to serve the vital, practical requirements of human life—to structure a society so as to perpetuate the species, to pass on the hard-earned knowledge and experience of generations past and centuries past to the young and inexperienced in order to spare the next generation the costly and dangerous process of learning everything all over again from scratch through trial and error—including fatal errors. Cultures exist so that people can know how to get food and put a roof over their head, how to cure the sick, how to cope with the death of loved ones, and how to get along with the living. Cultures are not bumper stickers. They are living, changing ways of doing all the things that have to be done in life.

Every culture discards over time the things that no longer do the job or which do not do the job as well as things borrowed from other cultures. Each individual does this, consciously or not, on a day-to-day basis. Languages take words from other languages, so that Spanish as spoken in Spain includes words taken from Arabic, and Spanish as spoken in Argentina has Italian words taken from the large Italian immigrant population there. People eat Kentucky Fried Chicken in Singapore and stay in Hilton Hotels in Cairo. This is not what some of the advocates of diversity have in mind. They seem to want to preserve cultures in their purity, almost like butterflies preserved in amber. Decisions about change, if any, seem to be regarded as collective decisions, political decisions. But this is not how cultures have arrived where they are. Individuals have decided for themselves how much of the old they wished to retain, how much of the new they found useful in their own lives.

In this way, cultures have enriched each other in all the great civilizations of the world. In this way, great port cities and other crossroads of cultures have become centers of progress all across the planet. No culture has grown great in isolation—but a number of cultures have made historic and even astonishing advances when their isolation was ended, usually by events beyond their control.

Japan was a classic example in the nineteenth century, but a similar story could be told of Scotland in an earlier era, when a country where once even the nobility were illiterate became, within a short time as history is measured, a country that produced world pioneers in field after field: David Hume in philosophy, Adam Smith in economics, Joseph Black in chemistry, Robert Adam in architecture, and James Watt, whose steam engine revolutionized modern industry and transport. In the process, the Scots lost their language but gained world preeminence in many fields. Then a whole society moved to higher standards of living than anyone ever dreamed of in their poverty-stricken past.

There were higher standards in other ways as well. As late as the eighteenth century, it was considered noteworthy that pedestrians in Edinburgh no longer had to be on the alert for sewage being thrown out the windows of people's homes or apartments. The more considerate Scots yelled a warning, but they threw out the sewage anyway. Perhaps it was worth losing a little of the indigenous culture to be rid of that problem. Those who use the term "cultural diversity" to promote a multiplicity of segregated ethnic enclaves are doing an enormous harm to the people in those enclaves. However they live socially, the people in those enclaves are going to have to compete economically for a livelihood. Even if they were not disadvantaged before, they will be very dis-advantaged if their competitors from the general population are free to tap the knowledge, skills, and analytical techniques Western civilization has drawn from all the other civilizations of the world, while those in the enclaves are restricted to what exists in the subculture immediately around them.

We need also to recognize that many great thinkers of the past—whether in medicine or philosophy, science or economics—labored not simply to advance whatever particular group they happened to have come from but to advance the human race. Their legacies, whether cures for deadly diseases or dramatic increases in crop yields to fight the scourge of hunger, belong to all people—and all people need to claim that legacy, not seal themselves off in a dead-end of tribalism or in an emotional orgy of cultural vanity.

Discussion Questions

1. Most Americans have grown up with the United States leading the world in many areas such as technology, standard of living, medicine, and education. Is it important that we always lead in these areas? How can diversity in the work-force help us advance? Have we made good use of our human resources in the past? Why or why not?

2. The United States regularly exchanges scientists, business and industry leaders, and technology with countries all over the world. Would the author think this is a good idea, or will this just help other countries get ahead of us?

3. In America, the management of workers by "assimilation into the workforce" is being replaced by the "integration of diversity." How would the author explain this shift in approach?

4. The author states that "What serves human purposes more effectively survives, while what does not, tends to decline or disappear." What aspects of American culture in general do you think may decline? What aspects of American business culture may decline?

5. List things that we have now or the ways things are done now that differ markedly from your parents' generation.

6. It has been said that English is the international language of business; Italian is the international language of music; French is the international language of diplomacy. What explanation would the author give for this? Might this change?

Assignment

Nobel Prizes are probably the most famous international awards. Nobel Prizes are awarded for contributions affecting all cultures in the areas of physiology/ medicine, chemistry, physics, literature, economics, and peace. Recipients receive a gold medal and diploma on December 10, the anniversary of the death of Albert Nobel. The Peace Prize is awarded in Oslo; the science and literature prizes in Stockholm.

In October 1999, *The Chronicle of Higher Education* carried an article entitled "U.S. Dominates Nobel Prizes in Science, But All Its Winners Are Foreign-Born." That article exemplified modern-day exchange among cultures and inspired this closer look at international contributions.

Instructions:

Group I:	Research the birth countries of Americans winning Nobel Prizes. Separately list the winners and their birth countries for each of the prize categories for the past 25 years. Record your findings on the form supplied by your instructor. Note the *different kinds* of contributions made to the United States by the foreign-born American winners.
Groups II–VII:	Research the nationalities (citizenship) of Nobel Prize winners. For the prize category assigned to your group, list the winners for the past 50 years. Record your findings on the form supplied by your instructor. Examine your findings for patterns of cultural concentrations.
All Groups:	The class will reassemble to compile findings and discuss trends and implications.

Sources: www.almaz.com/nobel/nobel.html   www.almaz.xom/nobel

TREASURE HUNT: CROSS-CULTURAL INVENTIONS AND CONTRIBUTIONS

M. June Allard
Worcester State College

David P. Harvey
Worcester, MA

Instructions

1. Guess the culture making the contribution shown in each box and write it on the line in the left column.
2. Research the contribution to determine the actual cultural source and the inventor if applicable, and write it on the line in the right column.

Source: www.historychannel.com

1. _____   _____

2. _____   _____

3. _____   _____

4. _____   _____

5. _____   _____

6. _____   _____

7. _____   _____

8. _____   _____

9. _____   _____

10. _____   _____

11. _____   _____

12. _____   _____

13. _____   _____

14. _____   _____

15. _____   _____

1. Toothbrush	2. Penicillin	3. Movable Type
4. Degree-Granting University	5. Nuclear Fission	6. Pendulum clock
7. Perspective Drawing	8. Computer with Memory	9. Eyeglasses
10. Digital Adding Machine	11. Steam Engine	12. Dynamite
13. Photograph	14. Wireless Transmission of Signal	15. Satellite

THE EMOTIONAL CONNECTION OF DISTINGUISHING DIFFERENCES AND CONFLICT

Carole G. Parker

Seton Hill University

In recent years, diversity in organizations has been an exciting, stimulating, frustrating, and intriguing topic. Some organizations continue to struggle for diversity whereas others have a fully integrated diverse workforce. The challenge to increase and manage diversity continues to be critical to organizational goals, particularly as more organizations, large and small, transact business internationally. Some organizations work to appreciate diversity and value differences, whereas others continue to discount differences and diversity. Smart managers today realize the importance of balance in work groups. Attempts to incorporate differences in age, gender, race, culture, sexual preference, and styles of being in their organizations to capitalize on the incredible potential diversity offers are occurring. Managing differences requires energy, commitment, tolerance, and finally, appreciation among all parties involved. Differences among people are not inherently good or bad; there is no one "right" way to deal with differences. Learning to manage and ultimately appreciate differences requires learning, emotional growth, and stretching the boundaries of all participants. Although differences can be challenging, they also lead to very important benefits, both to individuals, groups and organizations.

HOW DIFFERENCES ARE OFTEN MANAGED

What action and factors must be uppermost in selecting the most appropriate approach to addressing differences? Often avoidance or repressions are used to manage differences. The avoidance of differences often takes the form of associating with individuals of similar backgrounds, experiences, beliefs, and values. This strategy enables an environment of mutual support and predictability.

Those who are adverse to risk or challenges are apt to select this strategy. Another avoidance strategy is to separate individuals who create sparks between each other. Although this strategy may reduce tension, it minimizes the opportunity for individuals and the organization to learn and grow.

The repression of differences occurs when an individual or organization refuses to allow disagreements to emerge. Top management often influences the culture by stressing conformity, which naturally affects diversity. Statements by managers such as: "We must work on this project in a professional and collegial manner," or "By working together cooperatively, we will succeed during these difficult times," create the boundaries for behavior limited to cooperation, collaboration, and loyalty and limit the opportunity for challenging assumptions, testing new ideas, and strategies for success. Repression is quite costly. Resistances develop that have both organizational and individual consequences. Blocking strong feelings and repressing differences may result in desensitization and loss of productivity. When individual differences come together, managers exert control to reduce conflict.

Both appropriate times and dangers are associated with the use of avoidance and repression in managing differences. Teams or work groups faced with tight deadlines may want to limit the number and type of ideas generated. Avoidance may be an appropriate interim strategy for dealing with differences by enabling an individual to learn more about a person or situation before advancing a stance. The challenge to management is to decide when it is most appropriate to use these approaches. The skill level of the manager, rather than an overt choice, may also influence the decision. Avoidance can lead to groupthink, which occurs when everyone in a group agrees with everyone else, even though there are different opinions, values, beliefs, and perceptions among group members. Groupthink is the result of not challenging ideas, opinions, values, or beliefs. Individuals may not believe it is safe (concerns about advancing or retaining one's job) to challenge, particularly if management does not model this behavior.

Still another danger in avoiding differences is overcompatibility. When overcompatibility exists in an organization, it may be due to a strong need for support, reassurance, or security or a need to eliminate perceived threats. In an organization, this can severely hamper the development of new ideas, productivity, growth, and development. Avoidance and repression of differences are not viable solutions. When differences are present, they must be expressed and worked through. If not, unnecessary conflict will result.

POSITIVE ASPECTS OF DIFFERENCES

- Differences are opportunities. The old adage "Two heads are better than one" has merit. When combining multiple perspectives, one gains a richer set of experiences, and the variability of these often leads to a more creative approach than could be achieved independently.
- Differences are tests to the strength of a position. One needs to be sure all the aspects of a situation have been considered, all loops carefully closed. Multiple perspectives, opinions, and perceptions enhance the final product.

A healthy interaction among differences (gender, age, race, culture, etc.) could address the preceding concerns. Two factors influence the treatment of differences: first, the needs, wants and goals of the individual; and second, the value placed on the relationship. People are often motivated by the desire to meet their needs and satisfy their wants and desires. The stronger the motivation, the greater the likelihood of addressing differences. Furthermore, when the persons involved are important to each other, or valued, the tendency to manage the difference increases to preserve the relationship. The reverse is likely when there is no value in the relationship. Once these factors are assessed, it becomes necessary to recognize behavior and attitudes that *will* be helpful in managing the differences.

Differences are not problems to be solved; they are dilemmas to be managed. Successful managers of difference reduce their judgments and accept the difference as legitimate. Clear boundaries between self and others, a willingness and interest in being influenced, and an awareness of choice with the ability to make choices are also helpful. Using strong language such as *ought to, cannot, necessary, impossible, requirement,* or *mandate* will diminish success.

Differences are experienced from contact with others who are dissimilar. A range of life experiences and success in interpersonal relationships support the ability to deal with differences. Individuals who have traveled nationally and internationally or who have had unusual experiences beyond the normal scope of their daily activities tend to develop an appreciation for differences, even though at the time of initial contact there may have been challenges, fear, and longing for what is familiar. Managing differences is not an individual process; it is interactive among individuals. When only one individual is attempting to deal with the difference, the result is coping behavior. Dealing with differences evokes emotion. A range of emotions for human interaction that leads to awareness of differences is necessary. These emotions can lead to conflict but conflict is *not* a prerequisite to managing differences.

Differences evoke emotions at different levels, ranging from small or minor to large and major. An inverted triangle graphically shows the escalating intensity in each level of emotion as differences are encountered (see Figure 1).

This model is based on the assumption that difficulties will likely result from contact with differences. The first level involves an awareness of the difference. Here the parties exploring and learning about each other—what is similar—what is not and discomfort; the second level may result. One becomes uncomfortable with boundaries being pushed while values or beliefs are challenged. When the differences appear to be greater than the similarities, annoyance occurs. The parties are not able to appreciate how their differences may be beneficial to each other. Irritation, on the next level, may result from continued exploration, possibly through a dialectic process. Tension is heightening as more contact occurs; there is possibly an overlay of fear. The boundaries of self are threatened (What will happen to me if I continue with this encounter?), and frustration leading to open disagreement develops.

Anger, often a protective strategy, shifts the emotions to the next level, and hostility erupts while the dispute solidifies. Each party has a firm stance reflecting

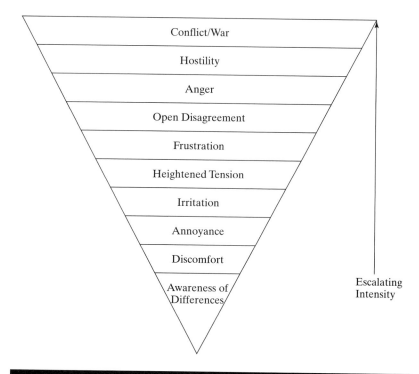

FIGURE 1   The Escalation of Differences into Conflict

their position. The final level is conflict or war, where each party works hard to repress, neutralize or destroy the other. In Figure 1, we suggest that an individual, group, organization, or society may, depending on the situation, traverse through each of these emotional levels when encountering differences. The process is not necessarily a linear one. Emotions run deep on various issues and could erupt immediately from awareness to hostility or anger or any other step on the triangle. In fact, awareness can lead to avoidance, tolerance, or appreciation.

Recent history lends itself to application to the triangle. In February 1993, terrorists, who have different values and beliefs than most Americans, bombed the New York City World Trade Center. The explosion caused six deaths, 1,042 injuries, and nearly $600 million in property damage. Americans were shocked, and then President Clinton declared that every effort should be taken to bring those responsible to justice. Swift actions lead to the prosecution and conviction of four of seven coconspirators. Yet, the American public, although outraged and frightened by the experience, only demonstrated minimal awareness that there were dramatic differences between the U.S. foreign policy and those on the receiving end of the policy. Not until seven years later, with the attacks on the World Trade Center again, along with the Pentagon in Washington D.C., did awareness shift to outrage, anger, hostility, and ultimately conflict/war.

During the aftermath of the events of September 11, 2001, when thousands of people from many countries met their peril in the attack on the

World Trade Center, the United States unified against all who would harm her. In many instances, those who disagreed with the policy to go to war against those responsible for this terrorist act were afraid to speak out. It was considered anti-American to express different opinions about how to handle terrorist activity focused on the United States. Such behavior is an example of groupthink, mentioned earlier in this chapter. The government is particularly susceptible to groupthink where patriotism must be at the highest, yet evidence of dissent tends to make its way to the media, newsprint, or television. Still, individuals may be reluctant to speak candidly against the actions of government policy.

Conflict, at the top of the triangle, may result or emerge from differences. There are many definitions of conflict. For our purposes, conflict is defined based on the experiences of participants in the Transcendus Exercise found in this text. From the moment Earthling groups come together to figure out how to explain conflict to their visitors, participants often find themselves confronting substantial differences with respect to both their ways of defining conflict and the positive and negative values attached to it. Listed here are typical examples of definitions generated by Earthling groups about conflict:

1. Conflict exists when two or more parties want the same thing or their wants are incompatible in some way.
2. Conflict must involve emotionality; it is a disturbing emotion within ourselves and may involve feelings of anger and frustration.
3. The higher the stakes, the greater the conflict; one must *care* to have conflict.
4. Conflict can be internal: within oneself, a group, or between groups. Conflict involves competition of wants and viewpoints.
5. Conflict can be enjoyable.

It is important to distinguish conflict from difference. Difference and conflict are both important and necessary ingredients in human interaction and, if valued, can lead to opportunity, creativity, and appreciation. Difference is a component of diversity, which is a constant in our environment. Managers and the workforce are grappling with this constant and learning that appreciating or valuing differences opens the door to new and creative ways of addressing organizational challenges. For example, when a group of salaried and union personnel from the automotive industry were invited to identify adjectives they associate with conflict, most of the language was highly charged, emotional, and violent. The list generated for differences was dramatically broader, more varied, and less emotionally charged and contained language of hope (see Table 1).

The autoworkers pointed out that differences can lead to conflict and cited examples including the inability to motivate employees to complete their assigned jobs, poor communication, pressures concerning time, inequity in work assignments, differences of opinions, and methods for getting work done. They further pointed out how important it is for people to listen to each other and pay attention to the difference, incorporating the difference in the

TABLE 1 Distinguishing Difference and Conflict	
Conflict	*Difference*
Anger	Opinions
War	Ideas
Tension	Options
Frustration	Methods
Kill	Skills
Hostility	Race
Shouting	Gender
	Jobs
	Age
	Interpretation
	Values
	Environment

process of solving a problem or completing a task, not just engaging in conflict because of the difference.

It was believed that when a diverse team worked together, there was greater creativity and innovation, a sense of connectedness, more risk taking, less boredom, higher productivity, and greater cooperation. On the other hand, the mismanagement of differences or engaging in conflictual behavior in the organization would most likely lead to higher stress, individual withdrawal, limited learning, less risk taking, overcompatibility, interpersonal tension, and decreased communication.

THE EMOTIONAL CONNECTION

Emotional intelligence is one key to developing the ability to manage and appreciate differences. Emotional intelligence involves at least five elements: awareness of self, the ability to recognize personal emotions when they are occurring; managing self, which involves awareness of and engaging in emotions that are appropriate to a situation; self-motivation, putting emotional energy into action for a useful person and controlling emotions when necessary; awareness of emotions in others, which involves empathy and demonstrating caring when appropriate; and finally, managing interpersonal relationships, which involves dealing with both self and others in social, professional and personal interactions (Goleman, 1995). Emotional intelligence, then, is the ability to be aware of, name, and manage individual experience of emotions. The triangle in Figure 1 illustrates the escalating intensity of emotions when differences are mismanaged or misunderstood and develop into conflict. Managers must recognize that it is the diversity in styles of interacting and the particular way a person or group makes meaning of their experience that creates the experience of difference. Difference enables choice and opportunity as much as it may create tension and insecurity; this also enables the organization to achieve its objectives. Differences provide opportunities to develop our emotional intelligence. According to Cherniss and Goleman (2001), managers and workers who develop their emotional intelligence may be able to improve their effectiveness at work and potential for advancement. In addition, personal relationships will also improve and strengthen when an individual develops emotional intelligence.

The family unit is an excellent and readily accessible unit for exploring and experimenting with emotional intelligence. Our home life is often a place where we must manage differences with significant consequences for either harmony or unrest. One answer to understanding the emotional impact of encountering differences at home or in the work environment may come with knowledge of three major transitions occurring in contemporary society. Fritz Capra (1982) suggests that a paradigm shift in the thoughts, perceptions, and values that form a particular view of reality is essential if the world is to survive. This is a pattern or paradigm shift involving moving from certainty to uncertainty, closed to open systems, truth to no truth, and a realization of multiple realities coexisting in a complex society. Recognition and mastery of this paradigm shift may prove to be a motivation for developing the emotional skills necessary for valuing diversity and managing differences.

Historically, it has not been acceptable for professionals to exhibit emotions in the workplace; with the introduction of emotional intelligence, there is more acceptance of the whole person and the resulting complexity. When managing diversity or differences, one has at least four options for guiding behavior: avoidance, conflict, tolerance, and appreciation. Avoidance provides an opportunity to learn more about the difference before declaring a stance. In this sense, avoidance as a strategy for managing differences may facilitate new learning and greater opportunity for future interaction of a productive nature. On the other hand, avoidance may be a survival strategy between different status levels within the organization. Clearly, a manager may tell a subordinate to "sit down and just be quiet." Under these circumstances, the worker could jeopardize their position with the organization if they chose to noncompliance.

Tolerance as a strategy may be influenced by status within the organization. Managers generally have the power and authority to get their viewpoints adopted. Nonmangers often must compromise or tolerate the views of their managers, even when they feel the freedom to express an opposing viewpoint. Oftentimes, adopting tolerance is necessary because it allows for the expression of differences; however, when there is an imbalance of power, the options for influence are limited. The upside of tolerance is an individual's opportunity to express a point of view that is active involvement rather than passive participation in an event. Conflict as a strategy may also serve some purpose. Conflict involves direct and active resistance to another and may involve judgments of good, bad, right, or wrong. Often conflict occurs more openly among managers, who have higher status and more latitude than subordinates in resisting a point of view or directives of each other and top management. Finally, appreciation of differences or diversity demonstrates a high degree of personal development and growth at the individual level. The process of appreciation involves a collaborative interaction among various parties with differences. When differences are appreciated, there are usually organizational norms that support the freedom of expression without fear of reprisal. With the ability to discuss differences openly, using a dialectical process, parties are often able to employ multiple strategies, resulting ultimately in appreciation. Appreciation results from applying the skills of emotional intelligence mentioned earlier.

CONCLUSION

Developing healthy ways to acknowledge and respond to diversity (differences) and the emotions evoked increases our ability to not only manage ourselves but also to manage others in workplace and personal settings. Employing a combination of strategies such as conflict, avoidance, tolerance, and appreciation may demonstrate the capacity of an individual to manage differences and value diversity.

Discussion Questions

1. How can one distinguish difference from conflict?
2. What are some of the dangers of avoiding and repressing differences?
3. Think of an experience that you had in an organization or social setting involving avoidance or repression of differences. What was the outcome? How did you feel about the outcome?
4. What are some positive aspects of difference?
5. What role do emotions play in our ability to manage differences?
6. How can you develop the skills needed to increase your emotional intelligence?

Bibliography

Cherniss, C., & Goleman, D. (2001). *The emotionally intelligent workplace.* San Francisco: Jossey-Bass.

Capra, F. (1982). *The turning point.* New York: Bantam.

Goleman, D. (1995). *Emotional intelligence.* New York: Bantam.

TRANSCENDUS EXERCISE

Carole G. Parker
Seton Hill University

Donald C. Klein
The Union Institute

Goals

1. To identify individual differences that may not be apparent among participants with respect to the nature and value of conflict.
2. To increase awareness of participants' assumptions, beliefs, values, biases, concerns, and preferences in relation to conflict that results from their experiences with differences.
3. To enable participants to manage more effectively their experience of diversity and conflict.

Instructions

1. Selection of Transcendents and Earthlings—the class is divided into small groups of 6–8, from which two persons will be identified as Transcendents and the rest as Earthlings. The instructor will provide more information about this process.
2. Planning and Role Preparation—approximately 10–15 minutes. Members of each group of Earthlings and pair of Transcendents meet separately to discuss their assignment and get into their role. Role assignments and information are provided by the instructor.
3. Meetings between groups of Earthlings and Transcendent pairs (approximately 10–15 minutes).
4. Small groups of Earthlings and pairs of Transcendents in their assigned roles come together to explore the nature and purpose of conflict.
5. Entire class is reformed for a discussion.

The original version of the Transcendus Exercise was created by Donald Klein in June 1984 for the use at the Beyond Conflict Training Laboratory in Bethel, Maine, Conducted by the NTL Institute for Applied Behavioral Science.

INTRODUCTION TO TRANSCENDUS

In another galaxy, far, far away, there is a planet called "Transcendus." The inhabitants on this planet are physically very similar to the people on Earth and differ from one another, just as Earthlings do. There is one major difference, however, between Transcendents and Earthlings: On Transcendus, there is no conflict.

Word has spread to Transcendus that Earth is a planet on which there is conflict that pervades relationships between individuals, groups, nations, and many other aspects of life. The Transcendent Governing Council has decided to send a team of anthropologists/sociologists to Earth to learn about conflict. Their instructions are to decide whether it would be advantageous to bring conflict, whatever it is, back to their home planet.

The Transcendents work in pairs as they meet with small groups of Earthlings to carry out their study.

INSTRUCTIONS FOR OBSERVERS

The task of the observer is to watch the behavior of group members and note how the group works together. Guidelines on what to look for include, but are not limited to the following:

Observations	Transcendents	Earthlings
1. Who speaks most and least? In what order do people talk?		
2. Does everyone contribute? What happens to the contributions of different members?		
3. What occurs when the Transcendents arrive? To what extent does the group stick to its original plan for interacting with the visitors? Does the plan change? If so, how does the change occur?		
4. What is the level of tension in the group before the Transcendents arrive and after they join the group?		
5. What kinds of emotions are expressed by group members and exhibited in their posture, facial expressions, and actions?		
6. What were your thoughts as an individual sitting on the sidelines observing?		
7. What, if any, emotions were stirred in you as an observer?		

INTERCULTURAL COMMUNICATION: A CURRENT PERSPECTIVE

Milton J. Bennett

The study of intercultural communication has tried to answer the question, "How do people understand one another when they do not share a common cultural experience?" Just a few decades ago, this question was one faced mainly by diplomats, expatriates, and the occasional international traveler. Today, living in multicultural societies within a global village, we all face the question every day. We now realize that issues of intercultural understanding are embedded in other complex questions: What kind of communication is needed by a pluralistic society to be both culturally diverse and unified in common goals? How does communication contribute to creating a climate of respect, not just tolerance, for diversity? The new vision and innovative competencies we bring to this changing world will determine the answer to another question about the global village posed by Dean Barnlund: "Will its residents be neighbors capable of respecting and utilizing their differences or clusters of strangers living in ghettos and united only in their antipathies for others?"[1]

DEALING WITH DIFFERENCE

If we look to our species' primate past and to our more recent history of dealing with cultural difference, there is little reason to be sanguine. Our initial response to difference is usually to avoid it. Imagine, if you will, a group of our primate ancestors gathered around their fire, gnawing on the day's catch. Another group of primates comes into view, heading toward the fire. I wonder how often the first group looked up and said (in effect), "Ah, cultural diversity, how wonderful." More likely it was fight or flight, and things have not changed that much since then. We flee to the suburbs or behind walls to avoid cultural difference, and if we are forced to confront it, there often is a fight.

52

Historically, if we were unsuccessful in avoiding different people, we tried to convert them. Political, economic, and religious missionaries sought out opportunities to impose their own beliefs on others. The thinking seemed to be, "If only people were more like us, then they would be all right to have around." This assumption can still be seen in the notion of the "melting pot" prevalent this century in the United States. It is difficult for many people to believe that any understanding at all is possible unless people have become similar to one another.

When we could not avoid or convert people who were different from ourselves, we killed them. Examples of genocide are not so very far away from us, either in time or distance, and individual cases of hate crimes are tragically frequent. Of course, one doesn't need to physically terminate the existence of others to effectively eliminate them. When we make their lives miserable in our organizations and neighborhoods, we also "kill" them—they cannot flourish, and often they do not survive.

Given this history of dealing with difference, it is no wonder that the topic of difference—understanding it, appreciating it, respecting it—is central to all practical treatments of intercultural communication. Yet, this emphasis on difference departs from the common approaches to communication and relationships based within a single culture.

Monocultural communication is *similarity based.* Common language, behavior patterns, and values form the base on which members of the culture exchange meaning with one another in conducting their daily affairs. These similarities generally allow people to predict the responses of others to certain kinds of messages and to take for granted some basic shared assumptions about the nature of reality. In monocultural communication, difference represents the potential for misunderstanding and friction. Thus, social difference of all kinds is discouraged.

Intercultural communication—communication between people of different cultures—cannot allow the easy assumption of similarity. By definition, cultures are different in their languages, behavior patterns, and values. So an attempt to use one's self as a predictor of shared assumptions and responses to messages is unlikely to work.[2] Because cultures embody such variety in patterns of perception and behavior, approaches to communication in cross-cultural situations guard against inappropriate assumptions of similarity and encourage the consideration of difference. In other words, the intercultural communication approach is *difference based.*[3]

UPPER-CASE CULTURE AND LOWER-CASE CULTURE

When people anticipate doing something *cultural* of an evening, their thoughts turn to art, literature, drama, classical music, or dance. In other words, they plan to participate in one of the *institutions* of culture—behavior that has become routinized into a particular form. I refer to this aspect of culture as "Culture writ large," with a capital "C." The more academic term that is used by most writers is *objective culture.*[4] Other examples of objective culture might include social, economic, political, and linguistic systems—the kinds of things that usually are included in area studies or history courses. The study of these institutions constitutes much of the curriculum in both international and multicultural education. For instance, courses in Japanese culture or African-American culture are likely to focus on the history, political structure, and arts of the groups. While this is valuable information, it is limited in its utility to the face-to-face concerns of intercultural communication. One can know a lot about the history of a culture and still not be able to communicate with an actual person from that culture. Understanding objective culture may create knowledge, but it doesn't necessarily generate competence.

The less-obvious aspect of culture is its *subjective* side—what we can call "culture writ small." Subjective culture refers to the psychological features that define a group of people—their everyday thinking and behavior—rather than to the institutions they have created. A good working definition of subjective culture is *the learned and shared patterns of beliefs, behaviors, and values of groups of interacting people.* Understanding subjective cultures—one's own and others'—is more likely to lead to intercultural competence.

Of course, social reality is constructed of both large and small "c" aspects of culture; people learn how to behave through socialization into the institutions of the culture, which leads them to behave in ways that perpetuate those same institutions.[5] As noted above, traditional international and multicultural education tends to focus only on the objective mode of this process; in contrast, intercultural communication focuses almost exclusively on the subjective mode. For instance, interculturalists are concerned with *language use* in cross-cultural relationships, rather than in linguistic structure. They study how language is modified or supplanted by culturally defined *nonverbal behavior,* how cultural patterns of thinking are expressed in particular *communication styles,* and how reality is defined and judged through cultural *assumptions and values.* In the following pages, examples in each of these areas will illustrate how understanding subjective culture can aid in the development of skills in cultural adaptation and intercultural communication.

LEVELS OF CULTURE

The definition of subjective culture also provides a base for defining *diversity* in a way that includes both international and domestic cultures at different *levels of abstraction.* National groups such as Japanese, Mexican, and U.S. American and pan-national ethnic groups such as Arab and Zulu are cultures at a high level of abstraction—the qualities that adhere to most (but not all) members of the culture are very general, and the group includes a lot of diversity. At this level of abstraction we can only point to general differences in patterns of thinking and behaving between cultures. For instance, we might observe that U.S. American culture is more characterized by individualism than is Japanese culture, which is more collectivist.

Analysis at a high level of abstraction provides a view of the "unifying force" of culture. The very existence of interaction, even through media, generates a commonality that spans individuals and ethnicities. For instance, despite their significant individual and ethnic differences, Mexicans spend more time interacting with other Mexicans than they do with Japanese. They certainly spend more time reading Mexican newspapers and watching Mexican television than they do consuming Japanese media. This fact generates Mexican "national character"—something that distinguishes Mexicans from Japanese (and from other Latin Americans as well).

U.S. Americans are particularly resistant to recognizing their national culture. Despite the fact that nearly everyone else in the world immediately recognizes them as Americans, many of them still insist on labeling themselves as "just individuals" or "a mixture of cultures." Of course, the very commonality of this tendency is an example of U.S. American national culture; no other people in the world but U.S. Americans are so quick to disavow their cultural affiliation. This is probably a manifestation of the individualism that is generally attributed to U.S. Americans.[6] Whatever the reason, it is perilous for U.S. Americans to fail to see the cultural force that unifies them. It leads them to see ethnic and other cultural differences as more of a threat to national unity than they are.

While cultural difference at a high level of abstraction provides a rich base for analyzing national cultural behavior, significant group and individual differences within each national group are concealed at this level. These differences provide a diversifying force that balances the unifying force of national culture.

At a lower level of abstraction, more specific groups such as ethnicities can be described in cultural terms.[7] In the United States, some of these groups are African American, Asian American, American Indian, Hispanic/Latino American, and European American. People in these groups may share many of the broad national culture patterns while differing significantly in the more specific patterns of their respective ethnicities.[8] It should be noted that in terms of subjective culture, ethnicity is a cultural rather than a genetic heritage; dark skin and other Negroid features may make one "black," but that person has not necessarily experienced African-American enculturation. Most black people in the world are *not* American in any sense. Similarly, "whites" are not necessarily European American, although in the United States it is difficult for them to escape being socialized in the patterns that are currently dominant in U.S. American society.

Other categories of subjective cultural diversity usually include gender, regionality, socioeconomic class, physical ability, sexual orientation, religion, organization, and vocation. The concept can embrace other long-term groupings such as single parents or avid sports fans, as long as the groups maintain the clear patterns of behavior and thinking of an "identity group."[9] By definition, individuals do not have different cultures; the term for patterns of individual behavior is *personality*.

STEREOTYPES AND GENERALIZATIONS

Whenever the topic of cultural difference is discussed, the allegation of stereotyping usually is not far behind. For instance, if cultural patterns of men and women are being compared, someone may well offer that she is a woman and doesn't act that way at all.

Stereotypes arise when we act as if all members of a culture or group share the same characteristics. Stereotypes can be attached to any assumed indicator of group membership, such as race, religion, ethnicity, age, or gender, as well as national culture. The characteristics that are assumedly shared by members of the group may be respected by the observer, in which case it is a *positive stereotype.* In the more likely case that the characteristics are disrespected, it is a *negative stereotype.* Stereotypes of both kinds are problematic in intercultural communication for several obvious reasons. One is that they may give us a false sense of understanding our communication partners. Whether the stereotype is positive or negative, it is usually only partially correct. Additionally, stereotypes may become self-fulfilling prophecies, where we observe others in selective ways that confirm our prejudice.

Despite the problems with stereotypes, it is necessary in intercultural communication to make *cultural generalizations.* Without any kind of supposition or hypothesis about the cultural differences we may encounter in an intercultural situation, we may fall prey to naive individualism, where we assume that every person is acting in some completely unique way. Or we may rely inordinately on common sense to direct our communication behavior. Common sense is, of course, common only to a particular culture. Its application outside of one's own culture is usually ethnocentric.

Cultural generalizations can be made while avoiding stereotypes by maintaining the idea *of preponderance of belief.*[10] Nearly all possible beliefs are represented in all cultures at all times, but each different culture has a preference for some beliefs over others.[11] The description of this preference, derived from large-group research, is a cultural generalization. Of course, individuals can be found in any culture who hold beliefs similar to people in a different culture. There just aren't so many of them—they don't represent the preponderance of people who hold beliefs closer to the norm, or "central tendency," of the group. As a specific example (see Figure 1), we may note that despite the accurate cultural generalization that U.S. Americans are more individualistic and Japanese are more group oriented, there are U.S. Americans who are every bit as group oriented as any Japanese, and there are Japanese who are as individualistic as any U.S. American. However, these relatively few people are closer to the fringe of their respective cultures. They are, in the neutral sociological sense of the term, "deviant."

Deductive stereotypes occur when we assume that abstract cultural generalizations apply to every single individual in the culture. While it is appropriate to generalize that U.S. Americans as a group are more

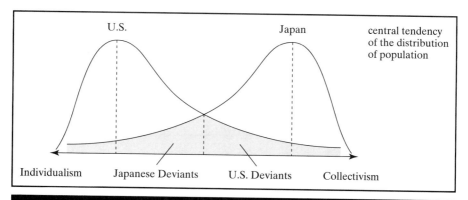

U.S.   Japan   central tendency of the distribution of population

Individualism   Japanese Deviants   U.S. Deviants   Collectivism

FIGURE 1 Generalization Distributions

individualistic than Japanese, it is stereotyping to assume that every American is strongly individualistic; the person with whom you are communicating may be a deviant. Cultural generalizations should be used tentatively as working hypotheses that need to be tested in each case: sometimes they work very well, sometimes they need to be modified, and sometimes they don't apply to the particular case at all. The idea is to derive the benefit of recognizing cultural patterns without experiencing too much "hardening of the categories."

Generalizing from too small a sample may generate an *inductive stereotype*. For example, we may inappropriately assume some general knowledge about Mexican culture based on having met one or a few Mexicans. This assumption is particularly troublesome since initial cross-cultural contacts may often be conducted by people who are deviant in their own cultures. ("Typical" members of the culture would more likely associate only with their cultural compatriots—that's how they stay typical.) So generalizing cultural patterns from any one person's behavior (including your own) in cross-cultural contact is likely to be both stereotypical and inaccurate.

Another form of inductive stereotype is derived from what Carlos E. Cortes calls the "social curriculum." He notes that schoolchildren report knowing a lot about Gypsies, even though few of the children have ever met even one member of that culture. According to Cortes's research, the knowledge was gained from old horror movies![12] Through media of all kinds we are besieged with images of "cultural" behavior: African Americans performing hip-hop or bringing warmth to medical practice; Hispanic Americans picking crops or exhibiting savvy in the courtroom; European Americans burning crosses or exercising altruism toward the homeless. When we generalize from any of these images, we are probably creating stereotypes. Media images are chosen not for their typicality, but for their unusualness. So, as with initial cross-cultural contacts, we need to look beyond the immediate image to the cultural patterns that can only be ascertained through research.

ASSUMPTIONS OF AN INTERCULTURAL COMMUNICATION PERSPECTIVE

Beyond its emphasis on cultural difference, intercultural communication is based on some assumptions that both identify it with and distinguish it from other social sciences.

Analysis of Personal Interaction

Like interpersonal communication, intercultural communication focuses on face-to-face (or at least person-to-person) interaction among human beings. For this kind of communication to occur, each participant must perceive him- or herself being perceived by others. That is, all participants must see themselves as potentially engaged in communication and capable of giving and receiving feedback. This assumption allows us to understand why interculturalists are not particularly focused on mass media. Even though the issues of international satellite broadcasting and culture-specific cable productions are fascinating, they are essentially one-way events. However, individual, mediated communication such as faxing, e-mailing, and Internet chat room dialogue does fit the definition of person-to-person communication.

It is surprising to some that intercultural communication does not often generate comprehensive descriptions of culture, or ethnographies. While such descriptions are crucial for any cross-cultural study, they do not in themselves constitute cases of cross-cultural interaction. An intercultural perspective leads researchers to hypothesize, given some difference in the described cultures, how members of the cultures might interact.

Another useful distinction in this context is that between *cultural interaction* and *cultural comparison*. When social science studies deal with culture at all, they frequently compare one aspect of a culture to a similar phenomenon in another. For instance, psychologists might compare how Northern European depth perception differs from that of Amazonian Indians. Or sociolinguists might analyze the differences in ritual greeting between European Americans and African Americans. While interculturalists use these kinds of comparisons for their knowledge base, they focus less on the differences themselves and more on how the differences are likely to affect face-to-face interaction.

This emphasis on interaction does not mean that interculturalists neglect knowledge about specific cultures. On the contrary, it is considered a prerequisite for interculturalists to have expert knowledge of at least their own cultures (an often-neglected skill in other academic fields). In addition, Most interculturalists are particularly knowledgeable about one or more cultures in addition to their own.

Culture-Specific and Culture-General Approaches

Interaction analysis and skill development can be undertaken at two levels. At the *culture-specific* level, differences between two particular cultures are assessed for their likely impact on communication between people of those cultures. For instance, the generalization that Hispanic-American patterns of cross-status communication differ from the more egalitarian patterns of European Americans'[13] could be analyzed for its possible effect on interaction between employees and managers from the two cultures. Training in alternative cross-status communication styles could then help members of both cultures appreciate and deal more effectively with each other in the workplace. This approach, based on specific ethnographies, is an intercultural form of "emic" cultural analysis.[14]

Culture-general approaches to interaction describe general cultural contrasts that are applicable in many cross-cultural situations. For instance, Edward T. Hall's definition of high-context and low-context cultures[15] is a culture-general contrast that suggests a source of miscommunication among many diverse cultures. Similarly, culture-general skills are communication competencies that would be useful in any cross-cultural situation. They usually include cultural self-awareness, nonevaluative perception, cultural adaptation strategies, and cross-cultural empathy. This approach, based on more abstract categories and generalizable skills, is the intercultural equivalent of "etic" cultural analysis.[16]

Emphasis on Process and the Development of Competence

The process of communication can be thought of as the mutual creation of meaning—the verbal and nonverbal behavior of communicating and the interpretations that are made of that behavior. The meaning itself, whatever it is, can be called the *content* of the communication. Everyday communication mainly stresses content, while studies of communication tend to emphasize the process and give less attention to the content. This is particularly true for intercultural communication, where apparently familiar or understandable content may mask radically different cultural processes.

Another implication of this assumption is that knowledge of content does not automatically translate into mastery of process. I have already noted that knowledge about objective cultural institutions does not necessarily yield competence in communicating with the people whose behavior maintains those institutions. Even knowledge about subjective cultural contrasts, while more directly applicable to communication, is still not sufficient in itself for intercultural competence. Specific knowledge of subjective culture needs to be framed in culture-general categories and coupled with an understanding of both the general and specific intercultural processes involved. Knowledge of the differences between U.S. American and Japanese decision-making styles is not, in itself, particularly useful. It needs to be framed in more general value contrasts (e.g., individualism and collectivism), linked with an understanding of how individualists and collectivists generally misconstrue each other's behavior, joined by an awareness of how those misunderstandings manifest themselves in dysfunctional communication patterns (e.g., negative spirals), and finally applied to avoiding negative spirals and other miscommunication in an actual joint decision-making effort.

Focus on Humanistic Phenomena

Most approaches to intercultural communication (and communication in general) treat it as a purely human phenomenon, not, for instance, as an expression of a divine plan. Any assumption of transcendental guidance to communication immediately runs afoul of cultural differences in religious beliefs. And if one believes that his or her communication style is dictated by a divine authority, adapting that style to a different cultural context will be difficult at best. Interculturalists generally leave questions of supernatural order to contexts where improving communication is not the goal.

In a similar vein, interculturalists tend to avoid purely ideological analyses of discourse. When communication behavior is labeled as "Marxist" or "imperialist" or "racist" or "sexist," the human aspects of that behavior are overshadowed by the reifications of principle. Polarization usually supplants any hope of inclusivity, and further exploration of communication differences is drowned out by the political commotion.[17]

I do not mean to say here that the abuse of power is inconsequential to communication. On the contrary, no improvement of intercultural relations is likely to occur in a climate of oppression and disrespect, and interculturalists have a role in changing that climate through their explication and facilitation of interaction. I do, however, mean to suggest that the professional work of interculturalists is not primarily ideological (except insofar as any action taken is inherently political, to some degree). Critical social analysis is an important part of political change. But when the question is how to understand and adapt to another culture more successfully, as it is in intercultural communication, purely ideological analyses yield little light and much heat.

Historical analyses of cultural behavior have some of the same disadvantages as ideological approaches. While it might be accurate to note that U.S. American individualism has Calvinistic roots nurtured in a wild frontier and that Japanese collectivism has grown out of Shintoism and close-knit agricultural communities, such an observation tells us little about how the values of individualism and collectivism are likely to affect the behavior of an American person with a Japanese person today. Similarly, understanding the history of immigration into the United States, while important for other reasons, is not particularly useful in analyzing the cross-cultural aspects of interethnic communication. In both cases, the immediate behavior and its cultural context may be occluded by a preoccupation with historical causes.

The avoidance of history as an analytical frame does not mean that interculturalists neglect the subject altogether. People of most cultures feel respected if the person they encounter knows something about the history of their group, and mutual respect is a major goal of intercultural communication. Also, the acknowledgment of history is particularly important if an oppressor/oppressed relationship existed (or continues to exist) between the communication partners. Any disavowal of that history on the part of a dominant culture member is likely to be interpreted as evidence of continuing (albeit possibly unintentional) oppression. For instance, the failure by European Americans to recognize the history of slavery or of American Indian genocide in the United States is often seen as racist. Knowledge of history is also important for interpreting those aspects of people's behavior that mainly are responses to past and present mistreatment. Scottish people, for instance, take particular umbrage at being confused with the English, their historical oppressors. But, while acknowledging historical context, interculturalists usually focus on patterns of behavior in the here and now. Specifically, they analyze the human interaction that is created each time different cultural patterns are brought into contact through face-to-face communication.

Another aspect of humanism is its assumption of personal and cultural relativity. This means that behavior and values must be understood both in terms of the uniqueness of each person and in terms of the culture of that person. Absolute judgments about the goodness or badness of behavior and values are avoided, as far as communication is concerned. Interculturalists generally consider that evaluations of culturally different behavior are likely to be ethnocentric and that in any case they interfere with the communication necessary to become informed about the worldview context in which the behavior must be interpreted. In the simplest terms, cultural relativity is a commitment to understanding all events in a cultural context, including how the event is likely to be evaluated in that context.

It is important to note here that cultural relativity is not the same as ethical relativity. The end result of understanding events in cultural context is not "whatever." Like most other people, interculturalists are both professionally and personally committed to ethical positions. They may be, however, particularly concerned that their ethical commitments are not based on ethnocentric absolutes.[18]

INTERCULTURAL COMMUNICATION PROCESSES

For the rest of this chapter, processes and skills of intercultural communication will be reviewed. In this section, the review will be restricted to the communication process. In the following sections, applications of these concepts to culture-general issues of intercultural adaptation and sensitivity will be considered.

Language and the Relativity of Experience

Many students (and some teachers) view language only as a communication tool—a method humans use to indicate the objects and ideas of their physical and social world. In this view, languages are sets of words tied together by rules, and learning a foreign or second language is the simple (but tedious) process of substituting words and rules to get the same meaning with a different tool.

Language does serve as a tool for communication, but in addition it is a "system of representation" for perception and thinking. This function of language provides us with verbal categories and prototypes that guide our formation of concepts and categorization of objects; it directs how we experience reality.[19] It is this "reality-organizing" aspect of language that engages interculturalists.

A memorable statement of how language organizes and represents cultural experience is now known as the Whorf/Sapir hypothesis:

> We dissect nature along lines laid down by our native languages. The categories and types that we isolate from the world of phenomena we do not find there because they stare every observer in the face; on the contrary, the world is presented in a kaleidoscopic flux of impressions which has to be organized by our minds—and this means largely by the linguistic systems in our minds.[20]

In this statement, Benjamin Lee Whorf advances what has come to be called the "strong form" of the hypothesis: Language largely determines the way in which we understand our reality. In other writings, Whorf takes the position that language, thought, and perception are interrelated, a position called the "weak hypothesis." Interculturalists tend to use the weak form of the hypothesis when they discuss language and culture.

An example of how various languages direct different experiences of reality is found in how objects must be represented grammatically. American English has only one way to count things (one, two, three, etc.), while Japanese and Trukese (a Micronesian language) each have many different counting systems. In part, these systems classify the physical appearance of objects. For instance, one (long) thing is counted with different words from one (flat) thing or one (round) thing in Trukese. We could imagine that the experience of objects in general is much richer in cultures where language gives meaning to subtle differences in shape. Indeed, Japanese aesthetic appreciation of objects seems more developed than that of Americans, whose English language has relatively simple linguistic structures to represent shapes.

In addition, both Japanese and Trukese count people with a set of words different from all others used for objects. We might speculate that research on human beings that quantifies behavior "objectively" (i.e., like objects) would not arise as easily in cultures where people were counted distinctly. And indeed, quantitative research on human beings is much more common in Western cultures, particularly U.S. American.

Another example of the relationship of syntax and experience can be found in the grammatical representation of space. In American English, things can be either "here" or "there," with a colloquial attempt to place them further out "over there." In the Trukese language, references to objects and people must be accompanied by a "location marker" that specifies their position relative to both the speaker and listener. A pen, for instance, must be called this (close to me but away from you) pen, this (midway between us) pen, that (far away from both of us but in sight) pen, or that (out of sight of both of us) pen. We may assume that Trukese people, who live on islands, experience "richer" space than do Americans, whose language does not provide so many spatial boundary markers and for whom space is therefore more abstract.

Language syntax also guides our social experience. Perhaps the simplest and best-known examples are linguistic differences in "status markers." Thai, Japanese, and some other Asian languages have elaborate systems of second-person singular (you) words that indicate the status of the speaker relative to the listener. In Thai, there are also variable forms of *I* to indicate relative status. Thus, I (relatively lower in status) may be speaking to you (somewhat higher in status) or to you (much higher in status), using a different form of *I* and *you* in each case. It seems apparent that cultures with languages that demand recognition of relative status in every direct address will encourage more acute experience of status difference than does the American culture, in which English provides only one form *of you.* European cultures, most of whose languages have two forms *of you,* indicating both status distinctions and familiarity, may represent the middle range of this dimension. Europeans are more overtly attentive to status than are Americans, but Europeans are no match for Asians in this regard.

The preceding examples indicate a relationship between language syntax and the experience of physical and social reality. The relationship between language and experience can also be found in the semantic dimension of language. Languages differ in how semantic categories are distinguished and elaborated. For instance, several stages of coconut growth are described with separate words in the Trukese language, while English has only one word to describe the nut. On the other hand, English has an elaborate vocabulary to describe colors, while Trukese describes only a few colors and does not distinguish between blue and green. It is clear that Americans without the extra vocabulary cannot easily distinguish coconuts in their different stages; that is, they do not have the experience of the coconuts as being different. Similarly it appears that Trukese people without additional color categories do not experience the difference between blue and green.

Other examples abound of how categories are differentiated to greater or lesser degrees. Wine connoisseurs maintain a highly differentiated set of labels for the experience of wine, as opposed to the two or three categories (red, white, and maybe blush) used by casual drinkers. Skiers distinguish more kinds of snow than do nonskiers, and so forth. Of even greater interest are situations where an entire kind of experience seems to disappear when the vocabulary for it is missing. For instance, while English has many words to describe boredom and ennui, Trukese seems to lack any reference to the entire concept. Although we cannot be sure, linguistic relativity would predict that Trukese people do not experience boredom in the same way as English speakers do until they learn to distinguish a category for it.

In summary, categories are constructed differently in different cultures and languages, and with the different constructions go different experiences of physical and social reality. These particular experiences are not *determined* by language, in the sense that other forms of experience are precluded without concomitant linguistic support. Research on color perception[21] and other phenomena indicate that distinctions can be made without a specific "naming strategy." Rather, linguistic relativity suggests that we are predisposed by our languages to make certain distinctions and not others—our language encourages habitual patterns of perception.

This formulation of linguistic and cultural relativity is central to intercultural communication. Without the assumption of relativity at the very root of our experience of reality, naive practitioners of intercultural relations veer toward itemizing different customs and providing tips for minor adjustments of behavior. More sophisticated interculturalists realize that their study is of nothing less than the clash of differing realities and that cultural adaptation demands the apprehension of essentially alien experience.

Perceptual Relativity

The Whorf/Sapir hypothesis alerts us to the likelihood that our experience of reality is a function of cultural worldview categories. At the basic level of perception, language and culture guide us in making *figure/ground distinctions.* From the "kaleidoscopic flux" (ground) of undifferentiated phenomena, we create a boundary that distinguishes some object (figure) from the ground.[22] These figures may literally be objects, or they may be concepts or feelings. Collections of figures are "categories." What we think exists—what is real— depends on whether we have distinguished the phenomenon as figure. And since culture through language guides us in making these distinctions, culture is actually operating directly on perception.

Micronesians, for example, are far more likely than Americans to see wave patterns—interactions of tide and current on the ocean surface that are used for navigation. To a typical American, the ocean is just "ground," and only boats or other objects are figures. But this same American may single out an automobile sound as indicating imminent mechanical failure, while to the Micronesian it is simply part of the background noise. In general, culture provides us with the tendency to perceive phenomena that are relevant to both physical and social survival.

The boundaries of constructed objects are mutable. For instance, as mentioned earlier, speakers of Trukese do not make a blue/green distinction. (One word, *avow,* refers to both colors, and "araw" is the response to either question, "What color is the sea?" or "What color is the grass?") Yet Trukese children are routinely taught to perceive the difference in color as part of their training in English as a second language. The mutability of perceptual boundaries supports the idea that perceivers actively organize stimuli into categories. And evidence from physiological studies of vision indicate that people do indeed see different objects when looking in the same direction.[23] The human eye and brain respond selectively to stimuli, depending on whether the visual system is tuned to the stimulus as figure or as ground.

The observation that perceptual figure/ground distinctions are learned and lead to different experiences of reality contradicts the traditional view of the perceiver who confronts a specific, objective reality. Instead, the perceiver is assumed to respond to culturally influenced categorizations of stimuli. Like the assumption of linguistic relativity, this assumption of perceptual relativity lies at the heart of intercultural communication. If we fail to assume that people of different cultures may sincerely perceive the world differently, then our efforts toward understanding are subverted by a desire to "correct" the one who has it wrong.

Nonverbal Behavior

There is an entire universe of behavior that is unexplored, unexamined, and very much taken for granted. It functions outside conscious awareness and *in juxtaposition to words.*[24]

Verbal language is *digital,* in the sense that words symbolize categories of phenomena in the same arbitrary way that on/off codes symbolize numbers and operations in a computer. Nonverbal behavior, by contrast, is *analogic.* It represents phenomena by creating contexts which can be experienced directly. For instance, it is digital to say, "I love you." It is analogic to represent that feeling with a look or a touch. Digital symbolizations are more capable of expressing complexity ("I love you twice as much now as I did last week"), but analogic representations are more credible because they are generally less easily manipulated.[25]

Some languages put more emphasis on the digital quality than others. English, for instance, is strongly digital in the way that it divides continua of human feeling and thought into discrete, abstract categories, providing speakers with many words to name particular affective and cognitive states. In contrast, Japanese is a more analogic language. It demands that its speakers imply and infer meaning from the context of relatively vague statements—the way it's said, by whom, to whom, where, at what time, and just before or after what other statement.[26]

Cultures such as Japanese that stress analogic communication are referred to as "high context."[27] Hall, who coined that term, defines it as a communication "in which *most* of the information is already in the person, while very little is in the coded, explicit, transmitted part of the message."[28] Cultures such as U.S. American that emphasize digital forms of communication are called "low context," defined as communication "where the mass of information is vested in the explicit code."[29]

In both high- and low-context cultures, all verbal messages in face-to-face interpersonal communication are accompanied by nonverbal behavior which provides an analogic background for the digital words.[30] Voice, gestures, eye contact, spacing, and touching all provide direct analogic expressions of emotion that modify (in low context) or supplant (in high context) the verbal message. Even in low-context cultures, only a small percentage of the meaning created in a social communication exchange is based on verbal language,[31] so understanding the more important nonverbal aspects of communication is vital to an overall comprehension of intercultural events.

In low-context cultures such as U.S. American, nonverbal behavior is unconsciously perceived more as a commentary on the verbal message than as a part of the message itself. This tendency is particularly noticeable in the use of voice tone, such as that used in the communication of sarcasm. Words such as, "My, what a nice tie," can be modified by a tone of voice that indicates to the listener, "Don't take these words seriously." In other words, the nonverbal cue (tone of voice, in this case) establishes the sarcastic relationship in which the words should be interpreted.

Paralanguage, which also includes the pitch, stress, volume, and speed with which language is spoken, lends itself readily to misinterpretation cross culturally. The potential for misunderstanding begins with perception. Is the communication stimulus even discriminated as figure from the ground of other behavior? U.S. Americans are likely to miss shadings of tone which in higher-context cultures would scream with meaning. Within the United States, European-American males are less likely than some African-American males to perceive the use of movement to signal a shift from talking to fighting. And conversely, black males may fail to discriminate the fighting cue of "intensity" in the tone of white male talk.[32]

In cross-cultural situations we may also perceive the appearance of a cue when none was intended. An example of this occurs around the American English use of a pitch drop at the end of sentences. The pitch of our voices goes up on the next to the last syllable and then down on the last syllable in a spoken statement. How quickly the pitch is dropped makes a difference. In even a short utterance such as "Come in," a medium pitch drop signifies normal interaction, while an abrupt drop may signify anger, frustration, anxiety, or impatience. Conversely, an elongated pitch drop usually indicates friendliness and relaxation, but an elongated pitch *increase* at the end of a statement can imply a manipulative or misleading intent. These implications are instantly recognized and reacted to by native speakers.

Nonnative English speakers may not respond to or generate voice tones in the same way. For instance, for native speakers of Cantonese, pitch changes are important within words but are not used to modulate sentences. So a Cantonese speaker of English as a second language may not generate an ending pitch drop. Additionally, Cantonese may sound rather staccato and a little loud to American ears. The combination of these factors leads some native English speakers to evaluate Chinese people as brusque or rude. If a native speaker generated loud, staccato, flat-pitch statements, it might indeed indicate rudeness. But when the native Cantonese speaker talks that way in English, it probably means that he or she is using the English language with Cantonese paralanguage. The failure to observe intended cues or the discrimination of nonexistent cues based solely on one's own culture can be termed *ethnocentric perception.*

Finally, we may correctly perceive that a nonverbal cue has been generated but misinterpret its meaning. This is most likely to occur when we assume (perhaps unconsciously) that particular behavior carries the same meaning in every culture. For example, the clipped speech of some British is noticed both by other British and by U.S. Americans. For the British, however, the paralanguage cues are likely to indicate social status, home region, or place of education. For the Americans, the cues may be interpreted simply as haughtiness. This tendency to assign meaning to events solely in the context of one's own culture can be called *ethnocentric interpretation.* Both ethnocentric perception and interpretation are consistent with the idea of cultural relativity—that our experience of reality differs culturally as well as individually.

The form of nonverbal interaction analysis used in the paralanguage examples above is also generally applied to the area of kinesics, or "body language." To illustrate this, we can imagine different degrees of gesturing placed on a continuum extending from the nearly motionless presentation of some Asians and Native Americans to the dramatic sweeps of Greeks and Italians. When they come into contact, people at contrasting positions on the continuum may fall prey to ethnocentric perception and interpretation. For instance, those in the middle of the continuum, such as European Americans, may interpret Native American reserve as "lacking ambition and self-esteem." Native Americans, on the other hand, may interpret European American gesturing as "intrusive and aggressive." African Americans, whose gesturing is a bit further along the continuum, may be interpreted by some Asians (Koreans, for example) as being "violent and unpredictable." The greater reserve of the Koreans might fit into an African-American interpretation of "unfriendly (perhaps because of racism)." As should be obvious from these examples, "simple" misinterpretations of nonverbal behavior may contribute to tragic failures in our educational system and terrible social strife.

Another practical consequence of nonverbal ethnocentrism occurs around turn taking in conversation, particularly in group discussion. The European-American pattern involves eye contact to cue turns. The speaker ends with his or her eyes in contact with the conversational heir apparent. If the speaker lowers her eyes at the end of an utterance, a confused babble of fits and starts may ensue. In contrast to this pattern, some Asian cultures routinely require averted eyes and a period of silence between speakers. In groups including more eye-intensive cultures, unacculturated Asians may never get a turn. And on the other end of this continuum, some forms of African-American, Middle Eastern, and Mediterranean cultures tend to prefer more of a "relay-race" pattern of turn taking. Whoever wants the turn next just begins talking, and eventually the conversational baton may be passed on to her. Both Asian and European Americans may interpret this last pattern as interrupting. The simple task of facilitating a group discussion increases dramatically in complexity when even this one intercultural dimension is introduced.

Communication Style

Habitual patterns of thought are manifested in communication behavior. Since our habits of thought are largely determined by culture, in cross-cultural situations we should see contrasts in these styles of communication. One of the most striking differences is in how a point is discussed, whether in writing[33] or verbally, as illustrated in the following example.

European Americans, particularly males, tend to use a *linear* style that marches through point *a,* point *b,* and point *c*; establishes links from point to point; and finally states an explicit conclusion. When someone veers off this line, he or she is likely to hear a statement such as "I'm not quite following you," or "Could we cut to the chase," or "What's the bottom line?" In many school systems, this style has been established as the only one indicative of clear critical thinking. It is, however, a culturally rare form of discourse.

An example of a contrasting style occurred in a group of international and U.S. American students. I had asked a question about early dating practices, and the Americans all answered with fairly concise statements that made some explicit connection to the question. When a Nigerian in the group replied, however, he began by describing the path through his village, the tree at the end of the path, the storyteller that performed under the tree, and the beginning of a story the storyteller once told, When, in response to the obvious discomfort of the Americans in the group, I asked the Nigerian what he was doing, he said, "I'm answering the question." The American students protested at that, so I asked, "How are you answering the question?" He replied, "I'm telling you everything you need to know to understand the point." "Good," said one of the Americans. "Then if we're just patient, you will eventually tell us the point." "Oh no," replied the Nigerian. "Once I tell you everything you need to know to understand the point, you will just know what the point is!"

What this student was describing is a circular, or *contextual,* discussion style. It is favored not only by many Africans but also typically by people of Latin, Arab, and Asian cultures. And in the United States, the more circular style is commonly used by African Americans, Asian Americans, Native Americans, Hispanic Americans, and others. Even among European Americans, a contextual approach is more typical of women than of men. The only natural cultural base for the linear style is Northern European and European American males. That doesn't make the style bad, of course, but it does mean that other, more prevalent styles need to be considered as viable alternatives. To some extent, this issue has been addressed in the context of gender differences,[34] and it is getting increasing attention in the context of multicultural classrooms.[35]

When people who favor a contextual approach generate an ethnocentric interpretation of the linear style, they may see it as simple or arrogant: simple because it lacks the richness of detail necessary to establish context, and arrogant because the speaker is deciding what particular points you should hear and then what point you should draw from them. On the other hand, proponents of a linear style are likely to interpret the circular style as vague, evasive, and illogical. Interculturalists sometimes approach this kind of mutual negative evaluation with the idea *of strengths and limits.* In this case, the strength of a linear style may be in efficient, short-term task completion, while its limit is in developing inclusive relationship. Conversely, the strength of a contextual style is its facilitation of team building and consensual creativity, while its limit is that it is slow. The goal of education and training in this area, in addition to developing awareness and respect for alternative styles, may be to develop "bistylistic" competency.

Another area where differences in communication style are particularly obvious is around confrontation. European and African Americans tend to be rather direct in their style of confrontation, compared with the indirectness of many Asians and Hispanics. Adherents of the direct style favor face-to-face discussion of problems, relatively open expression of feeling, and a willingness to say yes or no in answer to questions. People socialized in the more indirect style tend to seek third-person intermediaries for conducting difficult discussions, suggest rather than state feelings, and protect their own and others' "face" by providing the appearance of ambiguity in response to questions.[36]

I was once involved in an incident involving indirect style in Malaysia. The guide had provided our group with a wonderful day of sights and cultural insight, and we were anticipating a trip to the jungle the next day with him. Upon leaving us at the hotel, he stated somewhat offhandedly, "It will rain tomorrow." I joked back, "Oh, that's all right, we're used to getting wet." But he repeated the statement, this time adding, "It will rain really hard." More seriously this time, I said, "Our schedule is set, so we'll have to make this trip, rain or shine." He said okay and left. The next (sunny) morning, we arrived at our departure point to find a substitute guide who spoke no English. When someone in our party asked me why the original guide hadn't just said he couldn't make it the next day, I found myself ruefully explaining about indirectness and loss of face. Knowledge does not equal intercultural competence.

An elaboration of this basic contrast between direct and indirect styles can be applied to understanding a difficulty in communication between Northern Europeans and U.S. Americans. Northern Europeans (particularly Germans) tend to be direct about intellectual topics but relatively indirect about relational matters. For instance. Northern Europeans are more likely than most U.S. Americans to say, "That idea is the stupidest thing I've ever heard." But those same Northern Europeans are less likely than Americans to discuss their feelings about casual relationships with the people involved. In contrast, U.S. Americans are more likely to be indirect on intellectual topics, making comments such as "Perhaps there is another way to think about that" or simply "Hmmm, interesting." But those same Americans may be quick to state to his or her face how much they like a new acquaintance. So Americans often think that Northern Europeans are relationally haughty, while Northern Europeans may think that Americans are intellectually shallow. Ethnocentric perception leads U.S. Americans to fail to recognize indirectness in relational commentary, while Northern Europeans similarly fail to detect indirectness in intellectual discourse. Additionally, ethnocentric interpretation leads Americans to mistake normal Northern European argument for the intellectual arrogance it would represent in most U.S. contexts, and Northern Europeans to mistake normal American relational openness for the boorishness it would represent in many European contexts.

Values and Assumptions

Cultural values are the patterns of goodness and badness people assign to ways of being in the world. For instance, Japanese people typically assign goodness to being interdependent in groups (even if they often act individually), while U.S. Americans typically assign goodness to being independently self-reliant (even if they often act interdependently). To shorten this, we would state the generalization that, relative to the other culture, Japanese value collectivism and U.S. Americans value individualism. Conversely, Japanese tend to disvalue many manifestations of individualism as unnecessarily selfish, while U.S. Americans disvalue many forms of collectivism as unduly conformist.

Cultural assumptions are interrelated with values but refer to the existence of phenomena rather than the assignment of value to them. So, in terms of the above example contrasting Japanese and U.S. Americans, most Americans assume the existence of an individual identity, which is necessary for the self-reliance of individualism to exist. Most Japanese, on the other hand, assume the existence of a kind of collective consciousness ("we Japanese"), which is necessary for interrelationships of collectivism to occur. In most intercultural analyses of situations, it is necessary to ascertain both what cultural assumptions are being made in the situation and what values are being placed on those assumptions.

The system that has been used traditionally by interculturalists for analyzing cultural values is the one developed by Florence R. Kluckhohn and Fred L. Strodtbeck.[37] Based on research with several cultures, the system defines five dimensions of cultural assumptions: peoples' relationship to the environment, to each other, to activity, to time, and to the basic nature of human beings. Constituting each of these dimensions is a continuum of possible relationships that people might assume with the subject. For instance, people may assume that they can control the environment, that they can live in harmony with it, or that they are subjugated by the environment. Kluckhohn and Strodtbeck state that all positions on the continuum will be represented to some degree in all cultures, but that one position will be *preferred.* It is this general preference that constitutes a cultural value. For example, most U.S. Americans prefer to think that nature is controllable—witness their damming of rivers, their programs to conquer space, and so forth. We could say that, in general, U.S. Americans value being in control of their environment. Other assumptions about an appropriate relationship to nature are present in U.S. society, of course. But with some exceptions, those assumptions are not as yet preferred and so are not now considered general cultural values.[38]

Many modifications of the Kluckhohn and Strodtbeck approach have proved useful for intercultural value analysis. John C. Condon[39] has expanded the original five dimensions into a list that can be applied to a broader range of more specific cultural phenomena, as has L. Robert Kohls.[40] Edward C. Stewart has done the most to develop the theoretical potential of the approach by defining the contrast American approach to value analysis[41] and by redefining the original dimensions in particularly useful ways.[42]

Another approach to value analysis has been developed by Geert Hofstede.[43] As opposed to the deductive approach of Kluckhohn and Strodtbeck, Hofstede used the inductive technique of surveying a large number of people from various national cultures about their values and preferences in life. Using the statistical technique of factor analysis, he then isolated four dimensions (and later a fifth) that accounted for a large amount of the variation in answers. He named the four dimensions *Power-Distance,* referring to the assumption of status difference; *Masculinity,* referring to (among other things) the assumption of gender difference; *Individualism,* referring to the assumption of self-reliance; and *Uncertainty Avoidance,* referring to the assumption of intolerance of ambiguity. In later studies, he added the dimension of *Conjucian Dynamism* or *Long-Term Orientation,* referring to focus on future rewards.[44]

Returning to the data from each national culture, he was then able to rank-order the cultures in terms of each dimension. For instance, Japanese ranked 7th out of fifty countries on Uncertainty Avoidance, while the United States ranked 46th; on Individualism the United States scored 1st and Japan 22nd. By statistically combining factors, Hofstede was able to map clusters of cultures in several dimensions. Many contemporary studies of cultural values now use, at least in part, the Hofstede categories.

Cultural Adaptation

In many ways, the crux of intercultural communication is in how people adapt to other cultures. Yet the intercultural concept of adaptation is frequently misunderstood. To clarify the idea, it is useful to distinguish *adaptation* from *assimilation.* Assimilation is the process of resocialization that seeks to replace one's original worldview with that of the host culture. Assimilation is "substitutive." Adaptation, on the other hand, is the process whereby one's worldview is expanded to include behavior and values appropriate to the host culture. It is "additive," not substitutive. The assumed end result of assimilation is becoming a "new person," as Israel Zangwill wrote in his play, *The Melting Pot.*[45] The assumed end result of adaptation is becoming a bicultural or multicultural person. Such a person has new aspects, but not at the cost of his or her original socialization. The identity issues around adaptation are quite complex, and understanding them is one of the new frontiers of intercultural communication.

Developmental Approaches to Cultural Adaptation

Cultural adaptation is not an on/off phenomenon. Like many other human abilities, it appears that cultural adaptation develops through stages, in much the same way as does cognition as described by Jean Piaget[46] or ethicality as described by William G. Perry, Jr.[47] With descriptions of the stages of development, interculturalists who are responsible for facilitating cross-cultural encounters are able to diagnose learners' levels of development and thus design their interventions more effectively.

A straightforward form of developmental thinking can be illustrated with one of the best-known of all intercultural concepts: *culture shock.* The evolution of this concept began with a relatively simple statement of how disorientation can occur in a different cultural context, along with the implication that culture shock was something like a disease that could be prevented, or caught and cured.[48] From this distinctly nondevelopmental beginning, the concept gained complexity as it was described in terms of U or W curves extending through time.[49] Then Peter S. Adler[50] suggested that culture shock was a process that went through five stages: the euphoria of Contact, when cultural difference is first encountered; the confusion of Disintegration, when loss of self-esteem intrudes; the anger of Reintegration, when the new culture is rejected and the old self reasserted; the relaxed self-assuredness of Autonomy, when cross-cultural situations can be handled with relative ease; and the creativity of Independence, when choice and responsibility accompany a deep respect for one's own and others' cultures. These ideas were placed in an even broader developmental context by Janet M. Bennett,[51] who defined culture shock as a special case of the typical human response to any transition, loss, or change.

So when even a relatively simple aspect of cultural adaptation—culture shock—is cast in developmental terms, it attains a level of complexity that makes it a richer and more useful descriptor of peoples' experiences. When the broader topic of cultural adaptation in general is described in developmental terms, the result is even more descriptive of complex experience. One example of this attempt is the Developmental Model of Intercultural Sensitivity (DMIS).[52] Based on "meaning-making" models of cognitive psychology and radical constructivism,[53] the DMIS links changes in cognitive structure to an evolution in attitudes and behavior toward cultural difference in general. The DMIS is divided into *Ethnocentric Stages* and *Ethnorelative Stages.*

Ethnocentric is defined as using one's own set of standards and customs to judge all people, often unconsciously. *Ethnorelative* means the opposite; it refers to being comfortable with many standards and customs and to having an ability to adapt behavior and judgments to a variety of interpersonal settings. Following are short descriptions of each of six stages of development.

Denial

People at the denial stage are unable to construe cultural differences in complex ways. They probably live in relative isolation from other cultures, either by happenstance or by choice. Either they do not perceive cultural differences at all, or they can conceive only of broad categories such as "foreigner," "people of color," or "Africans." People at this stage may use stereotypes in their description of others that are not meant to denigrate but are based on knowing only one or two things about the other people. For instance, many U.S. Americans seem to think that all Africans live near jungles and have encounters with wild animals, or many Asians seem to think that all Americans from the Pacific Northwest live on ranches and ride horses.

In contrast to the complexity of our own worldview, the simplicity of these stereotypes makes "their" seemingly sparse experience seem less real than "our" demonstrably rich experience. Consequently, when actually confronted by cultural diversity, people in denial unconsciously attribute less than human status to the outsiders. They may then use power for purposes of

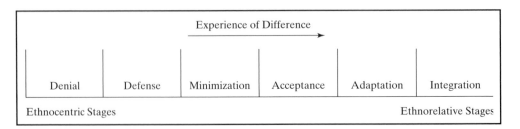

FIGURE 2 Development of Intercultural Sensitivity

exploiting the others, and in extreme cases of threat, they may further dehumanize the outsiders to enable genocide.

Defense

People at the defense stage have more ability to construe cultural difference, but they attach negative evaluations to it. They combat the threat of change to their stable worldview by denigrating others with negative stereotypes and by attaching positive stereotypes to themselves. Consequently, they view their own culture as the acme of "development" and tend to evaluate different cultures as "underdeveloped." A few people may enter a reversed form of defense, wherein they vilify their own culture and become zealous proponents of an adopted culture. For example, some U.S. Americans spurn their European roots while idealizing Native Indian cultures, and some U.S. Americans, when traveling, label most of their compatriots as "the ugly Americans." In all cases, however, defense is characterized by the polarization of a denigrated "them" with a superior "us."

People in defense consider themselves under siege. Members of socially dominant cultures may attempt to protect privilege and deny opportunities to outsiders, while nondominant culture members may aggressively protect their ethnic identity from suppression by the majority. Ironically, while personally directed violence may be more common in defense than in denial, the threat of systematic genocide is reduced by the greater humanity accorded one's enemy.

Minimization

People at the minimization stage try to bury cultural differences within already-familiar categories of physical and philosophical similarity. They recognize and accept superficial cultural differences such as eating customs and other social norms, but they assume that deep down all people are essentially the same—just human. As a consequence of this assumption, certain cultural values may be mistaken for universal desires; for instance, U.S. Americans may believe that people everywhere desire individual freedom, openness, and competition. Religious people may hold that everyone is a child of God, is subject to Allah's will, or acquires karma "whether they know it or not." Political and economic minimizers may suppose that we are all victims of historical Marxist forces or that we are all motivated by the private enterprise of capitalism. While people at the minimization stage are considerably more knowledgeable than those in denial and a lot nicer than those in defense, they are still ethnocentric in their adherence to these culture-bound universalistic assumptions.

In domestic intercultural relations in the United States, minimization is the classic "white liberal" position. It is usually accompanied by strong support for the "melting pot" idea, a distrust of ethnic and other labels for cultural diversity, and an abiding belief in the existence of equal opportunity. While eschewing power exercised through exploitation and denial of opportunity, people in minimization unquestioningly accept the dominant culture privileges built into institutions. People who do not enjoy these privileges— people of color and others who experience oppression in U.S. society—tend not to dwell at this somewhat self-congratulatory stage.

Acceptance

People at the acceptance stage enjoy recognizing and exploring cultural differences. They are aware that they themselves are cultural beings. They are fairly tolerant of ambiguity and are comfortable knowing there is no one right answer (although there are better answers for particular contexts). "Acceptance" does not mean that a person has to agree with or take on a cultural perspective other than his or her own. Rather, people accept the *viability* of different cultural ways of thinking and behaving, even though they might not like them. This is the first stage in which people begin to think about the notion of cultural relativity—that their own behavior and values are not the only good way to be in the world.

People in acceptance tend to avoid the exercise of power in any form. As a consequence, they may at times become paralyzed by the dilemmas posed by conflicting cultural norms. At this stage, people have moved beyond ethnocentric rules for behavior and may not yet have developed ethnorelative principles for taking action.

Adaptation

People at the adaptation stage use knowledge about their own and others' cultures to intentionally shift into a different cultural frame of reference. That is, they can empathize or take another person's perspective in order to understand and be understood across cultural boundaries. Based on their ability to use alternative cultural interpretations, people in this stage can modify their behavior in ways that make it more appropriate to cultures other than their own. Another way to think about this is that people in adaptation have increased their repertoire of behavior—they have maintained the skills of operating in their own cultures while adding the ability to operate effectively in one or more other cultures. This intercultural competence may include the ability to recognize how power is being exercised within a cultural context, and some people may themselves be able to exercise power in ways that are appropriate to the other culture. Advanced forms of adaptation are "bicultural" or "multicultural," wherein people have internalized one or more cultural frames in addition to that in which they were originally socialized. Bicultural people can completely shift their cultural frame of reference without much conscious effort.

Most people at the adaptation stage are generally interculturally sensitive; with varying degrees of sophistication, they can apply skills of empathy and adaptation of behavior to any cultural context. However, in some cases people have become "accidentally bicultural," wherein they received primary socialization in two or more cultural frames of reference. (Children of bicultural marriages and of long-term expatriates may fall into this category.) Sometimes these people are very good at shifting between the two cultures they have internalized, but they cannot apply the same adaptation skills to other cultures. In addition, some people in adaptation do not exhibit intercultural sensitivity toward groups that they do not consider cultures. For instance, some people who are otherwise interculturally skilled retain negative stereotypes of gay, lesbian, and bisexual people. When these groups are defined in cultural terms, people in adaptation are more likely to be able to relate to them in interculturally competent ways.

Integration

People at the integration stage of development are attempting to reconcile the sometimes-conflicting cultural frames that they have internalized. In the transition to this stage, some people become overwhelmed by the cultures they know and are disturbed that they can no longer identify with any one of them. But as they move into integration, people achieve an identity which allows them to see themselves as "interculturalists" or "multiculturalists" in addition to their national and ethnic backgrounds.[54] They recognize that worldviews are collective constructs and that identity is itself a construction of consciousness. As a consequence, they may seek out roles that allow them to be intercultural mediators and exhibit other qualities of "constructive marginality."[55] They also tend to associate with other cultural marginals rather than people from any one of the cultures they know.

People in integration are inclined to interpret and evaluate behavior from a variety of cultural frames of reference, so that there is never a single right or wrong answer. But, unlike the resulting paralysis of action that may occur in earlier stages, people in integration are capable of engaging in "contextual evaluation." The goodness or ethicality of actions is not given by absolute (and ethnocentric) principles but is constructed by human beings who thereby take responsibility for the realities they are creating. Thus, people in integration face the unending task of guiding their own behavior along the ethical lines that they themselves have created.

ETHNORELATIVE ETHICS

Much of the controversy surrounding the development of intercultural sensitivity is about ethics. Some people seem to think that being interculturally sensitive means giving up any set of ethical principles or moral guidelines. They think cultural relativity is the same thing as moral relativism or situational ethics. To understand that criticism, we can turn to yet another developmental model, the Perry Scheme of Cognitive and Ethical Development.[56]

Perry outlines a process whereby people develop ethical thinking and behavior as they learn more about the world. The model describes movement from "dualism" (one simple either/or way of thinking) to "multiplicity" (many ambiguous and equally good ways of thinking), and then on to "contextual relativism" (different actions are judged according to appropriate context) and "commitment in relativism" (people choose the context in which they will act, even though other actions are viable in different contexts).

People who are most critical of multiculturalism seem to be at Perry's stage of dualism. They think of ethics and morality as absolute, universal rules. In this dualistic view, the acceptance of different cultures leads only to multiplicity, where all options are equal and ethical chaos reigns. Therefore, goes the dualistic argument, either you choose the absolutist ethical path that rejects cultural relativism, or you accept cultural relativism and the only alternative it offers to absolutism, moral relativity, and situational ethics.

Interculturalists by and large reject this dualistic view in favor of a third alternative, one where ethnorelativism and strong ethical principles coexist. The reconciliation of culture and ethics occurs in parallel to the latter two stages of Perry's model. In contextual relativism, actions must be judged within context. Thus, at this stage, ethical actions must be judged within a cultural context. There is no universal ethical behavior. For instance, it is not universally ethical to be openly honest in dealing with others. That such is the case, however, does not imply that one should be dishonest whenever it is convenient or situationally normative (e.g., "Everyone else is lying to get those payments, so why shouldn't I?"). On the contrary, Perry's last stage suggests that we commit to acting within the context we wish to maintain. If we want a reality in which open honesty is normative, then it is ethical to act in ways that support the viability of that behavior. Perhaps this doesn't mean that someone with such an ethical commitment is openly honest in every situation. But it probably does mean that actions that contradict or undermine a context in which "honesty is the best policy" would be avoided.

Some antagonists of intercultural and multicultural thinking[57] have suggested that interculturalists are the same as any other ethical absolutist in their adherence to the "goodness" of contextual relativity. In so doing, these critics neglect that important aspect of language called "logical type."[58] The statement "It is good to have three wives" is different in logical type from the statement "It is good to know that forms of marriage are evaluated differently in different cultures." The latter statement is actually a "metastatement," a statement about other statements. Interculturalists would certainly think it was good to make that metastatement, but this thought is significantly different in type from thinking that it is good or bad to have one or three wives. Another such metastatement is "absolutists and relativists differ in their belief in the importance of contextual evaluation." It is good to be able to make this distinction, but doing so says nothing about the goodness of either absolutists or relativists. Absolutists might be judged as "bad" in the context of intercultural communication not for any particular beliefs they hold but because they reject seeing their own behavior in cultural context.

PERSONAL ENDNOTE

As you can see, I think an intercultural perspective offers more than an effective way to analyze interaction and facilitate adaptation. In my opinion, intercultural communication envisions a reality which will support the simultaneous existence of unity and diversity, of cooperation and competition in the global village, and of consensus and creative conflict in multicultural societies. In this vision, our different voices can be heard both in their uniqueness and in synergistic harmony. While there are many paths which can converge into this future, the focus brought by interculturalists rests on individuals and relationships. We strive to bring culture into individual consciousness and in so doing bring consciousness to bear on the creation of intercultural relationships.

Discussion Questions

1. (a) Based on material from Bennett's article and the previous readings in this section of the text, briefly describe a situation where you have formed an inductive stereotype (i.e., you based your generalizations on a small sample of a cultural experience such as some stereotype about Mexicans based on a spring break visit to Cancun, or a one-day trip over the border to Tijuana).
   (b) Using this situation, develop three or four inaccurate stereotypes that could be incorrectly generalized to all members of the group that you interacted with (for example, using this very specific and limited exposure to Mexicans in a resort area or a highly commercialized tourist area as characterizing the whole country and its people).
2. Bennett writes, "Knowledge does not equal intercultural competence." What does he mean by that statement? What connection does this statement have with the Nacirema reading?
3. Watch a foreign-language movie or foreign-language television show with the volume off. Apply Bennett's material on nonverbal communication to what you see. What did you learn from this experience?
4. Discuss the implications of Bennett's stages of cultural adaptation in terms of (a) a study abroad experience or (b) being sent to a foreign country for a short business trip.

Writing Assignments

1. Attend some function or event where "lowercase" cultural behavior can be easily observed (for example, an American student attended a social event held at a local Society of India group).
   (a) Analyze the behaviors and communications that you observed from the perspective of *traditional* North American cultural values.
   (b) *After* you have written part one of this assignment, perform library, and Internet research on this culture. If possible interview one or two people who may have a deeper understanding of this culture (students, coworkers, teachers who have lived and or worked with that culture).
   (c) Then, write an essay analyzing the source of your cultural misconceptions in section a.
2. Observe a class or a meeting, recording examples of the teacher or leader's high- or low-context behaviors. For example, did the teacher or leader give detailed instructions, use lots of wordy PowerPoint slides, and provide handouts repeating or clarifying the information presented (low-context communications). Also, take notes on the pitch, tone, of the verbal messages as well as the nonverbal behaviors. Make observations about the discussion/participation interactions of the class or meeting in terms of low-context or high-context verbal and nonverbal behaviors. Write a paper in which you analyze the meaning of what you saw and heard in terms of the theory presented in the Bennett reading.

Endnotes

1. Barnlund, D. (1998). Communication in a global village. In M.J. Bennett (Ed.), *Basic concepts of intercultural communication* (pp. 35–52). Yarmouth, ME: Intercultural Press.

2. Bennett, M.J. (1998). Overcoming the golden rule. In M.J. Bennett (Ed.), *Basic concepts of intercultural communication* (pp. 191–214). Yarmouth, ME: Intercultural Press.

3. Barna, L.M. (1998). Stumbling blocks in intercultural communication. In M.J. Bennett (Ed.), *Basic concepts of intercultural communication* (pp. 173–190). Yarmouth, ME: Intercultural Press.

4. For example, see Berger, P. L., & Luckmann, T. (1972). In H.C. Triandis (Ed.), *The analysis of subjective culture*, New York: John Wiley.

5. Berger, P.L., & Luckmann, T. (1966). *The social construction of reality: A treatise in the sociology of knowledge.* New York: Doubleday.

6. Stewart, E.C., & Bennett, M.J. (1991). *American cultural patterns: A cross-cultural perspective* (rev. ed.). Yarmouth, ME: Intercultural Press.

7. Some forms of ethnicity also exist at a higher level of abstraction than does national culture (e.g., Arab ethnicity, which cuts across many national boundaries: the Kurds of Iraq and Turkey, and many other groups in Europe, Asia, and Africa).

8. Each of these ethnic groups is, itself, at a relatively high level of abstraction. For instance, "African American" includes people from many places in Africa and its diaspora, such as the Caribbean, who arrived in America any time from a dozen generations to only one generation ago. (American Indians, of course, were here earlier.) Appropriately, "European American" and the other categories are at this same level of abstraction. More specific references, such as to Italian Americans or Mexican Americans, occur at a lower level of abstraction and should not be mixed with the higher-level generalizations. Care with these levels maintains a "conceptually level playing field" for interethnic relations.

9. Singer, M.R. (1998). Culture: A perceptual approach. In M. J. Bennett (Ed.), *Basic concepts of intercultural communication* (pp. 97–110). Yarmouth, ME: Intercultural Press.

10. Hoopes, D.S. (1980). Intercultural communication concepts and the psychology of intercultural experience. In M.D. Pusch (Ed.), *Multicultural education: A cross cultural training approach* (pp. 9–42). LaGrange Park, IL: Intercultural Press.

11. Kluckhohn, F.R., & Strodtbeck, F.L. (1973). *Variations in value orientations.* Westport, CT: Greenwood; Stewart, E.C., & Bennett, M.J. (1991). *American cultural patterns*: A cross-cultural perspective. Yarmouth, ME: Intercultural Press.

12. Cortes, C.E. (1992). Pride, prejudice and power: The mass media as societal educator on diversity. In J. Lynch, C. Modgil, & S. Modgil (Eds.), *Prejudice, Polemic or Progress?* (pp. 367–381). London: Falmer Press.

13. Stewart, E.C., & Bennett, M.J. (1991). *American cultural patterns: A cross-cultural perspective* (rev. ed.). Yarmouth, ME: Intercultural Press; Kras, E. S. *Management in two cultures: Bridging the gap between U.S. and Mexican managers* (rev. ed.). Yarmouth, ME: Intercultural Press; Condon, J.C. (1997). *Good neighbors: Communicating with the Mexicans* (2d ed.). Yarmouth, ME: Intercultural Press.

14. Martin, J.N., & Nakayama, T.K. (1997). *Intercultural communication in contexts.* Mountain View, CA: Mayfield.

15. Hall, E.T. (1976). *Beyond culture.* New York: Anchor/Doubleday.

16. Etic analysis as used by interculturalists does not assume the existence of universal categories. Rather, contrastive categories are created to generate

cultural distinctions that are useful for the purpose of communication.

17. Tannen, D. (1994). *Gender and discourse.* New York: Oxford University Press.

18. Perry, W.G., Jr. (1970). *Forms of intellectual and ethical development in the college years: A scheme.* Fort Worth, TX: Harcourt Brace.

19. Stewart, E.C., & Bennett, M.J. (1991). *American cultural patterns: A cross-cultural perspective* (rev. ed.). Yarmouth, ME: Intercultural Press.

20. Whorf, B.L. (1998). Science and Linguistics. In M.J. Bennett (Ed.). *Basic concepts of intercultural communication* (pp. 85–96). Yarmouth, ME: Intercultural Press.

21. Berlin, B., & Kay, P. (1969). *Basic color terms: Their universality and evolution.* Berkeley: University of California Press; Stewart E.C., & Bennett, M.J. (1991). *American Cultural Patterns: A cross-cultural perspective* (rev. ed.). Yarmouth, ME: Intercultural Press.

22. Brown, G.S. (1972). *Laws of Form.* Toronto: Bantam Books; von Foerster, H. (1984). On constructing a reality. In P. Watzlawick (Ed.), *The invented reality* (pp. 41–62). New York: Norton.

23. von Foerster, H. (1984). On constructing a reality. In P. Watzlawick (Ed.), *The Inverted Reality* (pp. 41–62). New York: Norton.

24. Hall, E.T. (1981). *The silent language.* New York: Anchor/ Doubleday.

25. Watzlawick, P., Beavin, J. H., & Jackson, D.D. (1967). *Pragmatics of human communication.* New York: Norton.

26. Hayashi, K. (1990, November). *Intercultural insights into Japanese business methods*, Senior Executive Seminar, Pacific University, Forest Grove, Oregon.

27. Hall, E.T. (1976). *Beyond culture.* New York: Anchor/Doubleday.

28. Hall, E.T. (1998). The power of hidden differences. In M.J. Bennett (Ed.), *Basic concepts of intercultural communication* (pp. 53–68). Yarmouth, ME: Intercultural Press.

29. Ibid.

30. Watzlawick, P., Beavin, J.H., & Jackson, D.D. (1967). *Pragmatics of human communication.* New York: Norton, p. 53.

31. Rosenfeld, L.B., & Civikly, J. (1976). *With words unspoken: The nonverbal experience.* New York: Holt, Rinehart & Winston, p. 5; Banks, J.A., & McGee Banks, C.A., (Eds). (1995). *Handbook of research on multicultural education.* New York: Simon and Schuster; Bennett, C.I. (1990). *Comprehensive multicultural education: Theory and practice* (2d ed.). Boston: Allyn & Bacon.

32. Kochman, T. (1981). *Black and white styles in conflict.* Chicago: University of Chicago Press, p. 47.

33. Kaplan, R.B. (1988). Cultural Thought Patterns. In J.S. Wurzel (Ed.), *Toward multiculturalism,* (pp. 207–221). Yarmouth, ME: Intercultural Press.

34. Belenky, M.F., Clinchy, B.M. Goldberger, N.R., & Tarule, J.M. (1997). *Women's ways of knowing: The development of self, voice, and mind* (New York: HarperCollins, 1997); Goldberger, N. et al., (1996). *Knowledge, difference, and power: Essays inspired by women's ways of knowing.* New York: HarperCollins.

35. Wurzel, J.S., & Fishman, N. (Producers), (1993). *A different place* and *Creating community: The intercultural classroom.* Boston: Intercultural Resource Corporation, 1993.

36. Ramsey, S.J. (1998). Interactions between North Americans and Japanese: Considerations of communication style. In M.J. Bennett (Ed.), *Basic concepts of intercultural communication* (pp. 111–130). Yarmouth, ME: Intercultural Press); Gudykunst, W. B., Ting-Toomey, S., & Chua, E. (1988). *Culture and interpersonal communication* (vol. 8). Newbury Park, CA: Sage.

37. Kluckhohn, F.R., & Strodtbeck, F.L. (1973). *Variations in value orientations.* Westport, CT: Greenwood.

38. The Kluckhohn and Strodtbeck system is used by interculturalists to generate convenient and useful contrasts among cultures, and not as the universal etic

categories that they were originally assumed to be.

39. Condon, J.C., & Yousef, F. (1975). *An introduction to intercultural communication.* New York: Macmillan.

40. Kohls, L.R. (1988). *Values Americans live by.* Duncanville, TX: Adult Learning Systems.

41. Stewart, E.C., Danielian, J., & Foster, R.J. (1998). Cultural assumptions and values. In M.J. Bennett (Ed.), *Basic concepts of intercultural communication* (pp. 157–172). Yarmouth, ME: Intercultural Press.

42. Stewart, E.C., & Bennett, M.J. (1991). *American cultural patterns*: A cross-cultural perspective (rev. ed.). Yarmouth, ME: Intercultural Press.

43. Hofstede, G. (1984). *Culture's consequences: International differences in work-related values* (abridged ed., vol. 5). Cross-Cultural Research and Methodology Series. Beverly Hills, CA: Sage.

44. Hofstede, G. (1991). *Cultures and organizations: Software of the mind.* London: McGraw-Hill.

45. Zangwill, I. (1921). *The melting pot: Drama in four acts.* New York: Macmillan.

46. Piaget, J. (1954). *Construction of reality in the child.* New York: Ballantine.

47. Perry, W.G., Jr. (1970). *Forms of intellectual and ethical development* in the college years: A scheme. Fort Worth, TX: Harcourt Brace.

48. Oberg, K. (1960). Cultural shock: Adjustment to new cultural environments. *Practical Anthropology 7,* 177.

49. Gullahorn, J., & Gullahorn, J. (1963). An extension of the U-curve Hypothesis. *Journal of Social Issues,* 19(3), 33–47.

50. Adler, P.S. (1972). Culture shock and the cross-cultural learning experience. In D.S. Hoopes (Ed.), *Readings in intercultural communication* (vol. 2, pp. 6–22).

Pittsburgh, PA: Regional Council for International Education.

51. Bennett, J.M. (1998). Transition shock: Putting culture shock in perspective. In M.J. Bennett (Ed.), *Basic Concepts of Intercultural Communication* (pp. 215–224). Yarmouth, ME: Intercultural Press.

52. Bennett, M.J. (1986). Towards ethnorelativism: A developmental model of intercultural sensitivity. In R.M. Paige (Ed.), *Cross-cultural orientation: New conceptualizations and applications* (pp. 27–69). New York: University Press of America.

53. Watzlawick, P. (Ed.). (1984). *The invented reality.* New York: Norton.

54. Adler, P.S. (1998). Beyond cultural identity: Reflections on multiculturalism. In M.J. Bennett (Ed.), *Basic concepts of intercultural communication* (pp. 225–246). Yarmouth, ME: Intercultural Press.

55. Bennett, J.M. (1993). Cultural marginality: Identity issues in intercultural training. In R.M. Paige (Ed.), *Education for the intercultural experience* (2d ed., pp. 109–136). Yarmouth, ME: Intercultural Press.

56. Perry, W.G., Jr. (1970). *Forms of intellectual and ethical development in the college years: A Scheme.* Fort Worth, TX: Harcourt Brace.

57. D'Souza, D. (1995). *The end of racism: Principles for a multiracial society.* New York; Free Press; Schlesinger A. M., Jr. (1998). *The disuniting of America: Reflections on a multicultural society.* New York: Norton; D'Souza, D. (1998). *Illiberal education: The politics of race and sex on campus.* New York: Random House.

58. Russell, B. (1948). *Human knowledge, its scope and limits.* New York: Simon & Schuster.

II

GROUP IDENTITY PERSPECTIVES ON DIVERSITY

The second section of the text addresses the topic of identity groups. Each person is unique but belongs to multiple groups that vary in terms of their salience or importance to one's self-identity. Even if an identity like age—such as being over 50, does not make much difference to an individual, it may affect how others perceive and interact with that individual.

Of course, there is a range of behaviors for members of any identity group, such as men differ in the degree to which they manifest assertiveness. However, individuals can be stereotyped by the most prevalent behavior patterns of their group. Members of identity groups may also experience "privileges" or lack of privileges because of their group memberships.

Section II is designed to give you more knowledge in terms of a variety of social identities: privilege (McIntosh), genders (Tannen, Harvey #16, Farough, Harvey #18), race (Baldino), cultural ethnicity (Allard #20, Aurelio & Novak), age (Holtzman, Kruger & Srock, Sherer #22, Harvey & Sherer #23), sexual orientation (Hunt #24, Ross & Whitty), physical/mental challenges (Allard #26, 27, 28, and 29; Oliver & Bartholomew), social class (Harvey #31), and religion (Rao, Harvey #33, Sherer #34). The capstone assignment (Allard #35) is designed to help students analyze group identities issues as they are communicated, often in stereotypical ways through various media.

Learning Outcomes for Section II

■ Students will gain in-depth knowledge about different types of identity groups.
■ Students will learn how social identities can impact in workplace interactions.

WHITE PRIVILEGE AND MALE PRIVILEGE: A PERSONAL ACCOUNT OF COMING TO SEE CORRESPONDENCES THROUGH WORK IN WOMEN'S STUDIES

Peggy McIntosh
Wellesley College

Through work to bring materials and perspectives from Women's Studies into the rest of the curriculum, I have often noticed men's unwillingness to grant that they are over privileged in the curriculum, even though they may grant that women are disadvantaged. Denials which amount to taboos surround the subject of advantages which men gain from women's disadvantages. These denials protect male privilege from being fully recognized, acknowledged, lessened, or ended.

Thinking through unacknowledged male privilege as a phenomenon with a life of its own, I realized that since hierarchies in our society are interlocking, there was most likely a phenomenon of white privilege which was similarly denied and protected, but alive and real in its effects. As a white person, I realized I had been taught about racism as something which puts others at a disadvantage, but had been taught not to see one of its corollary aspects, white privilege, which puts me at an advantage.

I think whites are carefully taught not to recognize white privilege, as males are taught not to recognize male privilege. So I have begun in an untutored way to ask what it is like to have white privilege. This paper is a partial record of my personal observations, and not a scholarly analysis. It is based on my daily experiences within my particular circumstances.

I have come to see white privilege as an invisible package of unearned assets which I can count on cashing in each day, but about which I was "meant" to remain oblivious. White privilege is like an invisible weightless knapsack of special provisions, assurances, tools, maps, guides, codebooks, passports, visas, clothes, compass, emergency gear, and blank checks.

Since I have had trouble facing white privilege, and describing its results in my life, I saw parallels here with men's reluctance to acknowledge male privilege. Only rarely will a man go beyond acknowledging that women are disadvantaged to acknowledging that men have unearned advantage, or that unearned privilege has not been good for men's development as human beings, or for society's development, or that privilege systems might ever be challenged and *changed*.

I will review here several types or layers of denial which I see at work protecting, and preventing awareness about, entrenched male privilege. Then I will draw parallels, from my own experience, with the denials which veil the facts of white privilege. Finally, I will list 46 ordinary and daily ways in which I experience having white privilege, within my life situation and its particular social and political frameworks.

Writing this paper has been difficult, despite warm receptions for the talks on which it is based.[1] For describing white privilege makes one newly accountable. As we in Women's Studies work to reveal male privilege and ask men to give up some of their power, so one who writes about having white privilege must ask, "Having described it, what will I do to lessen or end it?"

The denial of men's overprivileged state takes many forms in discussions of curriculum-change work. Some claim that men must be central in the curriculum because they have done most of what is important or distinctive in life or in civilization. Some recognize sexism in the curriculum but deny that it makes male students seem unduly important in life. Others agree that certain *individual* thinkers are blindly male-oriented but deny that there is any systemic tendency in disciplinary frameworks or epistemology to overempower men as a group. Those men who do grant that male privilege takes institutionalized and embedded forms are still likely to deny that male hegemony has opened doors for them personally. Virtually all men deny that male overreward alone can explain men's centrality in all the inner sanctums of our most powerful institutions. Moreover, those few who will acknowledge that male privilege systems have overempowered them usually end up doubting that we could dismantle these privilege systems. They may say they will work to improve women's status, in the society or in the university, but they can't or won't support the idea of lessening men's. In curricular terms, this is the point at which they say that they regret they cannot use any of the interesting new scholarship on women because the syllabus is full. When the talk turns to giving men less cultural room, even the most fair-minded of the men I know well tend to reflect, or fall back on, conservative assumptions about the inevitability of present gender relations and distributions of power, calling on precedent or sociobiology and psychobiology to demonstrate that male domination is natural and follows inevitably from evolutionary pressures. Others resort to arguments from "experience" or religion or social responsibility or wishing and dreaming.

After I realized, through faculty development work in Women's Studies, the extent to which men work from a base of unacknowledged privilege, I understood that much of their oppressiveness was unconscious. Then I remembered the frequent charges from women of color that white women whom they encounter are oppressive. I began to understand why we are justly seen as oppressive, even when we don't see ourselves that way. At the very least, obliviousness of one's privileged state can make a person or group irritating to be with. I began to count the ways in which I enjoy unearned skin privilege and have been conditioned into oblivion about its existence, unable to see that it put me "ahead" in any way, or put my people ahead, overrewarding us and yet also paradoxically damaging us, or that it could or should be changed.

My schooling gave me no training in seeing myself as an oppressor, as an unfairly advantaged person, or as a participant in a damaged culture. I was taught to see myself as an individual whose moral state depended on her individual moral will. At school, we were not taught about slavery in any depth; we were not taught to see slaveholders as damaged people. Slaves were seen as the only group at risk of being dehumanized. My schooling followed the pattern which Elizabeth Minnich has pointed out: Whites are taught to think of their lives as morally neutral, normative, and average, and also ideal, so that when we work to benefit others, this is seen as work which will allow "them" to be more like "us." I think many of us know how obnoxious this attitude can be in men.

After frustration with men who would not recognize male privilege, I decided to try to work on myself at least by identifying some of the daily effects of white privilege in my life. It is crude work, at this stage, but I will give here a list of special circumstances and conditions I experience which I did not earn but which I have been made to feel are mine by birth, by citizenship, and by virtue of being a conscientious law-abiding "normal" person of good will. I have chosen those conditions which I think in my case *attach somewhat more to skin-color privilege* than to class, religion, ethnic status, or geographical location, though of course all these other factors are intricately intertwined. As far as I can see, my Afro-American co-workers, friends, and acquaintances with whom I come into daily or frequent contact in this particular time, place, and line of work cannot count on most of these conditions.

1. I can if I wish arrange to be in the company of people of my race most of the time.
2. I can avoid spending time with people whom I was trained to mistrust and who have learned to mistrust my kind or me.

3. If I should need to move, I can be pretty sure of renting or purchasing housing in an area which I can afford and in which I would want to live.
4. I can be pretty sure that my neighbors in such a location will be neutral or pleasant to me.
5. I can go shopping alone most of the time, pretty well assured that I will not be followed or harassed.
6. I can turn on the television or open to the front page of the paper and see people of my race widely represented.
7. When I am told about our national heritage or about "civilization," I am shown that people of my color made it what it is.
8. I can be sure that my children will be given curricular materials that testify to the existence of their race.
9. If I want to, I can be pretty sure of finding a publisher for this piece on white privilege.
10. I can be pretty sure of having my voice heard in a group in which I am the only member of my race.
11. I can be casual about whether or not to listen to another woman's voice in a group in which she is the only member of her race.
12. I can go into a music shop and count on finding the music of my race represented, into a supermarket and find the staple foods which fit with my cultural traditions, into a hairdresser's shop and find someone who can cut my hair.
13. Whether I use checks, credit cards, or cash, I can count on my skin color not to work against the appearance of financial reliability.
14. I can arrange to protect my children most of the time from people who might not like them.
15. I do not have to educate my children to be aware of systemic racism for their own daily physical protection.
16. I can be pretty sure that my children's teachers and employers will tolerate them if they fit school and workplace norms; my chief worries about them do not concern others' attitudes toward their race.
17. I can talk with my mouth full and not have people put this down to my color.
18. I can swear, or dress in second-hand clothes, or not answer letters, without having people attribute these choices to the bad morals, the poverty, or the illiteracy of my race.
19. I can speak in public to a powerful male group without putting my race on trial.
20. I can do well in a challenging situation without being called a credit to my race.
21. I am never asked to speak for all the people of my racial group.
22. I can remain oblivious of the language and customs of persons of color who constitute the world's majority without feeling in my culture any penalty for such oblivion.
23. I can criticize our government and talk about how much I fear its policies and behavior without being seen as a cultural outsider.

24. I can be pretty sure that if I ask to talk to "the person in charge," I will be facing a person of my race.
25. If a traffic cop pulls me over or if the IRS audits my tax return, I can be sure I haven't been singled out because of my race.
26. I can easily buy posters, postcards, picture books, greeting cards, dolls, toys, and children's magazines featuring people of my race.
27. I can go home from most meetings of organizations I belong to feeling somewhat tied in, rather than isolated, out-of-place, outnumbered, unheard, held at a distance, or feared.
28. I can be pretty sure that an argument with a colleague of another race is more likely to jeopardize her chances for advancement than to jeopardize mine.
29. I can be pretty sure that if I argue for the promotion of a person of another race, or a program centering on race, this is not likely to cost me heavily within my present setting, even if my colleagues disagree with me.
30. If I declare there is a racial issue at hand, or there isn't a racial issue at hand, my race will lend me more credibility for either position than a person of color will have.
31. I can choose to ignore developments in minority writing and minority activist programs, or disparage them, or learn from them, but in any case, I can find ways to be more or less protected from negative consequences of any of these choices.
32. My culture gives me little fear about ignoring the perspectives and powers of people of other races.
33. I am not made acutely aware that my shape, bearing, or body odor will be taken as a reflection of my race.
34. I can worry about racism without being seen as self-interested or self-seeking.
35. I can take a job with an affirmative action employer without having my coworkers on the job suspect that I got it because of my race.
36. If my day, week, or year is going badly, I need not ask of each negative episode or situation whether it has racial overtones.
37. I can be pretty sure of finding people who would be willing to talk with me and advise me about my next steps, professionally.
38. I can think over many options, social, political, imaginative, or professional, without asking whether a person of my race would be accepted or allowed to do what I want to do.
39. I can be late to a meeting without having the lateness reflect on my race.
40. I can choose public accommodation without fearing that people of my race cannot get in or will be mistreated in the places I have chosen.
41. I can be sure that if I need legal or medical help, my race will not work against me.
42. I can arrange my activities so that I will never have to experience feelings of rejection owing to my race.
43. If I have low credibility as a leader I can be sure that my race is not the problem.

44. I can easily find academic courses and institutions which give attention only to people of my race.
45. I can expect figurative language and imagery in all of the arts to testify to experiences of my race.
46. I can choose blemish cover or bandages in "flesh" color and have them more or less match my skin.

I repeatedly forgot each of the realizations on this list until I wrote it down. For me, white privilege has turned out to be an elusive and fugitive subject. The pressure to avoid it is great, for in facing it I must give up the myth of meritocracy. If these things are true, this is not such a free country; one's life is not what one makes it; many doors open for certain people through no virtues of their own. These perceptions mean also that my moral condition is not what I had been led to believe. The appearance of being a good citizen rather than a troublemaker comes in large part from having all sorts of doors open automatically because of my color.

A further paralysis of nerve comes from literary silence protecting privilege. My clearest memories of finding such analysis are in Lillian Smith's unparalleled *Killers of the Dream* and Margaret Andersen's review of Karen and Mamie Fields' *Lemon Swamp.* Smith, for example, wrote about walking toward black children on the street and knowing they would step into the gutter; Andersen contrasted the pleasure which she, as a white child, took on summer driving trips to the south with Karen Fields' memories of driving in a closed car stocked with all necessities lest, in stopping, her black family should suffer "insult, or worse." Adreinne Rich also recognizes and writes about daily experiences of privilege, but in my observation, white women's writing in this area is far more often on systemic racism than on our daily lives as light-skinned women.[2]

In unpacking this invisible knapsack of white privilege, I have listed conditions of daily experience which I once took for granted, as neutral, normal, and universally available to everybody, just as I once thought of a male-focused curriculum as the neutral or accurate account which can speak for all. Nor did I think any of these perquisites as bad for the holder. I now think that we need a more finely differentiated taxonomy of privilege, for some of these varieties are only what one would want for everyone in a just society, and others give license to be ignorant, oblivious, arrogant, and destructive. Before proposing some more finely-tuned categorization, I will make some observations about the general effects of these conditions on my life and expectations.

In this potpourri of examples, some privileges make me feel at home in the world. Others allow me to escape penalties or dangers which others suffer. Through some, I escape fear, anxiety, or a sense of not being welcome or not being real. Some keep me from having to hide, to be in disguise, to feel sick or crazy, to negotiate each transaction from the position of being an outsider or, within my group, a person who is suspected of having too close links with a dominant culture. Most keep me from having to be angry.

I see a pattern running through the matrix of white privilege, a pattern of assumptions which were passed on to me as a white person. There was one main piece of cultural turf; it was my own turf, and I was among those who could control the turf. I could measure up to the cultural standards and take advantage of the many options I saw around me to make what the culture would call a success of my life. *My skin color was an asset for any move I was educated to want to make.* I could think of myself as "belonging" in major ways, and of making social systems work for me. I could freely disparage, fear, neglect, or be oblivious to anything outside of the dominant cultural forms. Being of the main culture, I could also criticize it fairly freely. My life was reflected back to me frequently enough so that I felt, with regard to my race, if not to my sex, like one of the real people.

Whether through the curriculum or in the newspaper, the television, the economic system, or the general look of people in the streets, we received daily signals and indications that my people counted, and that others *either didn't exist or must be trying not very successfully, to be like people of my race.* We were given cultural permission not to hear voices of people of other races, or a tepid cultural tolerance for hearing or acting on such voices. I was also raised not to suffer seriously from anything which darker-skinned people might say about my group, "protected," though perhaps I should more accurately say *prohibited,* through the habits of my economic class and social group, from living in racially mixed groups or being reflective about interactions between people of differing races.

In proportion as my racial group was being made confident, comfortable, and oblivious, other groups were likely being made inconfident, uncomfortable, and alienated. Whiteness protected me from many kinds of hostility, distress, and violence, which I was being subtly trained to visit in turn upon people of color.

For this reason, the word *privilege* now seems to me misleading. Its connotations are too positive to fit the conditions and behaviors which "privilege systems" produce. We usually think of privilege as being a favored state, whether earned, or conferred by birth or luck. School graduates are reminded they are privileged and urged to use their (enviable) assets well. The word *privilege* carries the connotation of being something everyone must want. Yet some of the conditions I have described here work to systemically overempower certain groups. Such privilege simply *confers dominance,* gives permission to control, because of one's race or sex. The kind of privilege which gives license to some people to be, at best, thoughtless and, and at worst, murderous should not continue to be referred to as a desirable attribute. Such "privilege" may be widely desired without being in any way beneficial to the whole society.

Moreover, though "privilege" may confer power, it does not confer moral strength. Those who do not depend on conferred dominance have traits and qualities which may never develop in those who do. Just as Women's Studies courses indicate that women survive their political circumstances to lead lives which hold the human race together, so "underprivileged" people of color who are the world's majority have survived their oppression and lived survivor's lives from which the white global minority can and must learn. In some groups, those dominated have actually become strong through *not* having all of these unearned advantages, and this gives them a great deal to teach the others. Members of the so-called privileged groups can seem foolish, ridiculous, infantile, or dangerous by contrast.

I want, then, to distinguish between earned strength and unearned power conferred systemically. Power from unearned privilege can look like strength when it is in fact permission to escape or to dominate. But not all of the privileges on my list are inevitably damaging. Some, like the expectation that neighbors will be decent to you, or that your race will not count against you in court, should be the norm in a just society and should be considered as the entitlement of everyone. Others, like the privilege not to listen to less powerful people, distort the humanity of the holders as well as the ignored groups. Still others, like finding one's staple foods everywhere, may be a function of being a member of a numerical majority in the population. Others have to do with not having to labor under pervasive negative steretyping and mythology.

We might at least start by distinguishing between positive advantages which we can work to spread, to the point where they are not advantages at all but simply part of the normal civic and social fabric, and negative types of advantage which unless rejected will always reinforce our present hierarchies. For example, the positive "privilege" of belonging, the feeling that one belongs within the human circle, as Native Americans say, fosters development and should not be seen as privilege for a few. It is, let us say, an entitlement which none of us should have to earn; ideally it is an *unearned entitlement.* At present, since only a few have it, it is an *unearned advantage* for them. The negative "privilege" which gave me cultural permission not to take darker-skinned Others seriously can be seen as arbitrarily conferred dominance and should not be desirable for anyone. This paper results from a process of coming to see that some of the power which I originally saw as attendant on being a human being in the United States consisted in *unearned advantage* and *conferred dominance,* as well as other kinds of special circumstance not universally taken for granted.

In writing this paper I have also realized that white identity and status (as well as class identity and status) give me considerable power to choose whether to broach this subject and its trouble. I can pretty well decide whether to disappear and avoid and not listen and escape the dislike I may engender in other people through this essay, or interrupt, take over, dominate, preach, direct, criticize, or control to some extent what goes on in reaction to it. Being white, I am given considerable power to escape many kinds of danger or penalty as well as to choose which risks I want to take.

There is an analogy here, once again, with Women's Studies. Our male colleagues do not have a great deal to lose in supporting Women's Studies, but they do decide whether to commit themselves to more equitable distributions of power. They will probably feel few penalties whatever choice they make; they do not seem, in any obvious short-term sense, the ones at risk, though they and we are all at risk because of the behaviors which have been rewarded in them.

Through Women's Studies work I have met very few men who are truly distressed about systemic, unearned male advantage and conferred dominance. And so one question for me and others like me is whether we will be like them, or whether we will get truly distressed, even outraged, about unearned race advantage and conferred dominance and if so, what we will do to lessen them. In any case, we need to do more work in identifying how they actually affect our daily lives. We need more down-to-earth writing by people about these taboo subjects. We need more understanding of the ways in which white "privilege" damages white people, for these are not the same ways in which it damages the victimized. Skewed white psyches are an inseparable part of the picture, though I do not want to confuse the kinds of damage done to the holders of special assets and to those who suffer the deficits. Many, perhaps most, of our white students in the United States think that racism doesn't affect them because they are not people of color; they do not see "whiteness" as a racial identity. Many men likewise think that Women's Studies does not bear on their own existences because they are not female; they do not see themselves as having gendered identities. Insisting on the universal *effects* of "privilege" systems, then, becomes one of our chief tasks, and being more explicit about the *particular* effects in particular contexts is another. Men need to join us in this work.

In addition, since race and sex are not the only advantaging systems at work, we need to similarly examine the daily experience of having age advantage, or ethnic advantage, or physical ability, or advantage related to nationality, religion, or sexual orientation. Professor Marnie Evans suggested to me that in many ways the list I made also applies directly to heterosexual privilege. This is a still more taboo subject than race privilege: the daily ways in which heterosexual privilege makes married persons comfortable or powerful, providing supports, assets, approvals, and rewards to those who live or expect to live in heterosexual pairs. Unpacking that content is still more difficult, owing to the deeper imbeddedness of heterosexual advantage and dominance, and stricter taboos surrounding these.

But to start such an analysis I would put this observation from my own experience: The fact that I live under the same roof with a man triggers all kinds of societal assumptions about my worth, politics, life, and values, and triggers a host of unearned advantages and powers. After recasting many elements from the original list I would add further observations like these:

1. My children do not have to answer questions about why I live with my partner (my husband).
2. I have no difficulty finding neighborhoods where people approve of our household.
3. My children are given texts and classes which implicitly support our kind of family unit, and do not turn them against my choice of domestic partnership.
4. I can travel alone or with my husband without expecting embarrassment or hostility in those who deal with us.
5. Most people I meet will see my marital arrangements as an asset to my life or as a favorable comment on my likability, my competence, or my mental health.
6. I can talk about the social events of a weekend without fearing most listener's reactions.

7. I will feel welcomed and "normal" in the usual walks of public life, institutional, and social.
8. In many contexts, I am seen as "all right" in daily work on women because I do not live chiefly with women.

Difficulties and dangers surrounding the task of finding parallels are many. Since racism, sexism, and heterosexism are not the same, the advantaging associated with them should not be seen as the same. In addition, it is hard to disentangle aspects of unearned advantage which rests more on social class, economic class, race, religion, sex, and ethnic identity than on other factors. Still, all of the oppressions are interlocking, as the Combahee River Collective statement of 1977 continues to remind us eloquently.[3]

One factor seems clear about all of the interlocking oppressions. They take both active forms which we can see and embedded forms which as a member of the dominant group one is taught not to see. In my class and place, I did not see myself as racist because I was taught to recognize racism only in individual acts of meanness by members of my group, never in invisible systems conferring unsought racial dominance on my group from birth. Likewise, we are taught to think that sexism or heterosexism is carried on only through individual acts of discrimination, meanness, or cruelty toward women, gays, and lesbians, rather than in invisible systems conferring unsought dominance on certain groups. Disapproving of the systems won't be enough to change them. I was taught to think that racism could end if white individuals changed their attitudes; many men think sexism can be ended by individual changes in daily behavior toward women. But a man's sex provides advantage for him whether or not he approves of the way in which dominance has been conferred on his group. A "white" skin in the United States opens many doors for whites whether or not we approve of the way dominance had been conferred on us. Individual acts can palliate, but cannot end, these problems. To redesign social systems we need first to acknowledge their colossal unseen dimensions. The silences and denials surrounding privilege are the key political tools here. They keep thinking about equality or equity incomplete, protecting unearned advantage and conferred dominance by making these taboo subjects. Most talk by whites about equal opportunity seems to me now to be about equal opportunity to try to get in to a position of dominance while denying that *systems* of dominance exist.

It seems to me that obliviousness about white advantage, like obliviousness about male advantage, is kept strongly inculturated in the United States so as to maintain the myth of meritocracy, the myth that democratic choice is equally available to all. Keeping most people unaware that freedom of confident action is there for just a small number of people props up those in power, and serves to keep power in the hands of the same groups that have most of it already. Though systemic change takes many decades, there are pressing questions for me and I imagine for some others like me if we raise our daily consciousness on the perquisites of being light-skinned. What will we do with such knowledge? As we know from watching men, it is an open question whether we will choose to use unearned advantage to weaken hidden systems of advantage, and whether we will use any of our arbitrarily-awarded power to try to reconstruct power systems on a broader base.

Discussion Questions

1. What does the author mean by the concept of "white privilege"?
2. Reread the author's list of 46 examples of white privilege. Select the five examples that seem the most significant in helping you to understand that white people are privileged. Explain your selections.
3. In addition to white privilege, the author also cites examples of heterosexual privilege. In a similar manner, develop a list of privileges that the able bodied enjoy that the physically challenged do not experience.
4. Most of us have experienced privilege in some form. Describe an example from your experience.
5. How does this article help you to understand the oppression that members of other groups may experience?

Notes

1. This paper was presented at the Virginia Women's Studies Association conference in Richmond in April 1986 and the American Educational Research Association conference in Boston in October 1986 and discussed with two groups of participants in the Dodge Seminars for Secondary School Teachers in New York and Boston in the spring of 1987.
2. Andersen, Margaret, "Race and the Social Science Curriculum: A Teaching and Learning Discussion." *Radical Teacher,* November 1984, pp. 17–20; Smith, Lillian. 1949. *Killers of the Dream.* New York: W.W. Norton.
3. "A Black Feminist Statement." The Combahee River Collective. In Hull, Scott, and Smith (eds.). *All the Women Are White, All the Blacks Are Men. But Some of Us Are Brave: Black Women's Studies.* The Feminist Press, 1982, pp. 13–22.

THE POWER OF TALK: WHO GETS HEARD AND WHY

Deborah Tannen

The head of a large division of a multinational corporation was running a meeting devoted to performance assessment. Each senior manager stood up, reviewed the individuals in his group, and evaluated them for promotion. Although there were women in every group, not one of them made the cut. One after another, each manager declared, in effect, that every woman in his group did not have the self-confidence needed to be promoted. The division head began to doubt his ears. How could it be that all the talented women in the division suffered from a lack of self-confidence?

In all likelihood, they didn't. Consider the many women who have left large corporations to start their own businesses, obviously exhibiting enough confidence to succeed on their own. Judgments about confidence can be inferred only from the way people present themselves, and much of that presentation is in the form of talk.

The CEO of a major corporation told me that he often has to make decisions in 5 minutes about matters on which others may have worked 5 months. He said he uses this rule: If the person making the proposal seems confident, the CEO approves it. If not, he says no. This might seem like a reasonable approach, but my field of research, sociolinguistics, suggests otherwise. The CEO obviously thinks he knows what a confident person sounds like. But his judgment, which may be dead right for some people, may be dead wrong for others.

Communication isn't as simple as saying what you mean. How you say what you mean is crucial, and differs from one person to the next, because using language is learned social behavior: How we talk and listen are deeply influenced by cultural experience. Although we might think that our ways of saying what we mean are natural, we can run into trouble if we interpret and evaluate others as if they necessarily felt the same way we'd feel if we spoke the way they did.

Since 1974, I have been researching the influence of linguistic style on conversations and human relationships. In the past 4 years, I have extended that research to the workplace, where I have observed how ways of speaking learned in childhood affect judgments of competence and confidence, as well as who gets heard, who gets credit, and what gets done.

The division head who was dumbfounded to hear that all the talented women in his organization lacked confidence was probably right to be skeptical. The senior managers were judging the women in their groups by their own linguistic norms, but women—like people who have grown up in a different culture—have often learned different styles of speaking than men, which can make them seem less competent and self-assured than they are.

WHAT'S LINGUISTIC STYLE?

Everything that is said must be said in a certain way—in a certain tone of voice, at a certain rate of speed, and with a certain degree of loudness. Whereas often we consciously consider what to say before speaking, we rarely think about how to say it, unless the situation is obviously loaded—for example, a job interview or a tricky performance review. Linguistic style refers to a person's characteristic speaking pattern. It includes such features as directness or indirectness, pacing and pausing, word choice, and the use of such elements as jokes, figures of speech, stories, questions, and apologies. In other words, linguistic style is a set of culturally learned signals by which we not only communicate what we mean but also interpret others' meaning and evaluate one another as people.

Consider turn taking, one element of linguistic style. Conversation is an enterprise in which people take turns: One person speaks, then the other responds. However, this apparently simple exchange requires a subtle negotiation of signals so that you know when the other person is finished and it's your turn to begin. Cultural factors such as country or region of origin and ethnic background influence how long a pause seems natural. When Bob, who is from Detroit, has a conversation with his colleague Joe, from New York City, it's hard for him to get a word in edgewise because he expects a slightly longer pause between turns than Joe does. A pause of that length never comes because, before it has a chance to, Joe senses an uncomfortable silence, which he fills with more talk of his own.

Both men fail to realize that differences in conversational style are getting in their way. Bob thinks that Joe is pushy and uninterested in what he has to say, and Joe thinks that Bob doesn't have much to contribute. Similarly, when Sally relocated from Texas to Washington, D.C., she kept searching for the right time to break in during staff meetings—and never found it. Although in Texas she was considered outgoing and confident, in Washington she was perceived as shy and retiring. Her boss even suggested she take an assertiveness training course. Thus, slight differences in conversational style—in these cases, a few seconds of pause—can have a surprising impact on who gets heard and on the judgments, including psychological ones, that are made about people and their abilities.

Every utterance functions on two levels. We're all familiar with the first one: Language communicates ideas. The second level is mostly invisible to us, but it plays a powerful role in communication. As a form of social behavior, language also negotiates relationships. Through ways of speaking, we signal—and create—the relative status of speakers and their level of rapport. If you say, "Sit down!" you are signaling that you have higher status than the person you are addressing, that you are so close to each other that you can drop all pleasantries, or that you are angry. If you say, "I would be honored if you would sit down," you are signaling great respect—or great sarcasm, depending on your tone of voice, the situation, and what you both know about how close you really are. If you say, "Your must be so tired—why don't you sit down," you are communicating either closeness and concerns or condescension. Each of these ways of saying the same thing—telling someone to sit down—can have a vastly different meaning.

In every community known to linguists, the patterns that constitute linguistic style are relatively different for men and women. What's "natural" for most men speaking a given language is, in some cases, different from what's "natural" for most women. That is because we learn ways of speaking as children growing up, especially from peers, and children tend to play with other children of the same sex. The research of sociologists, anthropologists, and psychologists observing American children at play has shown that, although both girls and boys find ways of creating rapport and negotiating status, girls tend to learn conversational rituals that focus on the rapport dimension of relationships whereas boys tend to learn rituals that focus on the status dimension.

Girls tend to play with a single best friend or in small groups, and they spend a lot of time talking. They use language to negotiate how close they are; for example, the girl you tell your secrets to becomes your best friend. Girls learn to downplay ways in which one is better than the others and to emphasize ways in which they are all the same. From childhood, most girls learn that sounding too sure of themselves will make them unpopular with their peers—although nobody really takes such modesty literally. A group of girls will ostracize a girls who calls attention to her own superiority and criticize her by saying, "She thinks she's something"; and a girl who tells others what to do is called "bossy." Thus, girls learn to talk in ways that balance their own needs with those of others—to save face for one another in the broadest sense of the term.

Boys tend to play very differently. They usually play in larger groups in which more boys can be included, but not everyone is treated as an equal. Boys with high status in their group are expected to emphasize rather than downplay their status, and usually one or several boys will be seen as the leader or leaders. Boys generally don't accuse one another of being bossy, because the leader is expected to tell lower-status boys what to do. Boys learn to use language to negotiate their status in the group by displaying their abilities and knowledge, and by challenging others and resisting challenges.

Giving orders is one way of getting and keeping the high-status role. Another is taking center stage by telling stories or jokes.

This is not to say that all boys and girls grow up this way or feel comfortable in these groups or are equally successful at negotiating within these norms. But, for the most part, these childhood play groups are where boys and girls learn their conversational styles. In this sense, they grow up in different worlds. The result is that women and men tend to have different habitual ways of saying what they mean, and conversations between them can be like cross-cultural communication: You can't assume that the other person means what you would mean if you said the same thing in the same way.

My research in companies across the United States shows that the lessons learned in childhood carry over into the workplace. Consider the following example: A focus group was organized at a major multinational company to evaluate a recently implemented flextime policy. The participants sat in a circle and discussed the new system. The group concluded that it was excellent, but they also agreed on ways to improve it. The meeting went well and was deemed a success by all, according to my own observations and everyone's comments to me. But the next day, I was in for a surprise.

I had left the meeting with the impression that Phil had been responsible for most of the suggestions adopted by the group. But as I typed up my notes, I noticed that Cheryl had made almost all those suggestions. I had thought that the key ideas came from Phil because he had picked up Cheryl's points and supported them, speaking at greater length in doing so than she had in raising them.

It would be easy to regard Phil as having stolen Cheryl's ideas and her thunder. But that would be inaccurate. Phil never claimed Cheryl's ideas as his own. Cheryl herself told me later that she left the meeting confident that she had contributed significantly and that she appreciated Phil's support. She volunteered, with a laugh, "It was not one of those times when a woman says something and it's ignored, then a man says it and it's picked up." In other words, Cheryl and Phil worked well as a team, the group fulfilled its charge, and the company got what it needed. So what was the problem?

I went back and asked all the participants who they thought had been the most influential group member, the one most responsible for the ideas that had been adopted. The pattern of answers was revealing. The two other women in the group named Cheryl. Two of the three men named Phil. Of the men, only Phil named Cheryl. In other words, in this instance, the women evaluated the contribution of another woman more accurately than the men did.

Meetings like this take place daily in companies around the country. Unless managers are unusually good at listening closely to how people say what they mean, the talents of someone like Cheryl may well be undervalued and underutilized.

One Up, One Down

Individual speakers vary in how sensitive they are to the social dynamics of language—in other words, to the subtle nuances of what others say to them. Men tend to be sensitive to the power dynamics of interaction, speaking in ways that position themselves as one up and resisting being put in a one-down position by others. Women tend to react more strongly to the rapport dynamic, speaking in ways that save face for others and buffering statements that could be seen as putting others in a one-down position: These linguistic patterns are pervasive; you can hear them in hundreds of exchanges in the workplace every day. And, as in the case of Cheryl and Phil, they affect who gets heard and who gets credit.

Getting Credit

Even so small a linguistic strategy as the choice of pronoun can affect who gets credit. In my research in the workplace, I heard men say "I" in situations where I heard women say "we." For example, one publishing company executive said, "I'm hiring a new manager. I'm going to put him in charge of my marketing division, as if he owned the corporation." In stark contrast, I recorded women saying "we" when referring to work they alone had done. One woman explained that it would sound too self-promoting to claim credit in an obvious way by saying, "I did this." Yet she expected—sometimes vainly—that others would know it was her work and would give her the credit she did not claim for herself.

Managers might leap to the conclusion that women who do not take credit for what they've done should be taught to do so. But that solution is problematic because we associate ways of speaking with moral qualities: The way we speak is who we are and who we want to be.

Veronica, a senior researcher in a high-tech company, had an observant boss. He noticed that many of the ideas coming out of the group were hers but that often someone else trumpeted them around the office and got credit for them. He advised her to "own" her ideas and make sure she got the credit. But Veronica found she simply didn't enjoy her work if she had to approach it as what seemed to her an unattractive and unappealing "grabbing game." It was her dislike of such behavior that had led her to avoid it in the first place. Whatever the motivation, women are less likely than men to have learned to blow their own horn. And they are more likely than men to believe that if they do so, they won't be liked.

Many have argued that the growing trend of assigning work to teams may be especially congenial to women, but it may also create complications for performance evaluation. When ideas are generated and work is accomplished in the privacy of the team, the outcome of the team's effort may become associated with the person most vocal about reporting results. There are many women and men—but probably relatively more women—who are reluctant to put themselves forward in this way and who consequently risk not getting credit for their contributions.

Confidence and Boasting

The CEO who based his decisions on the confidence level of speakers was articulating a value that is widely shared in U.S. businesses: One way to judge confidence is by an individual's behavior, especially verbal behavior. Here again, many women are at a disadvantage.

Studies show that women are more likely to downplay their certainty, and men are more likely to minimize their doubts. Psychologist Laurie Heatherington and her colleagues devised an ingenious experiment, which they reported in the journal *Sex Roles* (Volume 29, 1993). They asked hundreds of incoming college students to predict what grades they would get in their first year. Some subjects were asked to make their predictions privately by writing them down and placing them in an envelope; others were asked to make their predictions publicly, in the presence of a researcher. The results showed that more women than men predicted lower grades for themselves if they made their predictions publicly. If they made their predictions privately, the predictions were the same as those of the men—and the same as their actual grades. This study provides evidence that what comes across as lack of confidence—predicting lower grades for oneself—may reflect not one's actual level of confidence but the desire not to seem boastful.

These habits with regard to appearing humble or confident result from the socialization of boys and girls by their peers in childhood play. As adults, both women and men find these behaviors reinforced by the positive responses they get from friends and relatives who share the same norms. But the norms of behavior in the U.S. business world are based on the style of interaction that is more common among men—at least, among American men.

Asking Questions

Although asking the right questions is one of the hallmarks of a good manager, how and when questions are asked can send unintended signals about competence and power. In a group, if only one person asks questions, he or she risks being seen as the only ignorant one. Furthermore, we judge others not only by how they speak but also by how they are spoken to. The person who asks questions may end up being lectured to and looking like a novice under a schoolmaster's tutelage. The way boys are socialized makes them more likely to be aware of the underlying power dynamic by which a question asker can be seen in a one-down position.

One practicing physician learned the hard way that any exchange of information can become the basis for judgments—or misjudgments—about competence. During her training, she received a negative evaluation that she thought was unfair, so she asked her supervising physician for an explanation. He said that she knew less than her peers. Amazed at his answer, she asked how he had reached that conclusion. He said, "You ask more questions."

Along with cultural influences and individual personality, gender seems to play a role in whether and when people ask questions. For example, of all the observations I've made in lectures and books, the one that sparks the most enthusiastic flash of recognition is that men are less likely than women to stop and ask for directions when they are lost. I explain that men often resist asking for directions because they are aware that it puts them in a one-down position and because they value the independence that comes with finding their way by themselves. Asking for directions while driving is only one instance—along with many others that researchers have examined—in which men seem less likely than women to ask questions. I believe this is because they are more attuned than women to the potential face-losing aspect of asking questions. And men who believe that asking questions might reflect negatively on them may, in turn, be likely to form a negative opinion of others who ask questions in situations where they would not.

Conversational Rituals

Conversation is fundamentally ritual in the sense that we speak in ways our culture has conventionalized and expect certain types of responses. Take greetings, for example. I have heard visitors to the United States complain that Americans are hypocritical because they ask how you are but aren't interested in the answer. To Americans, "How are you?" is obviously a ritualized way to start a conversation rather than a literal request for information. In other parts of the world, including the Philippines, people ask each other "Where are you going?" when they meet. The question seems intrusive to Americans, who do not realize that it, too, is a ritual query to which the only expected reply is a vague "Over there."

It's easy and entertaining to observe different rituals in foreign countries. But we don't expect differences, and are far less likely to recognize the ritualized nature of our conversations, when we are with our compatriots at work. Our differing rituals can be even more problematic when we think we're all speaking the same language.

Apologies

Consider the simple phrase *I'm sorry*.

> CATHERINE: How did that big presentation go?
> BOB: Oh, not very well. I got a lot of flak from the VP for finance, and I didn't have the numbers at my fingertips.
> CATHERINE: Oh, I'm sorry. I know how hard you worked on that.

In this case, *I'm sorry* probably means "I'm sorry that happened," not "I apologize," unless it was Catherine's responsibility to supply Bob with the numbers for the presentation. Women tend to say *I'm sorry* more frequently than men, and often they intend it in this way—as a ritualized means of expressing concern. It's one of many learned elements of conversational style that girls often use to establish rapport. Ritual apologies—like other conversational rituals—work well when both parties share the same assumptions about their use. But people who utter frequent ritual apologies may end up appearing weaker, less confident, and literally more blameworthy than people who don't.

Apologies tend to be regarded differently by men, who are more likely to focus on the status implications of exchanges. Many men avoid apologies because they see them as putting the speaker in a one-down position. I observed with some amazement an encounter among several lawyers engaged in a negotiation on a speakerphone. At one point, the lawyer in whose office I was sitting accidentally elbowed the telephone and cut off the call. When his secretary got the parties back on again, I expected him to say what I would have said: "Sorry about that. I knocked the phone with my elbow." Instead, he said, "Hey, what happened? One minute you were there; the next minute you were gone." This lawyer seemed to have an automatic impulse not to admit fault if he didn't have to. For me, it was one of those pivotal moments when you realize that the world you live in is not the one everyone lives in and that the way you assume is the way to talk is really only one of many.

Those who caution managers not to undermine their authority by apologizing are approaching interaction from the perspective of the power dynamic. In many cases, this strategy is effective. On the other hand, when I asked people what frustrated them in their jobs, one frequently voiced complaint was wroking with or for someone who refuses to apologize or admit fault. In other words, accepting responsibility for errors and admitting mistakes may be an equally effective or superior strategy in some settings.

Feedback

Styles of giving feedback contain a ritual element that often is the cause for misunderstanding. Consider the following exchange: A manager had to tell her marketing director to rewrite a report. She began this potentially awkward task by citing the report's strengths and weaknesses and then moved to the main point: the weaknesses that needed to be remedied. The marketing director seemed to understand and accept his supervisor's comments, but his revision contained only minor changes and failed to address the major weaknesses. When the manager told him of her dissatisfaction, he accused her of misleading him: "You told me it was fine."

The impasse resulted from different linguistic styles. To the manager, it was natural to buffer the criticism by beginning with praise. Telling her subordinate that his report is inadequate and has to be rewritten puts him in a one-down position. Praising him for the parts that are good is a ritualized way of saving face for him. But the marketing director did not share his supervisor's assumption about how feedback should be given. Instead, he assumed that what she mentioned first was the main point and that what she brought up later was an afterthought.

Those who expect feedback to come in the way the manager presented it would appreciate her tact and would regard a more blunt approach as unnecessarily callous. But those who share the marketing director's assumptions would regard the blunt approach as honest and no-nonsense, and the manager's as obfuscating. Because each one's assumptions seemed self-evident, each blamed the other: The manager thought the marketing director was not listening, and he thought she had not communicated clearly or had changed her mind. This is significant because it illustrates that incidents labeled vaguely as "poor communication" may be the result of different linguistic styles.

Compliments

Exchanging compliments is a common ritual, especially among women. A mismatch in expectations about this ritual left Susan, a manager in the human resources field, in a one-down position. She and her colleague Bill had both given presentations at a national conference. On the airplane home, Susan told Bill, "That was a great talk!" "Thank you," he said. Then she asked,

"What did you think of mine?" He responded with a lengthy and detailed critique as she listened uncomfortably. An unpleasant feeling of having been put down came over her. Somehow she had been positioned as the novice in need of his expert advice. Even worse, she had only herself to blame, since she had, after all, asked Bill what he thought of her talk.

But had Susan asked for the response she received? When she asked Bill what he thought about her talk, she expected to hear not a critique but a compliment. In fact, her question had been an attempt to repair a ritual gone awry. Susan's initial compliment to Bill was the kind of automatic recognition she felt was more or less required after a colleague gives a presentation, and she expected Bill to respond with a matching compliment. She was just talking automatically, but he either sincerely misunderstood the ritual or simply took the opportunity to bask in the one-up position of critic. Whatever his motivation, it was Susan's attempt to spark an exchange of compliments that gave him the opening.

Although this exchange could have occurred between two men, it does not seem coincidental that it happened between a man and a woman. Linguist Janet Holmes discovered that women pay more compliments than men (*Anthropological Linguistics,* Volume 28, 1986). And, as I have observed, fewer men are likely to ask, "What did you think of my talk?" precisely because the question might invite an unwanted critique.

In the social structure of the peer groups in which they grow up, boys are indeed looking for opportunities to put others down and take the one-up position for themselves. In contrast, one of the rituals girls learn is taking the one-down position but assuming that the other person will recognize the ritual nature of self-denigration and pull them back up.

The exchange between Susan and Bill also suggests how women's and men's characteristic styles may put women at a disadvantage in the workplace. If one person is trying to minimize status differences, maintain an appearance that everyone is equal, and save face for the others while another person is trying to maintain the one-up position and avoid being positioned as one down, the person seeking the one-up position is likely to get it. At the same time, the person who has not been expending any effort to avoid the one-down position is likely to end up in it. Because women are more likely to take (or accept) the role of advice seeker, men are more inclined to interpret a ritual question from a woman as a request for advice.

Ritual Opposition

Apologizing, mitigating criticism with praise, and exchanging compliments are rituals common among women that men often take literally. A ritual common among men that women often take literally is ritual opposition.

A woman in communications told me she watched with distaste and distress as her office mate argued heatedly with another colleague about whose division should suffer budget cuts. She was even more surprised, however, that a short time later they were as friendly as ever. "How can you pretend that fight never happened?" she asked. "Who's pretending it never happened?" he responded, as puzzled by her question as she had been by his behavior. "It happened," he said, "and it's over." What she took as literal fighting to him was a routine part of daily negotiation: a ritual fight.

Many Americans expect the discussion of ideas to be a ritual fight—that is, an exploration through verbal opposition. They present their own ideas in the most certain and absolute form they can and wait to see if they are challenged. Being forced to defend an idea provides an opportunity to test it. In the same spirit, they may play devil's advocate in challenging their colleagues' ideas—trying to poke holes and find weaknesses—as a way of helping them explore and test their ideas.

This style can work well if everyone shares it, but those unaccustomed to it are likely to miss its ritual nature. They may give up an idea that is challenged, taking the objections as an indication that the idea was a poor one. Worse, they may take the opposition as a personal attack and may find it impossible to do their best in a contentious environment. People unaccustomed to this style may hedge when stating their ideas in order to fend off potential attacks. Ironically, this posture makes their arguments appear weak and is more likely to invite attack from pugnacious colleagues than to fend it off.

Ritual opposition can even play a role in who gets hired. Some consulting firms that recruit graduates from the top business schools use a confrontational interviewing technique. They challenge the candidate to "crack a case" in real time. A partner at one firm told me, "Women tend to do less well in this kind of interaction, and it certainly affects who gets hired. But, in fact, many women who don't 'test well' turn out to be good consultants. They're often smarter than some of the men who looked like analytic powerhouses under pressure."

The level of verbal opposition varies from one company's culture to the next, but I saw instances of it in all the organizations I studied. Anyone who is uncomfortable with this linguistic style—and that includes some men as well as many women—risks appearing insecure about his or her ideas.

Negotiating Authority

In organizations, formal authority comes from the position one holds, but actual authority has to be negotiated day to day. The effectiveness of individual managers depends in part on their skill in negotiating authority and on whether others reinforce or undercut their efforts. The way linguistic style reflects status plays a subtle role in placing individuals within a hierarchy.

Managing Up and Down

In all the companies I researched, I heard from women who knew they were doing a superior job and knew that their coworkers (and sometimes their immediate bosses) knew it as well, but believed that the higher-ups did not. They frequently told me that something outside themselves was holding them back and found it frustrating because they thought that all that should be necessary for success was to do a great job, that superior performance should be recognized and rewarded. In contrast, men often told me that if women weren't promoted it was because they simply weren't up to snuff. Looking around, however, I saw evidence that men more often than women behaved in ways likely to get them recognized by those with the power to determine their advancement.

In all the companies I visited, I observed what happened at lunchtime. I saw young men who regularly ate lunch with their boss, and senior men who ate with the big boss. I noticed far fewer women who sought out the highest-level person they could eat with. But one is more likely to get recognition for work done if one talks about it to those higher up, and it is easier to do so if the lines of communication are already open. Furthermore, given the opportunity for a conversation with superiors, men and women are likely to have different ways of talking about their accomplishments because of the different ways in which they were socialized as children. Boys are rewarded by their peers if they talk up their achievements, whereas girls are rewarded if they play theirs down. Linguistic styles common among men may tend to give them some advantages when it comes to managing up.

All speakers are aware of the status of the person they are talking to and adjust accordingly. Everyone speaks differently when talking to a boss than when talking to a subordinate. But, surprisingly, the ways in which they adjust their talk may be different and thus may project different images of themselves.

Communications researchers Karen Tracy and Eric Eisenberg studied how relative status affects the way people give criticism. They devised a business letter that contained some errors and asked 13 male and 11 female college students to role-play delivering criticism under two scenarios. In the first, the speaker was a boss talking to a subordinate; in the second, the speaker was a subordinate talking to his or her boss. The researchers measured how hard the speakers tried to avoid hurting the feelings of the person they were criticizing.

One might expect people to be more careful about how they deliver criticism when they are in a subordinate position. Tracy and Eisenberg found that hypothesis to be true for the men in their study but not for the women. As they reported in *Research on Language and Social Interaction* (Volume 2.4, 1990/1991), the women showed more concern about the other person's feelings when they were playing the role of superior. In other words, the women were more careful to save face for the other person when they were managing down than when they were managing up. This pattern recalls the way girls are socialized: Those who are in some way superior are expected to downplay rather than flaunt their superiority.

In my own recordings of workplace communication, I observed women talking in similar ways. For example, when a manager had to correct a mistake made by her secretary, she did so by acknowledging that there were mitigating circumstances. She said laughing, "You know, it's hard to do things around here, isn't it, with all these people coming in!" The manager was saving face for her subordinate, just like the female students role-playing in the Tracy and Eisenberg study.

Is this an effective way to communicate? One must ask, effective for what? The manager in question established a positive environment in her group, and the work was done effectively. On the other hand, numerous women in many different fields told me that their bosses say they don't project the proper authority.

Indirectness

Another linguistic signal that varies with power and status is indirectness—the tendency to say what we mean without spelling it out in so many words. Despite the widespread belief in the United States that it's always best to say exactly what we mean, indirectness is a fundamental and pervasive element in human communication. It also is one of the elements that vary most from one culture to another, and it can cause enormous misunderstanding when speakers have different habits and expectations about how it is used. It's often said that American women are more indirect than American men, but in fact everyone tends to be indirect in some situations and in different ways. Allowing for cultural, ethnic, regional, and individual differences, women are especially likely to be indirect when it comes to telling others what to do, which is not surprising, considering girls' readiness to brand other girls as bossy. On the other hand, men are especially likely to be indirect when it comes to admitting fault or weakness, which also is not surprising, considering boys' readiness to push around boys who assume the one-down position.

At first glance, it would seem that only the powerful can get away with bald commands such as "Have that report on my desk by noon." But power in an organization also can lead to requests so indirect that they don't sound like requests at all. A boss who says, "Do we have the sales data by product line for each region?" would be surprised and frustrated if a subordinate responded, "We probably do" rather than "I'll get it for you." Examples such as these notwithstanding, many researchers have claimed that those in subordinate positions are more likely to speak indirectly, and that is surely accurate in some situations. For example, linguist Charlotte Linde, in a study published in *Language in Society* (Volume 17, 1988), examined the black-box conversations that took place between pilots and copilots before airplane crashes. In one particularly tragic instance, an Air Florida plane crashed into the Potomac River immediately after attempting take-off from National Airport in Washington, D.C., killing all but 5 of the 74 people on board. The pilot, it turned out, had little experience flying in icy weather. The copilot had a bit more, and it became heartbreakingly clear on analysis that he had tried to warn the pilot but had done so indirectly. Alerted by Linde's observation, I examined the transcript of the conversations and found evidence of her hypothesis. The copilot repeatedly called attention to the bad weather and to ice buildup on other planes:

> COPILOT: Look how the ice is just hanging on his, ah, back there, see that? See all those icicles on the back there and everything?
>
> PILOT: Yeah.
>
> [The copilot also expressed concern about the long waiting time since deicing.]
>
> COPILOT: Boy, this is a, this is a losing battle here on trying to decide those things; it [gives] you a false feeling of security, that's all that does.

> [Just before they took off, the copilot expressed another concern—about abnormal instrument readings—but again he didn't press the matter when it wasn't picked up by the pilot.]
>
> COPILOT: That don't seem right, does it? [3-second pause]. Ah, that's not right. Well—
>
> PILOT: Yes it is, there's 80.
>
> COPILOT: Naw, I don't think that's right. [7-second pause] Ah, maybe it is.

Shortly thereafter, the plane took off, with tragic results. In other instances as well as this one, Linde observed that copilots, who are second in command, are more likely to express themselves indirectly or otherwise mitigate, or soften, their communication when they are suggesting courses of action to the pilot. In an effort to avert similar disasters, some airlines now offer training for copilots to express themselves in more assertive ways.

This solution seems self-evidently appropriate to most Americans. But when I assigned Linde's article in a graduate seminar I taught, a Japanese student pointed out that it would be just as effective to train pilots to pick up on hints. This approach reflects assumptions about communication that typify Japanese culture, which places great value on the ability of people to understand one another without putting everything into words. Either directness or indirectness can be a successful means of communication as long as the linguistic style is understood by the participants.

In the world of work, however, there is more at stake than whether the communication is understood. People in powerful positions are likely to reward styles similar to their own, because we all tend to take as self-evident the logic of our own styles. Accordingly, there is evidence that in the U.S. workplace, where instructions from a superior are expected to be voiced in a relatively direct manner, those who tend to be indirect when telling subordinates what to do may be perceived as lacking in confidence.

Consider the case of the manager at a national magazine who was responsible for giving assignments to reporters. She tended to phrase her assignments as questions. For example, she asked, "How would you like to do the X project with Y?" or said, "I was thinking of putting you on the X project. Is that okay?" This worked extremely well with her staff; they liked working for her, and the work got done in an efficient and orderly manner. But when she had her midyear evaluation with her own boss, he criticized her for not assuming the proper demeanor with her staff.

In any work environment, the higher ranking person has the power to enforce his or her view of appropriate demeanor, created in part by linguistic style. In most U.S. contexts, that view is likely to assume that the person in authority has the right to be relatively direct rather than to mitigate orders. There also are cases, however, in which the higher ranking person assumes a more indirect style. The owner of a retail operation told her subordinate, a store manager, to do something. He said he would do it, but a week later he still hadn't. They were able to trace the difficulty to the following conversation: She had said, "The bookkeeper needs help with the billing. How would you feel about helping her out?" He had said, "Fine." This conversation had seemed to be clear and flawless at the time, but it turned out that they had interpreted this simple exchange in very different ways. She thought he meant, "Fine, I'll help the bookkeeper out." He thought he meant, "Fine, I'll think about how I would feel about helping the bookkeeper out." He did think about it and came to the conclusion that he had more important things to do and couldn't spare the time.

To the owner, "How would you feel about helping the bookkeeper out?" was an obviously appropriate way to give the order "Help the bookkeeper out with the billing." Those who expect orders to be given as bold imperatives may find such locutions annoying or even misleading. But those for whom this style is natural do not think they are being indirect. They believe they are being clear in a polite or respectful way.

What is atypical in this example is that the person with the more indirect style was the boss, so the store manager was motivated to adapt to her style. She still gives orders the same way, but the store manager now understands how she means what she says. It's more common in U.S. business contexts for the highest-ranking people to take a more direct style, with the result that many women in authority risk being judged by their superiors as lacking the appropriate demeanor—and, consequently, lacking confidence.

WHAT TO DO?

I am often asked, what is the best way to give criticism or what is the best way to give orders? In other words, what is the best way to communicate? The answer is that there is no one best way. The results of a given way of speaking will vary depending on the situation, the culture of the company, the relative rank of speakers, their linguistic styles, and how those styles interact with one another. Because of all those influences, any way of speaking could be perfect for communicating with one person in one situation and disastrous with someone else in another. The critical skill for managers is to become aware of the workings and power of linguistic style, to make sure that people with something valuable to contribute get heard.

It may seem, for example, that running a meeting in an unstructured way gives equal opportunity to all. But awareness of the differences in conversational style makes it easy to see the potential for unequal access. Those who are comfortable speaking up in groups, who need little or no silence before raising their hands, or who speak out easily without waiting to be recognized are far more likely to get heard at meetings. Those who refrain from talking until it's clear that the previous speaker is finished, who wait to be recognized, and who are inclined to link their comments to those of others will do fine at a meeting where everyone else is following the same rules but will have a hard time getting heard in a meeting with people whose styles are more like the first pattern. Given the socialization typical of boys and girls, men are more likely to have learned the first style and women the second, making meetings more congenial for men than for women. It's common to observe women who participate actively in one-on-one discussions or in all-female groups but who are seldom heard in meetings with a large proportion of men. On the other hand, there are women who share the style more common among men, and they run a different risk—of being seen as too aggressive.

A manager aware of those dynamics might devise any number of ways of ensuring that everyone's ideas are heard and credited. Although no single solution will fit all contexts, managers who understand the dynamics of linguistic style can develop more adaptive and flexible approaches to running or participating in meetings, mentoring or advancing the careers of others, evaluating performance, and so on. Talk is the lifeblood of managerial work, and understanding that different people have different ways of saying what they mean will make it possible to take advantage of the talents of people with a broad range of linguistic styles. As the workplace becomes more culturally diverse and business becomes more global, managers will need to become even better at reading interactions and more flexible in adjusting their own styles to the people with whom they interact.

Discussion Questions

1. What evidence have you seen to support or refute Tannen's article in either students' behaviors in this class or at work?
2. What is the relationship between American corporate culture and the idea that women's learned conversation styles work against them in the workplace whereas men's conversation styles are an advantage?
3. Why does merely adding women to a team not necessarily result in women's points of views being equally represented in a discussion?
4. What is the relationship between conversational styles and sexual harassment in the work place?

BRIARWOOD INDUSTRIES

Carol P. Harvey
Assumption College

Diane Williamson sat at her desk at Briarwood Industries aimlessly staring out of her office window. Today was to be her big day; she expected to be promoted to vice president of marketing. Instead, she just wrote her letter of resignation. Impeccably dressed in her best navy blue suit, Diane looked successful but felt like a total failure.

When Diane came to Briarwood in 1989 as an experienced furniture sales rep, the company was already one of the largest manufacturers of upholstered living room furniture in the United States. However, the furniture industry was stagnant and sales in general were in decline. Assigned to the west coast region, Diane soon became one of the top sales reps in the country. She recognized the potential of warehouse merchandising and capitalized on having one of the major chain's national headquarters in her territory by securing a multimillion dollar contract to supply them with sofas and chairs.

In recognition, Diane was promoted to sales manager of the Seattle office in 1992 and to manager of new product and market development at corporate headquarters in North Carolina in 1995. Most recently, she moved the company into international markets by licensing Briarwood's designs to foreign manufacturers.

But the vice president's job went to Larry Jaccobi, a 12-year veteran of the company, who had the reputation of being efficient but not very creative in his management style. Larry was best known for implementing the company's order-entry system, which equipped the sales reps with portable computers that sent order data directly back to the plant. Having order data rapidly enabled Briarwood to implement a just-in-time inventory system that was projected to save the company millions of dollars over the next 5 years. Diane felt that Larry, although excellent at implementing other's ideas, lacked broad-based experience, and the vision to lead the department.

Diane was startled by a knock at her office door. Sandy McBride, the advertising manager and Diane's closest confidant at the company, heard through the office grapevine that Diane did not get the vice president's job. "What's plan B?" McBride asked. Welcoming the opportunity to talk, Diane expressed her shock and hurt at not getting the promotion. "I just don't understand how this could have happened," Diane lamented. "I came up through the sales ranks. I was the one who had the vision to diversify into office furniture, our most profitable product line. I wrote the marketing plan for our expansion into Canadian and European markets. What else could I have done?"

"Well, Diane, it was well known around here that Larry really wanted to be a vice president. He felt that he had paid his dues and that it was the next logical step. He never missed an opportunity to make his ambition very clear, or his work visible to the top brass. Remember that presentation he gave on just-in-time at the national sales meeting? Then there was the time that he volunteered to represent the company at the labor negotiations with the truck drivers union. Those reports went right to the top. I know that you and Larry never really got along . . . "

Diane abruptly cut Sandy off. "I don't work like that," Diane said. "I wouldn't want to take all the glory for something that was the product of a team effort. Larry looks out for Larry. My style is to do the best job that I can for the company. Good work gets noticed and rewarded. Look at the profit margins for the furniture division. Everyone knows that I am the brains behind that plan.

"And what about the 6 months that I spent in charge of production at the Atlanta plant. I filled in when the company was short-handed. I am not interested in running a manufacturing facility, but when the manager had a heart attack, I did it. I never complained about the assignment or about living away from my family for a year. I have always been there for Briarwood. Fine thanks I get.

"Well, it is too late now. I have resigned. It's Briarwood's loss. I am going to hand deliver this letter this morning."

An hour later, Diane sat in Gary Logan's office. As the retiring vice president of marketing and Diane's current boss read the letter, he expressed his surprise at Diane's action. "I think that you might want to reconsider your resignation. Although you have done a fine job here, quite frankly, your name was not even among the three top contenders for my job.

"We see you as a hard-working, loyal employee but not as corporate-level material. You seem to lack the competitiveness, independence, self-confidence, and level of comfort with risk that this job requires. In fact, this is the first time that you have even expressed an interest in being promoted to my job, and I announced my planned retirement date 3 months ago."

Diane felt her anger building, and said, "You can't be serious? Why wouldn't you realize that I considered myself a viable candidate to move into your position? I hinted at it during my last review. I clearly remember saying that I have done everything that this company has asked of me, and you agreed with me.

"What about the fact that I know that I am making $8,000 to $10,000 a year less than the other managers at my level of experience? I never complained about the salary differences. In fact, I never even brought it up. I thought being a team player counted for something here. I just might call my lawyer." With that statement, Diane left Gary's office but left her letter on his desk.

He left her letter on his desk, unsure how to handle the situation. Gary was glad that he had a lunch appointment with a good friend, Terry Wesley, the vice president of finance at Briarwood. Terry had a lot of female employees. Maybe Terry could help Gary understand Diane's behavior.

Discussion Questions

Note: You may be given special directions by your instructor for the discussion of this case.

1. Is Diane's reaction to Larry's promotion justified? Why or why not?
2. Does Diane have legal grounds to sue the company?
3. Who is mainly at fault in this situation? Why?
4. If Diane leaves Briarwood, what does she stand to lose? What will the company lose?
5. If you were Diane's best friend, Sandy, what advice would you give Diane about this situation?
6. If you were Gary Logan's best friend, Terry, what advice would you give Gary about this situation?
7. What can Diane learn from this experience?
8. What can Gary learn from this experience?
9. What are the lessons from this case for men and women working together in organizations?

THE NEGATIVE CONSEQUENCES OF MALE PRIVILEGE

Steven Farough
Assumption College

This piece argues that despite the privileges men receive from masculinity dominance, it is in their interest to work against it. As an entryway into this seemingly audacious claim, consider the following statements:

- "Do you want to fight?"
- "You throw like a girl!"
- "What are you, a fag?"
- "Be a *real* man."
- "Men are just more competitive and aggressive than women."

How often have we all heard such declarations? How often have we seen men use these challenges and declarations to other men and women? When such statements confront men, they realize that their *manhood* is on the line, that if they back down they will be seen as weak or feminine. Although this is only one part of masculinity and need not be the way masculinity is practiced, such comments are representative of a dominant form of masculinity in the United States that is defined as being tough, domineering, in control, and not feminine or gay (Connell, 1995). We are all familiar with this pervasive type of masculinity. We see it performed in the mass media and in our everyday lives. We might be scared by it. We might enjoy it, but we are surely aware of its centrality in our lives. However, what we are perhaps less familiar with is the proposition that men would greatly benefit from rejecting this dominant form of masculinity.

DOMINANT MASCULINITY

The aforementioned statements regarding the dominant culture of masculinity are by no means exhaustive, nor do they reflect the varieties of masculinities in the United States, other nations, or across history. Still, the word *dominant* is intended to suggest that although there are a variety of masculinities in every culture, some are more pervasive and powerful than others. In this case, dominant masculinity in the United States embodies the following characteristics.

- Men are expected to be physically powerful.
- Men are obliged to hide their emotions.
- Men are supposed to excel at competition.
- Men are to be in control of their lives and the situations they inhabit.
- Men are expected to earn income to support their families comfortably.
- Men are not to act feminine.
- Men should not be gay. (Connell, 1995; Kimmel, 2004; Messner, 1997)

What is particularly striking about dominant masculinity is that it is defined in part by what it is *not*. To be part of dominant masculinity means that one must not act in ways that are seen as feminine or gay; to be a "man" within the ideology of dominant masculinity is to be straight and unfeminine. It is also defined in a way that is associated with some of the key strategies for success in American enterprise: Competition, control, and withholding of emotions are all practices that many in the business world expect of their employees. The outcome of this widespread use of masculinity results in the gendering of work, where the key jobs and strategies for success are deeply linked to masculinity (Andersen, 2003; Pierce, 1995). For instance, to achieve financial and professional success, lawyers are expected to be intimidating and aggressive (Pierce, 1995). Bill collectors are expected to deflate the status of truant clients through an intimidation (Hochschild, 1983). Car salesmen are supposed to use their wits to talk customers into purchasing an automobile for more than it is really worth. A stockbroker's confident and assertive sales pitch to clients is imbued with a culture of dominant masculinity. Indeed, this dominant form of masculinity has provided untold wealth, power, and prestige for men as a group at the expense of women as a group. Dominant masculinity may be a stereotype, but it is one that is very powerful and successful.

Privileges of Dominant Masculinity
Before addressing the seemingly bold claim that it is in the interests of men to work against dominant forms of masculinity, attention should be given to the obvious benefits men receive from it, even if not all men share equally in the privileges of dominant masculinity. Of course, many have heard about men being the victims of "reverse discrimination" from affirmative action or how they have become the "new minority." Critiques against "political correctness" are pervasive as well, suggesting that men are consistently portrayed as the "bad guys" in the public sphere. Despite the public criticism of men, this has not prevented men, particularly white men, from maintaining disproportionate access to power and resources. Men continue to earn more than women in virtually every occupational category (U.S. Department of Labor, 2001). Even with high school degrees men earn almost as much as women with bachelor's degrees (U.S. Bureau of the Census, 1999).

Men are also overrepresented in the decision-making processes of business and government. White men comprise of 95% of senior managers, 90% of newspaper editors, and 80% of the wealthiest Americans (Rhode, 1997). The same holds true with elected officials. In 1997 men comprised 67.5% of all elected politicians (Hurst, 2001). The data clearly demonstrate that men continue to be disproportionately represented in key positions of power. Still, these generalized patterns tell us nothing about *why* men are overrepresented in such positions. To answer this, further attention must be given to the structural mechanisms that provide men as a group with greater access to economic and political power in the United States.

Upon a closer look at these generalized patterns, the data unequivocally demonstrate that white men in particular possess a whole set of advantages when compared to equally qualified white women and people of color. Research shows that people will rate resumes or work performance more critically if they think it belongs to women (Rhode, 1997). Men experience greater upward mobility than women in their occupations (Andersen, 2003; Lorber, 1994). Men have greater access to and control of networks for employment (Lorber, 1994). Men also receive greater access to mentoring relationships in business (Lorber, 1994). Mentoring and networking are key ways one moves up into better paying and more prestigious jobs. Federal government data on employment discrimination notes that white men are the least likely to experience discrimination in the workplace (Reskin, 1998). Men rarely face sexual harassment or other types of unwanted behaviors that make work a psychologically exhausting and painful experience (Andersen, 2003). In higher education, where it is noted that women now earn the majority of bachelor's degrees, men continue to earn more after graduation (U.S. Department of Labor, 2001).

In part, this has to do with structure of the American family and sex segregation in the workplace (Andersen, 2003; Rhode, 1997). Although changing, men's family roles continue to place them in positions of the primary income earner, whereas women continue to be forced into work that is more compatible with family life (Rhode, 1997). This contributes to the gender segregation of the workforce. For instance, men comprise of 72.1% of physicians, 70.4% of lawyers, and 91.9% of engineers (U.S. Department of Labor, 2001). In more "family friendly" occupations such as elementary teachers, nurses, and secretaries, women comprise over 80% of those employed (U.S. Department of Labor, 2001). In fact, the occupational structure is so segregated that in order to desegregate work, between 60% to 70% of men and women would have to change jobs (Lorber, 1994).

Women have made significant inroads into the work world, but they still run into the glass ceiling. This results in greater difficulty in gaining access to higher paying jobs dominated by men (Glass Ceiling Commission, 1995). Women in male-dominated occupations often experience sexual harassment (Andersen, 2003). It is also more difficult for women to move up into higher positions due to an alienating "male culture," because of the lack of network contacts, and/or fewer mentoring relationships (Lorber 1994; Pierce 1995). Women can also face the "mommy track": the practice of not hiring or promoting women during their childbearing years (Lorber, 1994). In these existing forms of discrimination and family obligations, women continue to be the primary caregivers of children, making it more difficult for women to move up the occupational ladder than men.

Even with passage of the 1993 Family and Medical Leave Act legislation designed to allow workers to take unpaid time away from work, only full-time employees working for organizations with more than 100 employees are covered. Ironically, more men are capable of taking advantage of this legislation because they are more often in full-time positions. Still, only between 1% and 7% of eligible men take advantage of the legislation (Rhode, 1997). Even in occupations in which women are the majority, men are often pushed up into better paying administrative jobs (Williams, 2004).

Some might argue that men and women freely choose family roles and occupations. However, the choices men and women make are the *result* of gender inequality, not a *cause*. Despite the significant gains by women over the past 30 years, discriminatory practices and structural constraints limit their chances for upward mobility and occupational choice. As one prominent philosopher said, "[People] make history, but they do not make it just as they please" (Marx, 1999/1852: 42). Such data also fly in the face of affirmative action critics, who claim white men are the "new minority" and experience "reverse discrimination." Even though there is variation in terms of race, class, and sexuality, when it comes to access to power and resources, men continue to do very well when compared to women. They are not the "new minority," and experiences of reverse discrimination are extraordinarily rare, although highly publicized (Reskin, 1998). Despite the gains of the civil rights and women's movements, men continue to be a privileged group in the United States.

Negative Consequences of Dominant Masculinity

Given the above-mentioned advantages of masculinity, some men might ask themselves why on earth they would want to give up such a wide range of advantages. These structural benefits are no doubt seductive to many men. High-status jobs, respect and deference from others, disproportionate influence, and accumulating wealth are but a few of the advantages of dominant masculinity and the infrastructure of privilege that supports it. Why give this up?

Accompanying these advantages comes a range of negative consequences for men who invest in dominant masculinity. Public health data clearly show some of the noticeable disadvantages. The average life span for men is 71.3 years, but for women it is 78.3 years (Sabo, 2004). Men are more likely to develop heart disease, have accidents, and be a victim of violent crime and homicide than women (Sabo, 2004). There are multiple reasons for this, but one key factor is the investment in dominant masculinity. Men who buy into it must engage in elaborate techniques of withholding their feelings and engage in behavior that puts them at greater physical risk (Sabo, 2004). To be a "man" is to deny physical pain, which can result in a failure to notify doctors of potentially life-threatening aliments. If one desires to be a "real man," one should be prepared for an early death.

Men who withhold their feelings also suffer psychologically. They experience higher rates of depression and suicide than women (Sabo, 2004). They also have more emotionally shallow relationships with families and friends. Men that cannot fit into dominant masculinity also suffer. Often denied access to living wages or control over their environment, working-class men, men of color, and gay men often cannot fit fully into dominant masculinity, leaving them subject to critiques of their self-worth. Dominant masculinity works as the underlying rationale for men bullying other men that do not conform to this norm. This results in significant numbers of men marginalized from and scarred by dominant masculinity, one that is often white, middle class, and straight. Dominant masculinity makes it more difficult to have a variety of legitimate masculinities in our society. Because dominant masculinity is defined as being superior to femininity (Connell 1995), men that invest in it suffer from being unable to have more egalitarian and emotionally open relationships with women. It also can result in creating discriminatory work environments. Dominant masculinity can even undermine meritocracy. Because men receive unearned advantages for being men in the workforce and political life, this makes it more difficult for equally qualified women and people of color to be rewarded for their hard work. Clearly, dominant masculinity has negative consequences, leaving men with shorter lives, higher rates of physical aliments, and less emotionally fulfilling experiences and contributes to the undermining of democratic principles. Greater access to power and resources may seem attractive, but when compared to the negative consequences, dominant masculinity becomes more problematic and undesirable.

WHERE DO WE GO FROM HERE? THE FEMINIST/SOCIOLOGICAL PERSPECTIVE

If men are both privileged by and suffer from dominant masculinity, we need a perspective that allows men (and women) to realize that it is in their interest to work against it. This way of thinking is what I call the feminist/sociological perspective. The feminist/sociological perspective shifts our thinking away from looking at dominant masculinity as solely a personality characteristic or biological disposition to focusing on how dominant masculinity is a *social construction* or a powerful stereotype created by social relations. For instance, consider again how some of the key elements of dominant masculinity are deeply associated with success in American enterprise mentioned earlier. The result of this association makes the business world deeply linked to dominant masculinity. If we can consciously realize how gendered American business is, it then becomes possible to work toward degendering the occupational structure. For instance, some of the key strategies of success in American business, such as competition and aggressiveness, may be important, but they need not be associated only with masculinity! Both men and women can be competitive and aggressive. By degendering such strategies, this would free the talent of women to move up the occupational ladder more fairly.

However, seeing dominant masculinity as a social construction also means that it should be seen as part of a broader social system of gender that privileges men who conform to it and marginalizes women and men that fail to participate in its performance. In other words, *gender should be viewed as a central institution in society*. As a social system or institution, we can also see how gender organizes virtually every aspect of our lives, including the economy, family, politics, and the nation–state, to name but a few. We can then also see how the institution gives men and women varying degrees of access to power. In order to alleviate these inequalities, the feminist/sociological perspective helps those in American businesses focus on these structural inequities as well as stereotypes. This means focusing on strategies and social policy designed to eliminate the glass ceiling and concentrating on how unequal family obligations lead to gender inequality and on how occupations are unfairly sex segregated.

Any discussion of gender inequality and identity would be severely limited without considering how *gender interacts with race, class, and sexual institutions*, the third key area of the perspective. Although women are often in subordinate positions in American business, race, class, and sexual institutions can vary the amount of oppression and privilege. In that same vein, despite men often possessing more social power in business, the institutions of class, race, and sexuality can temper or thwart such privileges in certain contexts. In our quest for gender equity it is imperative to consider how these factors impact one's opportunities as well.

The feminist/sociological perspective's attention to these aspects allows both men and women to see the constraints and benefits of the system. Although men who are sexist or resist transforming gender inequality should be held accountable for their actions, this perspective does not focus blame on individual men but rather on a social system. With its attention to the unequal distribution of power, the feminist/sociological perspective invites us to rally around one of the most foundational principles of the United States— democracy. If we see dominant masculinity as a standpoint in a broader social system of gender that unfairly benefits men, both men and women can fight against it for the sake of further developing a meritocratic system. The feminist/sociological perspective is an invitation for men to work with women to overcome these constraints. And as already pointed out, by noting the benefits and disadvantages of dominant masculinity, men can also see how this social system negatively affects men as well. Men can take pride in working to undermine it and refuse it. This can be achieved by highlighting the antimeritocratic aspects of dominant masculinity and its negative effects to men as a group. The feminist/sociological perspective is nothing less than a call for men to join with women to overcome the negative effects of dominant masculinity.

Discussion Questions

1. How do the key characteristics of dominant masculinity privilege men? How do these characteristics hurt men?
2. What other characteristics could be included in dominant masculinity?
3. If dominant masculinity is defined through such characteristics as physical strength, competition, control, and emotional distance, what does this say about femininity?

4. How do the key elements of the feminist/sociological perspective encourage men and women to work together against sexism?
5. Do you agree that the feminist/sociological perspective will help men and women work together to overcome sexism? Why or why not?
6. If the structure of the traditional family contributes to gender inequality, what can American business do so that women have the same chances for upward mobility as men?
7. How could the feminist/sociological perspective be implemented in American business?
8. What can be done to reduce the glass ceiling in American business?

Bibliography

Andersen, M. (2003). *Thinking about women: Sociological perspectives on sex and gender.* Boston: Allyn & Bacon.

Connell, R.W. (1995). *Masculinities.* Berkeley: University of California Press.

Glass Ceiling Commission. (1995). *Good for business: Making full use of the nation's human capital.* Washington, DC: U.S. Government Printing Office.

Hochschild, A. (1983). The Managed Heart: Commercialization of Human Feeling. Berkeley: University of California Press.

Hurst, C. (2001). *Social inequality: Forms, causes, and consequences.* Boston: Allyn & Bacon.

Kimmel, M. (2004). *The gendered society.* (2nd ed.). New York: Oxford University Press.

Lorber, J. (1994). *The paradoxes of gender.* New Haven, CT: Yale University Press.

Marx, K. (1999/1852). The eighteenth brumaire of Louis Bonaparte. In C. Lemert (Ed.), *Social theory: The multicultural & classic readings* (pp. 41–49). Boulder, CO: Westview Press.

Messner, M. (1997). *Politics of masculinities: Men in movements.* Thousand Oaks, CA: Sage.

Pierce, J. (1995). *Gender trails.* Berkeley: University of California Press.

Reskin, B. (1998). *The realities of affirmative action.* Washington, DC: American Sociological Association.

Rhode, D. (1997). *Speaking of sex: The denial of gender inequality.* Cambridge, MA: Harvard University Press.

Sabo, D. (2004). Masculinities and men's health: Moving toward post-superman era prevention. In M. Kimmel (Ed.), *The gendered society reader* (pp. 327–343). New York: Oxford University Press.

U.S. Bureau of the Census. (1999). *Statistical abstract of the United States.* Washington, DC: U.S. Government Printing Office.

U.S. Department of Labor. (2001). *Employment and earnings 2000.* Washington, DC: U.S. Department of Labor.

Williams, C. (2004). The glass escalator: Hidden advantages for men in the "female" professions. In M. Kimmel & M. Messner (Eds.), *Men's lives* (6th ed., pp. 285–299) Boston: Allyn & Bacon.

IS THIS SEXUAL HARASSMENT?

Carol P. Harvey
Assumption College

Goals

1. To help students to understand what is and what is not sexual harassment on the job.
2. To apply the federal government's sexual harassment guidelines to workplace situations. The Equal Employment Opportunity Commission's guidelines define sexual harassment as:

    . . . unwelcome sexual advances, requests for sexual favors, and other physical and verbal contact of a sexual nature when it affects the terms of employment under one or more of the following conditions: such an activity is a condition for employment; such an activity is a condition of employment consequences such as promotion, dismissal, or salary increases; such an activity creates a hostile working environment.

Instructions

Given the guidelines, which of the following incidents are examples of sexual harassment? Explain your reasons for your answers.

1. While teaching Gary how to run the new spreadsheet program on the computer, Lois, his supervisor, puts her hand on his shoulder.

2. Julie, the new secretary to the vice president of manufacturing, frequently has to go out into the plant as part of her job. Several of the machinists have been whistling at her and shouting off-color remarks as she passes through the shop. One of the other women in the company found Julie crying in the ladies' room after such an incident.

3. Paul and Cynthia, two sales reps, are both married. However, it is well known that they are dating each other outside of the office.

4. Jeanne's boss, Tom, frequently asks her out for drinks after work. She goes because both are single and she enjoys his company. On one of these occasions, he asks her out to dinner for the following Saturday evening.

5. Steve's boss, Cathy, frequently makes suggestive comments to him and has even suggested that they meet outside of the office. Although at first he ignored these remarks, recently he made it clear to her that he had a steady girlfriend and was not available. When she gave him his performance appraisal, much to his surprise, she cited him for not being a team player.

6. Jackie received a call at work that her father died suddenly. When she went to tell her boss that she had to leave, she burst into tears. He put his arms around her and let her cry on his shoulder.

7. Marge's coworker, Jerry, frequently tells her that what she is wearing is very attractive.

8. While being hired as a secretary, Amanda is told that she may occasionally be expected to accompany managers on important overnight business trips to handle the clerical duties at these meetings.

9. Joe, an elderly maintenance man, often makes suggestive comments to the young females in the office. His behavior has been reported to his supervisor several times but it is dismissed as, "Don't be so sensitive, old Joe doesn't mean any harm."

10. Jennifer frequently wears revealing blouses to the office. Several times she has caught male employees staring at her.

ONE MAN'S VIEWPOINT . . .

To the Editor:

In the arena of social justice, one of the most controversial issues confronting white America is the issue of affirmative action. One can expect conservatives to be against it, yet, even liberals can have a problem with the concept when it affects them personally, especially in regard to employment and college admissions. White America has a collective amnesia about the fact that people of color were denied jobs and school admissions for centuries, and that the color of their skin was the sole reason for their inability to access the American dream and achieve upward mobility.

A witty black woman I know often refers to a phenomenon about which white people are in complete denial, a phenomenon known as "white affirmative action." White affirmative action is the use of nepotism, favoritism, and political patronage by white people to achieve success and to exclude people of color from sharing the social, educational, and economic benefits society offers.

Nepotism is the practice of those with power or influence of favoring relatives or friends, especially by giving them jobs. Opponents of affirmative action descry the idea of anyone getting a job opportunity based on the color of his skin. They use the proverb "two wrongs don't make a right" as a basis for their opposition. This is very easy to say when you are a member of the group that is guilty of all the wrongdoing. One has to wonder where these moralists were when people of color and women were shut out of jobs solely because of the color of their skin or their gender.

Another defense is that the white people who are forced to share employment opportunities because of affirmative action weren't alive during the time of slavery or didn't participate in the abuses of the Jim Crow era. Why should they have to bear the burden of the sins of their ancestors? This is an interesting line of reasoning, and it would work if the logic behind it were consistent. If they are unwilling to be held accountable for the bad things done by the white people who came before them, they should also refuse to accept the benefits handed down by those same people. They should forfeit their inheritances and disavow all claims to any wealth, property, or privilege they have not earned themselves in their own lifetimes. This is especially true because much of the wealth in this country came from exploiting people of color, from the free labor of slaves to the ridiculously cheap labor of sharecroppers in the South and factory workers in the North.

The question that white people must ask themselves is this: What is the difference between a racial preference and a preference based on nepotism? Boston-based conservative talk show host Jay Severin said, "Every time a minority gets into college because of affirmative action, he takes the place of a more qualified white student." He made this statement during the presidency of George W. Bush, and shortly after the United States Supreme Court upheld, by a slim 5–4 margin, the use of affirmative action in the admission policy at the University of Michigan. This meant that a student of color with lower test scores could be admitted ahead of a white student with higher test scores. This might seem unfair until one is confronted with the fact that George W. Bush was accepted to Yale University with SAT scores that were approximately 200 points lower that the average incoming Yale freshman. Mr. Bush was accepted because of an advantage called "legacy" (i.e., his father, the former president, was a Yale alumnus, and his grandfather, Prescott Bush, was a former senator from Connecticut, the state in which Yale is located). Doesn't this mean that Mr. Bush took the place of a more qualified white student as well? He may have even taken the place of a more qualified student of color. One affirmative action opponent tried to explain this away by saying that "a college is a business, and the alumni donate money to the college, and therefore the college has to take care of the children of the alumni. It's a business decision." Yes, and two wrongs don't make a right.

Bill Belden, a human resource manager in a Midwestern plastics company, is opposed to affirmative action. " I hire anyone who can do the job," he said. "I don't believe in preferences." Needless to say, Bill's company consists of 400 white employees. What Bill doesn't realize is that he got his job opportunity through white affirmative action. Bill's father, Cal, had worked in the plant for 30 years, and he was able to get him a job. Bill became extremely irritated when it was suggested that he benefited from nepotism. "I was qualified," he said. That's true, but there are thousands of qualified people of color who don't have the opportunity he had. The plastics plant was loaded with family members: fathers and sons, uncles, cousins, and friends of family. The organization was a family affair, all white, and jobs were handed down from generation to generation, effectively locking out the minority population in the area. This is the unintended consequence of nepotism, and it results in a form of subconscious racism. Indeed, two wrongs do not make a right.

Four months after the 9/11 disaster at the World Trade Center, a controversy arose over a proposed memorial to New York City firefighters. A statue depicting one black, one white, and one Hispanic in the group of firefighters who raised the flag in the aftermath of the tragedy was bitterly criticized by syndicated columnist John Leo as the "falsifying of historical reality" because the "trio was all-white in real life." In his column Leo said, "An estimated 319 of 343 firefighters who gave their lives at the World Trade Center on September 11 were non-Hispanic whites, multiculturalism's villain class, white males."

The inference here is that somehow one is supposed to believe that white males deserve credit for bravery and heroism simply because 93% of the firefighters who died in the inferno were white. What Mr. Leo failed to consider was the fact that the overwhelming number of New York City firefighters are white because white people see these public-sector jobs as an entitlement. The jobs are theirs, and they are reluctant to allow others to obtain these jobs, even though people of color pay the taxes that pay the salaries for this type of employment. Go into any police, fire, or school department in this country and the list of employee names will read like a family tree. These are good-paying jobs for someone who didn't go to college, the benefits are wonderful, and there is job security and a generous pension after as little as 20 years of employment. Several months after Leo's article, another writer wrote an article about how poignant this tragedy was, citing the large number of sons, brothers, uncles, and cousins in the department who had lost relatives on 9/11. This underscored the fact that nepotism is as big a problem as affirmative action for white people who can't get jobs because they don't have family or political connections.

Many white people don't seem to be able to make this connection, however. Mary Mackenzie, an Irish-Catholic schoolteacher in Massachusetts, was scheduled for promotion to assistant principal in the elementary school in which she taught. Her colleagues even had a nameplate made up for her desk with her anticipated new title. The night before the decision was announced a high-ranking school department official arranged for his son-in-law, who had far less experience and far fewer credentials, to get the position. Mary was devastated, but eventually she took it in stride, citing "politics as usual." But when an experienced and qualified black woman was named principal at another school, Mary was vocally critical and angry, complaining of yet "another affirmative action hire." There is a psychological disconnect that revolves around this issue. Perhaps the explanation is that someday the critical white person can obtain a promotion through politics or favoritism, but he will never get ahead from being brown or black. Favoritism is fine, as long as it's the right kind of favoritism.

Patricia Grandone, a professor in a small New England college, reports that many of her white students are already complaining about how they won't be hired for jobs because of affirmative action. They need to realize that their chances for employment are far greater than those of their non-white peers. A recent study showed that résumés sent to prospective employers by people with African-American or Latino sounding names were rarely given consideration. They couldn't even get interviews because of the racial bias associated with their identities. White college students are sometimes naïve in their thinking, and they fail to realize that racism does indeed still exist. This résumé example is perhaps more subconscious than overt, but nevertheless it is racism based on society's stereotypes of blacks and Latinos.

White America is obsessed with test scores and qualifications, and in the area of affirmative action it tries to portray all affirmative action hires as unqualified, especially if test scores were a part of the hiring process. This is such a sensitive issue that many people in the minority community who get jobs try too hard to prove their competence. They tend to micromanage or they become paranoid. Their paranoia is often justified, for experience shows us that many of their white colleagues are just waiting for people of color to fail, thereby proving the negative effects of affirmative action. When white people in authority fail, however, it is not attributed to their race or the fact they got their positions through nepotism. They simply fail, and everybody moves on. It should be the same with people of color, but it isn't, and this is patently unfair.

If test scores were so important, we wouldn't need elections. We could simply appoint the MENSA members with the highest IQs to the presidency and the Congress. Most people would consider this to be ridiculous, because test scores are no indication that a person will be a competent worker or leader. We need to consider who makes up the tests and who decides how much weight or validity to give them. Generally speaking, white people design tests to benefit white people. Tests are often racially and gender biased. Research shows that people from certain cultures are simply better at taking tests than others. California once passed a law that banned any criteria other than test scores to be considered for admission to state medical and engineering schools. The group that lobbied for this thought it would be an effective way to keep white students from losing seats to minority students. The plan backfired, however, because Asian students were far better test takers than whites, and the schools that year were populated almost exclusively with Asians. The law was rescinded the following year.

For example, people apply for a position on the police department where the passing grade on the written exam is 85. A physical exam is also part of the qualifications, but that is given on a pass/fail basis. A black candidate who is an excellent physical specimen scores 86 on the written exam, but loses the job to a white applicant who barely passes the physical exam but scored 90 on the written test. The job is supposed to go to the person who scored higher on the written exam because white people decided that the written test was a more important factor for success as a police officer than physical prowess. If the black man got the job as a result of affirmative action, white people would convince themselves that the white man had been cheated.

Because many American cities, due to "white flight," have larger minority populations than white populations, it makes sense to encourage the appointment of minority police officers. One could assume that a white police officer would feel safer and more comfortable entering a black or Latino neighborhood with a black or Latino partner rather than another white officer.

In the aforementioned Supreme Court case, both the military and big business filed briefs with the court asking that affirmative action be continued. It is easy to see why the military would be in favor of a policy that has produced Secretary of State Colin Powell, who was the Chairman of the Joint Chiefs of Staff in the 1991 Gulf War with Iraq. Powell has stated that he would not be where he is today without affirmative action. He is not the only favorable voice in the military hierarchy, because we live in a society in which the lower socioeconomic classes make up the majority of the troops who serve our country. Because racism keeps people of color in the lower economic classes, they are the major component of our fighting forces, and the necessity of appointing military officers of color becomes of paramount importance. An army of color can't function efficiently with an all-white officer corps commanding it any more than an all-white police department can maintain order in a city that is predominantly black, Latino, or Asian.

Big business is in favor of affirmative action because it is good for business. Soon people of color will outnumber white people in the United States. The color businesses find most alluring is green, the color of money. Blacks, Latinos, and Asians must be persuaded to patronize white-owned businesses, and there is no better way to accomplish that than to have a rich supply of minority employees. People tend to shop in establishments that employ workers and managers who resemble them. These businesses have a large number of minority employees and a corresponding number of minority customers. The average white person doesn't notice this, but careful observation of these businesses and those that consciously or subconsciously hire mostly white employees would reveal a vast difference in their customer base. Smart businesses favor affirmative action, not necessarily out of altruism, but rather because of changing economic markets.

Let me close this with an anecdote that might be amusing. Earlier in the letter, I mentioned a witty black woman who coined a term describing nepotism, favoritism, and political patronage. After years of watching the antics and attitudes of white people toward people of color, she made the following observation: "White people are going to be shocked to find out that when they die and try to go to heaven they can't get in . . . unless God has an affirmative action plan."

Sincerely,
Carlo Baldino
Sutton, MA

Discussion Questions

1. What issues/perspectives has the author raised that you never thought of before reading his letter?
2. Cite examples from your own life when you have experienced an advantage due to the influence of family or friends.
3. How does this letter relate to the Nacirema reading?

BRIEFING PAPER

M. June Allard
Worcester State College

You have been assigned the task of preparing a briefing paper for teams preparing for an extended overseas assignment in _____. The briefing paper will present in very concise form important information about the country and its people—information that will aid visitors in understanding and in living in the country. Be inclusive in this paper. Assume that the team members know very little about the country to which they are being sent and assume further that many will have their families with them.

GENERAL COUNTRY INFORMATION

Include information such as: geographic location, climate, type of government, currency, religion, ethnicity/ethnic groups, relationships, class structure, sources of national pride, ratings on Hofstede's dimensions (Hofstede ratings may be included under Business Customs and Behaviors instead), etc.

http://cyborlink.com/besite/hofstede.htm

http://cyborlink.com/default.htm

http://www.itim.org

SOCIAL CUSTOMS AND MANNERS

Include information on greetings, forms of proper address, dress code, tipping, gift giving, attitudes toward foreigners, general etiquette and manners, etc.

BUSINESS CUSTOMS AND BEHAVIORS

Include information such as greetings, business card usage, gift giving, dress code, color significance, religious significance, communication and negotiation style, attitude toward women workers, attitude toward older workers, etc.

The paper should be about 6 to 8 double-spaced pages.

COUNTRIES

Middle East & Africa

Egypt
Saudi Arabia
South Africa
United Arab Emirates

Europe

Austria
Belgium
Finland
Germany
Greece
Iceland
Ireland
Italy
Netherlands
Portugal
Sweden

Asia

China
India
Indonesia
Japan
Malaysia
Russia
Singapore
South Korea
Thailand
Turkey

Central and South America

Argentina
Brazil
Chile
Colombia
Ecuador
Mexico
Peru
Venezuela

SUGGESTED INTERNET SOURCES

http://www.itim.org/4aba.html
http://globaledge.msu.edu
http://globaledge.msu.edu/ibrd/busresmain.asp?ResourceCategoryID=
17 (many links)
http://lcweb2.loc.gov/frd/cs/
http://www.state.gov/www/regions/background_info_countries.html
http://getcustoms.com
http://cyborlink.com
http://cyborlink.com/besite/hofstede.htm
http://cyborlink.com/default.htm
http://www.itim.org
http://memory.loc.gov/frd/cs/cshome.html

GENERATIONAL DIVERSITY ROLE-PLAY EXERCISE

Diane M. Holtzman

Evonne J. Kruger

Charles Srock

The Richard Stockton College of New Jersey

For the first time in history, four distinctively diverse generations are employed in our workforce: veterans, baby boomers, Gen Xers, and Gen Yers. These generations frequently collide in today's workplace, creating environments characterized by individual and generational enmity where attitudes of "Us" versus "Them" and "every man and woman for himself and herself" surface (Zemke, Raines, & Filipczak, 2000, p. 5). The adversarial atmosphere impedes the energies, productivity, teamwork, and collaborative problem solving required by complex and competitive global markets. To foster organizational environments that are positive and productive, individuals must be aware of the strengths and assets that each generation brings to the organization and skilled in dealing with multiple generations as both subordinates and supervisors. If generational framing is used to understand the values and work practices of others in the organization, greater understanding and cooperation will be fostered among the distinct cohorts.

According to Lancaster and Stillman (2002), " . . . different generations of employees won't become more alike with age. They will carry their 'generational personalities' with them throughout their lives. In fact, when hard times hit, the generations are likely to entrench themselves even more deeply into the attitudes and behaviors that have been ingrained in them" (p. 8).

Demographers agree about the overall profiles of the distinct cohorts in the workforce, but they do not agree on the years of birth or their names. The oldest workers, those born between 1922 and 1943 are termed "veterans", the swing generation, or the great generation, depending on the source. Those born between 1900 and 1945 tend to be called "traditionalists." The baby boom generation has been defined both as those born between 1943 and 1960 and those with births spanning the years 1946 through 1964. Generation Xers have been defined as being both born between 1965 and 1980, as well as between 1960 and 1980. The Generation Y cohort is also termed Millennials and Generation Nexters. Some place their births between 1980 and 2000, others between 1981 and 1999 (Lancaster & Stillman, 2002; Zemke, Raines, & Filipczak, 2000). Those born within a year or two of the start a new generation are called "cuspers" because they "stand in the gap between the two sides . . . [and] become naturals at mediating, translating, and mentoring" (Lancaster & Stillman, 2002, p. 39).

Each of these generations brings unique perspectives and values about work and the work environment. In traditional hierarchical organizations, generations tend to be more segregated as individuals rise to higher positions with experience. In general, older employees tend to be in upper and upper-middle management, middle-aged employees in middle management and occasionally in upper management, and younger employees in lower to more central levels. However, as organizations flatten into more horizontal structures, a "mixing" of generations occurs that profoundly influences organizational processes. As teamwork increases, intergenerational differences spark interpersonal conflict, creating issues surrounding collaborative problem solving, motivation, communication, training, and supervision. Thus, diversity of generations must be added to traditional discussions of diversity in the workplace and its impact on organizational effectiveness.

The nomenclature and the time frames for the cohorts that follow are those presented by Ron Zemke, Claire Raines, and Bob Filipczak (2000).

GENERATIONS IN THE WORKPLACE

The Profile for Veterans: Born between 1922 and 1943

- The core values of Veterans include dedication, discipline, sacrifice, hard work, duty before pleasure, delayed rewards, conformity, consistency and uniformity, sense of history, and oriented toward the past; respect for authority, adherence to the rules, preference for hierarchy; patience; conservative spending, and a deep sense of personal organizational and national honor.
- Veterans were influenced by world events that included the 1929 stock market crash, Dust Bowl, and Great Depression in the 1930s; Franklin Roosevelt's presidency, particularly his optimism and the New Deal, which brought Social Security and other social programs; the rise of Hitler and fall of Europe; Pearl Harbor and the United States at war; victory in Europe and Japan; and the Korean War.
- Assets of having Veterans in the workplace include their stability, orientation to detail, thoroughness, loyalty, and consistent hard work. Their liabilities include their difficulty coping with ambiguity and change, reluctance to buck the system, discomfort with conflict, and reticence to disagree.
- Messages that motivate Veterans include, "Your experience is respected here," "It's valuable to the rest of us to hear what has—and hasn't—worked in the past."

- In their leadership style, Veterans are directive, use command-and-control leadership, and use executive decision making. They want to take charge, delegate, and make the bulk of the decisions themselves (Aldisert, 2002, p. 25; Zemke, Raines, & Filipczak, 2000, pp. 29–62).

The Profile for Baby Boomers: Born between 1943 and 1960

- The core values of Baby Boomers include optimism, team orientation, personal gratification, health and wellness, personal growth, youth, hard work, and involvement.
- Boomers were influenced by: the McCarthy hearings in 1955; victories over polio and tuberculosis; the struggle for Civil Rights from Rosa Parks, through school integration, Martin Luther King, Jr., and the involvement of students in voter registration; bomb shelters and nuclear power; easily accessible birth control; John Fitzgerald Kennedy's presidency, including the establishment of the Peace Corps, the Cuban missile crisis, and astronauts in space; the assassinations of JFK, Martin Luther King, and Robert Kennedy; the Vietnam War and student protests that culminated in the Kent State University shootings; founding of the National Organization for Women; and the disgrace of Richard M. Nixon.
- Assets of having Boomers in the workplace include their service orientation, willingness to "go the extra mile," ability to establish and maintain good working relationships, desire to please, and team spirit. Liabilities include frequent lack of budget orientation, discomfort with conflict to the point of conflict avoidance, reluctance to disagree with peers for fear of harming working relationships, comfort with process frequently overshadows the need for goal attainment, overly sensitive to feedback, judgmental of those who see things differently, and self-centeredness.
- Messages that motivate Boomers include, "You're valued here," "We need you," "I approve of you," and "Your contribution is unique and important."
- In their leadership style, Boomers are collegial and consensual, but sometimes authoritarian. They are passionate and concerned about participation, spirit, humanity in the workplace, and creating a fair and level playing field for all. Because Boomers grew up with conservative parents and worked in their early careers for command-and-control supervisors, they often slip into that style when collegiality fails. Many Boomer managers lack sophisticated communication, motivation, supervision, and delegation skills (Aldisert, 2002, pp. 25–26; Zemke, Raines, & Filipczak, 2000, pp. 63–91).

The Profile for the Gen Xers: Born between 1960 and 1980

- The core values of the Gen Xers include appreciation of diversity, ability to think globally, the balance of work and home, technoliteracy, work should be fun, casual approach to authority, self-reliance, and pragmatism.

- The Gen Xers were influenced by the following events: the struggle for women's liberation and gay rights, the Watergate scandal, the energy crisis, personal computers, Three Mile Island meltdown, disenchantment with nuclear power, successive recessions accompanied by massive layoffs, the Iran hostages episode, erosion of America's world dominance and respect, the Challenger disaster, Exxon Valdez oil spill, AIDS, Operation Desert Storm, and the fall of Communism.
- Assets of having Xers in the workplace include that they are adaptable, technoliterate, independent, not intimidated by authority, voracious learners, financially savvy, multitask oriented, experienced team members, and creative. Liabilities include that they are impatient, have poor people skills, are cynical, have low expectations about job security, and are less willing to make personal sacrifices at work.
- Messages that motivate Gen Xers include, "Do it your way," "We've got the newest hardware and software," and "There are not a lot of rules around here."
- In their leadership styles, Xers are uncomfortable with bureaucratic rules and procedures and traditional chain-of-command systems. They know that sophisticated and demanding customers expect their needs to be met immediately. The Gen X leader is skilled at supporting and developing a responsive, competent team who can change direction, or projects, quickly. They are egalitarian and not hierarchical in their thinking. In addition, they are adept at accessing information on the Internet, via e-mail, and through the organization's information system (Aldisert, 2002, p. 26; Zemke, Raines, & Filipczak, 2000, pp. 92–126).

The Profile for Gen Y (the Nexters): Born between 1980 and 2000

- The core values for the Nexters include a sense of civic duty, confidence, optimism, achievement, sociability, morality, street smarts, and an appreciation of diversity.
- The Nexters' sphere of seminal events and trends includes violence such as the school yard shootings, Columbine, and the Oklahoma City bombing; the increased use of technology in schools and in the home; busy lives; the President Clinton and Monica Lewinsky scandal; and years of service learning throughout elementary and secondary school.
- Assets of having Nexters in the workplace include their optimism, tenacity, heroic spirit, multitasking capabilities, technological savvy, and collective action orientation. Liabilities include their need for supervision and structure and their inexperience in handling difficult interpersonal issues.
- Messages that motivate Nexters include, "You'll be working with other bright, creative people," "You and your colleagues can help turn this company around," and "Your boss is in his (or her) sixties."
- In their leadership style, Nexters combine the teamwork ethic of the Boomers with the can-do attitude of the Veterans and the technological savvy of the Xers. Resiliency is one of their strongest traits. They are very comfortable dealing with Boomers (Aldisert, 2002, pp. 27–28; Zemke, Raines, & Filipczak, 2000, pp. 127–150).

STUDENT INSTRUCTIONS FOR THE ROLE-PLAY EXERCISE/IN-CLASS ASSIGNMENT

You will be assigned to a group with other students. Your instructor will give you one of the role-play scenarios. These present work situations in which one manager is from the Baby Boom generation and has to make a personnel decision about an Xer employee. The other scenario is about an Xer employee who has to make a personnel decision about a Baby Boomer employee.

Read the role-play. Choose a group leader who will assign the roles of the manager, employee, and three members of the grievance committee who will propose a resolution to the conflict. The last role is that of observer, who will report to the class on the resolution arrived at by the grievance committee. Read the information provided in the article for the Baby Boomer and Xers roles. Do the role-play.

Following the exercise, the observers will report to the class on the resolution proposed by the grievance committee. Your instructor may have you write your answers for the questions that are asked at the end of the role-play.

ADDITIONAL ASSIGNMENTS

Your instructor will assign one of the topics presented in this section. In answering your topic, be sure to include specific information about the generational issues. Remember to support your statements using information from your experience or from the information presented in this text on diversity issues. For written assignments, research the topic using additional books and journals.

1. Compare and contrast the generational issues in the two role-play scenarios. In responding to this topic, discuss how individuals frame issues in terms of their generational cohort and how generational issues influence decisions in resolving intergenerational conflicts.
2. Discuss the issues of age discrimination and the political issues of the Boomer's relationship with the CEO in the Boomer–X role-play scenario.
3. Identify issues surrounding the ability of older individuals to adapt to changing technologies, as well as whether the organization has any responsibility to older, loyal employees and what that "responsibility" encompasses. One example would be the organization's responsibility to provide training.
4. What is the impact of any of the following on decision making for retention of employees: employee's age, length of employment, organizational position, and the individual's ability to change?
5. Write a reflective essay on your generational viewpoints about the role-play issues and discuss how your answers to the questions in the role-play may have been based on your generational framing.

6. What are the ethical and legal implications involved with generational issues that involve terminating employees in the Baby Boomer generation? Research legal cases and age discrimination legislation to support your viewpoints.

SCENARIO: X–BOOM

Sam, age 33, is the new Vice President for Information Services at the Davis Employment Agency. Sam rose quickly to the position of Assistant Vice President for Human Relations at the last job. Harry Davis, the founder of the firm, will retire in the next few years and hand the firm over to his son, Jim, 33. Recently, billings began to noticeably decline, even though industry billings were up. In response, Jim persuaded his father to hire several new employees to provide new and creative responses to clients' needs. One of these employees is Sam, now at Davis for four months.

Sam is having difficulty working with the employees, many of whom have been with the company for more than 10 years. Sam is particularly having problems with the Assistant Vice President, Lee, who started working for the company 30 years ago, right out of college. Lee worked up to Assistant VP. Lee, known for loyalty, commitment, and dedication to the company, is valued and respected by many in the agency.

Although Harry wanted Lee to move up to Vice President, Jim convinced his father that a younger person was needed in order to bring the firm into the 21st century. Over the past month, Sam has watched Lee's performance and is quite disturbed. Many of the employees say that "Lee's Way" seems antiquated by today's office procedures but that Lee is very competent and knowledgeable about everything in the office. Lee knows operations and each client's history. However, Lee's cumbersome and often-overlapping procedures frustrate newer employees who do not appreciate all the memos and correspondence being done on paper, rather than through electronic messaging, and the endless number of informational meetings. They prefer charts and aggregated data to long detailed memos and keep each other informed via e-mail, not face-to-face meetings.

Lee sees these procedures as time proven and cannot understand why Sam does not value going through channels, following the company procedures manual, documenting details, and articulating the "big picture" before proceeding.

Sam, in contrast, believes in getting things done efficiently, using technology to enhance productivity, finding shortcuts, and avoiding wasted time by being overly cautious. When Sam tries to explain how procedures can be improved or done more efficiently, Lee listens politely, expresses a look of frustration and tells Sam to "Trust me, I know from experience that this is the best way." Sam sighs and leaves mumbling.

One week Lee was working under a lot of pressure on projects Sam assigned with tight deadlines. It was clear Lee would not be able to complete them. Sam stayed late one night and outlined procedures for each project, and created data reporting templates. Jim stopped by and Sam explained the sophisticated charting of one project and how it graphed the data for clients. Jim was interested and commented about finally being able to communicate with clients on their wavelengths. The next day Sam showed Lee how the projects should be done. Lee's temper flared and a heated dialogue ensued.

Lee filed a harassment grievance with Human Resources, claiming that Sam is creating a harassing work environment so that Lee will quit and Sam can hire a younger person. Sam does not believe Lee to be capable of change and wants to write Lee up for insubordination and start documenting Lee's performance to move toward termination. Lee has requested a formal hearing. The hearing board is composed of three Human Resource members:

> Lou, age 56, is Vice President for Human Resources
> Fran, age 37, is the Assistant Vice President for Human Resources
> Jan, age 23, is the Human Resource Specialist

Both Sam and Lee have been asked to come in individually and explain what happened.

Role-Play Instructions
1. Role-play the meeting of the grievance committee with each of the two managers.
2. The grievance committee meets privately and decides how to resolve the issue.

Discussion: As a Group Discuss the Following Questions
1. What did your grievance committee recommend? How do you think this will be accepted by the two managers?
2. What generational issues are involved in this role-play?
3. What do you think will actually happen? Why?

For the class discussion, the group observers should report the decision by the grievance committee and how the committee arrived at the resolution for the conflict.

GENERATIONAL DIVERSITY ROLE-PLAY SCENARIO: BOOM–X

Pat, age 55, is Vice President for Customer Services at the Davis Employment agency. Pat started working for the company 33 years ago, right out of college, and advanced to a position under the mentorship of the founder, Harry Davis. Harry's son, Jim, 33, is now in charge of the agency. Upon retiring Harry announced, "I leave the company under the capable direction of my son and the sound management of Pat, who we all know is knowledgeable about the "Davis way." Pat, known for loyalty, commitment, and dedication to the company, is valued and respected by many in the agency.

Recently billings have begun to noticeably decline, even though industry billings are up. In response Jim has hired several new employees to provide new and creative responses to clients' needs. One of the new employees is 32-year-old Alex, Assistant Vice President for Customer Services under Pat. Alex manages the office and deals with clients. Alex has only been at Davis four months out of a six-month probationary period. Alex is having difficulty adapting to the coworkers, many of whom have been at the company for more than 10 years, and who are familiar and comfortable with Pat's management style. Alex has many good ideas, but is not empowered to enact any changes. This is frustrating to Alex, who believes incorporation of these ideas would bring the company "into the technological era of efficiency." Alex cannot convince Pat these ideas would enhance efficiency and more effectively met clients' needs.

Some of the office employees say that "Pat's Way" may seem antiquated by today's office procedures and technological advances, but Pat is very competent and on top of everything. Pat knows operations and each client's history. However, Pat's procedures create confusion with newer employees, who find them cumbersome and often overlapping. They do not appreciate all memos and correspondence being done on paper versus electronic messaging, and the endless number of informational meetings. They prefer charts and aggregated data to long detailed memos and keep each other informed via e-mail, not face-to-face meetings.

Pat sees the procedures as time proven and cannot understand why Alex does not value going through channels, following the company procedures manual, documenting details, and articulating the "big picture" before proceeding. Pat wonders why Alex doesn't take more time and care on projects. Alex, in contrast, believes in getting things done efficiently, using technology to enhance productivity, finding shortcuts, and avoiding wasted time by being overly cautious.

When Alex tries to explain how procedures could be improved or done more efficiently, Pat listens politely, expresses a look of frustration, and tells Alex to "Do it my way." Alex sighs and leaves the office, mumbling.

One week Alex was working under a lot of pressure on projects Pat had assigned with tight deadlines. Alex took charge, completed the assignments in the style to which he was accustomed. All the projects were completed on time. Alex did not ask to have Pat approve each step. "Surely Pat will appreciate me now," thought Alex. One night when Alex was working late, Jim stopped by the office and Alex explained the sophisticated charting of one project and how the data was presented in an easy-to-follow manner using spreadsheets created on Excel. Jim was interested and commented about finally being able to communicate with clients on their wavelengths. The next morning when Pat asked Alex how the projects were progressing, Alex stated that they were all done and on the way to clients. Pat's temper flared and a heated dialogue ensued.

Pat wrote a disciplinary letter to Alex citing insubordination. In addition, Pat wants to start documenting Alex's performance in order to eventually terminate Alex. Alex has requested a formal hearing regarding the disciplinary letter. The hearing board is composed of three HR members:

Lou, age 56, is Vice President for Human Resources
Fran, age 37, is the Assistant Vice President for Human Resources
Jan, age 23, is the Human Resources Specialist

Both Pat and Alex have been asked to come in individually to meet with the hearing board.

Role-Play Instructions
1. Role-play the meeting of the grievance committee with each of the managers.
2. The grievance committee should then meet privately and decide how to resolve the issue.

Discussion: As a Group Discuss the Following Questions
1. What did your grievance committee recommend? How do you think the two managers will accept this?
2. What generational issues are involved in this role-play?
3. What do you think will actually happen? Why?

Bibliography

Aldisert, L.M. (2002). *Valuing people: How human capital can be your strongest asset.* Chicago: Dearborn Trade Publishing.

Lancaster, L.C., & Stillman, D. (2002). *When generations collide: Who they are. Why they clash. How to solve the generational puzzle at work.* New York: Harper Collins.

Zemke, R., Raines, C., & Filipczak, B. (2000). *Generations at work: Managing the clash of veterans, boomers, Xers, and nexters in your workplace.* New York: American Management Association.

Additional Resources

Martin, C.A., & Tulgan, B. (2002). *Managing the generation mix: From collision to collaboration.* Amherst, MA: HRD Press.

Thiederman, S. (2003). *Making diversity work: Steps for defeating bias in the workplace.* Chicago: Dearborn Trade Publishing.

www.generationsatwork.com is the Website for "Generations at Work: The Online Home of Claire Raines Associates." The site includes links to resources on generational issues in the workplace.

THE AGING POPULATION: EXPLORING WORKPLACE ISSUES

Pamela D. Sherer
Providence College

Goals

- To familiarize you with age-related facts and workplace issues.
- To give you practice in identifying age-related resources available through the Internet.
- To provide an opportunity to explore and understand issues specifically related to the older worker.

Instructions

1. Preclass preparation time: 10 minutes to complete questionnaire; two hours for Internet research and group project planning.
2. In-class Activity: 50 minutes for review of questionnaire and short student presentations on previously assigned age-related topics.
   Prior to the day of the class discussion, your instructor will assign you to a group and topic for research. Topics may include

   - Age Discrimination in Employment Act (ADEA)
   - Age Discrimination Cases—A Brief Overview
   - Company Training Programs for Older Workers
   - Government Training Programs for Older Workers
   - Phased Retirement Programs
   - Recruitment Programs for Older Workers
   - Programs Targeted for Older Minorities
   - Temporary and Part-time Work for Older Workers

   Your group should be prepared to give a short presentation on your topic and provide the class with (a) a brief summary of your findings and (b) a one-page description identifying key issues and resources. Your instructor may ask you to post the one-page descriptions to your course Website. Possible Websites to begin your research:

Administration on Aging	http://www.aoa.dhhs.gov
National Council on Aging	http://www.ncoa.org
Age Discrimination in Employment Act	http://www.eeoc.gov/laws/adea.html
Committee for Economic Development	http://www.ced.org
American Society on Aging	http://www.asaging.org/
Employee Benefits Research Institute	http://www.ebri.org
American Association of Retired Persons	http://www.aarp.org
Experience Works	http://www.experienceworks.org/
The Older Women's League	http://www.owl-national.org
Green Thumb Inc.	http://www.greenthumb.org
Service Corps of Retired Executives (SCORE)	http://www.score.org/
National Older Worker Career Center	http://www.nowcc.org/

THE AGING POPULATION QUESTIONNAIRE

Indicate either **T** for true or **F** for false

_____ 1. Congress enacted the 1967 Age Discrimination in Employment Act (ADEA) to prevent employment discrimination against workers age 55 and over.

_____ 2. By 2030, there will be about 70 million older persons (65+), more than twice their number in 1998.

_____ 3. In the United States, only one third of workers approaching retirement believe that they could move into less-demanding work (at reduced pay) with their current employers. The remaining two-thirds do not expect their employers to accommodate such a transition.

_____ 4. In each of the past four fiscal years, age discrimination comprised about 5% of all discrimination charges filed with the Equal Employment Opportunity Commission (EEOC).

_____ 5. In 1998, about half (52%) of persons 65+ lived in nine states.

_____ 6. On average, age discrimination settlements and jury awards are substantially lower than those awarded for race discrimination, sex discrimination, or disability cases.

_____ 7. Minority populations are projected to represent 25% of the elderly (65+) population in 2030, up from 16% in 1998.

_____ 8. The most common situation provoking claims under the Age Discrimination in Employment Act of 1967 are reduction in force, which usually is caused by a merger, an acquisition, or a contracting-out of operations.

_____ 9. In 1950, there were seven working-age persons for every person age 65 and older in the United States; by 2030, there will be fewer than five.

_____ 10. Workers over the age of 55 are far more likely to receive training to improve their skills than any other age group.

INNOVATIVE WORK MODELS FOR OLDER WORKERS

Carol P. Harvey
Assumption College
Pamela D. Sherer
Providence College

Due to large numbers of baby boomers and increased life expectancies, people over 65 will represent 20 percent of the United States population by 2030 (Committee for Economic Development, 1999). Today, a fifty-five-year-old male can expect to live another 23 years and a female of the same age, 27 years (National Center for Health Statistics, 2001; Public Health Service, 1996). Unlike their parents and grandparents, who often made full retirement a life goal, a recent survey of baby boomers revealed that 70 percent of them expect to continue to work at least part-time after retirement (AARP, 1998).

Because the baby boomers are reaching traditional retirement ages at the same time that the United States is faced with a severe shortage of skilled and experienced labor, these economic, social, and demographic changes would seem to support the development of innovative programs to employ older workers. However, extensive research reveals that few organizations actually have programs in place that capitalize on the advantages of retaining or hiring older workers.

> American businesses do not yet regard the aging of the workforce as a compelling business issue. This lack of concern is further indicated by the small number of companies that have implemented programs or policies that could help employers fully utilize older employees. (AARP, 2000)

Most retirees who want or need to work have found it necessary to seek their own solutions. Typically, these jobs have taken the form of underemployment in low-level part-time service industries, like McDonald's, where 7% of the workforce is age sixty or older; seasonal employment; occasional consultant projects; or short-term placements through temporary work agencies.

Stereotypes about age still have considerable influence on workplace decisions. In a national survey, finding and keeping skilled employees was identified as the most important issue for human resource managers. They scored this item 8.9 on a 10-point scale. In the same survey, the respondents perceived older workers as having all but one of the top seven most desirable employee qualities. Older workers were identified as functioning well in a crisis; loyal; solid performers; experienced; having basic skills in reading, writing, and arithmetic; and possessing the ability to get along with coworkers. The only negative characteristic associated with older workers was their willingness to be flexible about performing different tasks, which scored a low mean rating of 4.5 (AARP, 2000).

"Age Works" author Beverly Goldberg warns corporate America that they must change their attitudes toward older workers or face the consequences of a shortage of skilled labor.

> As early as 2005, when some boomers begin retiring early, a sharp increase in the number of workers over 55 will be needed to maintain the percentage of the population that is employed.... A lot of companies will have to scramble to retain or hire older workers, many of whom are sitting atop of fat 401(k) accounts. Money alone will not lure them. An adjustment in corporate attitudes may be necessary. (Brock, 1999)

In addition, rigid government and organizational policies do not offer enough flexibility for innovative employment plans for older workers. Recently, Social Security liberalized restrictions to allow older workers to keep more of their income without docking their benefits. However, the IRS prohibits pension distributions to individuals who continue to work but have not reached traditional normal retirement ages (Watson Wyatt, 1999). So, a 55-year-old worker cannot retire gradually by reducing work hours and supplementing his/her income with pension benefits from the same employer, even if he or she has worked sufficient years to be eligible for the pension. For example, a recent early retirement plan offered to Massachusetts public school teachers with 30 or more years of service does not allow them to take substitute teaching assignments within the state public school system. So, the most qualified people in the state cannot work as substitute teachers. In addition, many organizations have retirement plans that calculate retirement benefits based on an employee's *last* 3 years of employment. So, employees who reduce their work hours also can lose pension benefits.

The few organizations that do have successful programs designed to capitalize on the strengths and advantages of older workers seem to share some common characteristics:

- Top management support
- Identification of their own organizational barriers
- Willingness to eliminate these barriers

- Flexibility
- Appreciation of the contributions of older workers

The Aerospace Corporation and Vita Needle are examples of two very different types of organizations that have successfully utilized the talents of older workers. The former is a $186 million a year corporation that employs over 3,000 employees, mostly highly educated scientists and engineers, to conduct government research. The latter is a small privately held manufacturer with 35 employees, located in a second-floor former theater. The Aerospace Corporation has a well-developed phased retirement program that allows the organization to retain the skills of a technical workforce. The Vita Needle Company simply values the contributions of older workers and has structured its operations around the needs of its older workforce.

THE AEROSPACE CORPORATION

Although individuals have always had the option of finding part-time or contract work to "bridge the gap" between full-time employment and retirement, few companies have instituted and maintained formalized phased retirement programs for their own employees. A notable exception is The Aerospace Corporation, El Segundo, CA, an independent nonprofit organization that receives yearly contracts that exceed $400 million in federally funded research.

The Aerospace Corporation was founded in 1960 at the request of the then Secretary of the Air Force. The organizational mission is to provide engineering services "objective technical analyses and asessments for space programs . . . [by operating] a federally funded research and development center (FFRDC) sponsored by the Department of Defense" (*1999 Annual Report*). The Department of Defense has identified five core competencies for The Aerospace Corporation: space launch certification, system-of-systems engineering, systems development and acquisition, process implementation, and technology application. Organized in a matrix structure, the heart of the $186 million corporation is the technical knowledge and expertise of its highly educated and skilled 3,000+ workforce. Consequently, it is to The Aerospace Corporation's advantage to retain this institutional memory on long-term projects.

This corporation has a "Retirement Transition Program" that offers its highly skilled technical employees four options: preretirement leaves of absence, part-time status in preparation for retirement, postretirement employment on a consulting basis, and postretirement employment on a "casual basis." The latter category is the most popular program. As a casual employee, the corporation's retirees can work in this phased retirement program up to 999 hours per year and still maintain their full pension benefits. Over 300 employees, 80 percent of them employed as engineers or scientists, take advantage of this program each year. In an interview on *Good Morning America*, Shirley McCarty, a participant in the plan, described it as a way to keep your "identity and self-esteem" (*Good Morning America*, February 8, 2000).

VITA NEEDLE

Innovative programs that utilize the talents and skills of older workers need not be limited to large organizations. Vita Needle, Needham, MA, is a manufacturer of stainless steel tubing and needles that has a reputation for quality and service and a policy of hiring primarily older workers. The average age of Vita Needle's 35 employees is 73 years. The oldest employee is 89 years old. The president, Fred Hartman, in an interview with Tom Brokaw for *NBC Nightly News*, said that he actively recruits older workers to assemble small metal components by hand because they are "extremely conscientious employees: loyal, dedicated, aware of quality requirements, and very reliable."

Founded in 1932 by the current president's great-grandfather, Oscar E. Nutter, a 68 year-old retiree from the textile industry, the company originally manufactured reusable medical needles, but these product lines now account for less than 20 percent of the business. Responding to the changing needs of a marketplace for disposable needles, Vita Needle expanded its product lines. The company now has more than 1,000 customers who use its products in medicine, sports equipment, and even the body-piercing business. The company produces some of the smallest needles in the world for eye surgery, most of the inflating needles for U.S. basketball manufacturers, and supplies 90 percent of the golf pro shops with needles used to inject solvent under golf club grips for repair and replacement. Stainless steel tube and wire products now make up 60–70 percent of the current sales. With yearly sales of $4 million, annual growth has averaged 20 percent over the past 5 years.

The Vita Needle Company's management practices illustrate how even a small business can simultaneously meet the employees' needs and its production and profit goals by utilizing flexible schedules and policies. Hartman allows his employees to work the ultimate in flextime. Each employee has a key to the factory and can start and finish work at any hour. It is common for workers to be on the job before 5 A.M. The first one in turns up the heat, and the last person who leaves is expected to put out the lights. Most workers put in 15 to 40 hours per week.

Rather than take advantage of such freedom, the production workers are so reliable and focused on quality that the company features them as a competitive advantage in its brochure. They are described as a "mature team of New England craftspeople (2/3 over age 70) with extraordinary attention to detail." Personnel costs are lower because the workers already have medical benefits through Medicare, do not need to take time off for child care needs, and have low turnover rates.

Employees join the company after retirement from careers such as nursing, engineering, and baking—one was even a circus performer. Some are there because they find Social Security and pension benefits inadequate and others because they find retirement boring and lonely. Hartman says it best, "There is a huge benefit to be gained from the experience, the values, [the] loyalty, and the dedication to quality that senior citizens bring to the workplace. We profit from it and so do our customers" (*Thomas's Register Trendletter*, 1999).

These two organizations illustrate that win-win solutions can be developed when there is an appreciation for the contributions of older workers. As the baby boomers moved through the stages of their lifetimes, their sheer numbers changed so many aspects of American society. As they move to retirement age, perhaps they will be the driving force that improves job opportunities for older workers.

Discussion Questions

1. List some of the stereotypes that often prevent older workers from having more employment opportunities. What are some of the things that managers could do to overcome these stereotypes? What are some of the things that older workers could do?
2. Make a list of the types of organizational barriers that could prevent organizations from developing programs like those at The Aerospace Corporation and Vita Needle. Then, make a list of the types of policies that could facilitate organizations developing similar programs.
3. Will the development of new uses for technology, like telecommuting, provide additional work opportunities for older workers? Why or why not?

References

Ackerman, Jerry. "Seniors Choosing Work over Retirement." *The Boston Globe*, October 15, 2000, pp. H1 and H6.

Anonymous. (1999). "Employees Inject Vitality into Needle Production." *Thomas's Register Trendletter*, #108, pp. 1–2.

American Association of Retired Persons (1998). "Boomers Approaching Midlife." Available at research.aarp.org

American Association of Retired Persons (AARP) (2000). "Companies Do Not Use Strategies That Would Better Utilize Older Workers." Available at www.aarp.org/press/2000.

Brock, Fred. "Labor Shortage: Color It Gray." *New York Times*, February 5, 1999, p. 7.

Committee for Economic Development. (1999). "New Opportunities for Older Workers." p. 2. Available at www.ced.org

Flaherty, Julie. "A Company Where Retirement is a Dirty Word." *The New York Times*, December 28, 1997. Section 3, pp. 1 and 11.

Good Morning America. Interview with Diane Sawyer, February 8, 2000.

Mason, Jon. "Time Stands Still Here." *The Boston Globe*, December 31, 1997, p. 1.

National Center for Health Statistics. (1992). Vol. 11, section 6 life tables. Available at www.lifeexpectancy.com/usle.html

Public Health Service and National Center for Health Statistics. (1996). Available at www.lifeexpectancy.com/usle.html

The Aerospace Corporation. *1999 Annual Report*, p. 4.

Watson, Wyatt. (1999). "Phased Retirement: Reshaping the End of Work." Available at www.watsonwyatt.com

CONTRADICTIONS AND MIXED MESSAGES: LESBIAN, GAY, BISEXUAL, AND TRANSGENDER ISSUES IN THE WORKPLACE

Gerald Hunt

Ryerson University

- Colleagues of a Colorado police officer refuse her calls for backup help when they learn she is a lesbian.
- An Oregon pest-control worker who has the highest sales record in the company is fired when his employer finds out he is gay.
- A Maine manufacturing company informs a senior manager he will be fired if rumors that he is gay are true—the manager quits rather than face dismissal.
- In 2001, American Airlines expanded their equal opportunities statement to include transgendered people.

These true stories illustrate the contradictions and mixed messages surrounding lesbians, gays, bisexuals, and transgendered (LGBT) issues in the workplace.[1] On the one hand, there have been important and supportive shifts in the legal situation, public opinion, and workplace cultures for sexual and gender minorities. LGBT characters have become an accepted part of situational comedy television (two of the key characters in the very successful *Will and Grace* are openly gay men). Some organizations fully embrace issues related to sexual and gender diversity and have removed as many discriminatory policies and procedures as possible. Influential organizations such as General Motors, AT&T, and IBM offer same-sex partner benefits; Disney holds an annual "gay day" in Orlando.

At the same time, negative bias in law, housing, the workplace, the media, and some churches is still a harsh fact of life if you are lesbian, gay, or bisexual and even starker if you are transgendered (dress and/or behave differently than the norms associated with one's birth sex). Most states do not ban job discrimination on the basis of sexual orientation or gender identity. The American military continues to proclaim that no openly gay men or lesbians should ever be allowed to serve in the defense of their country. The American Boy Scouts legally exclude gay men from their midst. For the casual observer, it is a bit confusing. Have LGBT minorities come a long way, just a little way, or no way at all? Are organizations legally and/or morally required to accommodate sexual and gender identity diversity?

LGBT ISSUES AT WORK

In the late 1940s, in his pioneering work on human sexuality, Kinsey (1948) found upwards of 10% of the American population to be engaged in homosexual activity. Recent American and Canadian studies have found that 5% to 6% of the population is predominately homosexual, identifying exclusively as gay or lesbian. That percentage rises to as high as 13% to 15% when bisexuals and transgendered people are included (Bagley & Tremblay, 1998). These figures mean that the LGBT population is higher than the number of Asian Americans (3.6% in the 2000 census) and greater than the number of Jewish people living in the United States (estimated at 3%). Unlike most minority groups, however, LGBT people are not readily visible, and many have chosen to remain invisible, especially at work, because they fear the negative consequences that might result from revealing their identity. As the murder of Matthew Shepard illustrated, being openly and visibly gay can still cost you your life (Matthew was an openly gay 21-year-old student at the University of Wyoming who was savagely murdered to make the point that homosexuals deserve to die). Throughout history are many examples of organizations harassing and dismissing employees when they learned, or even suspected, that these employees were homosexual.

The true case of Mark Sension illustrates the kind of dilemmas LGBT people can still confront within the labor market. Mark was hired by the University of Denver to be the Associate Director of Operations of the Ricks Center for Gifted Children. About a month after he was hired, his supervisor learned that he was a gay man. Soon after, Mark was fired without warning and escorted from the building by university security personnel. He was told his firing was an "issue of trust" because he did not make his sexual orientation clear during the hiring interview. However, if Mark had revealed his sexual orientation, he would not have been offered the job.

Despite the very real risks, in recent years, more and more LGBT people have come out to fight for equal rights. They find living in the closet too demeaning a price to pay for "protection" from discrimination. As a result, equality for LGBT people is now an issue of concern and an important rallying point for **all** people (straight and gay) who are concerned about equity and fairness at work.

Spokespersons offer a clear message: The gay, lesbian, bisexual, transgender community is discriminated against and treated inequitably at work. Change is demanded in human resources policies and practices concerned with recruiting, hiring, promotion, discipline, and benefits. Activists call for organizational leaders to foster and promote an environment that is positive and supportive of **all** human difference and diversity.

These demands closely parallel those made by women and Blacks, and in some ways the LGBT movement has only now caught up with other human rights movements. All these groups desire equal treatment—not special or exceptional treatment—and want the social and institutional barriers removed that prevent them from getting it.

The overwhelming difference between sexual orientation and gender identity and other types of diversity issues is that for some people sexual diversity at work is more controversial. Homosexuality and gender nonconformity make some people extremely uncomfortable and/or angry. Some conservative thinkers portray the LGBT minority as immoral and degenerate. Others feel that sexuality is a "private" issue and should not be exposed in the public domain. Some, guided by Christian teachings, quote from the Bible to defend their views (Leviticus 18:22 states that homosexuality is an abomination). These people fail to note that Leviticus 10:10 also indicates that eating shellfish is an abomination and that Exodus 35:2 clearly states that a neighbor who insists on working on the Sabbath should be put to death. Ultimately however, in countries based on secular governments where various religious and spiritual traditions coexist, the idea that the religious or moral philosophy of one group should override all others and directly influence the state and workplace becomes intolerable.

The polarization around homosexuality creates work situations characterized by a lack of consensus regarding the merit of appeals for equal treatment and justice being made by the LGBT community, thus resulting in a range of organizational responses. Some organizations have made extensive efforts to ensure that policies and benefits are equal for everyone and value their LGBT employees equally with other workers. In other settings, little if any accommodation exists. A few employers go so far as to dismiss these minorities if their identity becomes known.

SOCIAL, LEGAL, AND ECONOMIC DEVELOPMENTS

Despite controversies and differing perspectives, more and more LGBT people are open about their identities and vocal about their desire for change. This, combined with a changing social, legal, and economic environment, has convinced more and more organizations to rethink and overhaul policies and practices to accommodate LGBT employees.

Social Forces

With each passing year, the LGBT community has acquired a higher and more positive public profile. Yeager (1999) estimated there were 124 openly gay and lesbian elected officials serving at the federal, state, and municipal levels. These people ranged from member of Congress Barney Frank, to Margo Frasier, an elected sheriff in Austin, Texas, to Tim Mains, who serves on the Rochester City Council. Perhaps the greatest change, though, is from the devastating impact of AIDS, which has given the LGBT community a much stronger presence and voice in society.

Public opinion polls show a steadily increasing tolerance toward homosexuals in general and their workplace rights in particular. Wilcox and Wolpert (2000, p. 28), in a summary of polling data from throughout the 1990s, found that attitudes have moved in a positive direction since 1992, even though there remains a minority "voicing strongly negative reactions, often rooted in basic emotional reactions." Research conducted in 1998 (Yang, 1999) found that a majority of Americans supported the idea of gays and lesbians having equality in employment (84%), housing (81%), inheritance rights (62%), social security benefits (57%), and the military (66%). In other words, although there may not be widespread public involvement in fighting for LGBT rights, and some people continue to be extremely vocal in their opposition, there is no basis for believing that the majority of citizens in the United States support either overt or covert discrimination in the workplace on the basis of sexual orientation.

Legal Change

The increased visibility of LGBT people, combined with more assertive demands for equal rights, has generated considerable legal action. For the past decade, federal, state, and municipal legislators debated changes in legislation that would affect LGBT minorities in almost every aspect of their lives including violence and harassment, employment and housing discrimination, adoption and child care, domestic partner benefits, and the freedom to marry. In some jurisdictions, the legal changes are widespread; in others there has been little or no change.

At one time, all states had laws regulating and criminalizing consensual sexual activity between adults of the same sex. The beginning of 2003 found "sodomy" laws still on the books in 13 states. However, in a landmark case in June 2003, the Supreme Court struck down the sodomy law in Texas, effectively eliminating discriminatory sodomy laws throughout the country.

Increasing numbers of governments have passed bills to include sexual orientation as a protected ground, particularly in employment and housing. By the year 2003, 13 states (California, Connecticut, Hawaii, Maryland, Massachusetts, Minnesota, Nevada, New Hampshire, New Jersey, New York, Rhode Island, Vermont, and Wisconsin), as well as the District of Columbia, had civil rights laws prohibiting employment discrimination based on sexual orientation. An additional 10 states (Alaska, Colorado, Delaware, Illinois, Indiana, Kentucky, Montana, New Mexico, Pennsylvania, and Washington) had laws banning employment discrimination based on sexual orientation covering only the public sector. Seven other states had executive orders baring discrimination in public employment, and two states (Illinois and Michigan) had civil service rules prohibiting discrimination based on sexual orientation. In addition, 240 local governments had provisions banning such discrimination.

Laws protecting gender nonconformity in the workplace are spotty. Minnesota and Rhode Island are the only states specifically including gender identity in their antidiscrimination laws, but courts have ruled that transgendered people are protected under existing discrimination laws in Connecticut, Massachusetts, New Jersey, and New York. As well, a few cities such as Boulder, Atlanta, Dallas, and Houston prohibit employment discrimination based on gender identity.

One of the most spectacular developments arose in Vermont. In December 1999, the state made history by becoming the first American jurisdiction to equalize benefits for all people. Lesbians and gays who enter civil unions are eligible to receive the same protections and benefits that Vermont currently provides to married couples. Vermont was a logical place for this to happen because it was the first state to offer domestic partner benefits to state workers and one of the first to approve same-sex adoptions and prohibit discrimination on the basis of sexual orientation. To date there has not been a lineup of states to mirror Vermont's progressive initiatives, although some cities do have a mechanism for partner registration.

A very dramatic development occurred in San Francisco. In 1997, the city passed an Equal Benefits Ordinance Law requiring any company doing business with the city or county of San Francisco to offer the same benefits to the domestic partners of its employees as it offers to the legal spouses of employees. In response to San Francisco's law, many organizations such as Shell and United Airlines implemented domestic partner benefits (some companies such as FedEx complied only after they lost court challenges).

Labor Union Activity

Although initially unsupportive, some labor organizations now support LGBT rights (Bain, 1999; Frank, 1999; Krupat & McCreery, 2001). This support ranges from formal nondiscrimination clauses that include sexual orientation to the formation of subcommittees and caucuses focusing on issues of concern to LGBT workers. In 1997, the American Federation of Labor-CIO approved "Pride at Work" as a funded constituency group, and many state and local labor councils have adopted similar measures. A few unions, such as the American Federation of State, County, and Municipal Employees (AFSCME), Service Employees International Union (SEIU), and Union of Needletrades, Industrial, and Textile Employees (UNITE), have negotiated inclusive domestic partner benefits in areas such as health care insurance, bereavement leave, and pension coverage in their collective bargaining agreements.

One of the most dramatic examples of union activity is with the United Auto Workers (UAW). For a number of years, the issue of LGBT rights had been subject to some of the most divisive debate in the union's history. A 1997 *New Yorker* article, for example, profiled the story of Ron Woods, a UAW worker at Chrysler's Trenton, Michigan plant (Stewart, 1997). In the early 1990s, Ron helped organize a caucus with the goal of pressuring the union to take on LGBT issues. He also became involved in picketing a Cracker Barrel restaurant (a chain that had been openly firing gay and lesbian workers). After a newspaper photo of him in the picket line appeared in a Detroit paper, he began to experience very serious homophobic harassment, including physical assault, from his coworkers. Initially, the union's response was unsupportive, but gradually the tide turned. By 1998, the UAW had pressured General Motors and Ford to adopt a nondiscrimination policy that included sexual orientation, but Chrysler continued to refuse to take this step. By August 2000, the "Big Three" had all agreed not only to an inclusive non-discrimination policy, but also to medical, dental and prescription coverage for same-sex partners, covering about 466,000 workers throughout the United States.

Economic Forces

The LGBT community represents an important market segment and a group with considerable clout if it decides to boycott a product, service, or organization. Badgett (2001) argues that gays and lesbians are not as affluent as many believe, and on average earn no more than heterosexuals. However, this is a group (especially gay men) that is less likely to have children, probably making discretionary income levels higher than average and spending with more political sensitivity than most others. Buford (2000) points out that advertising for these so-called gay dollars in the media generally and the gay media in particular, is big business. Like Badgett, he argues that what matters about this group from a marketing point of view is not affluence, but slightly higher discretionary income, combined with more free time and desire to buy from LGBT-positive companies.

Activists affect the bottom line of anti-LGBT corporations in a variety of ways. They wage proxy contests against homophobic companies, urge public institutions to buy the shares of companies that prohibit antigay discrimination and to sell the shares of companies that do not, and lobby for legislation to prohibit states and municipalities from purchasing products and services from companies that discriminate against homosexuals. Boycotts of homophobic corporations such as Cracker Barrel Restaurants and Coors Beer provide indications that activists can have a direct impact on company policy. After years of condemnation and boycotts over the firing of openly gay and lesbian employees, Cracker Barrel finally added sexual orientation to its written nondiscrimination policy in 2002. In the early 1980s, the Coors organization went so far as to require lie detector tests to screen out prospective employees identified as gay or lesbian. This prompted countrywide boycotts of Coors Beer, leading to a significant reduction in the company's market share. Since then, Coors has taken steps to position itself as a more LGBT-positive company. Wal-Mart's addition of sexual orientation to its nondiscrimination policy in July 2003, after years of pressure from activists, is an important milestone, especially because Wal-Mart is the nation's largest employer, with over one million workers.

ORGANIZATIONAL RESPONSE

Corporate Sector

More and more organizations are responding positively to the concerns about discrimination raised by the LGBT community. Many large cities hold an annual Pride Day, with these events often partially sponsored by high-profile corporations such as breweries and clothing manufacturers. Increasing numbers of organizations have adopted antidiscrimination policies and instituted domestic partner benefit packages inclusive of same-sex partners. According to a recent survey, less than 24 employers offered same-sex, domestic partner benefits at the beginning of the 1990s, but this number rose to nearly 6,000 by the year 2003 (HRC, 2003). Put another way, nearly two employers a week have been instituting these kinds of benefits over the past decade. During the 1990s, the information technology sector led the way in implementing inclusive benefits, although by the end of the decade oil companies, major banks, hospitality firms, airlines, and accounting firms were leading the pack. As summarized in Table 1, many of the private-sector employers with LGBT-friendly policies are among the most prestigious and prosperous organizations in the United States. Included in the 169 *Fortune* 500 companies offering domestic partner health benefits are Ford, IBM, AT&T, Boeing, Chase Manhattan Bank, Walt Disney, American Airlines, Xerox, Eastman Kodak, Gap Inc., Nike, America Online, and New York Times Co. (see Table 1).

TABLE 1 Employers with LGBT-friendly Policies (2003)

A. *Employers with nondiscrimination policies that include sexual orientation:*
- *Fortune* 500 companies (304)
- Other private companies, nonprofit organizations, and unions (834)
- Colleges and universities (382)
- State and local governments (289)
- Federal government departments and agencies (38)

B. *Employers that offer domestic partner benefits that include same-sex partners:*
- *Fortune* 500 companies (169)
- Other private companies, nonprofit organizations, and unions (5,201)
- Colleges and universities (178)
- State and local governments (150)

C. *Employers with nondiscrimination policies that include gender identity:*
- Public sector (71)
- Private sector (127)

D. *Organizations with formal gay, lesbian, bisexual, and transgender employee groups (289)*

Source: www.hrc.org/worknet
Used with permission HRC Worknet, the Workplace Project Campaign Foundation

Public Sector

State and local governments, colleges, and universities were among the first organizations to institute nondiscrimination policies and offer benefits packages that included same-sex partners (see Table 1). By 2003, some state and local governments provided this level of protection. Among the post-secondary institutions with nondiscrimination policies are 44 of the top 50 national universities.

Business schools, long thought to be holdouts in developing LGBT-friendly environments for students and staff, are catching up. A 2002 survey of the top 20 business schools found that 100% had antidiscrimination policies based on sexual orientation, 86% had same-sex partner benefits, 86% had LGBT student groups, and 57% had at least one "out" professor (Aplomb Consulting, 2002).

FEDERAL GOVERNMENT

In 1998 President Clinton signed an executive order banning discrimination based on sexual orientation throughout the federal civil service. Even though the federal government does not yet offer same-sex benefits, all cabinet-level departments and 24 independent agencies have nondiscrimination policies. If the Employment Nondiscrimination Act currently before Congress passes, it will grant the same benefits currently available to legal spouses to all domestic partners, including same-sex couples.

LGBT EMPLOYEE NETWORK GROUPS

Many organizations now have groups or caucuses dealing with sexual orientation and gender identity issues. These groups provide a forum for LGBT people to meet each other and socialize and at the same time create a vehicle for pressuring their organizations to adopt LGBT-friendly policies and procedures. Some of these groups merged with race, gender, and disability activists to become "rainbow alliances." Nearly 300 organizations known to have LGBT employee groups include 3M, American Express, AT&T, the federal government, Ford, Levi Strauss, Kaiser Permanente, McKinsey and Co., Microsoft, NBC, and Warner-Lambert. The employee group at IBM, called EAGLE, has subgroups in Texas, California, and New York.

GENDER IDENTITY AND TRANSGENDER ISSUES

In recent years, workplace issues related to transgenderism and gender identity have developed a much higher profile. Trangenderism is "a broad term encompassing cross-dressers, inter-sexed people, transsexuals and people who live substantial portions of their lives as other than their birth gender. A transitioning transgendered person is one who is modifying his or her physical characteristics and manner of expression to—in effect—satisfy the standards for membership in another gender" (HRC, 2003, web). Transgendered and transgendering people pose a number of unique accommodation issues in the workplace, ranging from restroom use to dress codes. The response to these issues ranges from extreme hostility to full acceptance. Only 71 jurisdictions have implemented legal protection to prohibit employment discrimination based on gender identity, characteristics, or expression.

American Airlines expanded their equal opportunities statement in July 2001 to include gender identity, making them one of very few organizations with policies and guidelines specifically addressing transgendered issues in the workplace. For example, employees must use restrooms appropriate to their current gender, but have the right to access different restrooms if they alter their gender identity. American's policy stipulates that the attire of a transitioning employee should reflect the appropriate dress codes of the job they hold and the office where they work, underscoring that all employees are held to the same uniform appearance standards within their gender identity status.

THE SPECTER OF DISCRIMINATION CONTINUES

Some organizations steadfastly refuse to alter their human resources polices and practices to accommodate LGBT minorities. Other companies have even rescinded such protections and benefits after mergers and changes in ownership. In 1998, for example, Perot Systems Corporation became the first major American company to end its policy of offering domestic partner benefits to its gay and lesbian employees once Ross Perot returned to the CEO position after his absence to seek the presidency. Similarly, when Phillips Petroleum merged with Conoco in 2002, the new company rescinded Conoco's nondiscrimination policy covering sexual orientation. Prior to the merger of Mobil Oil and Exxon, Mobil had a nondiscrimination policy and offered domestic partner benefits, whereas Exxon did not. After the merger, a policy was put in place to allow same-sex partners of former Mobil employees to continue receiving benefits, but excluding former employees of Exxon or new employees of ExxonMobile from gaining access to these perks. The decision stood in stark contrast to the other major oil companies—Amoco, Chevron, and Shell—who offer benefits without prejudice.

Another organization that fights to retain homophobic policies is the Boy Scouts of America. The Supreme Court ruled in July 2000 that the Boy Scouts could maintain a policy excluding gay men from joining the organization. Several organizations such as Levi Strauss and the United Way discontinued contributions to the Scouts as a form of protest, and several churches, such as the United Methodists, have condemned the policy, but the Scouts remain adamant. In contrast, the Girl Scouts recently reaffirmed its inclusive nondiscrimination policy.

DEVELOPMENTS IN CANADA

The situation for LGBT people has undergone spectacular change in many other parts of the world. This is particularly the case in Canada. By most standards, Canada now ranks among the most favorable in the world for sexual minorities (along with Belgium, Denmark, and the Netherlands). The Charter of Rights and Freedoms (roughly equivalent to the American constitution) is interpreted to include sexual orientation and all human rights codes as protected grounds in housing and employment. Most provinces recognize same-sex relationships in family law, including the right to adopt children, and in June 2003, Canada became the third jurisdiction in the world to allow same-sex marriages (Belgium and the Netherlands were the first).

These legislative changes followed initiatives already under way in many Canadian organizations. As early as the mid-1980s, some unions, such as the Canadian Auto Workers and the Canadian Union of Public Employees, were fighting for nondiscrimination policies and negotiating same-sex benefit packages in collective bargaining agreements (Hunt, 1999, 2002). By the time they were legislatively mandated to do so, most universities, colleges, and public-sector organizations, and many in the private sector, had already moved toward inclusive policies and practices. One measure of the speed and depth of change is the Canadian military. Until the early 1990s, the armed forces could dismiss members found to be gay or lesbian. By 1998, they were advertising the same benefits, opportunities, and protections to all members and their families, regardless of sexual orientation (albeit only for those sufficiently brave to be open in what many believe is still an unwelcoming organizational culture in relation to sexual diversity).

Nevertheless, some employers seem to go out of their way to create an unfriendly and even negative environment for sexual minorities. Mitchell (1999) uses the expression "pink ceiling" to describe the macho culture of many organizations, especially in the financial sector, that discourage disclosure about sexuality altogether and/or punish nonconformity to the norm of silence by limiting advancement and career opportunities. Some Canadian institutions change their policies in relation to same-sex relationship-based benefit and pension packages only when confronted with litigation (which they invariably lose). One example is Dave Mitges' battle with Imperial Oil Ltd. For eight years, he presented his case for same-sex partner benefits at the annual meeting of the shareholders. Each time he asked, the answer was no. Only on the eve of a new Ontario law requiring it, did Imperial finally relent and agree to offer these benefits.

The Canadian situation highlights the fact that access to a legal system does not necessarily change a culture of exclusion and exclusivity. If organizational leaders, and the culture they produce, remain opposed to LGBT equality, then bias and subtle discrimination are likely to remain in force. As a result, people committed to diversity initiatives within Canada tend to focus their efforts on education in an effort to address the values and attitudes that underly prejudice.

CONCLUSIONS

Of all the diversity challenges an organization faces, accommodation to sexuality issues is the most contentious. This produces contradictions and mixed messages in the response LGBT people receive to their demands for equity, resulting in significant variation among states, local authorities, cities, and organizations.

On the one hand, unprecedented change occurred over the past decade. The majority of Americans now support equal rights for LGBT minorities, and a number of states and local governments prohibit employment discrimination. Increasingly organizations are taking steps to curb heterosexual bias in their human resources policies and practices, with some providing a welcoming environment for their LGBT workers.

In some settings, though, there has been no change at all. It is still legally possible to fire someone based on sexual orientation or gender nonconformity in most states. Few organizations offer equal employment benefits to same- and different-sex couples. Some organizations fight assertively for the right to fire LGBT people who might slip through their discriminatory fire walls. Others comply with legal changes but make no effort to create a safe and welcoming environment for LGBT minorities. The legal situation in Canada is more supportive than in the United States, but even there some organizations only implement change when forced.

Benchmark organizations with a broad-based commitment to diversity accept the challenges and opportunities associated with their LGBT employees. They discontinue discriminatory practices and alter human resources and benefit polices to ensure they are equal and fair for everyone. They ensure that LGBT issues are included in diversity education programs. Ultimately, a progressive organization must make clear through its disciplinary policies that homophobic behavior can no more be tolerated than sexist or racist behaviors.

Discussion Questions

1. Why have some states and local governments introduced protections for LGBT people and other states and local governments have not?
2. Why have some employers introduced protections for LGBT people and other employers have not?
3. You are working in the human resources department of a large manufacturing organization that likes to think it has excellent HR policies. You have been assigned the task of preparing a diversity training module on LGBT issues in the workplace. The module will be about 2 hours in length and is to be part of a longer course on diversity. This will be the first time that LGBT topics have been included in the course. Outline the topics that you will include in the module and your approach to teaching this topic.
4. You are the CEO in a large retail store. You have just completed a meeting with a delegation of religious leaders from the community who have indicated that they will recommend a boycott of your store to their parishioners if you go ahead with plans to offer same-sex benefits to your employees. How will you deal with this situation?

Note

1. These stories are taken from the Human Rights Campaign Foundation's project documenting discrimination. For information, go to www.hrc.org/worknet

Bibliography

Aplomb Consulting. (2002). *Report on the LGBT-friendliness of the nation's top business schools*. Aplomb Consulting. (Available online at www.aplomb.com)

Bagley, C., & Tremblay, P. (1998). On the prevalence of homosexuality and bisexuality, in a random community survey of 750 men Aged 18–27. *Journal of Homosexuality, 36*(2) 1–18.

Bain, C. (1999). A short history of lesbian and gay labor activism in the United States. In G. Hunt (Ed.), *Laboring for rights: Unions and sexual diversity across nations* (pp. 58–86). Philadelphia: Temple University Press.

Badgett, L. (2001). *Money, myths and change: The economic lives of lesbians and gay men*. Chicago: University of Chicago Press.

Buford, H. (2000, spring). Understanding gay consumers. *The Gay and Lesbian Review, VII*(2), 26–27.

Frank, M. (1999). Lesbian and gay caucuses in the U.S. labor movement. In G. Hunt (Ed.), *Laboring for rights: Unions and sexual diversity across nations* (pp. 87–102). Philadelphia: Temple University Press.

HRC. (2003). The state of the workplace for lesbian, gay, bisexual and transgender Americans 2002. Washington, DC: Human Rights Campaign Foundation.

Hunt, G. (2002). Organized labour, sexual diversity, and Union Activism in Canada. In F. Colgan & S. Ledwith (Eds.), *Gender, diversity and trade unions: International perspectives* (pp. 257–274). London: Routledge.

Hunt, G. (1999). No longer outsiders: Labor's response to sexual diversity in Canada. In G. Hunt (Ed.), *Laboring for rights: Unions and sexual diversity across nations* (pp. 10–36). Philadelphia: Temple University Press.

Kinsey, A., Pomeroy, W.B., & Martin, C.E. (1948). *Sexual behaviour in the human male*. New York: Saunders.

Krupat, K., & McCreery, P. (2001). *Out at work: Building a gay-labor alliance*. Minneapolis: University of Minnesota Press.

Mitchell, J. (1999, June). The pink ceiling. *The Globe and Mail Report on Business Magazine*, 78–84.

Stewart, J. (1997, 21 July). Coming out at Chrysler. *The New Yorker*, 38–49.

Yang, A. (1999). *From wrongs to rights, 1973–1999: Public opinion on gay and lesbian Americans moves toward equality*. Washington, DC: Policy Institute of the National Gay and Lesbian Task Force.

Wilcox, C., & Wolpert, R. (2000). Gay rights in the public sphere: Public opinion on gay and lesbian equality. In C. Rimmerman, K. Wald, & C. Wilcox (Eds.), *The politics of gay rights* (pp. 409–432). Chicago: University of Chicago Press.

Yeager, K. (1999). *Trailblazers: Profiles of America's gay and lesbian elected officials*. New York: The Hawthorn Press.

A LETTER FROM AN AMERICAN FACTORY WORKER

Dale G. Ross

Michael Whitty

University of Detroit Mercy

A former employee of a large Big Three auto supplier finally began to look at the situation he found himself in and drafted a letter to the president of the company. He wrote:

Dear Mr. President:

It has taken over a year to understand what happened to me on my job. I never wanted to really deliberately come out, but more, I wanted to try to downplay the seriousness of it all. I was hoping that most other people respected me and liked me well enough to accept me for who I am. But I was wrong. These people zeroed in on me when I admitted I was gay. In fact, the bosses' harassment started when I let only one person know my secret. It is now that I am learning how their discrimination has caused me to have low self-esteem, depression, dependencies, shame, guilt, on and on.

I also learned that it's all a pack of lies. I find it hard to write this down, so I have to put it down a little each day. I am usually depressed after I write. I am not doing well financially but I survive. I was soaring for about 2 years when I worked. Now I am barely able to work and pay taxes. I owe federal and local property taxes and I'm not making it. When I think that other peoples' ignorance did this to me, I feel just destroyed.

Let me tell you how it happened that I have the need to come out of the closet. I have always kept my private life to myself, but I do occasionally take on odd jobs for people. One day a person I only knew at work discussed a car problem that he had. I offered to fix it for him. So he had it towed over to my house, and I replaced the head gasket. During the few days his car was at my house, I invited him inside and he met my live-in lover. This was not a deliberate act of coming out, but more just common hospitality. A month or so later, I began being harassed by a production supervisor on the job. I didn't understand his attitude toward me. No matter how hard I tried, he constantly complained to my boss. I complained to the union, I complained to the department management, but I was not defended. So I used my seniority position to bump off to another department. Then weeks later I overhead my old boss talking. He said that I had screwed the department by quitting and they wasted all that training on me. Then the rumors started getting back to me about one bed at my house and two men living there. Where do you think all these strangers heard that? Some friend.

I do feel that you should know what happened to finally cause me to give up and quit. There were several different versions of the same threats against me. The most complete description was from an officer of my own union. He stopped me in the aisle as I was walking by. He asked me why I told everyone that I was gay. I told him that I am no longer willing to hide out and lie and I need to be truthful for myself. It is a hateful thing to have to deny your own identity out of shame, especially when that shame is placed on you by others who are adulterers, drunkards, crackheads, and downright lazy.

According to this union officer, "People who are smiling to your face, some of them you know really well, are talking about doing you bodily harm. Maybe possibly kill you, but I'm not going to tell you who said these things. I just don't want to see you get hurt. So be careful where you go around this plant and watch over your shoulder because some people are not who you think they are." By then, I had been harassed by the bosses and coworkers, I had my truck stolen from a company parking lot, and now a union official (who took an oath to stand by me) believed he was helping me by telling me to be afraid at work, going in and coming out of the shop. I can't even go fishing or hunting with anyone. This guy wants to hurt me, but no names; just hearsay.

I loved my job. I never made any kind of sexual advance in your plant in 4 years, yet so many people were worried that I would. I have never been so insulted in my life. My depression went haywire for awhile and I'm in therapy. It took me over a year to write this. I don't know whether to congratulate you on getting gays out of your shop, or to offer you my deepest sympathy for losing a man.

Bitterly, but with love,
XXXXX XXXXX

Discussion Questions

1. How do incidents such as this do harm to the business system as well as victimized individuals?
2. Does diversity training reach down to the frontline supervision in most companies that have some formal policies?
3. What are the special challenges to diversity training regarding inclusion of sexual orientation? What would be most effective in a "blue collar" setting? What is the union's role?
4. What might this factory worker's motivation(s) be for writing such a letter?

CHALLENGES

M. June Allard
Worcester State College

Goal
- To increase awareness of, and sensitivity to, the difficulties posed by physical challenges by *experiencing* such challenges.

MANIPULATION CHALLENGES

Directions
1. Take thick fat rubber bands and tie each thumb against its palm (or use latex gloves with thumbs not inserted in finger tubes, but resting against the palm).
2. Try the following exercises specified by your instructor:

- Thread a needle
- Tie a laced shoe
- Comb hair
- Button sweater, shirt, blouse
- Put on lipstick
- Unscrew a jar lid
- Peel a banana or orange
- Open a sealed cereal box
- Hold flip top can and open it
- Open can with nonelectric can opener

- Put on earrings
- Take class notes
- Open a potato chip bag
- Pare a potato
- Tie a bow
- Put on socks
- Brush teeth
- Get dressed
- Knit or crochet
- Buckle a belt

VISION CHALLENGES
- Thread a needle blindfolded
- Eat a meal blindfolded

HEARING CHALLENGES
- Watch a favorite TV show with the sound turned off and try to understand what is going on.

160

PERCEPTUAL-MOTOR CHALLENGE

Directions

1. Prop a mirror (8" by 10" or larger) on a table against some books or other object. Tilt mirror back slightly. Sit at the table facing the mirror.
2. Place the pattern supplied by your instructor flat on the table in front of the mirror.
3. Prepare to trace the pattern by looking at the pattern **only** in the mirror.
4. Cover the hand holding the pencil so that pattern cannot be viewed directly.
5. Looking at the pattern in the mirror, trace between the pattern bands *trying not to touch the outlines*. Record the time it takes to completely trace the pattern.

MUSICAL CHAIRS

M. June Allard
Worcester State College

Goal

To experience how it feels to be physically challenged; that is, unable to communicate with people in the traditional way.

Instructions

1. Form a group of four to six members and arrange your chairs in a circle.
2. Read the following passage to yourself.

   Fifty students reported for a class that had 35 student desk-chairs: 30 RH (right hand) and five LH (Left Hand). Fifteen RH students then volunteered to transfer to an honors section down the hall, thereby leaving everyone in the original class seated.

   After class, six RH students and one LH student reported their chairs were broken and needed replacing. Later that afternoon the honors instructor called saying eight of the transfer students were not eligible for the honors class and were, therefore, returning to the original class. How many additional RH and LH desk-chairs did the original instructor need for his class?

3. **Working as a group,** use **one** worksheet to come to some consensus on the answer to the question posed in the passage.
4. Your instructor will give you further special instructions on how your group will conduct the exercise.

MUSICAL CHAIRS WORKSHEET

Additional Chairs Needed: _____ *RH* _____ *LH*

ACCOMMODATING CHALLENGES

M. June Allard
Worcester State College

Under the ADA (Americans with Disabilities Act), employers may not discriminate in the hiring of persons with disabilities. Further, employers are required to provide reasonable accommodations to enable individuals with disabilities to perform their jobs and communicate effectively.

Notes: Tax incentives are provided for "qualified architectural and transportation barrier removal expenses." The employer is not required, however, to provide accommodations primarily for personal use such as hearing aids and wheelchairs.

Goal

- To raise awareness of physical challenges from the management perspective by focusing on *accommodating* such challenges.

Directions

1. Form groups of four or five.
2. Read the Sunday newspaper job ads. Select two ads for jobs. Make them as different as possible: different types of jobs, different levels, different industries. Try to select jobs for which someone in your group has some familiarity.
3. Your instructor will assign a physical challenge for each of your jobs.
4. Assume that someone with the physical challenge assigned to each of your jobs is by far the best-qualified candidate for the job. Research those disabilities, noting how many Americans are afflicted. Devise accommodations appropriate for the challenge.

SOURCES

The office of Disability Employment Policy, part of the U.S. Department of Labor, maintains JAN (Job Accommodation Network), a valuable resource on work site accommodations:

http://www.jan.wvu.edu/soar/disabilities.html
http://www.janweb.icdi.wvu/media

DILEMMAS AT VALLEY TECH

John E. Oliver

Sarah Ann Bartholomew

Valdosta State University

Dean Harold Warren sat in his office looking at his computer screen, which displayed the Department of Justice Americans with Disabilities Act (ADA) homepage. Dean Warren was wrestling with a real problem. "Does Dr. Johnson's abusive behavior result from a mental disorder that may make him eligible for protection under the ADA, or should I just deal with the abuse and sexual harassment complaints against him without regard to any mental disorder?"

That very morning, Dean Warren had received two complaints. The manager of an electronics store in the local mall had called to tell Dean Warren that Dr. Johnson had actually struck a female employee in the store. The second complaint was from a Valley Tech secretary, who said she had been sexually harassed by Dr. Johnson on a number of occasions.

DEAN HAROLD WARREN

Harold Warren obtained bachelor of science and master of science degrees from Ivy League colleges in New England and worked in industry for several years before attending one of the nation's finest engineering schools to pursue a doctorate. Upon completion of his Ph.D., he taught at a prestigious private university before taking the position of dean of faculties at Valley Tech, where he's been dean for over 10 years.

Dean Warren is known as a confident, incisive decision maker who studies issues thoroughly and solicited the participation of others before making decisions. Once he has heard the opinions of all concerned and makes his decision, he rarely changes his mind. Dean Warren is a goal-oriented leader, and most decisions lead toward the achievement of some objective. He has little patience for side issues that do not lead toward goal accomplishment. In the university culture, in which change comes slowly if ever, Dean Warren is known as an administrator who encourages change. His drive toward improvement sometimes leads those who are slow to adjust to feel stressed and pressured. Those resisting change are usually ignored; those who embraced change are rewarded for their efforts.

DR. RICHARD JOHNSON

Dr. Johnson is a tenured professor who has been at Valley Tech for over 20 years. He was hired during the late 1970s when Ph.D.s in his field were hard to find. Shortly after his arrival, complaints started coming in. It is said that Dr. Johnson is harsh and abusive to students, calling them lazy and stupid and refusing to answer "dumb" questions. Students often avoid his classes. Two foreign students awakened the college president one evening to complain that Dr. Johnson had called them "dumb *ucking" Indians. Faculty members complain of being yelled at and called names by Dr. Johnson. Several clients of the college's Research and Development Institute have called the institute director to complain that Dr. Johnson flirts with the female employees and speaks abusively to others. The wife of one faculty member saw Dr. Johnson ejected from a local health club by a sheriff's deputy for harassing a female member. Students who are employed as waiters and waitresses in the community say he is regularly abusive in his treatment of them.

Academic tenure is awarded to faculty members who are evaluated by their peers and supervisors to be competent in three areas—teaching, service, and professional development. Teaching is often measured by student evaluations and other criteria. Service is measured by positions on college committees, service to the profession, and service to the community. Professional development includes publication in professional journals and books as well as other criteria.

Dr. Johnson's teaching evaluations are the lowest in his department, as a result of his treatment of students. His service on college committees is also the lowest because of his abuse of fellow faculty and his sarcasm. Dr. Johnson's publication record, though, is exceptional and contributes to the national reputation and accreditation of the school. He regularly publishes several articles and books with a number of other faculty in the school. He seems to be nice to his coauthors as long as they provide help in his research. He shows little regard, however, for those who will not work with him. In spite of complaints like these, which began early in his career, Dr. Johnson was awarded tenure before Dean Warren arrived at Valley Tech.

THE RECENT COMPLAINTS

The two recent complaints are the most bothersome. A charge of sexual harassment of a secretary holds a potential high risk for Valley Tech. The secretary has been an excellent employee for 5 years. Her account of the incidents leading up to her reporting them to Dean Warren is particularly troubling. Over a period of time, Dr. Johnson's behavior toward her has become increasingly menacing. She states that Dr. Johnson's actions have made her physically ill and she has begun to have nightmares about him. Something has to be done.

In addition, the complaint from the store manager indicates that Dr. Johnson's behavior has progressed from verbal abuse to physical. The manager has not given Dean Warren specific details about the incident, but has indicated that he feels someone at Valley Tech "should be made aware of the danger." Dean Warren cannot imagine what would prompt a mature professional male to hit a young female clerk in a retail establishment. In fact, Dean Warren cannot imagine why a formal criminal charge has not been filed in the mail incident or in any of the other incidents involving Dr. Johnson over the years.

NARCISSISTIC PERSONALITY DISORDER

While talking with a psychologist at a cocktail party, Dean Warren asked what would cause a person to behave as Dr. Johnson behaved. "That behavior could be indicative of a serious personality disorder that is often associated with violence in the workplace." She continued, "People suffering from narcissistic personality disorder need the respect and admiration of others, but act in ways that tend to alienate those others. Narcissists are preoccupied with themselves and their own desires. They have no ability to see others' points of view or imagine their feelings. They are also alienated from their own feelings because those feelings are unacceptable even to themselves. They are filled with fear, anger, and self-loathing, but unconsciously deny these feelings and project them onto others. In this way, they avoid the intolerable pain that would be caused by owning those feelings. They create a self-image of themselves as good, smart, righteous, superior people.

"Narcissists justify their own unacceptable behavior through rationalization and distortion. They reinterpret events so that others are guilty and they are innocent. Their lack of empathy and respect for others come out as sarcasm and criticism. They overstimate their own abilities and accomplishments and devalue those of other people. They develop self-serving explanations in which positive outcomes are attributed to themselves and negative outcomes are attributed to others. Therefore, they feel free to exploit others to get what they want. Paradoxically, while narcissists need the admiration of others, they alienate them through exploitation, lack of empathy, criticism, and sarcasm. They themselves respond to criticism with either cool indifference or rage."

"What happens to a person to make him that way?" asked Dean Warren. About that time, the psychologist's spouse joined the conversation.

"Could be an abusive childhood," he said. "That's what seems to cause everything else! But don't worry, I think the ADA (Americans with Disabilities Act) makes everybody a victim, so there's probably nothing you can do about it."

"Is that true?" Dean Warren asked, turning to the psychologist.

"It is true that personality disorders are disabilities specifically mentioned in the ADA," said the psychologist, "but I think it's more complicated than that. If you think this guy might have narcissistic personality disorder, you might want to research it before you do anything."

ADA

Dean Warren left the cocktail party and went to his office. He got on the Internet and searched for the Americans with Disabilities Act which was part of the Department of Justice homepage (www.usdoj.gov/crt/ada/pubs/ada.txt). He found Title I of the ADA which was signed into law in 1990. He read and read, but it was difficult to find what he was looking for: clear definitions and information about what to do. He thought that maybe some of the other sites would be of more help.

Dean Warren found other Internet sites explaining the ADA, narcissistic personality disorder, and workplace violence by searching the web (see Figure 1). He also consulted Valley Tech's sexual harassment policy (see Figure 2) and statement on violent or criminal behavior (see Figure 3). After about an hour, Dean Warren began to understand his dilemma a lot better. "This information makes my decision a lot easier," he thought.

Discussion Questions

1. Before researching the issues in this case, what was your *initial* reaction to Dean Warren's dilemma?

After researching the issues, answer the following questions:

2. What useful information did you find on the Internet, in the library, or in other sources that will help you make your decision?
3. What did your sources say about personality disorders and the responsibilities of individuals and organizations in managing behavior and accommodations for emotional disabilities under the ADA?
4. If you were Dean Warren, what would you do? Your answers should be based on research findings.
5. What are the potential dangers to the organization of continued employment of Dr. Johnson? Of terminating Dr. Johnson?

FIGURE 1   Internet Sites Found by Dean Warren

a. Narcissistic Personality Disorder
   www.mhsource.com/disorders/nar.html
   www.cmhcsys.com/disorders/3×36t.htm

b. Americans with Disabilities Act (ADA)
   janweb.icdi.wvu.edu/Kinder/overview.htm
   www.ljextra.com/practice/laboremployment/0602psych.html

c. Workplace Violence
   members.aol.com/endwpv

It is the policy of Valley Tech to prevent and eliminate sexual harassment in any campus division, department, or work unit by any faculty or staff employee, administrator, supervisor, or student. It is further the college's policy not to tolerate any practice or behavior that constitutes sexual harassment.

1.   What is IT?

Sexual harassment occurs when advances are "unwelcome." It is defined as a form of sex discrimination which is illegal under Title VII of the Civil Rights Act of 1964 for employees and under Title IX of the Education Amendments of 1972.

Sexual harassment may be verbal, visual, or physical. It may be indirect or as overt as a suggestion that a person could receive a higher grade or pay raise by admission to sexual advances. The suggestion may not be direct, but implied from the conduct, circumstances, and relationship between the involved individuals. Sexual harrassment may consist of persistent, unwanted attempts to change a professional or educational relationship to a personal one. Sexual harrassment can range from sexual flirtations and put-downs to serious physical abuses such as sexual assault or rape.

Examples of harassment include unwelcome sexual advances; "repeated" sexually oriented kidding, teasing, joking, or flirting; verbal abuse of a sexual nature; graphic commentary about an individual's body, sexual prowess, or sexual deficiencies; derogatory or demeaning comments about women or men in general, whether sexual or not; leering, whistling, touching, pinching, or brushing against another's body; offensive crude language; or displaying objects or pictures which are sexual in nature that would create hostile or offensive work environments. Sexual harassment creates an atmosphere that is not conducive for effective teaching, learning, and working.

2.   WHO is affected?

It could happen to YOU! Sexual harassment is not limited to females only; males as well as females fall victim to sexual harassment daily. Research in higher education indicates that about 1/3 of females enrolled in research universities experience sexual harassment. At moderately sized universities, research indicates that about 1/4 of the female students experience sexual harassment from a professor or supervisor. Incidence research shows 3 to 12 percent of male students harassed (Roscoe, Goodwin, Repp, and Rose, 1987). Fitzgerald (1988) reports that administrative women experience more harassment, and between 20 and 49 percent of women faculty have experienced some level of sexual harassment at work.

3.   HOW can I protect myself?

Prevention is the best tool for the elimination of sexual harassment. You should be aware and have knowledge of the sexual harassment policy which has been set forth by Valley Tech, and should not be reluctant to express your strong disapproval of any action taken against you. If you are in a situation in which you feel sexually harassed, overwhelmed, or threatened . . . **do not ignore it, do not resign, and do not stop attending classes.** You should seek assistance at the OFFICE OF EQUAL EMPLOYMENT OPPORTUNITY.

4.   WHAT should I do, if confronted?

DO NOT GIVE UP! DO NOT GIVE IN!

You should:

a. Make it clear to the harasser you do not like his/her actions

b. Keep a written record of all harassing activities

c. Notify a few colleagues or fellow students of the problem. They can observe and corroborate your claims

d. Contact your Affirmative Action Officer

e. DON'T blame yourself!

5.   If I am a victim, how do I file a report? What can be done?

Any acts, or accusations, of sexual harassment should be reported as soon as possible. The incident will be discussed informally, professionally, and confidentially. If appropriate, an attempt will be made to resolve the problem through informal procedures. (No formal action on the alleged charge will be taken unless initiated by the complainant).

If informal efforts to resolve an incident are unsuccessful, formal procedures exist which allow parties an opportunity to pursue a resolution. A complete investigation will be conducted expeditiously, assuring maximum confidentiality. If a complaint is found to be valid and charges result, confidentiality is not guaranteed, and appropriate disciplinary action will be instituted.

FIGURE 2   Valley Tech Harassment Policy

The Public Safety Department provides police assistance 24 hours. Officers are certified police officers and have been trained to respond to hostile/violent actions. Immediately contact the Public Safety Department if hostile or violent behavior, actual or potential, is witnessed.

1. **Initiate immediate contact with the Public Safety Department to ensure that a timely response has begun before a situation becomes uncontrollable.**

2. **Leave the immediate area whenever possible and direct others to do so.**

3. **Should gunfire or explosives endanger the campus, you should take cover immediately using all available concealment. Close and lock doors when possible to separate yourself and others from the armed suspect.**

FIGURE 3   Violent or Criminal Behavior

DOES SOCIAL CLASS MAKE A DIFFERENCE?

Carol P. Harvey
Assumption College

Social class, which is usually determined by a combination of one's income, education, and occupation, may be less visible than other types of difference. However, in many countries where individualism is valued, it is common to believe that all people are created equal and that the same opportunities are available to everyone who has the innate talent and is willing to put in the effort. However, this position ignores the challenge of overcoming the social, educational, and networking resources of class origins. For example, the U.S. General Accounting Office reported that suburban school districts spend up to 10 times more on their public school systems than urban districts (U.S. GAO, 1997).

This exercise is designed to help you to understand how social class *could* affect a person's life experience due to differences in access and resources. Although social class in childhood does *not* necessarily determine status across one's life span, it may limit educational and career options. This may make it more difficult for a person to achieve his/her career and personal goals. Of course, individuals within a social class can have very different experiences due to a variety of factors.

DIRECTIONS

Complete the following two columns by thinking about what is apt to be the more common experience of a child growing up in Justin's or Clark's situation. Considering that Justin represents a child born into the lower socioeconomic class and Clark represents one born into the upper middle class, your answers should reflect what is likely to be the more common experiences for children born into these situations.

Justin was born to a 16-year-old single mother who lived with her family in an inner-city housing project. When he was born, she dropped out of high school to care for him. After he started school, she took a job

172

cleaning rooms in a local hospital. She is currently studying nights to get her General Equivalency Diploma (GED), so that she can get a better job.

Clark was born to a suburban couple in their mid-thirties. His mother has an MBA, and his father is a lawyer. Clark's mother quit her job when he was born. She returned to a managerial position when his younger sibling was in junior high.

	Justin	Clark
How might this child spend his time before he attends kindergarten?		
Why does this matter?		
When he goes to kindergarten, he is diagnosed with a learning disability. What types of help is he most likely to receive?		
Why might these resources be somewhat different for these two boys?		
During grammar school, how is he likely to spend his school vacations?		
Why does this matter?		
What types of after-school activities is he likely to participate in?		
What difference could this make in their lives?		
What role may sports play in his life?		

Why may these roles be quite different for these boys?		
As a teenager, who are most apt to be his role models?		
He needs help with math in high school. What types of resources are most apt to be available to him?		
Where can he learn about technology and develop computer expertise?		
If his College Board scores aren't too high, what resources may be available to help him raise his scores?		
What are his three most likely life choices after high school?		
Why may these differ? Who has a better chance of graduating from high school? Why?		
If he goes to college, how are his expenses paid?		
How could this impact his grades or experiences in college?		
If he needs an internship in college, who can help him secure one?		
Given the differences of growing up in different social classes, what job-related life and career skills may he have that give him workplace advantages or disadvantages?		

Discussion Questions

1. In terms of the workplace, how does social class matter?
2. Is social class *really* an invisible difference or are there ways that people often deduce other's social class origins? What can be the effect of this in job interviews, work related social situations, etc.
3. Do you think that the concept of "privilege" as explored in Peggy McIntosh's "White Privilege and Male Privilege. . . " article also apply to social class privilege? Why or why not?
4. What role does the media play in perpetuating both positive and negative social class stereotypes? Support your answer with examples.
5. In this exercise, both people were male and no specific race was suggested. Which of your answers might have been different, if the examples were female or nonwhite? Why?

Writing Assignments

1. There are many programs and organizations such as Head Start, the Nativity Schools, Big Brothers and Big Sisters, Boys and Girl's Clubs, Girls Inc., etc. that attempt to help individuals to overcome some of the effects of social class. Research and visit one of these organizations to better understand their mission and the roles that they play in providing access and opportunity. Specifically, how can these organizations change the life experiences and access to resources for children from lower classes?
2. Spend a day in a school that is the opposite from your own grammar or high school experience. If you attended a private school, arrange to visit an inner-city school. If you attended a school that was predominately lower or working class, arrange to visit a private school. Analyze any differences that you observe in terms of student body, dress, the academic experience, faculty, physical plant, athletic and after-school activities. Try to interview students and faculty about their perceptions of the total educational experience at the school. How does what you learned from this visit relate to this exercise? How does it translate into "privileges" in the workplace?

References

Anyton, J. (2003). Inner cities, affluent suburbs, and unequal educational opportunity. In J.A. Banks & C.A. McGee Banks (Eds.), *Multicultural education: Issues and perspectives* (pp. 85–102). New York: Wiley.

Mantsios, G. (1998). Media magic: Making class invisible. In P. Rothenberg (Ed.), *Race, class, and gender in the United States: An integrated study* (pp. 563–571). New York: St. Martin's Press.

U.S. General Accounting Office (GAO) (1997). *School finance: State efforts to reduce funding gaps between poor and wealthy districts*. Washington, DC: U.S. Government Printing Office.

RELIGION, CULTURE, AND MANAGEMENT IN THE NEW MILLENNIUM

Asha Rao

Rutgers University

Spirituality could be the ultimate competitive advantage.
—Ian Mitroff, A Spiritual Audit of Corporate America

Across the country, major-league executives are meeting for prayer breakfasts and spiritual conferences. In Minneapolis, 150 business chiefs lunch monthly at a private ivy-draped club to hear chief executives such as Medtronic Inc's William George and Carlson Co's Marilyn Carlson Nelson draw business solutions from the Bible. In Silicon Valley, a group of high-powered, high-tech Hindus—including Suhas Patil, founder of Cirrus Logic, Desh Despande, founder of Cascade Communications, and Krishna Kalra, founder of BioGenex—are part of a movement to connect technology to spirituality.
—Business Week, Nov. 1999

As we end a millennium and move into the twenty-first century, the world of business and management is turbulent and evolving faster than it has in the past. We live and work in "Internet time" where firms form, go public, and disband before decision trees and 5-year plans can be developed (Conlin, 1999). In this time of rapid change, there seems to be a renewed interest in old traditions: spirituality and religion in business. American CEOs and executives are drawing on the Bible, Bhagvad Gita, Talmud, and other scriptures for inspiration (Brahm, 1999; Conlin, 1999; Leigh, 1997).

The trend is not limited to the United States; Asian leaders have espoused the role of "Asian values" derived from Confucianism in the rapid economic development of the ASEAN region (*The Economist,* 1992; Hofstede and

Bond, 1988). In countries ranging from India to Burma to France, religion has played a part in management processes and economic development (or the lack thereof). At an individual level, we now truly live in a global village where more people than ever are internationally mobile or work in cross-cultural environments in global teams, which are often temporary or even virtual teams (Adler, 1997; Conlin, 1999). Consequently, people are directly affected by the cultural beliefs, religious norms, and practices of others.

This article examines the role of religion or faith in culturally derived values, beliefs, and management practices across the globe and discusses the implications for international managers. It focuses on work issues raised by major religions or faiths such as Christianity, Confucianism, Hinduism, Islam, and Judaism to examine their impact on management today, and potentially for the future. Although some of these religions directly affect the behavior of people at work, others have a more subtle effect through ethnic culture.

CONCEPTUAL FRAMEWORK

The statistics indicate that 95 percent of Americans say that they believe in God or a religious faith, and 48 percent bring religion into the workplace (Conlin, 1999). Our future global leaders, the presidential candidates in the current U.S. elections, report turning to the Bible for advice on a range of their decisions (*New York Times,* 2000). United State's attendance rates at religious services are among the highest in the world (Gannon, 1994). Recent reports suggest that top executives from a range of firms believe that faith has an impact on the bottom line (Conlin, 1999). Indeed, Ian Mitroff states that in the new millennium, spirituality could be the ultimate competitive advantage by raising productivity in the workplace (Mitroff, 1999).

The impact of religion is not always blatant or intentional. It can have an indirect, more subtle impact through national or ethnic culture. For instance, the concept of the 5-day workweek in the West is firmly rooted in Christianity, but most Christians or even Americans see this as an accepted business practice rather than a religious one. To understand the subtle impact of religion on business today, one needs to understand national or ethnic cultures.

CULTURE

Three critical mechanisms explain the origins of different cultures. They are religion, language, and geographical proximity (Ronen and Shenkar, 1985). Because religion is only one of three determinants of culture, it is clear that cultures sharing religious roots can differ because of variations in the latter two mechanisms. This explains the differences in cultures between the Latin American cluster and the Anglo cluster. The power of religion is evident in the similarities of culture in the Islamic nations and in the overseas Chinese. Cultural bonds, or the collective programming, is usually difficult to break even later in adulthood. We maintain culturally derived values, beliefs, and behavior

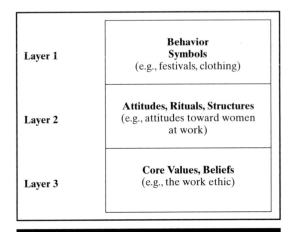

Layer 1	**Behavior** **Symbols** (e.g., festivals, clothing)
Layer 2	**Attitudes, Rituals, Structures** (e.g., attitudes toward women at work)
Layer 3	**Core Values, Beliefs** (e.g., the work ethic)

FIGURE 1   The Culture Pit and Religion

in the workplace and even when traveling across cultures as demonstrated by much research in the field of cross-cultural management (Adler, 1997).

Cultures have several layers, as depicted in Figure 1.

Elements in layer one change with time. These include language, clothing, or appearance and behavior. These elements are based on the deeper levels of culture. At the next level lie attitudes and rituals—key among them being the attitude toward women in the workplace. These too can change with time, but they adapt at a much slower pace. At the core of the culture, in the third layer, lie values and beliefs that are stable, often across generations, and relatively impermeable to the passage of time. Religious beliefs and practices can be linked to each layer of culture. The following discussion begins with the bottom layer and draws upon it in examining the upper layers of culture.

RELIGION AND CULTURAL VALUES

The impact of religion at the level of core values and beliefs is strong. Take for instance the meaning of work in different cultures, cultural assumptions, and ethics. Religions differ in their emphasis on the role of work in life. Much has been written about the Protestant Work Ethnic, which helps explain the critical- ity of work in the United States. Succinctly, the ethic holds that a good Protestant will work hard on earth and be successful in order to reap rewards later in heaven. A person's work, or their calling, comes from God. In working hard, people make evident their worth to both God and themselves. In the United States, the Protestant ethic was joined by Social Darwinism, as so well expressed by Russell Conwell, a Methodist minister and the first president of Temple University (Burr, 1917). He extolled his followers, "I say you ought to be rich; you have no right to be poor . . . I must say that you ought to spend some time getting rich." He went on to conclude that it was absurd to believe that peo- ple should not want wealth, because wealth enables people to truly accomplish something of value on earth (Gannon, 1991). In this fashion, the work value is united with both drive and a high need for achievement in the United States.

Other religions also speak of the value of work. The book of Islam, the Quran, indicates that work is an obligation. Indeed, the prophet Muhammad was a trader by profession. But Islam also breeds an element of fatalism in the workplace, letting employees off the hook, because destiny is in the hand of God, who is the ultimate creator of wealth (Rice, 1999). Hindu philosophy offers *dharma* (duty) as one of the four means to salvation. This aspect of Hindu religion espoused in the *Bhagvad Gita* as *karma,* which represents work or duty without an attachment towards immediate rewards. Kalra, founder and CEO of BioGenex laboratories says, "The *Bhagvad Gita* teaches that I have rights on action, but no rights on the fruits of action, nor should I be attached to inaction as a result. So I have the right to be the best CEO but no right to how much money I can earn . . . As a result of this, I have no fear of failure, and I can take risks," (Brahm, 1999).

Work helps the Hindu earn a living, satisfy worldly interests, gain power and status, and take care of the family (Gannon, 1994). But, Hinduism dictates that the role of work changes during different stages in life. The role of work is strongest in the second stage of life, where the *grahasta* is obliged to work and fulfil his duty to society. At later stages, the Hindu needs to withdraw from worldly accomplishments such as work to focus on the search for the truth.

Differences in power relations can also be traced back to religions. For instance, Confucius declared that the stability of society is based on unequal relationships and listed five basic and unequal relationships as follows: father–son, husband–wife, ruler–subject, older brother–younger brother, older friend–younger friend. This philosophy helps explain the power differentials between men and women, bosses and subordinates, and the relevance of seniority in cultures such as China, Japan, and Korea. Also, these relationships are held together by mutual and complementary obligations, which helps explain the power of *guanxi* in Chinese business (Leong and Tung, 1998).

Religion and culture have been linked to economic development. In one analysis, cultures where long-term values of persistence, ordered relationships, thrift, and a sense of shame were dominant tended to experience rapid economic growth. Cultures that clung to short-term Confucian values of personal steadiness, face, tradition, and reciprocity of favors tended to be slow developers (Hofstede and Bond, 1988). Taking this a level higher, the rulers of South Korea and Singapore have long used Confucian principles as a means of societal change and control.

Religion and Ethics

Religious values and management interface in discussions of ethics and social responsibility but surface in different forms in different cultures (Laczniak, 1999; Rice, 1999; Vogel, 1992). U.S. firms today are formulating codes of ethical conduct for their employees worldwide. In trying to explain why the level of public interest in business ethics in the United States exceeds that in the rest of the world, Vogel (1992) draws upon America's Protestant heritage, which makes the creation of wealth "God's work"; it raises people's expectations of the moral behavior of businesspeople. Most Americans also believe that these ethics are or should be universal, compared to Eastern cultures that allow for situational or contextual variations (Trompenaars, 1993).

In discussing Islamic ethics, Rice (1999) states that Islam requires the free-market system to be complemented by a moral filter so that scarce resources are equitably distributed in society. The religion stresses brotherhood, equality, and socioeconomic justice for all. In the Gulf countries, oil has brought amazing wealth to a few, but interestingly that wealth has also trickled down to the masses through social welfare programs. *Zakat,* or alms tax, is one of the five pillars of Islam.[1] According to Rice, the Quranic injunction "there is no compulsion in religion" leads people to follow a strong moral code.

Jewish business ethics also acknowledge the centrality of the community (Pava, 1998) as reflected in three talmudic principles. First is the recognition of different levels of responsibility for charity; second, the *Kofin* principles "formalize a minimum standard. If B's situation can improve at no cost to A, A should willingly waive legal rights." Third, *lifnim mishurat hadin* calls for ethical conduct beyond meeting legal norms. The emphasis on community over wealth is apparent in Brahm's (1999) account of Arron Feuerstein's (President/CEO, Malden Mills Industries) decision to keep his mill open and his employees on the payroll even after the mill burned down. Feuerstein drew on the teachings of the Talmud, which stress that money is not as crucial as taking care of others and acquiring a good name, which is "the greatest treasure a man can acquire." Feuerstein paid his employees for the next few months and was rewarded with his employees' motivation and loyalty.

These contrasting approaches show that global religions focus on different aspects of ethics. It is interesting to note that in the United States the focus is on creating ethical codes of conduct to control managerial behavior such as bribery and the misuse of resources, whereas Islamic societies focus on the welfare of all, that is, socioeconomic issues.

ATTITUDES, SOCIAL STRUCTURES AND THE CONCEPT OF TIME

The concepts discussed in this section are based on the values and core assumptions described in the previous one, but these include rituals or artifacts that are observable as well as discernable attitudes that are based on core values. Some of the key concepts include attitudes such as those towards women and work, and structures such as the Hindu caste system, Islamic banking, and ethical codes such as Catholic Social Teaching (Laczniak, 1999).

Women in Management

Sadly, most religions can be held accountable for the lower status of women in the workforce. Christianity, Islam, Hinduism, Judaism, and Confucianism all assign women to nurturing, family primary roles, allowing for power differentials between men and women. In the United States, the Southern Baptist Convention recently declared that wives should be submissive to their husbands (*New York Times,* 2000). Fundamentalist leaders in different cultures have used religion to drastically limit the ability of women to acquire an education and to participate in the workforce (for example, the Taliban in Afghanistan).

The beliefs on the appropriate role of women in society affect state policy. For instance, until 1977 the Federal Republic of Germany had laws that gave husbands the right to prevent their wives from working outside the home. In South Africa, a husband could control his wife's right to negotiate and undertake contracts until 1984 (Adler and Israeli, 1988). In a more indirect fashion, the family primary role advocated for women legitimizes the social limits to their career choices along with business practices such as unequal pay for equal work prevalent in most cultures (Adler and Israeli, 1988).

Social Hierarchies and Business Codes

Although educated Indians deem caste a medieval degeneration, it has been a basic feature of Hindu society. The caste system mandated a religious division of labor into four castes of priests (*brahamans*), warriors (*kshatryias*), businessfolk (*vaishyas*) and workers (*sudras*). The discriminatory negative consequences of this inherited division of labor are well known. Yet, much of Indian enterprise, in India and overseas, can be traced to the business families belonging to the *viashya* clans (Saha, 1993). The knowledge that it was their mandated role in society and centuries of specialization helped the *vaishya* business houses develop their skills.

In Islamic countries such as Saudi Arabia, business law is derived from the Quran and the Hadith. The fact that the prophet Mohammad prohibited *riba*, or unearned profit, has lead to the development of systems of Islamic banking where banks invest in business or enter into partnership so that the lender and borrower share the same risk and reward rather than profit from another's work.

SURFACE CULTURE

Values, core assumptions, attitudes, and rituals are manifested in the surface culture. This layer is paradoxically the most evident, yet the most mutable layer of culture. Some evident manifestations of the cultural layers include schedules and calendars, festivals, and the concept of the workweek.

Calendars, Schedules, and the Workweek

Although the 5-day workweek is common in many countries, it is most accepted in Christian ones. In 1992 when merchants in Montreal sought to overturn legislation that kept stores closed on Sunday, people raised the issue that even God rested on Sunday after creating the world and so should Quebec residents. The president of YKK (North America) found this to be a point of conflict between American and Japanese employees. The former hated working over weekends, which was a common practice for Japanese expatriates. He traced the difference to differences in faith or religion because the Japanese picked up the workweek concept from the Americans after World War II, and didn't take it too seriously (Ishino, 1994). Sunday has no religious significance for much of the world. In the Islamic world, the weekend begins on Thursday. In predominantly Hindu India, the workweek is 5-1/2 days.

Devout Christians go to church on Sunday, a holiday in the Western world, but Jews and Muslims have to make adjustments to manage the clash between their religious rituals and work. Given that Orthodox Jews cannot operate machines (such as cars) from Friday sundown to Saturday sundown, it poses a challenge for people who are asked to work late on Fridays. Prayer is one of the five pillars of Islam, and a devout Muslim must pray five times a day. A colleague in Princeton keeps a prayer mat rolled up in his drawer at work and schedules his prayer times between meetings.

Religious days for many groups including the Hindus and Muslims are determined by the lunar calendar and change from year to year. This is important for the modern business traveler because, across the globe, most mandated holidays are religious ones. Mapping them has become a business necessity and enterprise. Work slows down in the Muslim world during the month of Ramadan (the ninth month in the Islamic calendar) when people generally fast from sunrise to sunset and focus on prayer. A similar phenomenon occurs around Christmas in the United States and Diwali in India. In an interesting development in international negotiations, South Americans realized that U.S. businesspeople were tempted to make concessions and close deals so that they could return home for Christmas. They then scheduled negotiations around the holidays to gain an advantage (Adler, 1997).

Finally, religious norms often dictate dress in the workplace. In Islamic cultures where modesty is a virtue, women wear loose-fitting clothing in public. Women often wear the veil, which represents honor, dignity, chastity, purity, and integrity, to work. Devout Muslim men often have beards and wear skull caps. Jewish men, too, may wear skullcaps to work. In both religions, the cap is viewed as a symbol of subservience to their God.

Causes

The popular press suggests many motives for the current interest in religion and spirituality in the workplace. For one, the changing nature of business, especially in the high-technology area, leads managers into uncharted territory. Although the formal attendance rates at churches in the United States is high, the number usually increases during periods of crisis (Gannon, 1994). A potential explanation for the interest in religion is that the pace of change in the business environment, and the stress of working in this environment, creates an internal crisis that draws people to their religion.

Consequences

In sum, the impact of religion on management is widespread through its impact on culture. However, what we see happening today is a more direct application of religion and spirituality in the workforce by executives, rather than the incidental application through culture. The current belief is that this is conducive to the workplace because it spurs the development of employee programs such as on-site day care and flextime, enhances motivation, and increases productivity (Mitroff, 1999). But what of its consequence in a global economy? To some extent, it is positive because managers can theoretically schedule work to take advantage of religious differences—such as having non-Christians work over Christmas, and non-Muslims over Ramadan. But, on another level, it is bound to create conflict when different religious practices and beliefs collide. Conflicts that emerge from differences in beliefs and values are usually difficult to resolve because people become committed to positions based on principles and will not compromise (Lewicki, Litterer, and Saunders, 1988). Managers need to consider the implications of these trends and consider ways to deal with the negative consequences. Because religion and culture have many layers, some are more critical to people than others. Mapping the similarities and differences of dominant religions will help managers reduce conflict and build on universal norms. Unlike other management trends, religion is a personal issue at the core of most people's values. The inappropriate application of religious principles can have potentially dangerous consequences.

Discussion Questions

1. Identify a belief, value, or attitude of yours that you can attribute to your religion.
2. Examine its impact on your work and career.
3. How could your religion affect your role and performance in a multicultural workplace?
4. In small-group discussions, map some of the similarities and differences in religious beliefs, attitudes, and behavior of people following different world religions and faiths. Present your findings to the class.

References

Adler, N.J. (1997). *International Dimensions of Organizational Behavior*, Ohio: South Western.

Adler, N.J., and D.N. Israeli. (1988). *Woman in Management Worldwide*, Sharpe: Armonk, N.Y.

Alexandrin, G. (1993). "Elements of Buddhist Economies." *International Journal of Social Economics*, 20(2), pp. 3–11.

Ananth, S. (1998). *Vaastu: The Classical Indian Science of Architecture and Design*, Penguin: India.

Brahm, J. (1999). "The Spiritual Side." *Industry Week*, 248(3), pp. 48–56.

Burr, Agnes Rush. (1917). *Russell H. Conwell and His Work, One Man's Interpretation of Life*. Philadelphia: John C. Winston Company.

"Motorola's Cultural Sensitivity Pays Off from Hong Kong to Texas." *Business Week*, 1991.

Conlin, M. (1999). "Religion in the Workplace: The Growing Presence of Spirituality in Corporate America." *Business Week*, Nov. 1, pp. 151–159.

Copeland, L., and L. Griggs. (1985). *Going International*. New York: Random House.

Digh, P. "Religion in the Workplace: Make a Good-Faith Effort to Accommodate." *HR Magazine*, 43(13), pp. 84–91.

Ferraro, G.P. (1994). *The Cultural Dimensions of International Business*, Upper Saddle River, N.J.: Prentice Hall.

Flynn, G. (1988). "Accomodating Religion on the Job: Few Rules, Lots of Common Sense." *Workforce*, 77(9), pp. 94–97.

Gannon, M. (1994). *Understanding Global Cultures: Metaphorical Journeys Through 17 Countries*. Thousand Oaks, Calif: Sage.

Hofstede G. (1980). *Cultures Consequences: International Differences in Work Related Values*. Beverly Hills: Sage.

Hofstede, Geert, and Michael Harris Bond. "The Confucius Connection: From Cultural Roots to Economic Growth." *Organizational Dynamics*, Spring 1988, 16(4), pp. 4–22.

Ishino, Y. "Religion in Management," presented at McGill University, 1994.

Laczniak, G.R. (1999). "Distributive Justice, Catholic Social Teaching, and the Moral Responsibility of Marketeers." 18(1), pp. 125–129.

Leigh, P. (1997). "The New Spirit at Work." *Training and Development*, 51(3), pp. 26–33.

Lloyd, Bruce, and Trompenaars, Fons. (1993). "Culture and Change: Conflict or Consensus?" *Leadership and Organizational Journal*, 14(6), p. 17.

Mitroff, I. (1999). *A Spiritual Audit of Corporate America.* San Francisco: Jossey-Bass.

Pava, M.I. (1998). "The Substance of Jewish Business Ethics" *Journal of Business Ethics*, 17(6), pp. 603–617.

Rice, G. (1999). "Islamic Ethics and the Implications for Business." *Journal of Business Ethics*, 18(4), pp. 345–358.

Ronen, S., and O. Shenkar. (1985). "Clustering Countries on Attitudinal Dimensions: A Review and Synthesis." *Academy of Management Review*, 19(3), pp. 435–54.

Saha, A. (1993). "The Caste System in India and Its Consequences." *International Journal of Sociology and Social Policy*, 13(3), pp. 1–76.

"Teaching New Values." *The Economist*, Nov. 28, 1992, 325(7787), p. 31.

"The 2000 Campaign: Al Gore's Journey." *The New York Times*, October 22, 2000, p. 20.

Vogel, D. (1992). "The Globalization of Business Ethics: Why America Remains Distinctive." *California Management Review*, 35(1).

Yeung, I., and R. Tung. (1996). "Achieving Business Success in Confucian Societies: The Importance of Guanxi." *Organizational Dynamics*, 25(2), pp. 54–65.

Endnotes

1. The other four pillars are the belief in one God, *salat* or prayer, the observance of *ramadan,* and pilgrimage to Mecca in one's lifetime.

Internet Assignments

1. Examine the holidays and observances listed in the society and culture section of Yahoo! Compare the holidays for Buddhists, Christians, Hindus, Muslims, and Jews.

2. Examine the Web sites of some *Fortune* 500 firms to learn about their policy on religion in the workplace.

3. Universities often describe their policies on religious accommodation on their Web sites. (for example, www.uwo.ca/univsec/handbook/general/religiou.html) What is your university's policy on religious accommodation?

RELIGION AND WORK

Carol P. Harvey
Assumption College

In today's global society, it is useful to learn more about the religions that may be practiced by coworkers. Without some knowledge, individuals may attribute incorrect meanings to others' behaviors. In addition, organizations may have policies and practices that inadvertently conflict with their employees' religious beliefs. For example, some organizations do not allow vacation time to be accrued, thus preventing pilgrimages that may require a month of leave. Others require all workers to take Christian holidays and do not capitalize on the opportunity to have non-Christians work on days that have no significance to them. Jewish employees, for example may choose to work on Christmas Eve in exchange for having Yom Kippur off with pay. Because many individuals may be reluctant to discuss their religion or to explain its practices in a work setting, misunderstanding of behavior can result.

The following scenarios depict workplace incidents in which others are not aware of the religious basis for the individual's behavior. In each case, the employee is put in the limelight because of his/her religion. The supervisor or coworker, who has little or no knowledge of the religious practices that are at the root of these actions, may attribute an incorrect reason for the behavior that they see. These scenarios illustrate that lack of knowledge can lead to conflict, decreased productivity, and diminished motivation for workers as well as managers.

DIRECTIONS

Each scenario illustrates the intersection between religion and the workplace. Form small groups and through the sharing of information (or if given as a research assignment, through library and Web sources) answer the following questions.

  A. Using only the information provided in the scenario, list the *possible* attributions (i.e., explanations of why this person is behaving as he/she is without knowing the real reasons behind the behavior) that coworkers and managers in the case could use to explain the person's behavior.
  B. Discuss the negative and/or positive effects of these attributions on the work organization.

C. What should a manager do in this situation?
D. If someone in your group has some knowledge about religions, ask him/her to explain the religious significance of this worker's behavior. **(NOTE: It is important to this exercise that this is the last step in the discussion.)**

1. Mary Ellen comes to work with a dark spot on her forehead. Several times during the day, coworkers tease her about forgetting to wash her face and suggest that she visit the ladies room.

2. David sits with his coworkers at a luncheon provided during a meeting. Chicken, with a creamy sauce, salad, and rice are served but he declines to eat and only sips water. People at the table ask him if he is feeling well. He keeps assuring them that he is fine.

3. Kaleen never attends any company informal or formal social events (drinks after work, trips to a nearby casino, holiday parties, etc.). In addition, in an organization where "open doors" are a strong cultural norm, his door is often closed for short periods of time. During his performance appraisal, his boss tells Kaleen that he needs to become more sociable and accessible if he expects to move into a management position.

4. Tyler works full time as an assistant manager in a large retail chain store that is open 12 hours a day, 7 days a week. It is company policy that all managers must rotate working on weekends. Tyler has been using many different excuses to avoid working on Saturdays. Although Tyler is a good worker, his boss no longer believes Tyler's stories and will be noting this behavior in his next performance review.

Writing Assignments

1. Using the Internet, research a religion that you are unfamiliar with and write an original scenario like those in this exercise, in which an employee's work behavior, based on religious beliefs and practices, is misunderstood by a boss or coworker.
2. First, conduct research through the library, Web, etc. into the history, beliefs, dietary practices, ethical standards, and implications for workplace behavior of a religion with which you are *totally* unfamiliar. Ideas include: Assemblies of God, Buddhism, Shintoism, Confucianism, Eastern Rite Catholicism, Taoism, Sikhism, Hinduism, Seventh-day Adventists, Mennonite/Amish, Roman Catholicism, Quaker (Religious Society of Friends), Hassidic Judaism, Bahai, and Native American-First Nation, beliefs, etc.

   After you have researched this religion, plan to attend a service at the temple, church, or meeting place of the religion you have researched. You should contact the priest, minister, rabbi, or leader to ask permission, check on the time of the service, and inquire about any dress codes that may be necessary to observe. Be prompt, dress appropriately, and be able and willing to stay for the entire service.

   Write a 5 to 6-page double-spaced paper that explains what a manager should know about this religion to better understand his/her workers who practice this faith. What did you learn about those who practice this religion from attending the service? Emphasis should be placed on understanding the cultural and historic roots of the faith, discussion of the behavioral and work-related implications of the values, ethical beliefs, and practices of the religion.

   Information and links to many additional resources on the major religions of the world can be found at http://www.religioustolerance.org. An excellent book on the subject of religious practices is "How to Be a Perfect Stranger" (2003), 3rd edition, by Stuart M. Matlins and Arthur J. Magida, Skylight Paths Publishing: Woodstock Vermont.

EXPLORING RELIGIOUS DIVERSITY: AN EXERCISE

Pamela D. Sherer

Providence College

BACKGROUND INFORMATION

It's Friday. The office staff is gathered in the conference room for an employee recognition lunch. There's a choice of ham, roast beef or salami and cheese sandwiches. There's also a julienne meat salad and soda. Most think of the lunch as a nice gesture to show the workers they're appreciated. But there are a few who feel left out. The Muslims aren't there at all because the lunch is being held during one of their required prayer times. A Jewish worker looks at the display of food and moves away from the table. Meat together with cheese is not kosher. His colleague, a Hindu, cannot eat meat at all. And a couple of Christians complain to one another because the lunch is taking place during Lent. They, therefore, cannot eat meat either. With all the best intentions, a gesture of appreciation has become a medium for exclusion. (Bennett, 2001)

The preceding situation exemplifies how unfamiliarity with other religions and their practices can create situations that reflect an insensitivity to coworkers and that can result in an uncomfortable and/or exclusionary environment for some employees. If the planners of this event had had an awareness, understanding, and sensitivity to these different religious practices, they could have planned an event that was welcoming to all.

According to the Tanenbaum Center for Interreligious Understanding, "New immigration patterns and age demographics have changed the religious make-up of the labor force in the United States. Today, America is a culture that is shaped not only by Christians and Jews, as in the past, but also by Muslims, Hindus, Buddhists, Sikhs and adherents of many other religions, including different denominations, and new and non-traditional variants of all of the above. As a result, religious diversity in the workplace has become one of the most important social issues of our time" (www.tanenbaum.org).

According to *The Encyclopedia of American Religions* (Melton, 2003), there are over 2,000 different primary religious organizations in the United States. These include churches, sects, cults, temples, societies, and missions. Of these, there are more than 1,000 Christian denominations. The Harvard University Pluralism Project provides descriptions and statistics, gleaned from numerous sources, on the major religions in the United States (http://www.fas.harvard.edu/~pluralsm/).

Today's enlightened organizations know they must pay attention to the realities of increased religious diversity. In addition to the previously mentioned sensitivity issue, there are the potential legal ramifications for business practices that are not in concurrence with relevant laws. Organizational members, especially managers, need to be aware of those laws and related human resource practices associated with religious accommodation and discrimination in the workplace. Data compiled by the U.S. Equal Employment Opportunity Commission document that religious-based discrimination charges filed under Title VII of the Civil Rights Act of 1964 have increased from 1,388 in 1992 to 2,572 in 2002 (www.eeoc.gov/stats/religion.html).

Title VII of the Civil Rights Act of 1964 states that employers must reasonably accommodate employees' religious beliefs unless it creates an undue hardship for the employer (http://www.eeoc.gov/laws/vii.html). The duty to accommodate is triggered if an employee notifies an employer of a conflict between his or her sincerely held religious beliefs and a job requirement (see the Anti-Defamation League Website, which provides further information on what constitutes an undue hardship: http://www.adl.org/issue_religious_freedom/religious_ac/accommodation_QA.asp).

For example, an employee may request not to work on his or her Sabbath. The Equal Employment Opportunity Commission (EEOC), "Guidelines on Discrimination Because of Religion," suggest three common methods for accommodating conflicts between an employer's work schedule and an employee's religious needs (Wolf, Freidman, & Sutherland, 1998, p. 89):

1. Voluntary substitution and "swaps" of work assignments between employees
2. Flexible scheduling work hours, breaks, and holiday leave
3. Lateral transfers of employees with religious conflicts to different assignments or locations

With the increase in discrimination suits and with the increase in religions and variety of practice in the United States, it is not surprising that organizations find it necessary to review relevant laws and their own organizational practices concerning religious accommodation and discrimination at work (Lindsay & Bach, 1999; Wolf, Freidman, & Sutherland, 1998). And, as religious diversity in the United States continues to grow, organizations know they must increase their awareness and understanding of the religious beliefs and practices of their workforce (Bennett, 2001; Brotherton, 2001; Sheler, 2002; Spognardi & Ketay, 2000).

Bibliography

Bennett, G. (2001). Religious diversity in the workplace — an emerging issue. *Diversity Factor, 9*(2), 15–20.

Brotherton, P. (2001). Religious diversity initiatives foster respect and understanding. *Society for Human Resources (SHRM) Moasics, 7*(2), 1–4.

Lindsay, R., & Bach, E. (April, 1999). Prohibiting discrimination based on religion: An employer's obligation. Society for Human Resource Management White Paper. Available from http://www.shrm.org/

Melton, J. (2003). *Encyclopedia of American religions* (7th ed.). New York: Thompson-Gale.

Sheler, J. (2002, May 6). Faith in America, *U.S. News & World Report, 15*(10), 41–49.

Society for Human Resource Management (SHRM) and The Tanenbaum Center for Interreligious Understanding. (2001). *Religion in the workplace survey.* Available from http://www.shrm.org and http://www.tanenbaum.org/

Spognardi, M., & Ketay, S. (2000). In the lion's den: Religious accommodation and harassment in the workplace. *Employee Relations Law Journal, 25*(4), 7–27.

Wolf, M., Freidman, B., & Sutherland, D. (1998*). Religion in the workplace: A comprehensive guide to legal rights and responsibilities.* Chicago: America Bar Association.

ASSIGNMENT

The goals of this exercise are to

- Increase student familiarity with various religions and their practices
- Develop student awareness of current opportunities and challenges related to religious diversity in the workplace
- Foster classroom discussion on developing organizational strategies to educate managers and employees about sensitivity to and accommodations of religious diversity

Outside-of-Class Activities

Individually or in groups you will be responsible for selecting a religion (other than your own) and completing the Comparative Religion Chart. You will need to research the following:

A. The specific religion and its practices
B. Specific past or current workplace issues that have been raised with respect to this religion and/or its practices
C. Strategies that organizations have used to educate employees about workplace religious diversity in general

The following articles and Internet resources will be helpful in beginning your research.

Digh, P. (1998, December). Religion in the workplace: Make a good-faith effort to accommodate. *HR Magazine, 43*(13), 84–91. Provides a brief overview of the major religions in the United States and workplace accommodations.

Kosmin, B., & Mayer, E. (2001). America religious identification survey. (The Graduate Center: The City University of New York). Available from http://www.gc.cuny.edu/studies/aris_index.htm

Sheler, J. (2002, May 6). Faith in America. *U.S. News & World Report, 15*(10), 41–49.
   Describes current religious affiliation in the United States and highlights
   Buddhism, Christianity, Hinduism, Islam, and Judaism.

http://www.adl.org/issue_religious_freedom/religious_ac/accommodation_QA.asp
The Anti-Defamation League Website link offers a Religious Freedom section with
   frequently asked questions about Religious Accommodation in the Workplace and
   Religious Discrimination.

http://www.eeoc.gov/laws/vii.html
Title VII of the Civil Rights Act of 1964

http://www.pluralism.org/resources/links/index.php
The Pluralism Project at Harvard University was developed to study and document
   the growing religious diversity of the United States, with a special view to its new
   immigrant religious communities. The resource site provides links to information
   on several religions, organizations, and reports.

http://religions.rutgers.edu/vri/
Virtual Religion Index, maintained by the Religion Department at Rutgers
   University, provides links to many Internet sources related to religion, including
   comparative religion.

http://uwacadweb.uwyo.edu/religionet/er/DEFAULT.HTM
University of Wyoming Program of Religious Studies. Exploring Religions:
A Website introducing five world religions: Hinduism, Buddhism, Judaism,
   Christianity, and Islam.

http://www.wabashcenter.wabash.edu/
The Wabash Center: Guide to Internet Resources for Teaching and Learning in
   Theology and Religion, includes a substantial section on world religions.

In-Class Activities

You will be asked to give a short presentation sharing your findings on the
religion you have researched. Class members will be asked to fill out the
chart during student presentations.

Discussion Questions

1. Based on the information from your presentations and recorded on
   your Comparative Religion Chart, which major issues appear to be
   most salient in addressing workplace religious diversity? Why?
2. Based on your discussion, predict future major organizational religious
   diversity challenges and opportunities.
3. Based on your research, identify some major strategies that organizations or managers might utilize in educating employees about religious
   diversity in the workplace. Be specific.

Comparative Religion Chart

Religion Description	Buddhism	Christianity	Hinduism	Islam	Judaism	Another Religion
Brief history						
Beliefs						
Calendar & other faith-based time considerations						
Diet						

Comparative Religion Chart

Religion	Buddhism	Christianity	Hinduism	Islam	Judaism	Another Religion
Description						
Attire						
Varieties of practice within this religion						
Other religious practices of specific importance for the workplace						
Examples of specific workplace legal cases related to this religion						
Other issues						

*Categories based on *Religion in the workplace: A guide to navigating the complex landscape.* (2002). Tanenbaum Center for Interreligious Understanding, New York.

ACCEPTING DIVERSE PRACTICES

Jeanne M. Aurelio

Bridgewater State College

Michael A. Novak

University of Massachusetts Boston

National cultures vary in major ways, the most well documented being differences in individualism/collectivism, acceptance of ambiguity, power distance, masculinity/femininity, and time orientation.[1,2] So pervasive is socialization into any culture or subculture that it can prevent us from being able to think like or understand people from different cultures. We tend to interpret diverse practices from our own culturally learned points of view rather than understanding them in their cultural context. Social conformity, for example, may be seen as a sign of weakness in American culture, but as inner strength to the Japanese, whose culture values the ability to suppress self-interest in favor of the group.[3] Besides including national cultures, this exercise treats groups such as the disabled and the gay community as subcultures.

Goals

- To enable you to examine cultural practices in the contexts of the cultures from which they emerge
- To generate ways to increase acceptance of such behaviors

INSTRUCTIONS

Writing Assignment for Participants Prior to Class

Pretend that each following numbered scenario pertains to you personally. Answer **Questions A, B, and C** (as in Scenario #1) in the first person for each situation. Your answers will form the basis of class discussion. An example is given for Scenario #1.

Scenarios

1. Due to your religion, about which you feel very strongly, you need to have a place at work where you can pray several times a day. Other

people take several cigarette breaks a day in a designated place, so what's the difference?

Question A: What personal feelings are you likely to have about your practice?

If I were Muslim, for example, I would probably feel that I was a good person because I observe my religion by praying five times a day, even at work, when it's inconvenient. I am proud of being Muslim and want to show people that Islam is not a religion of extremism. I would not understand why work concessions are more easily made to people who smoke than to people who try to practice their religion.

Question B: What cultural implications do you believe are present in the situation?

(Note: This answer is based on the respondent's knowledge or lack of knowledge about the situation. It may be or not be correct. Notice that the example contains the word guess). *Someone who is a Muslim could come from a different culture; therefore, I may not understand his values as well as I understand my values. I guess someone who is Muslim may be very family oriented and may not be as materialistic.*

Question C: What reactions might you expect from coworkers, supervisors, and customers/clients (if applicable) because of your practice?

I would probably find some coworkers and supervisors who accept my practice. I know that some people might be somewhat afraid of Muslims, given the events of 9/11. Others may be afraid because they don't know anything about Islam except what they learn from the media, which is often negative.

2. You prefer to eat home-cooked ethnic meals at work, so you heat them up in the common microwave in the employee lounge at lunchtime. Some people comment on hating the smell of your delicious food.
3. You have been raised to look at people steadily when you are talking and to look away while they are talking. People have asked you to not to stare at them when you are talking and to look at them when they are talking, but you can't seem to retrain yourself.
4. As a woman brought up in a patriarchal culture, you believe that women should perform quiet, helping roles in society. In your professional job, your boss has repeatedly asked you to become more assertive, but that would make you very uncomfortable.
5. You and your gay or lesbian partner have adopted a child. You have placed several pictures of your family on your desk. You've noticed that few people ask you about your family, whereas you overhear them inquiring about each other's families at every opportunity.
6. In your culture, people express themselves by being loud. You are often forward, assertive, and intense. In your organization, you've noticed not only that people generally are more reserved than you are, but also that they act like you are overbearing.

7. You are legally blind. Your workstation has been modified to allow you to use it. You have some state-of-the art computer peripherals that you hear other people saying they wish they had.

8. (Instructor may assign another situation.) (Space intentionally left blank.)

Instructions to Follow in Class

Step 1: Scenarios (30 minutes) As a class discuss each of the assigned scenarios, answering questions A, B, and C.

Step 2: Discussion Questions

I. What connections did you make between personal behavior and cultures? (Reflect back on your answers to written question B.) How do you foresee your new understanding helping you at work or school?

II. If you notice differences between yourself and various people at work, what can you do to become more accepting of them?

III. If you were different in any of the ways mentioned in the scenarios, what would you do to help people understand you better? Differentiate among cultural, ethnic, sexual preference, religion, disability, and other types of differences.

Endnotes

1. Hofstede, G. (1980). *Culture's consequences: International differences in work-related values.* London: Sage.

2. Hofstede, G., & Bond, M. (1988). The Confucius connection: From cultural roots to economic growth. *Organizational Dynamics, 16*(4) 4–21.

3. Gannon, M.J. (1994). *Understanding global cultures: Metaphorical journeys through 17 countries.* Thousand Oaks, CA: Sage.

MEDIA MESSAGES

M. June Allard
Worcester State College

> ... Cultures have enriched each other in all the great civilizations
> of the world ... No culture has grown great in isolation. (Sowell,
> 1991, p. 44)

Sowell makes a compelling case for the importance of contact among cultures and one that modern cultures have been quick to appreciate. The last
decades have witnessed the exponential expansion of communication
among cultures with modern technological and electronic advances that
transcend geographic barriers to provide limitless opportunities for cultural
interaction and advancement. Cultures enrich each other through communication in the broadest sense—communication that occurs through the
medium of travel and migration and communication through print and
electronic media.

"TRAVEL AS MEDIA"

Travel is the traditional medium of culture contact. Such in-person contacts are especially important in high-context cultures such as those in Asia
and South America, where it is the social situation that provides the "cues"
to the meaning of the words and silences in communication. From the
United States, travel to nearly all parts of the world is constantly increasing
in the form of tourism, cultural and scientific exchanges, study abroad,
business trips, and other short-term more transitory cross-cultural contacts. Most of this business and personal travel are cultural contact avenues
restricted to the more "privileged, industrialized first-world subject"
(Nakamura, 2003).

Migration and immigration travel provide longer term, more sustained
cultural contact. Unlike travel and tourism, migration occurs for people of all
economic levels. Rich and poor alike leave home countries in turmoil. For
whatever reasons that they leave one culture for another, immigrants bring
with them their home cultures—customs, religions, languages and ways of
looking at the world—and the process of cultural enrichment begins.

ELECTRONIC MEDIA

Print and electronic media play an important role in transmitting culture in low-context cultures such as the United States, where meaning and messages are derived mostly from the words themselves and much less from the situation in which they occur.

In "developed" countries TV, like radio, is universal. By 1990, more than 98% of all U.S. households owned at least one television set, with preschool children watching TV more than 27 hours per week and their teenage siblings watching in excess of 21 hours (Bennett, 1994). Today the Internet, e-mail, and fax provide additional electronic means of cultural contact. Although these electronic advances are widespread in developed countries, they are the media of the more privileged, and even within the United States, the "digital divide" often denies the less affluent these newest avenues of cultural exchange.

"PRINT" AND ENTERTAINMENT MEDIA

Newspapers and magazines, although not as widely read as before the advent of television and electronic media, are still very influential. Millions of U.S. adults read national circulation newspapers and magazines with substantial percentages of all cultural groups reading magazines. Even the entertainment media, most particularly films and videos, are far-reaching conveyers of culture as are other cultural products such as art, music, books, video games and toys, and the knowledge and products of science and technology.

THE SHAPING OF CULTURE

What role does the communication media play in the shaping of culture today? How do newspapers, magazines, books, TV, radio, Internet, e-mail, and fax function to influence and enrich cultures? The answer is complex for the media serve as agents of transmission and cultural maintenance by passing down the culture to new generations and conveying it to newcomers. Media also become shapers of culture by serving to unite cultures and subcultures and at the same time dividing cultural groups from each other.

The complexity of the role is easily seen in the case of immigrants in the United States, where mass media (newspapers, radio, and television) serve to unite by teaching immigrants about the larger culture and teaching the larger culture about them. Although the larger culture dominates the national news, ethnic-cultural and religious festivals are presented in feature stories locally. At the same time, however, e-mail, telephone, and broadcast media allow newcomers to maintain their ethnic and social class identity by providing easy contact with their home culture. This contact includes not only the home country, but also fellow immigrants and other cultural enclaves within the United States as well. In recent years language programs and radio and TV stations and newspaper and magazines targeted to specific cultural groups further serve to maintain these cultures and at the same time infuse into them elements of the larger culture. In the process, ethnic media serve to separate the ethnic cultures from the mainstream culture.

THE MEDIA AND WHO IT REACHES

One size does not fit all groups. The interaction of the media with various segments of society is not uniform. Just as international travel and electronic media are available to only part of the society, other media forms are accessed in differing degrees by different segments of the society. All groups do not "tune in" to TV to the same extent nor do they read newspapers and magazine (much less the same papers and magazines) to the same extent.

There are approximately 102 million TV households and 262 million TV viewers in the U.S. In 1999–2000, Americans spent more than 53 hours per week on the average watching TV. According to the Nielsen ratings, both total Hispanic-American and Spanish-dominant households watch even more television (57+ and 55+ hours, respectively) every week and African Americans, the largest minority segment of TV viewers, generally spend more time watching television than other population groups. Some 21% of African and Asian Americans also watch cable TV, compared to 14% of Latinos and 8% of whites (Nielson, 2003a, 2003b).

Americans also spend countless hours reading newspapers and magazines, listening to the radio, and going to the movies. In 2002, more than 143,668,000 adults read news papers (Newspaper Association of America, 2003). In addition, a recent survey found that 59% of Asian Americans, 45% of African Americans, 43% of whites, and 30% of Latinos read a magazine the previous day (DiversityInc, 2003).

There are historical as well as cultural reasons for ethnic differences in media use. Over the last decades of the 20th century, the growing diversity in the United States led some media to avoid dealing with people of color as they moved into cities and to try to build audiences based on those who fit a desired age, education, income, racial, or gender target market. Minority concerns were frequently ignored. Thus mass media developed into a segmented media—selective in *who* it transmits to and in *what* it transmits. Advertisers, the driving force behind the audiences targeted by newspapers, wanted predominantly affluent Anglo readers. In practical terms this means selectivity in terms of which stories are aired and which are not. In some places stories about African, Latino, and Asian Americans have actually been kept off the air.

As a result of this selectivity, the media *maximized* racial and ethnic division. As diversity numbers in the United States have grown, however, this exclusion from national media has given rise to newspapers and TV channels specifically targeting the excluded minorities. Spanish-language TV channels are now common in urban areas, and in September of 2003, large mainstream English-language newspapers launched several

Spanish-language daily newspapers (*Hoy, Diario La Estrella, Al Dia*) to complement the small Spanish-language weeklies.

In addition to Spanish-language TV channels, satellite dishes now bring in stations from Mexico and Colombia, CNN (in Spanish), and Fox Sports (in Spanish). Cable operators serve geographically defined markets with programming geared to those areas. Smaller ethnic and cultural groups that are more diffused geographically, such as the Arabic, Russian, and Korean language groups, are serviced by satellite television.

WHAT THE MEDIA TRANSMITS

The ethnic-targeted media focus on culture-specific entertainment and news. Aimed at the young Americanized Latinos, two Spanish-language networks now feature Spanish-language soap operas *(telenovelas)* that provide satire and moral dilemmas focusing on issues distinct to U.S. Latinos. The new Spanish-language dailies are far more than translations of English-language papers. They cover local, national, and international news concentrating on sports relevant to the group such as soccer, good classified ads, and Latino countries—topics of high interest to U.S. Latinos. Late in 2003, Comcast, the nation's largest cable company, launched new packages of Spanish-language programming. The Associated Press quotes Mauro Panzera, Senior Director of Multicultural Marketing at Comcast, Philadelphia:

> We launched the package to give them the best possible way of keeping a lifeline not only to the Hispanic market here but also back home, to connect with their heritage and what's important in their lives. (Associated Press, 2003)

Stereotypes

All forms of media engage in the transmission of cultural stereotypes. Traditional typecasting of African Americans and Native Americans by advertisers has decreased markedly in broadcast and print media. Unfortunately other forms of stereotyping are alive and well, often in the character roles portrayed in TV dramatizations. In the last few decades, many studies have examined the stereotypes fostered by media. A sample of the stereotypes emerging from Nielson and other studies include:

> *Youth.* Positive images are largely absent. Youth are stereotyped by exclusion from mass media suggesting their lack of importance. In local news they are often portrayed in the context of crime and other at-risk behaviors. A considerable gender imbalance in youth stories occurs with most stories about males. Racial imbalance occurs with 35% of the news about white youth involved in crime compared to 52% for nonwhite youth.
> *Businessmen.* Compared to characters in other occupations, this group was portrayed twice as often in a negative way. They committed 40%

    iii. What audience do you think the commercials target? Why?

    iv. What stereotype and cultural messages do you think the commercials send? Explain.

Print Media: Magazines

2. Visit a library or bookstore. Select three magazines, one from each of the following columns. Use the Recording Form for your observations of the ethnicity, gender, social class, and the tone of the commentary. You will need several copies of the Recording Form for each magazine.

Cosmopolitan	Money	Elle
Family Circle	Brides	Time
Good Housekeeping	Travel & Leisure	Jet
Martha Stewart Living	Sports Illustrated	Vogue
Shape	Seventeen	Consumer Reports
Woman's Day	AARP	Fortune
Redbook	Gentlemen's Quarterly	Forbes

After you have recorded your observations, analyze the media messages and answer the following questions for each magazine.

  a. What group(s) (gender, class, race/ethnicity, age, etc.) does each magazine seem to target? Explain. Give examples.

  b. What group(s) (gender, class, race/ethnicity, age, etc.) do the advertisements in each magazine seem to target? Give examples.

  c. Are the groups treated in proportion to their numbers in the population? Explain.

  d. Are the groups treated equally in tone? Explain.

  e. What messages (cultural values, stereotypes, etc.) does each magazine seem to convey? Explain. Give examples.

  f. What messages (cultural values, stereotypes, etc.) do the advertisements in each magazine seem to convey? Explain. Give examples.

Print Media: Mass Circulation Newspapers

3. Examine a single issue of a mass circulation daily or Sunday newspaper and record your observations of the ethnicity, gender, social class, and tone (i.e., positive, negative, neutral) of the commentary in the (a) stories or (b) features on the Recording Form. You will need several copies of the form.

  a. Newspaper stories

  b. Features including wedding, engagement, op-ed, anniversary, and death notices; financial reporting; clothing; travel articles; etc.

After you have recorded your observations, answer the following questions.

  a. Are the groups treated in proportion to their numbers in the population? Explain.

  b. Do you think the groups are treated equally in tone (i.e., positive, negative, neutral)? Explain.

  c. What audience do you think they may target? Explain.

  d. What stereotypes do you think they may foster? Explain.

Other Cultural Products

4. Transmission of cultural expectations for both genders begins at birth and continues throughout childhood. Verify this firsthand by making one of the following observations. Your instructor will supply Recording Forms to aid you in making your observations. You will need several copies of the Recording Form.

   a. *Baby cards.* Visit a store selling baby cards and record the gender differences in color, design, and message. Use separate Recording Forms for male and female cards. Do not use cards from the Internet.*

   b. *Toys.* Visit a large toy store and record gender and racial differences in color, design, and message. Use separate Recording Forms for male and female toys.

   c. *Comic books.* Examine three different comic books and record social identities information such as gender and race about the principal and secondary characters on the Recording Form. Use separate forms for each comic book.

   d. *Children's books or elementary school textbooks.* Visit a library or bookstore and examine the textbooks used in a single grade or examine subject textbooks (e.g., social sciences) for several grades, recording information about the characters in the book on the Recording Form. Use separate forms for each book.

   e. *Video games.* Examine three different video games, noting information about the principal and secondary characters on the Recording Form. Use separate forms for each game.

   After making the observations answer the following questions.

   i. What stereotypes and cultural messages do you think are being sent? Explain.

   ii. How are ethnic and racial groups represented? As leading characters? As villains? Heroes? What are the gender roles? Explain.

Additional Assignments

Newspaper

Anatomy of a newspaper.

Dissect a newspaper:

1. Select one newspaper. A different person should examine each of the following for a single day. Assign individuals from other groups to examine the paper on different days. Use Recording Form to make observations.

   a. Comic strips
   b. Advertising
   c. Letters to the editors
   d. Features
   e. News stories
   f. Photographs

2. Group members will combine their observations into a "profile" of the newspaper.

Anatomy of Ethnic Newspapers

Dissect ethnic newspapers in the same fashion as national circulation newspapers.

---

*Do not use cards from the Internet as it offers a very limited choice.

Magazines

Select an unusual magazine (such as a biking magazine or skiing magazine or *Travel Over 50*) and analyze it to determine what segment of society it targets in terms of race/ethnicity, age, social class, gender, etc.

Television

Select TV networks targeting special groups such as the Home and Garden Channel or ESPN and compare their programming (messages) to those of mass TV.

Bibliography

American Society of Newspaper Editors. (2001, April 3). *2001 ASNE census finds newsrooms less diverse: Increased hiring of minorities blunted by departure rate.* Retrieved November 11, 2003, from http://www.asne.org

Associated Press. (2003, October 7). *Cable TV seeks Spanish-speaking customers.* Retrieved November 26, 2003, from http://www.diversityinc.com

Barnes, K., & DeBell, C. (1995, August). *The portrayal of men and women workers in Sunday comics: No laughing matter.* Paper presented at the American Psychological Association Convention, New York.

Bennett, W. (1994). *The index of leading cultural indicators.* New York: Touchstone, pp. 102–106.

Brown, C.S. (2003, August 12). *Univision/Hispanic broadcasting merger: What's at stake for marketers, Latinos?* Retrieved November 26, 2003, from http://www.diversityinc.com

Center for Media and Public Affairs. (2003). *Factoids. Demographics of network reporters 1989–1999.* Retrieved on November 18, 2003, from http://www.cmpa.com/factoid/diverse.htm

Center for Media and Public Affairs. (2003, February 28). *Minorities, women make network news history.* Retrieved November 17, 2003, from http://www.cmpa./preeerel/MinRelease2003.htm

Cole, Y. (2003, July 21). *U.S. "telenovelas": Bringing Latino generations together.* Retrieved November 26, 2003, from http://www.diversityinc.com

DiversityInc. (2003, September 10). *Diversity factoids.* Retrieved November 26, 2003, from http://www.diversityinc.com

Fitzgerald, M. (2003, January 8). *Newspaper outlook 2003.* Retrieved November 27, 2003, from http://www.editorandpublisher.com.

Government goes down the tube: Images of government in TV entertainment. Executive summary. Retrieved November 18, 2003, from http://www.cmpa.com

Huang, T. T. (2003, November 17). Poynter Online. *The battle for inclusiveness.* Retrieved November 18, 2003, from http://www.poynter.org

Italian-American characters in television entertainment. Executive summary. (2003). Retrieved November 18, 2003, from http://www.cmpa.com

Lichter, S. R., & Amundson, D. (2003). *Distorted reality: Hispanic characters in TV Entertainment 1955–1992. Executive Summary.* Retrieved November 18, 2003, from http://www.cmpa.com

Lichter, S. R., Lichter, L., & Rothman, S. (2003). *Video villains: the TV businessman 1955–1986. Executive summary.* Retrieved November 17, 2003, from http://www.cmpa.com

Lopez, E. M. (2003, September 4). *Can new Spanish-language dailies help save the newspaper industry?* Retrieved November 26, 2003, from http://www.diversityinc.com

Mantsios, G. (1998). *Media magic. Making class invisible.* In P. Rothenberg (Ed.), *Race, class, and gender in the United*

States: An integrated study (4th ed., pp. 510–519). New York: St. Martin's.

Mitchell, B. (2003, November 17). *It's about hiring, too.* Retrieved November 18, 2003, from http://www.poynter.org

Media Monitor. (2002, September/October). *What's the matter with kids today? Images of teenagers on local and national TV news.* Retrieved November 17, 2003, from http://www.cmpa.com

Nakamura, L. (2003). "Where do you want to go today?" Cybernetic tourism, the Internet and transnationality. In G. Dines & J. Humez (Eds.), *Gender, race and class in media: A text-reader* (2nd ed., pp. 684–687). Thousand Oaks, CA: Sage.

Newspaper Association of America. (2003, November 27). *News briefs.* Retrieved November 27, 2003, from http://www.naa.org

Newspaper Association of America. (2003). *Trends and numbers.* Retrieved December 1, 2003, from http://www.naa.org

Nielsen Media Research. (2003a). *The African-American television audience.* Retrieved November 18, 2003, from http://www.nielsenmedia.com/ethnicmeasure

Nielsen Media Research. (2003b). *Hispanic-American television audience.* Retrieved November 18, 2003, from http://www.nielsenmedia.com/ethnicmeasure

Online NewsHour. (1999, August 23). *Diversity in the newsroom.* Retrieved November 27, 2003, from http://www.pbs.org/newshour

Readership Institute. (1999) *Newspaper staffing, diversity and turnover.* Retrieved November 27, 2003, from http://www.readership.org

Seitz, M. Z. (2002, July 16) Despite some progress, minorities remain an unseen presence. *Star Ledger,* p. 28.

Shaheen, J. G. (1989) TV Arabs. From new worlds of literature, Jerome Beatty and J. Paul Hunter, eds. In P. Rothenberg, *Race, class and gender in the United States. An Integrated Study* (6th ed., pp. 356–357). New York: Worth.

Smith, Ron. (2003, October 24). *Copy editing for diversity.* Poynter Online. Retrieved November 18, 2003, from http://www.poynter.org

Sowell, T. (1991). A world view of cultural diversity. *Society, 29* (1), 37–44.

Television's impact on ethnic and racial images: A study of Howard Beach adolescents Executive summary. (2003). Retrieved November 17, 2003, from http://www.cmpa.com

UNITY: Journalists of Color, Inc. (2003, April 7). *Unity: Newspapers face diversity crisis and need crisis reaction.* Retrieved November 27, 2003, from http://unityjournalists.org/news3a.html

Wilson C. C., II, Gutierrez, F., & Chao, L. (2003). *Racism, sexism, and the media: The rise of class communication in multicultural America* (3rd ed.). Thousand Oaks, CA: Sage.

Zafar, S. (2003, January) Going beyond words. *Managing Diversity, 12* (4), p. 1.

PART

III

ORGANIZATIONAL PERSPECTIVES ON DIVERSITY

The last section of the text is designed to illustrate how complicated it is to make diversity initiatives workable within organizational contexts. This situation is further complicated in a culture that has a short-term orientation and is prone to measuring business success primarily in terms of achieving financial goals.

Section III opens with an exercise that challenges us to look at diversity initiatives within our own organizations (Harvey #36) and continues with an exploration of the three paradigms that can be used to categorize organizational responses to workplace diversity (Thomas & Ely). Additional issues in diversity management are explored in terms of the ethical rationale (McNett), the business case for diversity (Robinson & Dechant), and diversity issues in Canada (Mentzer).

Six true cases involving the issues and challenges of diversity management follow: Coca-Cola (Harvey #41), Ford in Mexico (Muller), law enforcement (Diodati), Wall Street (Ligos), Air Force (Dawson & Chunis), and Cracker Barrel (Howard). The section closes with two evaluation assignments: one for Websites and the second a capstone diversity audit.

Learning Outcomes for Section III

- Students will learn how diversity is implemented in organizational settings.
- Students will learn about the human, public relations, and legal costs of not dealing with diversity as a systemic organizational change.
- Students will perform a diversity audit that enables them to evaluate organizational diversity initiatives.

EXPLORING DIVERSITY IN YOUR ORGANIZATION

Carol P. Harvey
Assumption College

A good beginning to a course in diversity is to analyze how diversity or lack of diversity could impact an organization with which you are quite familiar. Your instructor can assign either Option A, which is relevant to exploring diversity on a college campus, or Option B, which is appropriate for an organization where you are or have been recently employed.

Goals
- To understand that having diverse people in organizations is only a starting point for diversity initiatives
- To analyze the impact of organizational diversity or lack of diversity on one's experiences

INSTRUCTIONS

Option A—Exploring Diversity on Your College Campus

1. **Organizational Leadership.** Using the catalog, Web page, or other resources, research your college to determine who has the power to make important decisions in the organization. How diverse is this college in terms of its board of trustees and senior staff such as vice-presidents, provosts, deans, and above?

2. **Faculty.** Using the catalog, Web page, or other resources, research your college's faculty to determine how diverse they are. Contrast

the effects of having a more homogeneous faculty and a more heterogeneous faculty in terms of: (a) your learning experiences,
(b) your advising/mentoring experiences, or (c) any other aspects
of your college life such as athletics, extracurricular activities, and
so on.

3. **Student Body.** Compare the student body to the organizational leadership and faculty. In most cases, the students are younger and less
educated but are there other obvious differences such as race, gender,
or ethnicity?

How does the student body compare with the community in which the
college is located? (www.census.gov) If there are major differences,
how can these be an advantage or a disadvantage to your college experience? Explain your answer.

4. If your college is diverse in terms of leadership, faculty, and/or students, how does diversity contribute to your learning experience
and/or personal development?

or

5. If your college isn't diverse, how does the lack of diversity impact your
learning experience and/or personal development?

INSTRUCTIONS

Option B—Exploring Diversity in Your Work Organization

1. **Organizational Leadership.** Using the organizational chart, Web page, or other resources, research your company to determine who has the power to make important decisions in the organization. How diverse is this organization in terms of its board of directors and senior managers such as vice-presidents, area managers, and above? *(Note: Their criteria for defining diversity may be related to the location and the mission your company. For example, if you are working in a racially diverse city such as Detroit, you may find more African Americans. If you are working in fashion retail, you may find more women in leadership positions. Although many aspects of diversity aren't visible, the purpose here is more to determine if there are obvious groups that are not represented in the leadership of the company.)*

2. **Lower-level and/or hourly workers.** How does the diversity of the board and management of your organization compare to the composition of the various levels of your organization? What types of issues does this raise? Provide specific examples.

3. **Customers.** If your organization works with consumers and clients, how do your target markets compare with the management and staff of your organization in terms of diversity?

4. In the future, how could diversity or lack of diversity impact your career and/or the ability of the organization to meet customer/client needs?

MAKING DIFFERENCES MATTER: A NEW PARADIGM FOR MANAGING DIVERSITY

David A. Thomas

Robin J. Ely

Why should companies concern themselves with diversity? Until recently, many managers answered this question with the assertion that discrimination is wrong, both legally and morally. But today managers are voicing a second notion as well. A more diverse workforce, they say, will increase organizational effectiveness. It "will lift morale, bring greater access to new segments of the marketplace, and enhance productivity. In short, they claim, diversity will be good for business.

Yet if this is true—and we believe it is—where are the positive impacts of diversity? Numerous and varied initiatives to increase diversity in corporate America have been under way for more than two decades. Rarely, however, have those efforts spurred leaps in organizational effectiveness. Instead, many attempts to increase diversity in the workplace have backfired, sometimes even heightening tensions among employees and hindering a company's performance.

This article offers an explanation for why diversity efforts are not fulfilling their promise and presents a new paradigm for understanding—and leveraging—diversity. It is our belief that there is a distinct way to unleash the powerful benefits of a diverse workforce. Although these benefits include increased profitability, they go beyond financial measures to encompass learning, creativity, flexibility, organizational and individual growth, and the ability of a company to adjust rapidly and successfully to market changes. The desired transformation, however, requires a fundamental change in the attitudes and behaviors of an organization's leadership. And that will come only when senior managers abandon an underlying and flawed assumption about diversity and replace it with a broader understanding.

Most people assume that workplace diversity is about increasing racial, national, gender, or class representation—in other words, recruiting and retaining more people from traditionally underrepresented "identity groups." Taking this commonly held assumption as a starting point, we set out six years ago to investigate its link to organizational effectiveness. We soon found that thinking of diversity simply in terms of identity-group representation inhibited effectiveness.

Organizations usually take one of two paths in managing diversity. In the name of equality and fairness, they encourage (and expect) women and people of color to blend in. Or they set them apart in jobs that relate specifically to their backgrounds assigning them, for example, to areas that require them to interface with clients or customers of the same identity group. African American MBAs often find themselves marketing products to inner-city communities; Hispanics frequently market to Hispanics or work for Latin American subsidiaries. In those kinds of cases, companies are operating on the assumption that the main virtue identity groups have to offer is knowledge of their own people. This assumption is limited—and limiting—and detrimental to diversity efforts.

What we suggest here is that diversity goes beyond increasing the number of different identity-group affiliations on the payroll to recognizing that such an effort is merely the first step in managing a diverse workforce for the organization's utmost benefit. Diversity should be understood as the *varied perspectives and approaches to work* that members of different identity groups bring.

Women, Hispanics, Asian Americans, African Americans, Native Americans— these groups and others outside the mainstream of corporate America don't bring with them just their "insider information." They bring different, important, and competitively relevant knowledge and perspectives about how to actually *do work*—how to design processes, reach goals, frame tasks, create effective teams, communicate ideas, and lead. When allowed to, members of these groups can help companies grow and improve by challenging basic assumptions about an organization's functions, strategies, operations, practices, and procedures. And in doing so, they are able to bring more of their whole selves to the workplace and identify more fully with the work they do, setting in motion a virtuous circle. Certainly, individuals can be expected to contribute to a company their firsthand familiarity with niche markets. But only when companies start thinking about diversity more holistically—as providing fresh and meaningful approaches to work—and stop assuming that diversity relates simply to how a person looks or where he or she comes from, will they be able to reap its full rewards.

Two perspectives have guided most diversity initiatives to date: the *discrimination-and-fairness paradigm* and the *access-and-legitimacy paradigm.* But we have identified a new, emerging approach to this complex management issue. This approach, which we call the *learning-and-effectiveness paradigm* incorporates aspects of the first two paradigms but goes beyond them by concretely connecting diversity to approaches to work. Our goal is to help business leaders see what their own approach to diversity currently is and how it may already have influenced their companies' diversity efforts. Managers can learn to assess whether they need to change their diversity initiatives and, if so, how to accomplish that change.

The following discussion will also cite several examples of how connecting the new definition of diversity to the actual *doing* of work has led some organizations to markedly better performance. The organizations differ in many ways—none are in the same industry, for instance—but they are united by one similarity: Their leaders realize that increasing demographic variation does not in itself increase organizational effectiveness. They realize that it is how a company defines diversity—and *what it does* with the experiences of being a diverse organization—that delivers on the promise.

THE DISCRIMINATION-AND-FAIRNESS PARADIGM

Using the discrimination-and-fairness paradigm is perhaps thus far the dominant way of understanding diversity. Leaders who look at diversity through this lens usually focus on equal opportunity, fair treatment, recruitment, and compliance with federal Equal Employment Opportunity requirements. The paradigm's underlying logic can be expressed as follows:

> Prejudice has kept members of certain demographic groups out of organizations such as ours. As a matter of fairness and to comply with federal mandates, we need to work toward restructuring the makeup of our organization to let it more closely reflect that of society. We need managerial processes that ensure that all our employees are treated equally and with respect and that some are not given unfair advantage over others.

Although it resembles the thinking behind traditional affirmative-action efforts, the discrimination-and-fairness paradigm does go beyond a simple concern with numbers. Companies that operate with this philosophical orientation often institute mentoring and career-development programs specifically for the women and people of color in their ranks and train other employees to respect cultural differences. Under this paradigm, nevertheless, progress in diversity is measured by how well the company achieves its recruitment and retention goals rather than by the degree to which conditions in the company allow employees to draw on their personal assets and perspectives to do their work more effectively. The staff, one might say diversified, but the work does not.

What are some of the common characteristics of companies that have used the discrimination-and-fairness paradigm successfully to increase their demographic diversity? Our research indicates that they are usually run by leaders who value due process and equal treatment of all employees and who have the authority to use top-down directives to enforce initiatives based on those attitudes. Such, companies are often bureaucratic in structure, with control processes in place for monitoring, measuring, and rewarding individual performance. And finally, they are often organizations with entrenched, easily observable cultures, in which values like fairness are widespread and deeply inculcated and codes of conduct are clear and unambiguous. (Perhaps the most extreme example of an organization in which all these factors are at work is the United States Army.)

Without doubt, there are benefits to this paradigm: it does tend to increase demographic diversity in an organization, and it often succeeds in promoting fair treatment. But it also has significant limitations. The first of these is that its color-blind, gender-blind ideal is to some degree built on the implicit assumption that "we are all the same" or "we aspire to being all the same." Under this paradigm, it is not desirable for diversification of the workforce to influence the organization's work or culture. The company should operate as if every person were of the same race, gender, and nationality. It is unlikely that leaders who manage diversity under this paradigm will explore how people's differences generate a potential diversity of effective ways of working, leading, viewing the market, managing people, and learning.

Not only does the discrimination-and-fairness paradigm insist that everyone is the same, but, with its emphasis on equal treatment, it puts pressure on employees to make sure that important differences among them do not count. Genuine disagreements about work definition, therefore, are sometimes wrongly interpreted through this paradigm's fairness-unfairness lens—especially when honest disagreements are accompanied by tense debate. A female employee who insists, for example, that a company's advertising strategy is not appropriate for all ethnic segments in the marketplace might feel she is violating the code of assimilation upon which the paradigm is built. Moreover, if she were then to defend her opinion by citing, let us say, her personal knowledge of the ethnic group the company wanted to reach, she might risk being perceived as importing inappropriate attitudes into an organization that prides itself on being blind to cultural differences.

Workplace paradigms channel organizational thinking in powerful ways. By limiting the ability of employees to acknowledge openly their work-related but culturally based differences, the paradigm actually undermines the organization's capacity to learn about and improve its own strategies, processes, and practices. And it also keeps people from identifying strongly and personally with their work—a critical source of motivation and self-regulation in any business environment.

As an illustration of the paradigm's weaknesses, consider the case of Iversen Dunham, an international consulting firm that focuses on foreign and domestic economic-development policy. (Like all the examples in this article, the company is real, but its name is disguised.) Not long ago, the firm's managers asked us to help them understand why race relations had become a divisive issue precisely at a time when Iversen was receiving accolades for its diversity efforts. Indeed, other organizations had even begun to use the firm to benchmark their own diversity programs.

Iversen's diversity efforts had begun in the early 1970s, when senior managers decided to pursue greater racial and gender diversity in the firm's higher ranks. (The firm's leaders were strongly committed to the cause of social justice.) Women and people of color were hired and charted on career paths toward becoming project leaders. High performers among those who had left the firm were persuaded to return in senior roles. By 1989, about 50% of Iversen's project leaders and professionals were women, and 30% were people of color. The 13-member management committee once exclusively white and male included five women and four people of color. Additionally, Iversen had developed a strong contingent of foreign nationals.

It was at about this time, however, that tensions began to surface. Senior managers found it hard to believe that, after all the effort to create a fair and mutually respectful work community, some staff members could still be claiming that Iversen had racial discrimination problems. The management invited us to study the firm and deliver an outsider's assessment of its problem.

We had been inside the firm for only a short time when it became clear that Iversen's leaders viewed the dynamics of diversity through the lens of the discrimination-and-fairness paradigm. But where they saw racial discord, we discerned clashing approaches to the actual work of consulting. Why? Our research showed that tensions were strongest among midlevel project leaders. Surveys and interviews indicated that white project leaders welcomed demographic diversity as a general sign of progress but that they also thought the new employees were somehow changing the company, pulling it away from its original culture and its mission. Common criticisms were that African American and Hispanic staff made problems too complex by linking issues the organization had traditionally regarded as unrelated and that they brought on projects that seemed to require greater cultural sensitivity. White male project leaders also complained that their peers who were women and people of color were undermining one of Iversen's traditional strengths: its hard-core quantitative orientation. For instance, minority project leaders had suggested that Iversen consultants collect information and seek input from others in the client company besides senior managers—that is, from the rank and file and from middle managers. Some had urged Iversen to expand its consulting approach to include the gathering and analysis of qualitative data through interviewing and observation. Indeed, these project leaders had even challenged one of Iversen's long-standing, core assumptions: that the firm's reports were objective. They urged Iversen Dunham to recognize and address the subjective aspect of its analyses; the firm could, for example, include in its reports to clients dissenting Iversen views, if any existed.

For their part, project leaders who were women and people of color felt that they were not accorded the same level of authority to carry out that work as their white male peers. Moreover, they sensed that those peers were skeptical of their opinions, and they resented that doubts were not voiced openly.

Meanwhile, there also was some concern expressed about tension between white managers and nonwhite subordinates, who claimed they were being treated unfairly. But our analysis suggests that the manager-subordinate conflicts were not numerous enough to warrant the attention they were drawing from top management. We believed it was significant that senior managers found it easier to focus on this second type of conflict than on midlevel conflicts about project choice and project definition. Indeed, Iversen Dunham's focus seemed to be a result of the firm's reliance on its particular diversity paradigm and the emphasis on fairness and equality. It was relatively easy to diagnose problems in light of those concepts and to devise a solution: just get managers to treat their subordinates more fairly.

In contrast, it was difficult to diagnose peer-to-peer tensions in the framework of this model. Such conflicts were about the very nature of Iversen's work, not simply unfair treatment. Yes, they were related to identity-group affiliations, but they were not symptomatic of classic racism. It was Iversen's paradigm that led managers to interpret them as such. Remember, we were asked to assess what was supposed to be a racial discrimination problem. Iversen's discrimination-and-fairness paradigm had created a kind of cognitive blind spot; and, as a result, the company's leadership could not frame the problem accurately or solve it effectively. Instead, the company needed a cultural shift—it needed to grasp what to do with its diversity once it had achieved the numbers. If all Iversen Dunham employees were to contribute to the fullest extent, the company would need a paradigm that would encourage open and explicit discussion of what identity-group differences really mean and how they can be used as sources of individual and organizational effectiveness.

Today, mainly because of senior managers' resistance to such a cultural transformation, Iversen continues to struggle with the tensions arising from the diversity of its workforce.

THE ACCESS-AND-LEGITIMACY PARADIGM

In the competitive climate of the 1980s and 1990s, a new rhetoric and rationale for managing diversity emerged. If the discrimination-and-fairness paradigm can be said to have idealized assimilation and color- and gender-blind conformism, the access-and-legitimacy paradigm was predicated on the acceptance and celebration of differences. The underlying motivation of the access-and-legitimacy paradigm can be expressed this way:

> We are living in an increasingly multicultural country, and new ethnic groups are quickly gaining consumer power. Our company needs a demographically more diverse workforce to help us gain access to these differentiated segments. We need employees with multilingual skills in order to understand and serve our customers better and to gain legitimacy with them. Diversity isn't just fair; it makes business sense.

Where this paradigm has taken hold, organizations have pushed for access to—and legitimacy with—a more diverse clientele by matching the demographics of the organization to those of critical consumer or constituent groups. In cases, the effort has led to substantial increases in organizational diversity. In investment banks, for example, municipal finance departments have long led corporate finance departments in pursuing demographic diversity because of the typical makeup of the administration of city halls and county boards. Many consumer-products companies that have used market segmentation based on gender, racial, and other demographic differences have also frequently created dedicated marketing positions for each segment. The paradigm has therefore led to new professional and managerial opportunities for women and people of color.

What are the common characteristics of organizations that have successfully used the access-and-legitimacy paradigm to increase their demographic diversity? There is but one: such companies almost always operate in a business environment in which there is increased diversity among customers, clients, or the labor pool—and therefore a clear opportunity or an imminent threat to the company.

Again, the paradigm has its strengths. Its market-based motivation and the potential for competitive advantage that it suggests are often qualities an entire company can understand and therefore support. But the paradigm is perhaps more notable for its limitations. In their pursuit of niche markets, access-and-legitimacy organizations tend to emphasize the role of cultural differences in a company without really analyzing those differences to see how they actually affect the work that is done. Whereas discrimination-and-fairness leaders are too quick to subvert differences in the interest of preserving harmony, access-and-legitimacy leaders are too quick to push staff with niche capabilities into differentiated pigeonholes without trying to understand what those capabilities really are and how they could be integrated into the company's mainstream work. To illustrate our point, we present the case of Access Capital.

Access Capital International is a U.S. investment bank that in the early 1980s launched an aggressive plan to expand into Europe. Initially, however, Access encountered serious problems opening offices in international markets; the people from the United States who were installed abroad lacked credibility, were ignorant of local cultural norms and market conditions, and simply couldn't seem to connect with native clients. Access responded by hiring Europeans who had attended North American business schools and by assigning them in teams to the foreign offices. This strategy was a marked success. Before long, the leaders of Access could take enormous pride in the fact that their European operations were highly profitable and staffed by a truly international corps of professionals. They took to calling the company "the best investment bank in the world."

Several years passed. Access's foreign offices continued to thrive, but some leaders were beginning to sense that the company was not fully benefiting from its diversity efforts. Indeed, some even suspected that the bank had made itself vulnerable because of how it had chosen to manage diversity. A senior executive from the United States explains:

> If the French team all resigned tomorrow, what would we do? I'm not sure what we could do! We've never attempted to learn what these differences and cultural competencies really are, how they change the process of doing business. What is the German country team actually doing? We don't know. We know they're good, but we don't know the subtleties of how they do what they do. We assumed—and I think correctly—that culture makes a difference, but that's about as far as we went. We hired Europeans with American MBA's because we didn't know why we couldn't do business in Europe—we just assumed there was something cultural about why we couldn't connect. And ten years later, we still don't know what it is. If we knew, then perhaps we could take it and teach it. Which part of the investment banking process is universal and which part of it draws upon particular cultural competencies? What are the commonalities and differences? I may not be German, but maybe I could do better at understanding what it means to be an American doing business in Germany. Our company's biggest failing is that the department heads in London and the directors of the various country teams have never talked about these cultural identity issues openly. We knew enough to use people's cultural strengths, as it were, but we never seemed to learn from them.

Access's story makes an important point about the main limitation of the access-and-legitimacy paradigm: under its influence, the motivation for diversity usually emerges from very immediate and often crisis-oriented needs for access and legitimacy—in this case, the need to broker deals in European markets. However, once the organization appears to be achieving its goal, the leaders seldom go on to identify and analyze the culturally based skills, beliefs, and practices that worked so well. Nor do they consider how the organization can incorporate and learn from those skills, beliefs, or practices in order to capitalize on diversity in the long run.

Under the access-and-legitimacy paradigm, it was as if the bank's country teams had become little spin-off companies in their own right, doing their own exotic, slightly mysterious cultural diversity thing in a niche market of their own, using competencies that for some reason could not become more fully integrated into the larger organization's understanding of itself. Difference was valued within Access Capital—hence the development of country teams in the first place—but not valued enough that the organization would try to integrate it into the very core of its culture and into its business practices.

Finally, the access-and-legitimacy paradigm can leave some employees feeling exploited. Many organizations using this paradigm have diversified only in those areas in which they interact with particular niche-market segments. In time, many individuals recruited for this function have come to feel devalued and used as they begin to sense that opportunities in other parts of the organization are closed to them. Often the larger organization regards the experience of these employees as more limited or specialized, even though many of them in fact started their careers in the mainstream market before moving to special markets where their cultural backgrounds were a recognized asset. Also, many of these people say that when companies have needed to downsize or narrow their marketing focus, it is the special departments that are often the first to go. That situation creates tenuous and ultimately untenable career paths for employees in the special departments.

THE EMERGING PARADIGM: CONNECTING DIVERSITY TO WORK PERSPECTIVES

Recently, in the course of our research, we have encountered a small number of organizations that, having relied initially on one of the above paradigms to guide their diversity efforts, have come to believe that they are not making the most of their own pluralism. These organizations, like Access Capital, recognize that employees frequently make decisions and choices at work that draw upon their cultural background—choices made because of their identity-group affiliations. The companies have also developed an outlook on diversity that enables them to *incorporate* employees' perspectives into the main work of the organization and to enhance work by rethinking primary tasks and redefining markets, products, strategies, missions, business practices, and even cultures. Such companies are using the learning-and-effectiveness paradigm for managing diversity and, by doing so, are tapping diversity's true benefits.

A case in point is Dewey & Levin, a small public-interest law firm located in a northeastern U.S. city. Although Dewey & Levin had long been a profitable practice, by the mid-1980s its all-white legal staff had become concerned that the women they represented in employment-related disputes were exclusively white. The firm's attorneys viewed that fact as a deficiency in light of their mandate to advocate on behalf of all women. Using the thinking behind the access-and-legitimacy paradigm, they also saw it as bad for business.

Shortly thereafter, the firm hired a Hispanic female attorney. The partners' hope, simply put, was that she would bring in clients from her own community and also demonstrate the firm's commitment to representing all women. But something even bigger than that happened. The new attorney introduced ideas to Dewey & Levin about what kinds of cases it should take on. Senior managers were open to those ideas and pursued them with great success. More women of color were hired, and they, too, brought fresh perspectives. The firm now pursues cases that its previously all-white legal staff would not have thought relevant or appropriate because the link between the firm's mission and the employment issues involved in the cases would not have been obvious to them. For example, the firm has pursued precedent-setting litigation that challenges English-only policies—an area that it once would have ignored because such policies did not fall under the purview of traditional affirmative-action work. Yet it now sees a link English-only policies and employment issues for a large group of women—primarily recent immigrants—whom it had previously failed to serve adequately. As one of the white principals explains, the demographic composition of Dewey & Levin "affected the work in terms of expanding of what are [relevant] issues and taking on issues and framing them in creative ways that would have never been done [with an all-white staff]. It's really changed the substance—and in that sense enhanced the quality—of our work."

Dewey & Levin's increased business has reinforced its commitment to diversity. In addition, people of color at the firm uniformly report feeling respected, not simply "brought along as window dressing." Many of the new attorneys say their perspectives are heard with a kind of openness and interest they have never experienced before in a work setting. Not surprisingly, the firm has had little difficulty attracting and retaining a competent and diverse professional staff.

If the discrimination-and-fairness paradigm is organized around the theme of assimilation—in which the aim is to achieve a demographically representative workforce whose members treat one another exactly the same—then the access-and-legitimacy paradigm can be regarded as coalescing around an almost opposite concept: differentiation, in which the objective is to place different people where their demographic characteristics match those of important constituents and markets.

The emerging paradigm, in contrast to both, organizes itself around the overarching theme of integration. Assimilation goes too far in pursuing sameness. Differentiation, as we have shown, overshoots in the other direction. The new model for managing diversity transcends both. Like the fairness paradigm, it promotes equal opportunity for all individuals. And like the access paradigm, it acknowledges cultural differences among people and recognizes the value in those differences. Yet this new model for managing diversity lets the organization internalize differences among employees so that it learns and grows because of them. Indeed, with the model fully in place, members of the organization can say, we are all on the same team, *with* our differences—not *despite* them.

EIGHT PRECONDITIONS FOR MAKING THE PARADIGM SHIFT

Dewey & Levin may be atypical in its eagerness to open itself up to change and engage in a long-term transformation process. We remain convinced, however, that unless organizations that are currently in the grip of the other two paradigms can revise their view of diversity so as to avoid cognitive blind spots, opportunities will be missed, tensions will most likely be misdiagnosed, and companies will continue to find the potential benefits of diversity elusive.

Hence the question arises: What is it about the law firm of Dewey & Levin and other emerging third-paradigm companies that enables them to make the most of their diversity? Our research suggests that there are eight preconditions that help to position organizations to use identity-group differences in the service of organizational learning, growth, and renewal.

1. **The leadership must understand that a diverse workforce will embody different perspectives and approaches to work, and must truly value variety of opinion and insight.** We know of a financial services company that once assumed that the only successful sales model was one that utilized aggressive, rapid-fire cold calls. (Indeed, its incentive system rewarded salespeople in large part for the number of calls made.) An internal review of the company's diversity initiatives, however, showed that the company's first- and third-most-profitable employees were women who were most likely to use a sales technique based on the slow but sure building of relationships. The company's top management had now made the link between different identity groups and different approaches to how work gets done and has come to see that there is more than one right way to get positive results.
2. **The leadership must recognize both the learning opportunities and the challenges that the expression of different perspectives presents for an organization.** In other words, the second precondition is a leadership that is committed to persevering during the long process of learning and relearning that the new paradigm requires.
3. **The organizational culture must create an expectation of high standards of performance from everyone.** Such a culture isn't one that expects less from some employees than from others. Some organizations expect women and people of color to underperform—a negative assumption that too often becomes a self-fulfilling prophecy. To move to the third paradigm, a company must believe that all its members can and should contribute fully.
4. **The organizational culture must stimulate personal development.** Such a culture brings out people's full range of useful knowledge and skills—usually through the careful design of jobs that allow people to grow and develop but also though training and education programs.
5. **The organizational culture must encourage openness.** Such a culture instills a high tolerance for debate and supports constructive conflict on work-related matters.
6. **The culture must make workers feel valued.** If this precondition is met, workers feel committed to—and empowered within—the organization and therefore feel comfortable taking the initiative to apply their skills and experiences in new ways to enhance their job performance.
7. **The organization must have a well-articulated and widely understood mission.** Such a mission enables people to be clear about what the company is trying to accomplish. It grounds and guides discussions about work-related changes that staff members might suggest. Being clear about the company's mission helps keep discussions about work differences from degenerating into debates about the validity of people's perspectives. A clear mission provides a focal point that keeps the discussion centered on accomplishment of goals.
8. **The organization must have a relatively egalitarian, nonbureaucratic structure.** It's important to have a structure that promotes the exchange of ideas and welcomes constructive challenges to the usual

way of doing things—from any employee with valuable experience. Forward-thinking leaders in bureaucratic organizations must retain the organization's efficiency-promoting control systems and chains of command while finding ways to reshape the change-resisting mind-set of the classic bureaucratic model. They need to separate the enabling elements of bureaucracy (the ability to get things done) from the disabling elements of bureaucracy (those that create resistance to experimentation).

FIRST INTERSTATE BANK: A PARADIGM SHIFT IN PROGRESS

All eight preconditions do not have to be in place in order to begin a shift from the first or second diversity orientations toward the learning-and-effectiveness paradigm. But most should be. First Interstate Bank, a midsize bank operating in a midwestern city, illustrates this point.

First Interstate, admittedly, is not a typical bank. Its client base is a minority community, and its mission is expressly to serve that base through "the development of a highly talented workforce." The bank is unique in other ways: its leadership welcomes constructive criticism; its structure is relatively egalitarian and nonbureaucratic; and its culture is open-minded. Nevertheless, First Interstate had long enforced a policy that loan officers had to hold college degrees. Those without were hired only for support-staff jobs and were never promoted beyond or outside support functions.

Two years ago, however, the support staff began to challenge the policy. Many of them had been with First Interstate for many years and, with the company's active support, had improved their skills through training. Others had expanded their skills on the job, again with the bank's encouragement, learning to run credit checks, prepare presentations for clients, and even calculate the algorithms necessary for many loan decisions. As a result, some people on the support staff were doing many of the same tasks as loan officers. Why, then, they wondered, couldn't they receive commensurate rewards in title and compensation?

This questioning led to a series of contentious meetings between the support staff and the bank's senior managers. It soon became clear that the problem called for managing diversity—diversity based not on race or gender but on class. The support personnel were uniformly from lower socioeconomic communities than were the college-educated loan officers. Regardless, the principle was the same as for race- or gender-based diversity problems. The support staff had different ideas about how the work of the bank should be done. They argued that those among them with the requisite skills should be allowed to rise through the ranks to professional positions, and they believed their ideas were not being heard or accepted.

Their beliefs challenged assumptions that the company's leadership had long held about which employees should have the authority to deal with customers and about how much responsibility administrative employees should ultimately receive. In order to take up this challenge, the bank would have to be open to exploring the requirements that a new perspective would impose on it. It would need to consider the possibility of mapping out an educational and career path for people without degrees—a path that put such workers on road to becoming loan officers. In other words, the leadership would have to transform itself willingly and embrace fluidity in policies that in times past had been clearly stated and unquestioningly held.

Today the bank's leadership is undergoing just such a transformation. The going, however, is far from easy. The bank's senior managers now look beyond the tensions and acrimony sparked by the debate over differing work perspectives and consider the bank's new direction an important learning and growth opportunity.

SHIFT COMPLETE: THIRD-PARADIGM COMPANIES IN ACTION

First Interstate is a shift in progress; but, in addition to Dewey & Levin, there are several organizations we know of for which the shift is complete. In these cases, company leaders have played a critical role as facilitators and tone setters. We have observed in particular that in organizations that have adopted the new perspective, leaders and manager—and, following in their tracks, employees in general—are taking four kinds of action.

They are making the mental connection. First in organizations that have adopted the new perspective, the leaders are actively seeking opportunities to explore how identity-group differences affect relationships among workers and affect the way work gets done. They are investing considerable time and energy in understanding how identity-group memberships take on social meaning in the organization and how those meaning manifest themselves in the way work is defined, assigned, and accomplished. When there is no proactive search to understand, then learning from diversity, if it happens at all, can occur only reactively—that is, in response to diversity-related crises.

The situation at Iversen Dunham illustrates the missed opportunities resulting from that scenario. Rather than seeing differences in the way project leaders defined and approached their work as an opportunity to gain new insights and develop new approaches to achieving its mission, the firm remained entrenched in its traditional ways, able to arbitrate such differences only by thinking about what was fair and what was racist. With this quite limited view of the role race can play in an organization, discussions about the topic become fraught with fear and defensiveness, and everyone misses out on insights about how race might influence work in positive ways.

A second case, however, illustrates how some leaders using the new paradigm have been able to envision—and make—the connection between cultural diversity and the company's work. A vice president of Mastiff, a large national insurance company, received a complaint from one of managers in her unit, an African American man. The manager wanted to demote an African American woman he had hired for a leadership position from another Mastiff division just three months before. He told the vice president he was profoundly disappointed with the performance of his new hire.

"I hired her because I was pretty certain she had tremendous leadership skill," he said. "I knew she had a management style that was very open and empowering. I was also sure she'd have a great impact on the rest of the management team. But she hasn't done any of that."

Surprised, the vice president tried to find out from him what he thought the problem was, but she was not getting any answers that she felt really defined or illuminated the root of the problem. Privately, it puzzled her that someone would decide to demote a 15-year veteran of the company—and a minority woman at that—so soon after bringing her to his unit.

The vice president probed further. In the course of the conversation, the manager happened to mention that he knew the new employee from church and was familiar with the way she handled leadership there and in other community settings. In those less formal situations, he had seen her perform as an extremely effective, sensitive, and influential leader.

That is when the vice president made an interpretive leap. "If that's what you know about her," the vice president said to the manager, "then the question for us is, why can't she bring those skills to work here?" The vice president decided to arrange a meeting with all three present to ask this very question directly. In the meeting, the African American woman explained, "I didn't think I would last long if I acted that way here. My personal style of leadership—that particular style—works well if you have the permission to do it fully; then you can just do it and not have to look over your shoulder."

Pointing to the manager who had planned to fire her, she added, "He's right. The style of leadership I use outside this company can definitely be effective. But I've been at Mastiff for 15 years. I know this organization, and I know if I brought that piece of myself—if I became that authentic—I just wouldn't survive here."

What this example illustrates is that the vice president's learning-and-effectiveness paradigm led her to explore and then make the link between cultural diversity and work style. What was occurring, she realized, was a mismatch between the cultural background of the recently promoted woman and the cultural environment of her work setting. It had little to do with private attitudes or feeling, or gender issues, or some inherent lack of leadership ability. The source of the underperformance was that the newly promoted woman had a certain style and the organization's culture did not support her in expressing it comfortably. The vice president's paradigm led her to ask new questions and to seek out new information, but, more important, it also led her to interpret existing information differently.

The two senior managers began to realize that part of the African American woman's inability to see herself as a leader at work was that she had for so long been undervalued in the organization. And, in a sense, she had become used to splitting herself off from who she was in her own community. In the 15 years she had been at Mastiff, she had done her job well as an individual contributor, but she had never received any signals that her bosses wanted her to draw on her cultural competencies in order to lead effectively.

They Are Legitimating Open Discussion

Leaders and managers who have adopted the new paradigm are taking the initiative to "green light" open discussion about how identity-group memberships inform and influence an employee's experience and the organization's behavior. They are encouraging people to make explicit use of background cultural experience and the pools of knowledge gained outside the organization to inform and enhance their work. Individuals often do use their cultural competencies at work, but in a closeted, almost embarrassed, way. The unfortunate result is that the opportunity for collective and organizational learning and improvement is lost.

The case of a Chinese woman who worked as a chemist at Torinno Food Company illustrates this point. Linda was part of a product development group at Torinno when a problem arose with the flavoring of a new soup. After the group had made a number of scientific attempts to correct the problem, Linda came up with the solution by "setting aside my chemistry and drawing on my understanding of Chinese cooking." She did not, however, share with her colleagues—all of them white males—the real source of her inspiration for the solution for fear that it would set her apart or that they might consider her unprofessional. Overlaid on the cultural issue, of course, was a gender issue (women cooking) as well as a working-family issue (women doing home cooking in a chemistry lab). All of these themes had erected unspoken boundaries that Linda knew could be career damaging for her to cross. After solving the problem, she simply went back to the so-called scientific way of doing things.

Senior managers at Torinno Foods in fact had made a substantial commitment to diversifying the workforce through a program designed to teach employees to value the contributions of all its members. Yet Linda's perceptions indicate that, in the actual day-to-day context of work, the program had failed—and in precisely one of those areas where it would have been important for it to have worked. It had failed to affirm someone's identity-group experiences as a legitimate source of insight into her work. It is likely that this organization will miss future opportunities to take full advantage of the talent of employees such as Linda. When people believed that they must suggest and apply their ideas covertly, the organization also misses opportunities to discuss, debate, refine, and build on those ideas fully. In addition, because individuals like Linda will continue to think that they must hide parts of themselves in order to fit in, they will find it difficult to engage fully not only in their work but also in their workplace relationships. That kind of situation can breed resentment and misunderstanding, fueling tensions that can further obstruct productive work relationships.

They Actively Work Against Forms Of Dominance And Subordination That Inhibit Full Contribution

Companies in which the third paradigm is emerging have leaders and managers who take responsibility for removing the barriers that block employees from using the full range of their competencies, cultural, or otherwise. Racism, homophobia, sexism, and sexual harassment are the most obvious forms of dominance that decrease individual and organizational effectiveness—and third-paradigm leaders have zero tolerance for them. In addition, the leaders are aware that organizations can create their own unique patterns of dominance and subordination based on the presumed superiority and entitlement of some groups over others. It is not uncommon, for instance, to find organizations in which one functional area considers itself better than another. Members of the presumed inferior group frequently describe the organization in the very terms used by these who experience identity-group discrimination. Regardless of the source of the oppression, the result is diminished performance and commitment from employees.

What can leaders do to prevent those kinds of behaviors beyond explicitly forbidding any forms of dominance? They can and should test their own assumptions about the competencies of all members of the workforce because negative assumptions are often unconsciously communicated in powerful—albeit nonverbal—ways. For example, senior managers at Delta Manufacturing had for years allowed productivity and quality at their inner-city plants to lag well behind the levels of other plants. When the company's chief executive officer began to question why the problem was never addressed, he came to realize that, in his heart, he had believed that inner-city workers, most of whom were African American or Hispanic, were not capable of doing better then subpar. In the end, the CEO and his senior management team were able to reverse their reasoning and take responsibility for improving the situation. The result was a sharp increase in the performance of the inner-city plants and a message to the entire organization about the capabilities of its entire workforce.

At Mastiff, the insurance company discussed earlier, the vice president and her manager decided to work with the recently promoted African American woman rather than demote her. They realized that their unit was really a pocket inside the larger organization: they did not have to wait for the rest of the organization to make a paradigm shift in order for their particular unit to change. So they met again to think about how to create conditions within their unit that would move the woman toward seeing her leadership position as encompassing all her skills. They assured her that her authentic style of leadership was precisely what they wanted her to bring to the job. They wanted her to be able to use whatever aspects of herself she thought would make more effective in her work because the whole purpose was to do the job effectively, not to fit some preset traditional formula of how to behave. They let her know that, as a management team, they would try to adjust and change and support her. And they would deal with whatever consequences resulted from her exercising her decision rights in new ways.

Another example of this line of action—working against forms of dominance and subordination to enable full contribution—is the way the CEO of a major chemical company modified the attendance rules for his company's annual strategy conference. In the past, the conference had been attended only by senior executives, a relatively homogeneous group of white men. The company had been working hard on increasing the representation of women and people of color in its ranks, and the CEO could have left it at that. But he reckoned that, unless steps were taken, it would be ten years before the conferences tapped into the insights and perspectives of his newly diverse workforce. So he took the bold step of opening the conference to people from across all levels of the hierarchy, bringing together a diagonal slice of the organization. He also asked the conference organizers to come up with specific interventions, such as small group meetings before the larger session, to ensure that the new attendees would be comfortable enough to enter discussions. The result was that strategy-conference participants heard a much broader, richer, and livelier discussion about future scenarios for the company.

They Are Making Sure That Organizational Trust Stays Intact

Few things are faster at killing a shift to a new way of thinking about diversity than feelings of broken trust. Therefore, managers of organizations that are successfully shifting to the learning-and-effectiveness paradigm take one more step: they make sure their organizations remain "safe" places for employees to be themselves. These managers recognize that tensions naturally arise as an organization begins to make room for diversity, starts to experiment with process and product ideas, and learns to reappraise its mission in light of suggestions from newly empowered constituents in the company. But as people put more of themselves out and open up about new feelings and ideas, the dynamics of the learning-and-effectiveness paradigm can produce temporary vulnerabilities. Managers who have helped their organizations make the change successfully have consistently demonstrated their commitment to the process and to all employees by setting a tone of honest discourse, by acknowledging tensions, and by resolving them sensitively and swiftly.

Our research over the past six years indicates that one cardinal limitation is at the root of companies' inability to attain the expected performance benefits of higher levels of diversity: the leadership's vision of the purpose of a diversified workforce. We have described the two most dominant orientations toward diversity and some of their consequences and limitations, together with a new framework for understanding and managing diversity. The learning-and-effectiveness paradigm we have outlined here is, undoubtedly, still in an emergent phase in those few organizations that embody it. We expect that as more organizations take on the challenge of truly engaging their diversity, new and unforeseen dilemmas will arise. Thus, perhaps more than anything else, a shift toward this paradigm requires a high-level commitment to learning more about the environment, structure, and tasks of one's organization, and giving improvement-generating change greater priority than the security of what is familiar. This is not an easy challenge, but we remain convinced that unless organizations take this step, any diversity initiative will fall short of fulfilling its rich promise.

Discussion Questions

1. According to this article, why might an organization that is operating in (a) the discrimination-and-fairness paradigm or (b) the access-and-legitimacy paradigm have trouble recruiting and retaining the most qualified diverse workers?
2. Review the eight preconditions for an organization to be in the third paradigm—learning and effectiveness. Which of these eight could be considered good management practices even if diversity were not part of the issue?
3. Think of an organization where you have worked. Explain which of the three paradigms this organization was operating in and justify your answer.

BUILDING A BUSINESS CASE FOR DIVERSITY

Gail Robinson

Kathleen Dechant

Abstract: Business experts have often overlooked the significance of diversity initiatives despite the profound impact it creates on organizational effectiveness. Problems are further aggravated by the lack of understanding concerning payback on investments. Diversity initiatives offer corporate leaders an optimal tool for increasing their resources and at the same time creating a conducive working atmosphere for workers.

A phenomenal surge in the growth of emerging markets, extensive use of cross-functional, heterogeneous teams to produce creative solutions to business problems, an increased reliance on non-traditional workforce talent—the realities of today's workplace clearly demonstrate that diversity management has become a critical aspect of operating a business.[1] Yet, a 1992 survey by the Hay Group showed that only five percent of 1,405 companies thought they were doing a very good job of managing the diversity of their workforces.[2] The reason companies aren't doing a better job stems from the way management determines and prioritizes a firm's time and resources. Although top management views diversity integration as important, there are usually more tangible and compelling business priorities that win out in the short run. The shift to lean organizational structures and the forces of Wall Street favor short-term investments with clear returns. In contrast, diversity integration requires a long-term commitment and the payback is often not as tangible or predictable as, say, investing in new product development.

Just as the head of Research and Development must present a compelling, fact-based business case to top management to gain the necessary commitment and resources from the organization to pursue a product initiative, so too must the head of Human Resources develop a cue for diversity integration based on the competitive edge gained by optimizing the people resources of a firm.

Developing a business case for diversity is more difficult than for other business issues because evidence of diversity's impact on the bottom line has not been systematically measured and documented for easy retrieval and use. The human resource executive who tries to build such a case confronts a vast array of information and advice on diversity management, but finds little guidance on how to pull this data together to present a compelling and fact-based business case.

This article outlines, describes, and updates the competitive and business reasons for managing diversity. Citing best practices as well as the most recent research, the approach presented builds upon the seminal work done in 1991 by Cox and Blake linking diversity and organizational performance.[2] As a whole, it demonstrates that a compelling rationale can be created for making diversity a top business priority.

WHAT DO WE MEAN BY DIVERSITY AND DIVERSITY MANAGEMENT?

Some companies still use the traditional Equal Employment Opportunity Commission (EEOC) definition of diversity, which deals with differences in gender, racioethnicity, and age. Others employ definitions that are broader and include different physical abilities, qualities, and sexual orientation. Still others focus on the heterogeneity of attitudes, perspectives, and backgrounds among group members. Finally, some businesses have broadened their definition of diversity even further to include people from different hierarchical levels, functions, and backgrounds. The Pillsbury Company, for instance, defines diversity as "all the ways in which we differ."[3]

Companies competing in today's fast-paced global markets tend to favor the broadest definitions of diversity—ones that encompass differences in gender, racioethnicity, age, physical abilities, qualities, and sexual orientation, is well as differences in attitudes, perspectives and background.

BUSINESS REASONS FOR MANAGING DIVERSITY

Since the publication of the Workforce 2000 study, cost savings and winning the competition for talent are frequently cited as strong arguments for the pursuit of diversity initiatives.[4] More recently, they have been supplemented with a third, even more forceful argument—the opportunity to drive business growth by leveraging the many facets of diversity. All three reasons surfaced as significant in a recent survey of *Fortune* 100 company human resource executives.[5]

HR Executives Cite Business Reasons for Diversity

Human Resource executives from 15 *Fortune* 100 companies were asked to identify the primary business reasons for engaging in diversity management. The results focus more on reasons that leverage the opportunities diversity management offers than on those having to do with avoiding the penalties of mismanagement (e.g., turnover costs and lawsuits).

Top five reasons:

1. Better utilization of talent (93 percent)
2. Increased marketplace understanding (80 percent)
3. Enhanced breadth of understanding in leadership positions (60 percent)
4. Enhanced creativity (53 percent)
5. Increased quality of team problem-solving (40 percent)

EXHIBIT 1   Diversity Rationale Poll

Cost Savings

The first argument for diversity focuses on the negative impact of diversity mismanagement on the bottom line.

Higher Turnover Costs

Turnover among women and people of color is a significant and costly problem for many companies. The turnover rate for blacks in the U.S. workforce is 40 percent higher than the rate for whites, and turnover among women is twice as high as for men.[6] The added recruiting, staffing, and training costs per person are estimated at $5,000 to $10,000 for an hourly worker and between $75,000 to $211,000 for an executive at around the $100,000 salary level. Mary Mattis, Vice President of Catalyst, an organization that works with corporations to foster the career and leadership development of women, estimates that replacement costs total 93 percent of the departing employee's annual salary.[7] In addition, such a revolving-door situation means employees are constantly climbing the learning curve instead of performing at full potential.

Women have higher turnover rates than men at all ages, not just during their childbearing years. Mobil, for example, discovered that its high potential women were leaving the company at two and a half times the rate of comparable men.[8] A *Fortune* 500 utility company with 27,000 employees found it was losing $15.3 million per year because of the costs associated with systematic gender bias, such as turnover and loss of productivity. This high figure did not even include sexual harassment costs.[9] The lack of opportunity for career growth is the primary reason that professional and managerial women leave their jobs.[10]

Higher Absenteeism Rates

Absenteeism, like turnover, can rack up significant costs for the organization. One *Fortune* 500 financial services corporation estimated the cost of absenteeism for 440 of their blue collar and clerical workers at $100,000.[17] Absenteeism rates are often higher among women and non-white men than they are for white males. A study of absence rates in the U.S. workforce found that rates for women are 58 percent higher than for men.[11] In many cases, family responsibilities, including child and elder care, are key factors underlying such high absenteeism.

Other studies have tied employees' perceptions of the workplace to elements of productivity, which may help to explain the notable level of absenteeism among non-white men. For example, Robert Eisenberger and his colleagues found a positive relationship between employees' perceptions of being valued and cared about by their organization and their attendance, dedication, and job performance.[12] Workers must feel secure about their status to fully engage themselves at work. This is a particular issue for low-status members of an organization, who cannot engage themselves deeply in their work when the organizational values do not fit their own.[13]

A Gallup poll found that often mothers employed full-time, would prefer part-time employment, flexible hours, or telecommuting.[14] Companies are beginning to respond to work/family balance issues by offering changes in benefits, day care facilities, and flexible hours. There is some evidence that these approaches can result in lower absenteeism rates. For example, in one study, companies were assigned an accommodation score based on the adoption of four benefit-liberalization changes associated with pregnant workers. Analysis revealed that the higher a company's accommodation score, the lower the number of sick days taken by pregnant workers and the more willing they were to work overtime during pregnancy.[15]

The addition of an in-house child care facility in one organization improved organizational commitment and job satisfaction and lowered absenteeism rates. Greater use of flextime work scheduling caused both short- and long-term absence to decline significantly. Work efficiency measures also increased significantly.[16]

Lawsuits on Sexual, Race and Age Discrimination

With employee sexual harassment complaints on the rise, the EEOC faces a backlog of 97,000 cases.[17] Lawsuits increase in frequency as employees become more aware of discriminatory practices. For example, there were 20 times more discrimination lawsuits in 1990 than 1970. Plaintiffs win two-thirds of the cases that go to trial. The average jury award for a discrimination lawsuit is $600,000.[18] Texaco settled a race discrimination lawsuit November, 1996 for $176.1 million.[30] In addition, Texaco agreed to allow the EEOC to monitor every detail of its hiring and promotion practices for the for the next five year to ensure there is no discrimination against minority employees.[19] A lawsuit filed in May 1996, against Smith-Barney claims that women make up less than 5 percent of the company's 11,000 brokers and fewer than 10 branch managers out of 440 branch offices.

Foreign-owned companies can't escape liability either. Mitsubishi faces $120 million damages as a result of a sexual harassment lawsuit filed by the

EEOC.[20] In response, the firm decided to implement a comprehensive training program for dealing with sexual harassment and appointed a senior manager to promote advancement for minorities and women.

Winning the Competition for Talent

Winning the competition for talent means attracting, retaining, and promoting excellent employees from different demographic groups. As women and minorities increase in representation in the labor pool, organizations are competing to hire, retain, and utilize the best employees from these groups. Companies cited as the best places to work for women and minorities reported an increased inflow of applications from women and minorities, which is evidence of their ability to attract talent. According to Niall FitzGerald, Co-Chairman of Unilever, "We need the best people available. If we directly or indirectly restrict our choice, or make it more difficult to find the very best management available now and in the future, this is not only short sighted it will also be short-lived!"[21]

Attracting good talent is one thing; retaining it quite another. Women and minorities most often leave firms out of frustration over finding career opportunities and advancing up the corporate ladder.[22] A possible explanation for this problem can be attributed to the reluctance of management to coach and counsel these employees. Employees need feedback on the effectiveness of their behavior. However, women and people of color tend to receive less feedback than men. Feedback given to men is two-and-a-half to three times lengthier than that given to women, according to Kate Butler of American Human Management Association. Conversely, women in successful mentoring relationships report an increase of nearly 94 percent to their professional effectiveness.[23]

Women are more likely to be placed in unchallenging jobs than men and to be limited by sexual bias in promotion opportunities. Racially motivated job treatment discrimination and promotion discrimination against minorities are factors that affect minority employees. The subtle biases present in promotion decisions often result in less than optimal utilization of the best talent in organizations.[24]

Sustaining competitive advantage depends on optimizing valuable human resources. Companies that are better able to recruit, develop, retain and promote diverse employees have an edge. Talented people will be attracted to corporations that value their capabilities and will be more willing to invest themselves in productive activity if they believe they are treated fairly and that career opportunities are available.

Driving Business Growth

A powerful new impetus for managing diversity centers on driving business growth by leveraging opportunities associated with increased marketplace understanding, greater creativity, higher quality team problem-solving, improved leadership effectiveness, and better global relations.

The Women of Microsoft

Bill Gates, CEO of Microsoft, and his senior management team boast that they only hire smart people. In the early days of the firm, this mostly meant male software engineers; Microsoft was not a particularly hospitable place for women. Today, the future growth of the company depends in no small part on the women of the Interactive Media Division. As the corporate market for PCs slows, Microsoft is looking to the consumer market; its U.S. Multimedia Division is looking to come up with creative CD-ROMs to engage this growing segment of the market. The requirements for these home CD-ROMs differ considerably from corporate computer and spreadsheet programs. They demand talents found mainly in a female talent pool. Microsoft has begun to leverage its skills to attract and retain women in a industry where such talent is scarce and is fast becoming a determinant of competitive success.[25]

EXHIBIT 2   Diversity and Microsoft

Improving Marketplace Understanding

The consumer market for goods and services is becoming increasingly diverse. Given the increase in ethnocultural diversity within the U.S. marketplace, formerly small market niches are becoming substantial ones that large corporations want to pursue. The spending power of African-Americans, Asian-Americans, and Hispanics together was estimated at $424 billion in 1990 and is expected to reach $650 billion by the year 2000.[26]

The cultural understanding needed to market to these demographic niches resides most naturally in marketers with the same cultural background. Joanie Miller, director of the Center for the New American Work Force, Queens College, says, "The power of cultural knowledge and individual contact inherent in diversity is vastly underestimated in the fight to gain share in today's segmented marketplace."[27]

Several companies have taken advantage of their diverse talent to improve marketplace understanding. Avon Company, for example, was able to turn around its unprofitable inner city markets by putting African-American and Hispanic managers in charge of marketing to these populations. In the early 1990s, Maybelline, Inc., launched a new product line, Shades of You, for women of darker skin tones. With no minorities working in marketing or in middle or upper management, Maybelline hired people of color into marketing to concentrate on promoting the line. Shades of You captured 41 percent of the $55 million ethnic cosmetics market, making Maybelline the dominant player in the ethnic marketplace. Maybelline has since folded the line into an expanded product portfolio, having discovered that women in general prefer a wide range of color choices.[28]

Dupont recently leveraged the cultural savvy of a group of African-American workers in opening up promising new markets for its agricultural products. Another multicultural team recommended changes in the development and marketing of the company's decorating materials and garnered $45 million in business worldwide as a result.[29]

Besides gaining market penetration, companies can benefit from the good will of diverse consumers who prefer to spend their dollars on products produced by a diverse workforce or to give patronage to businesses with a diverse sales force. As Liz Minyard of Minyard Food Stores states, "Most people in the [supermarket] industry are beginning to realize that your workplace should reflect your consumer base. It just makes good business sense."[30]

Finally, customers and suppliers, as well as consumers, are becoming more diverse. The Food Marketing Institute's Board of Directors formed a Task Force on Managing Diversity with the goal of increasing representation and utilization of females and minorities in the industry at both the store and corporate levels.[31] Companies are likely to benefit from matching the diversity of their customers and suppliers for the same reasons as from matching the diversity of their consumer bases.

Increasing Creativity and Innovation

Along with increasing marketplace understanding, the optimization of a diverse workforce can stimulate creativity and innovation.[32] Attitudes, cognitive functioning, and beliefs are not randomly distributed in the population, but tend to vary systematically with demographic variables such as age, race, and gender. Therefore, an expected consequence of increased cultural diversity in organizations is the presence of different perspectives for the performance of creative tasks. In addition, employees who feel valued and supported by their organizations tend to be more innovative.[33]

Producing Higher Quality Problem-Solving

Research shows that heterogeneous teams produce more innovative solutions to problems. For example, differences among team member allow them to see problems from a variety of perspectives based on a range of experiences. The variety of perspectives and natural conflict that surface from their interaction ensure that differing views surface and are discussed. It also ensures that a wide range of possible solutions is entertained, and that there is a wide-ranging exploration of the possible consequences of each option considered.

Heterogeneity initially creates difficulties for team members in communicating, understanding, and functioning as a team. While diverse groups experience more conflict in agreeing on what is important and in working together at the outset, they ultimately outperform homogeneous groups in identifying problem perspective and alternative solutions.[34]

Enhancing Leadership Effectiveness

The demographic composition of top management teams affects competitive strategy and financial effectiveness. In a study of 199 top management teams in the banking industry, organizational innovation positively correlated with team heterogeneity.[35] Homogeneity at the top results in a more myopic perspective at senior levels. According to Niall FitzGerald of Unilever, "It is important for any

---

The CanadianOxy Experience

Two years ago, a fierce civil war broke out in the Republic of Yemen between two factions with divergent philosophies. CanadianOxy owns a 52 percent interest in and operates the Masila Block Development program in Yemen. The firm's facilities were not attacked, and it was able to continue operations during the war. CEO Bernard F. Isautier believes that the efforts of his people to build very strong relationships with all interested parties were what saved the organization's installation. "We have been successful in integrating our staff with the Yemeni population ... (they) know that we are interested in the development of the country and that we would continue this whoever won the war. . . . It was in no one's best interests to damage our facilities."[38]

EXHIBIT 3 Diversity during Civil War

---

business, operating in an increasingly complex and rapidly changing environment to deploy a broad range of talents. That provides a breadth of understanding of the world and environment within which business operates—and a fusion of the very best values and different perspectives which make up that world."[36]

Building Effective Global Relationships

A critical challenge for top management today is to turn ethnocultural diversity into a differentiating advantage in an increasingly competitive global marketplace. Companies that in the past dealt primarily with the customs and people of North America now find it critical to incorporate ethnocultural diversity into marketing, sales, and customer service strategies throughout the world.

Cultural competence must be recognized as a key management skill. American managers who have been highly successful in the national market may find that their tried and true management practices just don't work in the global arena. They now have to adjust to a world of extraordinary variety in consumer preferences and work practices.[37] The increased cultural awareness developed by a firm's adaptation to diversity can help it become more effective in cross-cultural business situations. Cultural issues have impact on dealing with international customers or managing a group of local nationals.

PULLING IT ALL TOGETHER: STRUCTURING THE BUSINESS CASE

Diversity management can have an impact on both a firm's long-term financial performance and its short-term stock performance.[39] However, the most successful business case for diversity is one that focuses on attaining a firm's specific business objectives. For example, a labor-intensive business, such as a restaurant chain or retail sales operation, may need to reduce turnover and

Early in the 1980s, Corning realized that women and people of color were resigning from the company at more than twice the rate of white men, costing the company $2 to $4 million a year to recruit, train, and relocate replacements. Two quality teams were set up in 1987 to identify and address the issues facing women and black employees. They found that the barriers or challenges facing white males were not the same as those facing women and people of color.

Corning embarked on a systemic intervention to change things. Then CEO Jamie Houghton was appalled that people in the corporation did not feel valued and felt they were not able to contribute. The intervention included mentoring, career development opportunities, a more progressive approach to child care and other work life balance programs, and training. Targets were set to raise the critical mass in the organization. An examination of performance and reward systems was conducted to ensure they were free of bias.

The business case for this systemic intervention rested on the cost of replacement, the shrinking talent pool, and changing market demographics. Using a conservative estimate of $50,000 as the cost of turnover for an average employee. Corning estimated a savings of $5 million by reducing the attrition rate by 100 people. Corning's goal was to have an employee population that mirrored the face of the country. Given the demand for diverse talent, it maintained that a company that was not diversity-friendly would have a difficult time attracting and retaining such talent.

Finally, the company saw the changes taking place in marketplace. As the population it was selling to changed, the marketing and sales strategies had to be shaped by a workforce that thought, acted like, and understood the marketplace. After five years the company has realized the necessary critical mass. Thirty five percent of the management workforce was female, up from almost none in the early 1980s. A relatively recent climate survey showed that the views of the corporation by men and women employees are virtually the same on 40 key questions having to do with career development, fairness, and employee value, among other things.[40]

EXHIBIT 4   The Business Case for Diversity at Corning

absenteeism. A consumer goods or financial services firm may need to improve its understanding and management of enthnoculturalism. Corning's business case for diversity provides an excellent example of linking a company's goals with its diversity initiative.

Creating a business case for diversity involves four steps.
- Determining business objectives or needs
- Identifying actions required for each objective or need

- Conducting a cost/benefit analysis
- Developing tracking mechanisms to assess progress and financial impact

Determining objectives starts with consideration of the business strategy and identifies the highest leverage business opportunities or needs that require diversity. McDonald's business strategy, for example, calls for providing a consistent customer experience across all McDonald's restaurants. For many years this strategy was achieved by employing and training energetic teenagers who were in abundant supply. During the 1980s, the company noticed that the workforce demographics were beginning to change. Teenagers who had for so long formed the basis of the consistent McDonald's experience were dwindling in supply.

The second step identifying what is required to achieve these objectives or needs means deciding whether the nature and magnitude of the initiative will be focused or comprehensive in scope. A focused approach has targeted, specific objectives that seek a particular short-term payback of investment dollars. For example, McDonald's decided to pursue a focused initiative and tapped into the growing numbers of older workers as its new labor pool. It realized that it would have to manage this population differently and took the actions required to do so.[41] A comprehensive strategy has multiple targets and objectives involving a significant investment of time and money. Such a strategy requires integration across the organization, touching multiple systems, levels and cultures.

The third step calls for specifying the costs involved in the implementation of the initiative and the expected returns. Part of the cost/benefit derived from using senior citizens is that they require little or no special training.

The fourth and final step requires that a company identify up front and along the way all the activities of progress that can be measured and evaluated. Building in such measures replicates the way most organizations assess business performance. It also suggests the need for including measures and monitoring processes in strategic business plans that have timetables and for assigning accountability and rewarding and recognizing progress. McDonald's diversity initiative of recruiting MacSeniors has been so successful that the company has gone on to actively recruit older workers for management jobs.

In presenting a business case for a comprehensive approach to diversity, however, diversity management generally involves a long-term culture change requiring a significant commitment of time, resources, and leadership attention. Therefore, the corresponding return on investment may take years. To develop process measures, which track the progress of the diversity interventions, and outcome measures, which track the impact of diversity on business results, can be used to demonstrate progress.

Process can be measured by involving employees in focus groups, surveys, interviews, and various culture audits or needs assessments. Process measures might also include company statistics on recruitment, retention, and promotions, including adverse impact. Process indicators enable top management to see signs of progress, even when business results are not yet visible.

Outcome measures, on the other hand, provide validation and ultimate justification for a long-term investment in diversity. These include measures produced by initiatives designed to achieve specific business objectives, such as new market penetration results as well as broader measures of financial results.

CONCLUSION

The bottom-line focus of today's business environment requires that diversity initiatives be treated like any other business investment, e.g., technology or advertising. This requires human resources executives to create a clear, compelling business case for diversity linked to the company's strategic business objectives. By providing top management with a better understanding of the expected return on investment, HR executives can more successfully compete for the company's scarce resources, resulting in better funded and supported diversity initiatives.

Discussion Questions

1. Which of the authors' arguments for diversity would be the most compelling reason for increased diversity in your organization or at your college?
2. Select an organization where you work or visit a large corporate Website (one of the cases from this text like Ford, Coca-Cola, or Cracker Barrel could also be used here) to determine if they seem to be using any of the authors' reasons for diversity as a business advantage. How well does this reason fit with the organization's stated mission and goals?
3. How does this article help to explain why many diversity-training programs, although well intentioned, often don't really make much of a difference to an organization?

Endnotes

1. Rice, F. (1994). How to make diversity pay. *Fortune*, August 8, 79–86.
2. Cox, T. H., & Blake, S. (1991). Managing cultural diversity: Implications for organizational competitiveness. *Academy of Management Executive, 3,* 45–56.
3. Hayles, R., & Russell, A. (1997). *The diversity directive*. Chicago: Irwin. See Chapter 2 for more definitions of how companies are currently defining diversity. See Chapter 6 for more details relative to identifying the nature of actions to take in both focused and comprehensive initiatives.
4. Johnston, W. B., & Packer, A. E. (1987). *Workforce 2000: Work and workers for the twenty-first century*. Indianapolis, IN: Hudson Institute.
5. Dechant, K. (1995). *HR executives cite business reasons for diversity*. Unpublished manuscript. University of Connecticut.
6. Schwartz, F. (1989). Management, women and the new facts of life. *Harvard Business Review*, January/February, 65–76; Cox and Blake, ibid.
7. Auster, E. R. (1988). Behind closed doors: Sex bias at professional and managerial levels. *Employee Responsibilities and Rights Journal, 1,* 129–144; Stuart, P. (1992). What does the glass ceiling cost you? *Personnel Journal*, November, 70–80.
8. Trost, C. (1989). Firms heed women employees needs: new approach forced

by shifts in population. *Wall Street Journal*, November 22, B 1.

9. Stuart, ibid.

10. Tashjian, V. W. (1990). *Don't blame the baby: Why women leave corporations.* Wilmington, DE: Wick and Company.

11. Meisenheimer, J. R. (1990). Employee absences in 1989: A new look at data from the CPS. *Monthly Labor Review*, August, 28–33.

12. Eisenberger, R., Fasolo, P., and DavisLaMatro, V. (1990). Perceived organizational support and employee diligence, commitment, and innovation. *Journal of Applied Psychology*, 75, 51–59.

13. Kahn, W. A. (1990). Psychological conditions of personal engagement and disengagement at work. *Academy of Management Journal, 33*, 692–724.

14. Hudson Institute. (1988). *Opportunity 2000: Creative Affirmative Action Strategies for a Changing Workforce.* Indianapolis, IN: Hudson Institute; *USA Today*, 1987.

15. Helping pregnant workers pays off. December 2, 1987. USA Today.

16. Youngblood, S. A., & Chambers-Cook, K. (1984). Child care assistance can improve employee attitudes and behavior. *Personnel Administrator*, February, 93–95; Kim, J. S. & Campagna, A. F. (1981). Effects of flextime on employee attendance and performance: A field experiment. *Academy of Management Journal, 24*, 729–741.

17. Spiro, L. N. (1996). Smith Barney's woman problem. *Business Week, June 3*, 102 & 106.

18. Gillespie, J. F., & Volpi, W. M. (1992). *Harnessing the power of cut diversity at Lever: Brief and action plan.* New York: Lever Brothers Company.

19. Eichenwald, C. (1997). Texaco to let U.S. check bias-law compliance. *New York Times*, January 4, p. 36.

20. Cole, R. E., & Deskins, D. R., Jr. (1988). Racial factors in site location employment patterns of Japanese auto firms in America. *California Management Review, 31*, 9–22.

21. Feinstein, S. (1989). Being the best on somebody's list does attract. *Wall Street Journal*, October 10; FitzGerald, N. W. A. (1993). Managing a key resource. London, U.K.: Unilever.

22. Cox, T. H., & Nkomo, S. (1991). A race and gender group analysis early career experience of MBAs. *Work and Occupations, 18*(4), 43 446,

23. Morrison, A. M. (1992). The new leaders: Guidelines on leadership diversity in America. San Francisco: Jossey-Bass, p. 137.

24. Taylor, M. S., & Ilgen, D. R. (1981). Sex discrimination against women in initial placement decisions: A laboratory investigation. *Academy of Management Journal. 24*, 859–865; Hitt, M. A., & Barr, S. H. (1989). Managerial selection decision models: Examination of configural cue processing. *Journal of Applied Psychology, 74*, 53–61; Greenhaus, J. H., Parasuraman, S., & Wormley, W. M., (1990). Effects of race on organizational experiences, job performance evaluations, and career outcomes. *Academy of Management Journal, 33*, 64–86; Ilgen, D. R., & Youtz, M. A. (1986). Factors affecting the evaluation and development of minorities in organizations. In K. Rowland & G. Ferris (Eds.) Research in personnel and human resource management: A research annual (pp. 307–337). Greenwich, CT: JAI Press.; Killingsworth, M. R., & Reimers C. W. (1983). Race, ranking, promotions and pay at a federal facility: A logit analysis. *Industrial and Labor Relations Review, 37*, 92–107; Crosby, F. J., & Blanchard, F. A., (1989). Introduction: Affirmative action the question of standards. In F. A. Blanchard & F. J. Crosby (Eds.), *Affirmative action in perspective* (pp. 37–46). New York: Springer-Verlag.

25. Cushmano, M., & Solby, R. (1995). *Microsoft secrets*. New York: Free Press; Moody, F. (1996). Wonder women in the rude boys paradise. *Fast Company*, June–July, 85–98.

26. Copeland, L. (1988). Valuing workplace diversity: Ten reasons employers recognize the benefits of a mixed workforce. *Personnel Administrator*, November, 38–40.

27. Wilson, M. (1995). Diversity in the workplace. *Chain Store Age Executive*, June, 21–23.

28. Dreyfuss, J. (1990). Get ready for the new workforce. *Fortune*, April 23, 165–181; *Wall Street Journal*, 1996. Cosmetic Firms find women blur color lines, July 3, B1.

29. Labich, K. (1996). Making diversity pay. *Fortune*. September, 177.

30. Wilson, ibid.

31. Wilson, ibid.

32. Filley, A. C., House, R. J., & Kerr. S. (1976). *Managerial process and organizational behavior*. Glenview, IL: Scott, Foresman.

33. Eisenberger, et al., ibid.

34. Jackson, S. E., May, K. E. & Whitney, K. (1995). Understanding the dynamics of diversity in decision-making teams. In R. Guzzo, E. Salas & Associates (Eds.), *Team effectiveness and decision making in organizations*. San Francisco: Jossey-Bass.

35. Eisenhardt, K. M., & Schoonhoven, C. B. (1990). Organizational growth: Linking founding team, strategy, environment, and growth among U.S semiconductor ventures, 1978–1988. *Administrative Science Quarterly, 35*, 504–529.

36. Fitzgerald, ibid.

37. O'Hara-Devereaux, M., & Johansen, R. (1994). *Global work: Bridging distance, culture, and time*. San Francisco: Jossey-Bass.

38. Benimadhu, P. (1995). Adding value through diversity: An interview with Bernard F. Isavtise. *Canadian Business Review*, Spring.

39. Wright, P. Ferris, S. P., Hiller, J. S., & Kroll, M. (1995). Competitiveness through management of diversity: Effects on stock price valuation. *Academy of Management Journal, 38*, 272–287.

40. Schmidt, P. (1988). Women and minorities: Is industry ready? *New York Times*, Oct. 16, 25–27.

41. Ladickt, K. (1996). Making diversity pay. *Fortune* September, 1977.

DIVERSITY IN THE WORKPLACE: ETHICS, PRAGMATISM, OR SOME OF BOTH?

Jeanne McNett

Assumption College

When, in reference to diversity issues, Spike Lee suggested in his 1989 film that we "do the right thing," most of us tend to agree, either from personal conviction, if we have taken the time to think the matter out, or because we ascribe to the politically correct values of our day.[1] But what of the more philosophical, normative approach that Spike Lee's comment suggests? What are the *ethical underpinnings* of diversity? It is this issue that interests us here: the ethics of diversity in the workplace. In our investigation, we briefly will examine the economic arguments for diversity. In contrast to the ethics arguments, the economic arguments offer us rational, pragmatic reasons for business decision making in the diversity area. They probably will be familiar to most of us because there are many good arguments for diversity from a strictly business perspective. We then explore what ethical theories might offer support for diversity in the workplace. We conclude with an attempt to bridge between the practical (business) and the good (ethics).

The first task in any discussion is to define the terms so that we know we are talking about similar ideas. By *diversity* we mean valuing, respecting, and appreciating the differences (such as age, culture, education, ethnicity, experience, gender, race, religion, and sexual orientation, among others) that make people unique. Note that our definition has to do with *valuing* differences, so it is a frame of mind, a way of thinking, rather than a result. This is an important distinction because thinking of diversity as only a result and not a process, a way of thinking, might lead to incorrect conclusions. For example, we might observe that a workforce is diverse and assume that a valuing of diversity led to the workforce composition, when in reality, other factors such as differential wages, poor work conditions, and business location led to the diversity.

ECONOMIC ARGUMENTS FOR DIVERSITY

The economic arguments for a diverse workforce are based on an assumed connection between diversity and desired business outcomes. They are all good arguments, but none seems to rest on an ethical claim or justification. Most compelling is the connection made between a workforce that brings valuable and different perspectives and abilities to connect with a wide spectrum of customers. This market-driven argument for diversity becomes increasingly important because globalization has strengthened the role relationships play in business transactions. Globalization has led managers to realize that business is all about relationships. The more diverse the workforce is, the deeper the business communication ability across cultures is likely to be and the greater the potential for deep, long-lasting relationships. An additional economic argument for diversity is that when the firm is recruiting from a larger, more diverse labor pool, the likelihood of hiring capable managers increases.[2]

There is also the idea that a diverse workforce is nontraditional, and therefore more creative and more capable of instituting and accepting change because diverse workgroups tend to be more accepting of ambiguity.[3] Other researchers[4] suggest that the Western assumption that innovation comes from the center of the firm (that is, traditionally, the less diverse part) is a dying vestige of what has been identified as essentially an imperialist way of thinking. They conclude that "over time . . . as multinationals develop products better suited to the emerging markets, they are finding that those markets are becoming an important source of innovation." That is a good example of diversity's potential for creativity.

These arguments rest on a way of thinking about business known as the resource-based theory of the firm.[5] According to this theory, the firm is thought of as a bundle of resources that is poised, ready to take advantage of opportunities in the external environment. The more distinctive these firms resources are, the more difficult they would be for a competitor to imitate. A diverse workforce with established customer relationships is an example of such a difficult to imitate resource. Lord Browne, Group Chief Executive (CEO) of British Petroleum, offers an example of these economic rationales for diversity and their primacy over the ethical justifications in a recent keynote address:

> For BP the issue is no longer about whether diversity is a good thing . . . the issue is how to deliver strategy. How to take immediate, real actions . . . We're competing for resources. . . . And we're competing for markets. . . . And therefore we're competing for talent. If we can get a disproportionate share of the most talented people in the world, we have a chance of holding a competitive edge. That is the simple strategic logic behind our commitment to diversity and to the inclusion of individuals—men and women regardless of background, religion, ethnic origin, nationality or sexual orientation. We want to employ the best people,

everywhere, on the single criterion of merit. And the importance of that goal as a part of our overall business strategy has grown as competition has intensified.[6]

BP is an energy company that needs to establish relationships that will allow it to extract oil and gas in Mexico, Indonesia, West Africa, and Russia, while it competes for markets in America, China, South Africa, and Europe. BP's approach to diversity, based as it is on economic market arguments, makes a lot of sense because they focus on strategic outcomes desired by the business. Such arguments, perhaps good for diversity, are not in and of themselves *ethical* arguments. They go to an assertion that the purpose of business is to increase profits, not to do good. This position is best articulated by the economist Milton Friedman: "There is one and only one social responsibility of business—to use its resources and engage in activities designed to increase its profits so long as it stays within the rules of the game, which is to say, engages in open and free competition without deception or fraud."[7] In contrast, an ethical approach would consider judgments about right and wrong, good and bad, what ought to be in our world.[8]

Another difference between the pragmatic, economic arguments for diversity and the ethical ones would be their criteria for judgment. In economic arguments, the criteria are the results. So judging an approach or decision about diversity is, at a superficial level, seemingly quite easy: We look at the business results the implementation of such a decision produces. In marked contrast, to examine the ethics of a decision, we need to know the analysis on which the decision rests. The ethical dimension of such decisions will not always be obvious from the surface of that decision.

CATEGORIES OF ETHICAL THEORIES

So what *would* an ethical approach to diversity look like? In order to get to that question's answer, it will be helpful to examine the three categories into which Western ethical inquiry can be sorted, the first two traditional categories and the third recently added. This categorization scheme will remind us that the assumptions on which ethical decisions are made can vary widely. Awareness of these assumptions is an important first step in understanding the complexities of what we consider to be right and good and just actions with regard to diversity. One category looks at the *process* or the means of a decision; another addresses what is good and bad by looking at likely *outcomes* or consequences of a decision; and the final category looks at the *caring aspects* of such a decision.

F. Neil Brady has developed a matrix[9] for these distinctive categories of ethical theories that offers a cogent, helpful summary. His correlation of these approaches with the three virtues of faith, hope, and charity is an added benefit as we think about ethics and workplace diversity. Our modification of Brady's chart is Exhibit 1. The horizontal axis describes the three main theoretical bases for ethical judgment, with Brady's suggested equivalents in parentheses. We'll discuss each of them and their likely application to a diversity claim. Such a claim would be that the valuing of difference—our definition of diversity—is good or produces the quality of goodness by process (deontological) or outcomes (teleological), or care for others (charity). We also consider whether the claim for the theory is universal in nature, for all times and all places, or particular, depending on the context.

Three Categories of Ethical Theories			
	Deontology (Faith)	**Teleology** (Hope)	**Caring** (Charity)
Universal application (all times, all places)	Universal duty: universal principles, The Way	Universal ends: Character ethic, utilitarianism, other -isms	Universal care love for humanity
Particular Application (depends on context)	Particular duties: situation ethic, case by case approach	Particular ends: self-actualizaiton	Particular care: personal relationships

EXHIBIT 1   Matrix of Ethics Theories

The reason for a consideration of universal or particular applications of an ethical theory is that the context in which a diversity decision is made may well change the assumptions on which actions understood to be ethical are based. A short example of such differences is found in the consideration of differences in Japan. The Japanese culture is homogeneous to a large degree, and the introduction of difference is generally not seen as good. In fact, families and an individual's company will conduct background investigations of an engaged employee's potential spouse to make certain he or she is pure Japanese and not from an outcast group such as the *borakumin*. Such an action in North America, especially on the part of the employer, would be regarded not as a moral duty but as an immoral action on the grounds of both privacy and what we in North America would consider racial prejudice.

Thus, Brady's categorization describes various ethical theories based on the claims that their application makes: Is the theory universally applicable (*the* rule, built on understood similarities) or does it claim a situational focus (it all depends, built on differences)? This distinction is helpful as we consider the ethical bases for diversity because it incorporates the idea of the decision's context. We now look at applications of these various ethical theories to diversity in the workplace. The ethical assertion would be that the differences diversity brings to the company are good or produce the quality of goodness by process (deontological, faith), outcomes (teleological, hope), or care for others (charity).

Deontological Category of Ethics Theories

The first category of ethics theories in our framework is deontological, stemming from duties and moral obligations (the Greek *deont* means duty). Probably the most well-known deontological theory is Immanuel Kant's categorical imperative, which dictates that one has a duty to "act only on that maxim by which you can at the same time will that it should become a universal law,"[10] popularly paraphrased as the Golden Rule. Deontological theories are based on duties, rules, and obligations that lie outside the person. Religious practice tends to rest on a deontological approach to ethics. For example, we can think of the Ten Commandments as a series of duties, and thus, Brady's use of the term *faith*.

Deontological Ethics and Diversity

Can a claim that workplace diversity rests on duty be made in a convincing way? Such a claim would establish that we have a duty to tolerate differences. Note that this tolerance would be not because of the *results* of these differences, but because having differences is good in itself.

To explore our sense of duty in this regard, we use a situation of which all U.S. readers are a part, the U.S. housing market. We all live somewhere. Consideration of the nature of the U.S. housing market, segregated as it is by race and economic class, might suggest that there is no widely accepted duty to incorporate or tolerate difference, at least in this narrow but universally inhabited sector. At the particularist level, though, we can recognize that we might have specific duties we hold to one another with regard to diversity, depending on the context. For example, when we find ourselves part of a public group, say, a search committee, we may well accept that there is a duty to diversify the committee membership, simply for the sake of diversity and not for a pragmatic reason. Of course, we may well want to diversify for reasons other than duty, such as to meet legal obligations, ensure compliance with the choice by including various constituencies or stakeholders and their varied points of view in the search process, and so on. We can see that in some situations, diversity may be understood to be a duty, a good in and of itself. Yet on balance, deontological approaches to diversity are probably few in the work situation.

This observation is in accord with sociologist William Julius Wilson's application of Blalock's theory of social power to an understanding of diversity, which suggests that when majority members change their beliefs about minority members, these changes are initially a result of power shifts (in this case, Civil Rights legislation); the value shift follows. Increasingly diversified workplaces developed initially as a response to federal legislation (for example, Title VII of the Civil Rights Act of 1964, the Americans with Disabilities Act of 1990, the Equal Pay Act of 1963, the Age Discrimination in Employment Act of 1967) rather than as a response to a changed belief system about what is right.

In our discussion of deontological approaches, we have considered individuals as the location of ethical decisions. This approach is justified because it is in the minds of individual managers that decisions are made. We must note that at the same time, though, organizations have a limited kind of personhood, at least in a legal sense. Considered from this perspective, the organization may be seen as capable of ethical decision making. The ethics codes of these organizations are essentially rule based (deontological); the corporate citizen is bound by duty to follow the rules, some of which may address valuing diversity.

Teleological Category of Ethics Theories

The second category of ethical approaches is teleological, addressing the good that comes from a focus on the ends achieved by a contemplated action (Greek *telos*, end). The teleological approach holds that decisions are right or good if they produce a desired goodness and bad if they produce some undesirable state (badness or pain). So teleological approaches are action based, in contrast to the deontological approaches, which concern the process.[11] Utilitarianism, the greatest good for the greatest number, illustrates such an approach. A business example of such outcome or consequence-based morality can be found in cost-benefit analysis, where the benefit is weighed against the cost and the decision made to follow the path that provides the greatest overall gain. In fact, research suggests that many American managers hold to utilitarian principles in their decision making.[12] For example, a manager might structure a layoff list with the least trained and newest members of the organization as the first to face cuts, on the basis that keeping people with seniority will lead to the retention of higher levels of knowledge, which in turn may lead to better results long term for a larger number of people (the company's stakeholders).

Distributive justice, concerned with fair and equitable outcomes, is another ethical theory within the teleological category. Distributive justice suggests that ethical decisions are those that lead to a fair distribution of goods. Philosopher John Rawls has developed a test for distributive justice: Is the decision the one that we would make if we were cloaked in a *veil of ignorance*? This veil of ignorance would not allow us to know our status and position and, thus, protects us from self-interest playing a role in decisions on distribution of goods. Laura Hartman describes how Rawls sees the veil of ignorance working and the ends it would achieve.[13] First of all, we would make decisions unaware of their immediate consequences to ourselves. We would develop a cooperative system in which the benefits would be distributed unequally only when doing so would benefit all, especially those who were least advantaged. Ethical justice would be measured by the capacity of the decision to enhance cooperation among all, by its fairness. Because these theories rely on outcomes that depend on actions, but we don't know the outcomes of an action often until well after it is completed, Brady connects these approaches to *hope*.

Teleological Ethics and Diversity

Utilitarianism, in its assertion that a good or ethical decision is one that produces the greatest good for the greatest number, seems on first examination to be business friendly. As a justification for diversity, a utilitarian approach might argue that valuing differences would lead to behaviors that themselves would be likely to lead to better results for the company's stakeholders, through a diverse workforce that is, perhaps, better at decision making and that possesses increased creativity, better knowledge of markets, and increased communication abilities. Such a work team is likely to produce better results for a broader array of people, the various stakeholders. We would expect utilitarian approaches to the valuing of diversity in the workplace to be frequent because both the management environment and utilitarianism share a focus on results. Note, though, that for an ethical decision, results have to show greater good, not simply bottom-line good.

An example of the distributive justice theory applied to diversity is found in HR processes that rest on principles of fairness and justice: All employees, regardless of level and type of contract (part time and temporary), receive medical and other benefits, profit sharing, retirement contributions, and bonuses. Selection, compensation, and promotion systems also offer examples of distributive justice in the area of diversity. The ethical rationale would be that we take this decision because it is the right thing to do in order to produce equity, not that it will be good for business. These are all examples of universal application. Teleological theories in a particularist context would be theories that apply to differences among people and also focus on the ends or outcomes to judge the ethical nature of a decision. Self-actualization might be considered an example here, that we have a moral duty to fully develop skills and talents, and that organizational decisions that lead in that direction (support for education, training programs, mentoring systems) are ethical ones. This approach, on a case-by-case basis, would have powerful application to diversity because it would support individual learning and development within the company. That the increased learning could be thought to lead to improved results for the company would be a utilitarian justification. Another application of distributive justice theories in a particularist context is found in the justification (or failure of justification) of affirmative action. The desired outcomes (more social equity universally) were argued to outweigh what some understood to be unfair processes (individual, particular decisions).

Caring Theories of Ethics

The final category of our ethical framework addresses caring, which involves, unlike deontology and teleology, a nonrational, emotional claim. These are the theories that come not from a reasoned sense of duty nor from desired outcomes, but because they are psychological and emotional in nature, "from an interpersonal connectedness"—an ethic of *charity*, as Brady suggests.[14] On the universal side of this theory, examples drawn from religious situations and philanthropy come to mind readily: belief systems that value a love for humanity, for example, and a love for individuals because they are a part of that humanity. On the particular side, someone who joins the Peace Corps to do volunteer work in a specific setting or who does community volunteer work in a specific effort based on caring might offer us examples of particularized caring ethics. The layoff situation we discussed as an example of teleological ethics (the greatest good is achieved by keeping those who have been with the company longest and know the most) may also rest on an ethics of caring (the manager keeps the people whom he/she cares about most, those with the most seniority).

Caring Theories and Diversity

We can find a caring ethics basis for diversity at work in Pope John Paul's belief that "the evil of our times consists in the first place in a kind of degradation, indeed in a pulverization, of the fundamental uniqueness of each person." He argues that the fundamental error of socialism is that it tries to reduce humans to something less than they are, as did the Nazis (racial makeup) and the Marxists (class status).[15] The Pope's claim is that our human diversity is a good and that we are fundamentally unique in our personhood. This uniqueness should be recognized and loved. Such ethical arguments for diversity would be strong in the workplace because they would offer the individual liberation from the crushing anonymity of a cubicle existence, for example. The ethics of caring leads to powerful emotional connections among people. Although we may not find it often at an official, articulated level (How does a CEO convincingly claim to care about 25,000 employees personally and convincingly?), it may be more common, unarticulated, yet in the minds of organization members, than we realize, as a tacit part of the organizational culture. The college at which I teach is infused with the ethics of caring, among faculty and staff and about our students. When students come on campus, they feel this emotional connection and are often drawn to the school by it. Yet, as is frequently the case with ethics of caring, we don't yet know how to talk about it.

The diversity claim offered by ethics of caring might be stated as follows: We value diversity in our organization because we value every individual and his/her dignity and right to contribute and be a part of our organization. This particularist approach in a business setting seems more likely than does the universal aspect, which would be generalized over a larger population. Perhaps organizations that intentionally adopt religious-based values systems (Islamic banks) offer an example of a universal approach if their values include reverence for all people.

BUSINESS PRAGMATISM AND AN ETHICAL APPROACH

The economic arguments for diversity with which we began our exploration are based on the resource-based view of the firm and are *pragmatic* in that they are concerned with *what works best* to meet business objectives. William James captured pragmatism's essence in slightly different words: "Pragmatism asks its usual question. 'Grant an idea or belief to be true,' it says, 'what concrete difference will its being true make in anyone's actual life? How will the truth be realized? What experiences will be different from those which would obtain if the belief were false? What, in short, is the truth's cash-value in experiential terms?'" (from Pragmatism, 1907)[16]

We examine pragmatism here because it may offer us a way to better understand and pin down the ethical claims for workplace diversity. Such an approach to decision making, including that about diversity, is the cornerstone of business practice: *If it works, do it*, or as James suggested, if it works, it is true. Note that James is concerned with what is true, not good. The question that now faces us is, how does a pragmatic approach square with the ethical options we have just reviewed? In order to summarize this issue, we use a four-square grid with the horizontal axis representing ethics (highly ethical to unethical), and the vertical axis representing the level of pragmatism (fully pragmatic to nonpragmatic). We now have a way to categorize our theoretical justifications of workplace diversity that considers their practical aspect, "the cash-value," to quote James. We will see which of our ethical theories can offer what is good and good for business at the same time.

The matrix in Exhibit 2 is a useful way to think about possible relationships between pragmatism and ethical choices.[17] Quadrant I is where most business-people would like to be, pragmatic (good numbers, good business results) and ethical (good process, creating goodness). Quadrant I is also where the teleological ethical theories we have reviewed would be, utilitarianism and distributive justice. They are concerned with outcomes and the good that constitutes those outcomes. What we see by considering Quadrant I is that an argument for diversity in the workplace can be pragmatic (good for business) and also ethical. Such an argument might be, for example, that diversity is good, the right way to select personnel, because when we have a diverse team, we communicate better with diverse markets and are more innovative within the organization because we are always trying to question our unarticulated assumptions. Such an environment is good for its participants and for business results.

The argument for a diverse workplace because it is simply beneficial for business (the bottom line) is an example of a pragmatic and nonethical argument, which is where the economic arguments for diversity that we reviewed

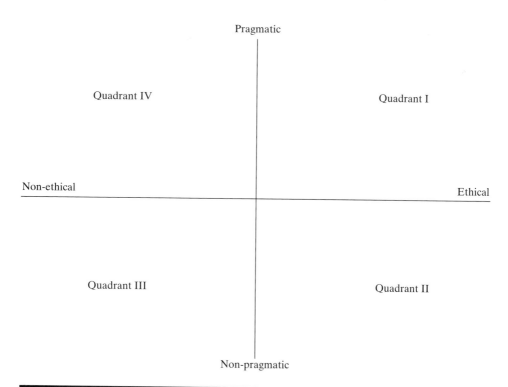

EXHIBIT 2 The Pragmatic and the Ethical with Regard to Diversity

earlier are located, Quadrant IV. Such arguments would be nonethical because they do not consider the treatment of people in ethical terms; people are inputs, parallel to semiconductors and motherboards.

Note that the arguments in Quadrant I (teleological) and IV (pragmatic without an ethical base) are close and yet a world apart. The danger of the pragmatic nonethical approach is that it might do harm to people. One can imagine a woman engineer being assigned to a project in the mainly male profession of construction engineering because the company wants to qualify to compete on projects that require a diverse workforce. In such a case, the woman engineer is there on the project for the business ends, almost as a token, but the company does nothing to support her integration into the work team. The hostile work environment that might result from the company's unconsidered approach to building a diverse workforce would be a harm.

In passing, we note that Quadrant III is where we would locate nonpragmatic, nonethical efforts, a combination difficult about which to think. Perhaps some business decisions with regard to diversity are the result of personal prejudice that considers neither the practical aspects of the market nor the decision's ethical content. Consider a family business in an area that attracts many gays and a decision maker whose unexamined, homophobic values affect personnel selection. Such an example would be nonpragmatic and nonethical.

Quadrant II represents ethical, nonpragmatic approaches. Because a for-profit business has to take care of the bottom line, has to show that outputs have added value over inputs, such approaches would be unusual, but they exist. Ben and Jerry's Ice Cream sources ingredients for their product from worker collaboratives in impoverished areas in the United States, Africa, and Latin America. This commitment to businesses in developing economies may increase production costs, but it appears to be a cost consumers are willing to subsidize. One could argue that Ben and Jerry's has changed the nature of the product; it is not premium ice cream that consumers purchase, but premium ice cream *and* a contribution to greater good in the world (eating premium ice cream as an ethical act!). In contrast to the for-profit sector, in the nonprofit sector ethical nonpragmatic approaches would be abundant. Think of the local art museum, symphony, opera, and other community efforts that by their very natures are nonpragmatic.

Our analysis illustrates that Quadrant I is where most of the ethical arguments for diversity in the workplace are likely to be located. These teleological ethical arguments, because they focus on outcomes, are similar on the surface to the pragmatic economic justifications for diversity. The ethical analysis adds an important dimension, though, a consideration that is missing in the economic, pragmatic approach. It appears that when there is ethical analysis in the decision-making stage, business can do well and do good.

DOING WELL AND DOING GOOD

In concluding, we now consider briefly how decision making about diversity in the workplace might maintain a practical focus and at the same time an ethical one. One key assumption we can draw from our earlier discussion is that if there is an ethical consideration present in a diversity-related decision,

1.	**Have you defined the problem accurately?** A moral decision cannot be built on convenient ignorance.
2.	**How would you define the problem if you stood on the other side of the fence?** Explore the role of self-interest in a decision and the relationship between expedient and responsible actions.
3.	**How did this situation occur in the first place?** This course of questioning helps to distinguish the symptoms from the disease and to work against the tendency to ignore problems until they become crises.
4.	**To whom and what do you give your loyalties as a person and as a member of the corporation?** The area of divided loyalties is a difficult one in the diversity area. The first steps to addressing such issues are to articulate and then examine them.
5.	**What is your intention in making this decision?**
6.	**How does this intention compare with the likely results?** Intentions do matter. Because they can have effects on attitudes inside and outside the organization, their communication is important
7.	**Whom could your decision or action injure?** This question helps to discover whether any resulting injury would be intentional.
8.	**Can you engage the affected parties in a discussion of the problem before you make your decision?** Stakeholder participation ensures that affected parties can discuss what among the alternatives may be in their best interests and see the issues in a larger context.
9.	**Are you confident that your position will be as valid over a long period of time as it seems now?** Articulation of values should anticipate good and bad times. A difference in time frame can make a huge impact on the problem's meaning.
10.	**Could you disclose without a qualm your decision or action to your boss, your CEO, the board of directors, your family, or society as a whole?** This test, aka the billboard test, helps to uncover conscience and loyalties.
11.	**What is the symbolic intention of your action if understood? If misunderstood?** How the symbol is perceived or misperceived is what matters. Getting intent out there early (see nos. 5 and 6) helps to frame how the action is understood.
12.	**Under what conditions would you allow exceptions to your stand?** It is important to discuss under what conditions the rules of the game may be changed.

EXHIBIT 3   Questions for a Discussion of Ethical Aspects of Decisions

it is often tacit, unarticulated, in the decision maker's private thoughts. What gets articulated is the economic justification for the decision (see Exhibit 3). Laura Nash calls for discussion-based ethical analysis to become part of any organizational decision[18] and offers a series of 12 questions to encourage such discussion. Their review is helpful in surfacing the frequently hidden assumptions found in diversity-related decisions. Now that we understand what ethical decisions are, we now have an approach so that we can "do the right thing" as we implement diversity in the workplace, by making good, ethical, pragmatic, business results-focused decisions.

Discussion Questions

1. Describe an approach to a business diversity program that would be pragmatic and ethical, that would involve a consideration of doing the right thing and taking actions that make good business sense.
2. What are some possible explanations for the hesitancy to discuss ethics in the workplace?
3. This discussion's definition of diversity rests on a valuing of differences across many groups of people. Explain why valuing (the process) is what should serve as the foundation for diversity and not the results.
4. Which of the final 12 discussion areas would be most difficult for you as a manager to discuss in the organization with your colleagues? Why?

Endnotes

1. Ana Marta Gonzalez in her "Ethics In a Global Business and in a Plural Society," *Journal of Business Ethics,* 44(1), 23–34, suggests that political correctness is an attempt to avoid the socially uncomfortable discussions often brought on by a careful consideration of diversity.
2. Schraeder, C., Blackburn, V., & Iles, P. (1997). Women in management and firm financial performance: An exploratory study. *Journal of Management Issues* 9(3), 355–372. A more complex analysis is found in the Diversity Research Network's report, The effects of diversity on business performance. *Human Resource Management, 42*(1), 3–21. This report addresses the complex research issues related to identifying and measuring causal outcomes of diversity.
3. Rosener, J. (1995). *America's competitive secret: Utilizing women as a management strategy.* New York: Oxford University Press. Quoted in Schraeder. On diversity

and creativity, see Goleman, D., Kaufman, P., & Ray, M. (1992). *The creative spirit.* New York: Dutton.
4. Prahalad, C., & Lieberthal, K. (1998). The end of corporate imperialism. *Harvard Business Review, 76*(4), 68–79. See also /www.nytimes.com/marketing/diversity/
5. Barney, J. (1991). Firm resources and sustained competitive advantage. *Journal of Management, 17*(1), 99–120.
6. "The Strategic Logic of Diversity," keynote speech at Women in Leadership Conference, Hotel Intercontinental, Berlin, June 19, 2002. /www.bp.com/centres/press/s_detail_p.asp?id=161/
7. Milton Friedman's frequently cited and anthologized essay, "The social responsibility of business is to increase its profits." /http://ca.geocities.com/busa2100/miltonfriedman.htm/
8. This definition is based on a more complete exploration of ethics found in Hartman L. P. (2002). *Perspectives in*

business ethics (2nd ed.). Burr Ridge, IL: McGraw-Hill/Irwin.

9. Brady, F. N. (1996). Introduction: A typology of ethical theories. *Ethical universals in international business* (p. 6). Berlin: Springer.

10. Kant, I. (1785). *The foundations of the metaphysics of morals*, section one.

11. Hopkins, W. (1997). *Ethical dimensions of diversity*. Thousand Oaks CA: Sage.

12. Fritzsche, D., & Becker, H. (1984). Linking management behavior to ethical philosophy: An empirical investigation. *Academy of Management Journal, 27*(1), 166–176.

13. Hartman, L. (2002). *Perspectives in business ethics*. Burr Ridge, IL: McGraw-Hill/Irwin.

14. Brady, N. (1996), p. 5.

15. Quoted by Brooks, D. (2003). Bigger than Nobel. *The New York Times*, October 11. See /http://www.nytimes.com/2003/10/11/opinion/11BROO.html/

16. William James (1842–1910), an American intellectual whose work bridges psychology and philosophy, was one of the members of the American group of philosophers known as the pragmatists. He helped to develop a theoretical basis for pragmatism. Consideration of this interesting work is, however, beyond the scope of the relationship of workplace diversity to ethics. The setup material for the James quote is from professor Frank Pajares' Website on William James (Emory University): http://www.emory.edu/EDUCATION/mfp/james.html

17. A similar matrix idea using ethics and legality was developed by Verne Henderson ("The Ethical Side of Enterprise," in *Sloan Management Review* 23:1982, 37–47) to categorize ethical and legal behaviors, an adaptation of which was used in Lane, H., DiStefano, J., & Maznevski, M. (2000). *International management behavior* (4th ed.). Malden, MA: Blackwell, p. 435.

18. Nash, L. (1981). Ethics without the sermon. *Harvard Business Review, 56*(6), 79–90. The questions are summarized from Nash's more extensive and richer discussion. The commentary with applications to diversity is added.

HOW CANADA PROMOTES WORKPLACE DIVERSITY

Marc S. Mentzer

University of Saskatchewan

When an American visits Canada, at first glance Canada is just like the United States, except a bit colder and with money in funny colors. Even though Canada is outwardly similar to the United States, there are deeply rooted differences in history and in society's values that are not immediately evident to the visitor.

To begin to comprehend the differences between the two countries, we must go back to the time of the American Revolution. The American revolutionaries expected that present-day Canada would join them in the fight against the English king, but the area that makes up present-day Canada stayed loyal to the king, and continued under British rule until Canada became independent in 1867. As a result, Canadians have a faith in government that's very different than the usual skepticism and suspicion toward government that one sees in the United States.

Another key difference is that the Canadian federal government has less power than the U.S. government, especially where employment regulation is concerned. Canadian government law on employment issues affects only those industries that are federally regulated according to the Canadian constitution. These are broadcasting, telecommunications, banking, railroads, airlines, shipping, other transport across provincial boundaries, uranium mining, and crown corporations. (A crown corporation is a company in which the government owns all the stock, such as Canada Post or the Canadian Broadcasting Corporation.) All other businesses are beyond the jurisdiction of the Canadian government and are affected only by laws passed by the province in which they operate.

As an example, consider Sears, the department store chain. In the United States, Sears must obey the U.S. federal law regarding nondiscrimination, minimum wage, and so on. Each state has its own laws, but with some exceptions, a company as large as Sears can ignore the state laws because they're overridden by U.S. federal law.

In Canada, Sears also has stores throughout the country. But retailing is not federally regulated under the Canadian constitution. Therefore, Sears in Canada must obey the laws of each province in which it operates. A Sears store in Ontario must obey Ontario laws, a store in Quebec must obey Quebec laws, and so on. Overall, this makes the task of obeying the law much more complicated for Sears in Canada than it is for Sears in the United States.

THE CANADIAN HUMAN RIGHTS ACT

In 1977, Parliament passed the Canadian Human Rights Act, which forbids discrimination by federally regulated employers on the basis of race, gender, and certain other grounds. This act prohibits systemic (indirect) discrimination, as when an employer asks an applicant about her childbearing plans or engages in sexual harassment, as well as direct discrimination, as when an employer says women will not be considered. Instead of complaints being heard in court, as is the U.S. practice, discrimination complaints are made to the Canadian Human Rights Commission. This allows victims to have a hearing without having to hire a lawyer, although monetary damages tend to be much lower than they would be in a U.S. court. In severe cases of discrimination, the Commission has the power to impose a hiring quota, as in 1984, when it ordered Canadian National Railways that women had to comprise one fourth of all new hires for blue-collar jobs. The Commission rarely uses this power, but it remains in the background as a powerful tool for punishing employers who are the worst offenders.

Another feature of the Canadian Human Rights Act is that it requires comparable worth in pay policies, which in Canada is known under the label of pay equity. Every covered employer must ensure that predominantly female occupations are paid the same as predominantly male occupations of equal importance or difficulty in the same organization. For example, secretaries working for a railroad might claim that their job is of equal importance or difficulty as that of a track maintenance worker, and thus could demand that their pay be the same. Pay equity or comparable worth is a type of law that does not exist in the United States at the federal level because it is seen as interfering with market forces, but it's a fact of life for organizations under the jurisdiction of the Canadian federal government. At the provincial level, Ontario and Quebec also have pay equity laws that cover employers, and most other provinces have pay equity laws limited to public-sector organizations such as universities and hospitals.

EMPLOYMENT EQUITY LEGISLATION

Initially it was hoped that the Canadian Human Rights Act would be sufficient to break down the barriers that prevent the economic progress of women and minorities. However, with the passage of time, it became apparent that simply forbidding discrimination was not enough. In 1984 a parliamentary commission recommended legislation that would push employers to take proactive or aggressive measures to increase the numbers of women and minority employees (Canada, 1984). This commission noted that in the United States, affirmative action has been divisive because it pits men against women and whites against minorities. Thus, to avoid the ill will surrounding the term *affirmative action,* a new term, *employment equity,* was created to cover such proactive measures as aggressive recruiting among women and minorities, providing child care facilities, accommodating the needs of people with disabilities, and so on.

The resulting legislation, the Canadian Employment Equity Act of 1986, was mainly symbolic, relying on persuasion and embarrassment so that employers would be more serious about creating workplaces that value diversity. Covered employers submit their data to the federal government, which then assigns grades (A, B, etc.) to each employer. A later version of the law, the Canadian Employment Equity Act of 1995, put in place modest fines (up to $50,000) for employers not meeting their targets, although in practice these fines are rarely if ever imposed.

The Four Protected Groups

In the United States, initially, the main thrust of civil rights legislation was to end discrimination against blacks. This has never been the burning issue in Canada that it is in the United States, because blacks comprise only 2% of the Canadian population, versus 13% in the United States. Similarly, Hispanics comprise only 1% of the Canadian population, compared to 13% in the United States. Therefore, when Canada introduced employment equity legislation, there was some question as to which groups should be chosen for special protection. In the end, the government designated four protected groups:

1. **Women:** As in the United States, Canadian women lag behind men in income and representation in high-paying jobs. Thus, women were identified as one of the groups to be targeted under employment equity.
2. **Aboriginal peoples:** This group includes Indians, Inuit (the aboriginal people of the Arctic regions), and Métis (those of mixed French-Indian ancestry in western Canada). Aboriginal people constitute 3% of the Canadian population, which is double their percentage in the United States. The low Canadian percentage is deceptive, because there are large regions of Canada where aboriginal people are the majority. The plight of aboriginal people is of deep concern in Canadian society. Many live in isolated villages or remote reservations, whereas others have moved to the cities but still have difficulty entering the economic mainstream. Aboriginal people frequently overcome barriers to gain education and achieve success in Canadian society, but the pace of change is not what it should be.
3. **People with disabilities:** Both Canada and the United States define disabilities to include psychological conditions such as mental illness, as well as physical conditions such as blindness or use of a wheelchair.
4. **Visible minorities:** This is the most interesting, and most controversial, of the four protected groups under Canadian law, and it has no exact

equivalent in U.S. law. "Visible minorities" refers to those of black, Asian, Arab, Pacific Islander, or Latin American ancestry. Chinese Canadians, comprising 4% of the Canadian population, are the largest of the ethnic groups in this category. The visible minority category includes some groups, such as Japanese Canadians, that have very high income levels today, but had historically been the target of discrimination. "Visible minorities" includes other groups, such as Pacific Islander Canadians or Southeast Asian Canadians, that are very recent arrivals in Canada, with high unemployment rates and, on average, very low incomes. In short, the category of visible minorities is quite an assortment of ethnic groups that have very little in common with one another. Altogether, visible minorities comprise 13% of the Canadian population. In percentage terms, people of black or Hispanic ancestry are more numerous in the United States than in Canada, whereas there is a larger percentage of people of Asian ancestry in Canada than in the United States.

There were some other minorities that sought to be included as protected groups under the Employment Equity Act, but were excluded, although their rights are protected elsewhere under Canadian law. For example, note that lesbians and gays are not a protected group. Also, French-speaking people in predominantly English-speaking areas wanted to be treated as a protected group, but were not. (One fourth of the population speaks French as their first language, and in some areas they feel they're at a disadvantage in an English-language-dominated society.) Because these minority groups are covered by the Human Rights Act, it is still illegal to discriminate against someone on the basis of their sexual orientation or whether they learned French before English. However, employers are not required to engage in proactive or aggressive actions to increase their representation in the workforce.

There have been some glitches in the implementation of employment equity (Mentzer, 2002). An employee cannot be counted as a member of a minority group unless he or she identifies as such on a questionnaire administered by the employer. For example, let's suppose some minority employees don't complete the questionnaire due to a desire to blend in and not draw attention. Yet, the employer can't count them in employment equity statistics unless they self-identify on their questionnaires. Another dilemma is that people of Latin American or Arab descent often don't realize that the government defines them as being in the visible minority category, and hence the resulting statistics are likely to undercount visible minority employees.

In the United States, some white individuals have won lawsuits claiming reverse discrimination, which has caused the unraveling of some of the U.S. affirmative action initiatives. A claim of reverse discrimination cannot be made in the Canadian legal system. Section 15 of the Charter of Rights and Freedoms, which is part of the Canadian constitution, states that discrimination is illegal. It then goes on to state that policies that improve the situation of disadvantaged groups are an allowable exception to the antidiscrimination clause. This is a key difference between the U.S. and Canadian constitutions, with far-ranging implications for affirmative action and employment equity policies in the two countries.

EMPLOYMENT EQUITY IN ACTION

Employment equity, when properly implemented, goes far beyond merely increasing the number of women and minority employees. Instead, the focus of employment equity should be to encourage flexibility and create a workplace in which people of all backgrounds feel comfortable.

For example, Pelmorex, which owns specialized cable channels, regularly does employee recruiting at aboriginal events and in campus offices for students with disabilities. Pelmorex takes pride in how it accommodates employees with disabilities, for instance, by having an employee with a mental health condition work in a quiet area of the office, or by providing large computer screens for employees who are visually impaired (Vu, 2003).

Another success story in employment equity is Cameco, a uranium company operating in northern Saskatchewan, where aboriginal people, many living in isolated villages, make up four fifths of the local population. When hiring miners, Cameco gives preference to local residents, and students in northern Saskatchewan are hired each year by Cameco for summer employment. As well, Cameco gives preference to suppliers from northern Saskatchewan, sometimes allowing them to skip the usual bidding process. Cameco's long-term goal is to build up a base of local businesses in this predominantly aboriginal region (Cameco, 2003, communication from company).

Canada's largest bank, the Royal Bank, is highly regarded for its outreach toward people with disabilities. Making arrangements for employees with disabilities occasionally involves substantial expenses; hence, Royal Bank has created a central fund for these, so that individual managers don't have to worry about such expenses coming out of their departmental budgets (Young, 2000).

When properly implemented, employment equity changes the organization's internal culture to one in which people will be accepting of diversity in all its forms, instead of the old-fashioned approach of expecting all employees to come from the same mold.

CANADA'S PROVINCES AND TERRITORIES

Canada is divided into 10 provinces and 3 territories, which, generally speaking, have more power than U.S. state governments. Each of the 10 provinces and 3 territories has its own human rights laws forbidding discrimination. With a few exceptions, these laws also include provisions for imposing hiring quotas on employers who are chronic offenders, similar to the features of the Canadian Human Rights Act, although the provisions for punitive hiring quotas are rarely used. Although every province and territory forbids discrimination, none of them have any laws that require employers to engage in proactive measures in the spirit of employment equity or affirmative action.

The result is that only those employers in federally regulated industries are required by legislation to have employment equity programs. Such household names as Wal-Mart, McDonald's, or General Motors are not in federally regulated industries, and therefore are not covered by the Canadian Employment Equity Act, although they certainly may create *voluntary* employment equity plans if they wish. In addition, such companies must obey the antidiscrimination laws of the provinces and territories in which they operate.

Thus we see how executives of companies operating in both the United States and Canada face a particular challenge, because they must be knowledgeable about two countries' sets of laws, and in most instances the laws of Canada's 10 provinces and 3 territories as well. Frequently, a human resource policy that is legal in the United States will be illegal in Canada, or vice versa, and such companies have to obey the laws of the jurisdiction in which they operate. Two countries, similar in so many ways, have entirely different legal structures to address the issue of increasing diversity in the workplace.

Discussion Questions

1. How is the power of the Canadian federal government different in relation to the provinces, from the power of the U.S. federal government in relation to the states?
2. (a)   If a U.S.-based retail chain has stores throughout Canada, which laws apply — those of the U.S. government, those of the Canadian federal government, or those of each province?
   (b)   If a Canadian chain has stores throughout the United States, which laws apply — those of the United States, those of the Canadian federal government, or those of the province in which it is based?
3. What is the difference between employment equity and pay equity?
4. How does the Canadian constitution affect affirmative action-type programs?
5. (a)   Make an argument that it is easier for employers to comply with diversity legislation in Canada than it is in the United States.
   (b)   Make an argument that it is *not* easier for employers to comply with diversity legislation in Canada than in the United States.

Bibliography

Canada. Minister of Supply and Services. (1984). *Report of the commission on equality in employment.* Judge Rosalie Silberman Abella, Commissioner. Ottawa.

Mentzer, M. S. (2002). The Canadian experience with employment equity legislation. *International Journal of Value-Based Management, 15*, 35–50.

Vu, U. (2003, 19 May). Sunny spot for the disadvantaged. *Canadian HR Reporter, 16*(10), 2.

Young, L. (2000, 27 March). Leveraging diversity at Royal Bank financial group. *Canadian HR Reporter, 13*(6), 9.

Note: U.S. statistics are from the 2000 census, as reported by the U.S. Census Bureau (http://www.census.gov, accessed June 2003). Canadian statistics are from the 2001 census, as reported by Statistics Canada (http://www.statcan.ca, accessed June 2003).

Websites

"About Canada"
http://canada.gc.ca/acanada

Canadian (Federal) Human Rights Commission
http://www.chrc-ccdp.ca

Ontario Human Rights Commission
Ontario is the most populous of the provinces (Toronto is the capital).
http://www.ohrc.on.ca

Also, of all the provinces, Ontario has the strictest pay equity (comparable worth) laws: http://www.gov.on.ca/lab/pec

Quebec: Commission des droits de la personne et des droits de la jeunesse
Quebec is the only predominantly French-speaking province. For this Website, French is the default language, but there is a link that can be clicked on to get the English version.
http://www.cdpdj.qc.ca

WHAT HAPPENED
AT COCA-COLA?

Carol P. Harvey
Assumption College

Coca- Cola . . .

- is considered the world's most recognized brand name
- controls 53% of the world's soft-drink market
- was an international brand by 1900
- was instrumental in the racial integration movement in Atlanta in the 1960s
- was rated 32nd on *Fortune*'s 2002 list of the 50 Best Companies for minorities
- agreed to spend $200 million to settle recent racial and gender bias lawsuits

How did a company with a history of international business, that long targeted many of its products to minority groups, that is headquartered in a state where 28% of the population is black lose the largest racial discrimination lawsuit (*Ingram et al. The Coca-Cola Company*) in U.S. history? The case illustrates the contrast between a corporation's public image and the acceptance of racism within its organizational culture. Although Coca-Cola contributed to civil rights groups such as the Southern Christian Leadership Conference and the Rainbow Push Coalition, according to Foust (2000b)

> When it came to its own workforce, the story was quite different. . . . According to allegations filed in the discrimination lawsuit, former CEO Ivestor told a transferee stunned by the latent racist culture, at its headquarters that it would take "15 to 20 years before blacks would be fairly represented in the company" (p. 58)

However, this was not the first time that racism at Coca-Cola had been an issue.

> The company's Southern bottlers taunted and terrorized Coke's first black salesman. Privately, legendary Chief Executive, Robert S. Woodruff questioned civil rights legislation in the 1960's. And if the

worst excesses of the past are gone, according to internal Coke documents released as part of a current lawsuit, even today the median salary for black employees is 44% less than that for whites." (Foust, 2000b, p. 58)

INDUSTRY BACKGROUND

The soft-drink industry has its roots the United States when physicians in the 1800s began prescribing the bubbling waters discovered in New York as a cure for ailments ranging from arthritis to headaches and including everything in between. Later, the development of artificial carbonated water by laboratory scientists, the addition of flavors like lemon and root beer by pharmacists, and the growing popularity of the local pharmacy's soda fountain as a social gathering spot, led to increased demand for these products.

From its humble beginnings, the soft-drink industry enjoyed a phenomenal growth rate. One in every four beverages consumed in the United States is a soft drink, which amounts to an annual consumption of 53 gallons for every man, woman, and child in the country (www.nsda.org, 2003). However, due to the consumer shift to bottled waters, teas, fruit juices, and product variations in coffee, the consumption rate for soft drinks has become stagnant in the United States. To increase sales, soft-drink producers diversified into other bottled beverage products and aggressively compete in a market that is highly saturated, except in developing countries.

EARLY COMPANY HISTORY

The history of the Coca-Cola Corporation, the producer of two of the world's three most popular carbonated drinks, parallels the industry trends in terms of growth and product lines. Pioneering a sophisticated distribution system of local bottlers who purchase the coke syrup from the corporation and implementing aggressive growth strategies of 7% to 8% a year, Coke now controls 51% of the carbonated beverage sales in the world and 18% of the noncarbonated beverage market. In 2002, the corporation had $19 billion in operating revenues and netted $3.9 billion from its 300 brands sold in over 200 countries. (www.coca-cola.org, 2003).

However, the organization had humble beginnings when John S. Pemberton began a patent medicine business in Atlanta, Georgia, in 1886, where he invented such products as liver pills, hair dye, and the beverage known today as Coca-Cola. With caffeine and cocaine in his sugary syrup concentrate, the product was marketed as a cure-all remedy. Pemberton and his partners grossed a mere $50 in sales during the first year. In 1891 they sold the business and its secret formula for coke syrup for $2300 to Asa Candler. The new owner, a druggist, improved the original formula, removed the cocaine, and hired a sales force that blanketed the United States and beyond selling syrup concentrate to local bottlers. He promoted the business using such progressive marketing techniques as free samples and product logo premiums and by 1904 the company had sold a million gallons of syrup, and by 1969 six billion gallons (Derdak, 1988).

During WWII, General Eisenhower requested that Coke be made available to American soldiers serving in North Africa and Europe. So the company set up multiple foreign bottling plants that paved the way for a global business presence after the war. During the 1950s the company expanded rapidly internationally and opened 15 to 20 plants per year. As early as the 1950s Coke recognized the potential of minority markets and included racial minorities in their advertisements. (Pendergast, 2000)

Although Coca-Cola was a one-product company until the 1960s, it quickly became synonymous with the American way of life with its growing success and in its promotional messages. The company's "advertising never reflected the problems of the world, only a good and happy life" (Derdak, 1988, p. 233).

For Coke the 1960s were a time of diversification, product development, and increased competition. Because Pepsi began to aggressively challenge Coke for market share, Coke bought Minute Maid and Belmont Springs Water and launched Tab, Sprite, and Fresca, making significant inroads into the diet soda market. During the 1970s Coca-Cola focused on foreign expansion, particularly into China and Russia. As a result, by 1984 Pepsi outsold Coke with a 22.8% market share compared to Coke's 21.6% (Derdak, 1988, p. 234). Although the introduction of Diet Coke, now the world's #1 diet beverage, pumped up sales, the introduction of a reformulated "New Coke" was a marketing and public relations disaster. "Coke's great (financial) returns in the 1990s were based on the notion that it could keep increasing earnings at 20% or more per year. It can't" (Sivy, 2000, p. 42).

CORPORATE CULTURE AND LEADERSHIP

Fueled by phenomenal marketing and financial successes, Coca-Cola was "run by bureaucrats and accountants focused more on getting the most out of what they had . . . than of thinking of new ideas" (New Doug, 1999, p. 55). Described as "insular" and "predominated by the "good ol' boys from the University of Georgia" (Foust, 2000a, p. 56), the organization was "a marketing machine that created desire for the Coke brand (at whatever price), rather than a sales company that gave consumers what they wanted" (Feldman, 2000, p. 33). In some parts of the world, Coca-Cola was seen as representing American imperialism. This attitude is exemplified by former CEO Roberto Goizueta's wish that one day Coke should replace tap water. In 1997 when Goizueta suddenly died, the board replaced him with his protégé, M. Douglas Ivestor. Refusing to appoint a chief operating officer, "Ivestor did what accountants do best, he put his head down and carried on with the old way of doing things" (New Doug, 1999, p. 55). Over the next two years, Ivestor, described as "arrogant and insecure" (Morris & Sellers, 2000 p. 15), inherited many problems, including a tainted Coke scare in Europe that resulted in the largest product recall in company history

(Europe Shuns, 1999), a decline in earnings for two straight years, and the need to steeply increase the price of Coke syrup sales to bottlers in an attempt to bolster profits.

THE LAWSUIT

In 1999, just when things seemed like they couldn't get worse for Ivestor, Coca-Cola was served with a lawsuit that accused the company of systemically discriminating against black employees in promotions, evaluations, terminations, and pay. "Publicity surrounding the case troubled Coke, whose U.S. customer base is disproportionately made up of African Americans and Latinos" (Mokhiber, 2000, p. 30).

Could this lawsuit have been prevented? Earlier when black employees shared their complaints with the Rev. Joseph Wheeler, president of the local NAACP, he brought these concerns to Coca-Cola officials. He was told that the company was under no obligation to talk to him because he was not a lawyer. Greg Clark, one of the plaintiffs, said, "that he would never have sued had he felt that his concerns were taken seriously: 'They ignored me, ignored me, ignored me, to the point where I felt that I had no other recourse' " (Harrington, 2000, p. 188).

In response to the lawsuit, Ivestor appointed Carl H. Ware, the highest-ranking black executive in the company, as the co-chair of the Diversity Advisory Council along with Senior Vice-President Jack Stahl. Ware, a Harvard graduate, joined the company in 1974 to work in the area of urban and government affairs. As vice-president of the Africa group, Ware focused on "cultivating African governments and bridging cultural hurdles so that the company can do business, often in partnerships, with local governments" (Holsendolph, 1999, p. 1). He is credited with influencing Coca-Cola's decision to divest its South African assets in support of the antiapartheid cause. In 1994, Ware helped to organize Nelson Mandela's fund-raising tour in the United States, which is credited with smoothing the way for Coke sales in postapartheid South Africa, where Coke sales now exceed 400 million cases a year (Foust, 2000b, p. 138). Having worked 26 years at the company, Ware was known for his ability to defuse problems before they became full-blown crises. In 1981, Jesse Jackson, critical of Coke's hiring record and its weak support for black-owned businesses, was set to kick off a "Don't choke on Coke" boycott. Jackson called it off after Ware helped craft a $50 million program to help support black vendors (Foust, 2000b, p. 138).

As the lawsuit wound its way through the court system, the number of plaintiffs increased, and both sides turned up the pressure. What began with four current and ex-employees (administrative assistant Motisola Abdallah, security officer Gregory Clark, consumer information specialist Linda Ingram, and a former director, Kimberly Orton) eventually became a major class-action suit with approximately 2,000 plaintiffs. The claim was that Coca-Cola had "systematically discriminated against African-Americans by paying them lower salaries, than whites for the same work, passing over them for promotions, and subjecting them to harassment" (Mokhiber, 2000, p. 30), since at least 1995. Coincidentally, 1995 was the same year that Carl Ware presented Ivestor, then Coke's COO with a report documenting racial disparities in pay, performance evaluations, and promotions for black employees. The plaintiffs asked both for monetary damages and a court order that required the company to change some of its employment practices. The lead co-counsel in the case was Cyrus Mehri, a 37-year-old lawyer, who had successfully won the $176 million Texaco racial discrimination lawsuit.

Coca-Cola denied the charges of discrimination, claiming that the plaintiffs' claims had nothing in common but their race. Carl Ware said, "I think we've made great strides in developing a gold standard for diversity management" (Foust, 1999, p. 2) and "I myself am a good example, a proof that glass walls do not exist at the Coca-Cola Company" (Holsendolph, 1999, p. 1). However, "the company's dithering continued even after the suit was filed. For starters, rather than pursue the almost inevitable settlement, Coke first engaged in a vigorous pre-trial defense" (Harrington, 2000, p. 188) and attempted to stop the class-action status of the lawsuit. U.S. District Court Judge Richard Story instructed the company to add a disclaimer to company e-mails to employees about the case that read, "The foregoing represents Coca-Cola's opinion of the lawsuit. It is unlawful for Coca-Cola to retaliate against employees who choose to participate in this case" (Unger, 1999a). The company did not add the statement.

In October 1999, while the case was pending, Ivestor effectively demoted Ware, the company's highest-ranking black executive, by having him report to a fellow senior vice-president. "In response, Ware announced that he would retire at the end of the year. The episode fueled questions about Coke's commitment to diversity" (Smith, 2000, p. 52).

Although Ivestor's tenure was fraught with financial problems, the demotion of Ware seemed to be one of the catalytic events/public relations problems that moved influential board members to strongly suggest to Ivestor that he was no longer the man to run Coke. On December 5, 1999 Ivestor submitted his resignation at an emergency board meeting called on a Sunday evening. Morris and Sellers wrote

> Ivestor's sudden fall from one of the world's premier corporate jobs is more than just a tale of bad luck or plans gone wrong. It is a management story full of leadership lessons. It features colossal arrogance and insecurity. Its main character was blind to his own weaknesses and unwilling to take advice. . . . But the ultimate measure of a CEO is how he handles crises, and again and again, in the view of certain directors and the powerful bottling executives, Ivestor was a day late and a dollar short. . . . He took pride in being a substance-over-style guy but that translated into taking no heed of image and perception issues, which are merely all important to a company like Coke. (2000 p. 78)

The board elected Douglas Daft, a 56-year-old Australian with 30 years experience at Coke, primarily in their Asian and Middle-Eastern markets, as president and CEO. In contrast to his predecessor, Daft was a delegator, who spoke of repositioning the company from three perspectives: building brand, thinking and acting locally in global business relations, and being seen as a model citizen. In a speech delivered to the Chief Executive's Club in Boston, he said, "I want the Coca-Cola Company to be one of the most desired employers in the world. I have told our people that we are going to take our company to the head of the class when it comes to the diversity of our workforce and our business" (Daft, 2000, p. 606). He quickly mended fences with Carl Ware by naming him Vice-President for Global Public Affairs, reporting directly to him and adopted two of the suggestions from Ware's 1995 report: clear support for diversity from the top executives and tying compensation increases to the achievement of diversity goals. As a result, Ware rescinded his retirement plan

In November 2000, as a result of a court-ordered mediation, Coca-Cola settled the lawsuit with almost all of the 2,200 plaintiffs for $192.5 million. Approximately 1% of the plaintiffs decided to "opt-out" of the settlement agreement. On June 7, 2002, the U.S. District Court for the Northern District of Georgia approved the Settlement Agreement in what is formally known as *Ingram et. al. v. The Coca-Cola Company.* The Agreement applied to all non-hourly U.S.-based employees of the company but not to employees of its bottlers. The terms of the Agreement called for back pay to current and former employees, future pay equity adjustments, linkage between senior managers' compensation and the company's EEO performance and the creation of an outside seven-member Task Force to provide independent oversight of Coca-Cola's compliance. The Task Force was responsible for preparing four annual reports evaluating the implementation of these programs. Cyrus Mehri, head of the plaintiffs' legal team, summed up his opinion of the case.

> The biggest problems at Coke were their HR practices. They had almost as many job titles as they did jobs, there was no consistent form of job posting, and promotional practices were not consistently applied. This gave undue discretion to managers and prevented employees from having a fair chance to compete for these positions. Coke had cultivated an image of being extraordinarily progressive and generous in the African-American community. Unfortunately, Coke—like so many companies—got very arrogant and believed their own PR. They valued minorities as consumers, but not as employees. (Wiscombe, 2003, p. 34)

When asked to comment on the case, Coca-Cola corporate media relations spokesperson Karyn Dest wrote

> Clearly we learned a valuable lesson from the lawsuit. But, in addition to the learning around diversity, another great learning for us was that we had no documented proof when it came to the lawsuit of our efforts. We didn't measure the growth and development of minorities and women at the company. (personal communication, November 5, 2003)

AFTER THE LAWSUIT

Alexis Herman, a former U.S. Secretary of Labor, chaired the Task Force that issued its first report in September 2002. Since the settlement, Coca-Cola implemented numerous systemic changes in its policies and procedures. (See Exhibit 1) with measurable results (see Exhibit 2). Although the report was generally positive, the Task Force cited key areas that needed additional work: identification of employees for senior management positions and improvement in the perceptions of minority employees that their career opportunities are comparable to those of white employees. Currently, "about a third of Coke's employees are minorities but most top employees are white. . . . All minorities, the report said, are over represented in lower-paying support jobs" (Wyatt, 2002, p. 1).

The Task Force also chided the corporation for missing an opportunity to diversify the board of directors, which was then composed of nine white men, two white women, and one African-American man. In the spring of 2002, when the board membership was expanded from 12 to 14 members, two white men were selected. "The company's failure to consult with the task force with respect to the nominations undermined its diversity efforts and suggested a lack of sensitivity to diversity goals" (Bean, 2002b, p. 1).

Shortly after the report was published, CEO and Chairman Daft wrote a memo to employees that said, "There is still work to do. Our commitment to diversity is a journey not an endpoint. Diversity is not an initiative; it is a fundamental element of our business success" (Day, 2002, p. 3). In 2002, Coca-Cola began a five-year $800 million dollar supplier diversity program. That year alone $181 million worth of goods and services were purchased from women and minority-owned businesses. In 2003, Coca-Cola extended health benefits to same-sex domestic partners and named the first Hispanic female, Maria Elena Lagomasino, Chief Executive of J. P. Morgan, a private bank, to its board of directors. Coca-Cola is currently ranked number 25 on *Fortune* magazine's list of Best Companies for Minorities and at number 18 on DiversityInc.'s survey of the top 50 companies for diversity (Dest, personal communication, November 5, 2003).

However, Coca-Cola's public relations problems with diversity were far from over. A recent article on the DiversityInc Website questioned Coca-Cola's commitment to diversity in terms of the company's minority supplier program in contrast to the amount spent by other *Fortune* 100 companies. In addition, it was mentioned that a recent article written by Johnnie Booker and published in *Corporate Corridors* magazine on Coke's supplier diversity programs progress neglected to state in the byline that Booker was Coca-Cola's director of supplier diversity (Cole, 2002).

At the 2002 annual shareholders meting at Madison Square Garden, some African-American employees protested because they believed that blacks remain underrepresented in the top corporate ranks, get fired more often, and are still paid less than white employees. "Protesters handed out material claiming that 16% of the Coke workforce is black but that blacks have just 1.5% of the top jobs" (White, 2002, E03).

In May of the same year, some employees in Texas accused Coca-Cola of repackaging nearly out-of-date soda, marking it down, and then reselling it in minority neighborhoods since 1993. Coca-Cola management denied the allegation.

On May 24, 2002, The Coca-Cola Company, in a conciliation agreement with the U.S. Department of Labor, agreed to pay $ 8.1 million in back pay to over 2,000 female employees. The agreement followed an audit by the Office of Federal Contract Compliance (OFCCP), which enforces federal rules against discrimination at companies holding government contracts. The audit revealed wage disparities between male and female employees between 1998 and 2000 (Bean, 2002a).

- Established uniform processes for employee reviews
- Required that all job postings attract at least three candidates, one of whom must be a woman or minority
- Implemented mandatory diversity training for managers and employees
- Conducted human resources audits and adverse impact analyses
- Tied performance appraisals and compensation for managers to their effectiveness in performance management
- Implemented a uniform compensation system based on job-related measures, including a market-based salary structure, a common review date, and additional compensation training for managers
- Established a mentoring program
- Initiated executive briefings for senior management concerning diversity strategy
- Implemented a "Solutions" program that included an ombudsman and an hot-line to resolve employee disputes

Adapted from the *First Annual Report of the Task Force* (Herman et al., 2002)

EXHIBIT 1   Programs and Policies Implemented by Coca-Cola since the Settlement Agreement Was Accepted

---

- Of the 6,864 nonhourly U.S. Coke employees, 30% are minorities, up 4% since 12/00. Two thirds of the minorities are African Americans
- In the first 6 months of 2002, white men were promoted at the rate of 4.7%, women at 5%, and minorities at 5.7%; of the 301 new hires 29% were minorities, and 55% were women.
- Minorities make up only 20% of the workforce at the executive level and are overrepresented at 47% among the lowest paid support personnel

Adapted from the *First Annual Report of the Task Force* (Herman et al., 2002)

EXHIBIT 2   Key Findings from the First Annual Report of the Task Force

Discussion Questions

1. Considering that minority groups are one of Coca-Cola's major target markets in the United States and that the company sells its products all over the world, how could a diverse workforce be considered a strategic advantage to the organization?
2. With all of the positive changes that have been instituted at Coca-Cola since the settlement of the lawsuit in 2000, how is it possible that the survey administered by the Task Force revealed that minority employees still perceive that their career opportunities are not comparable to those of whites?
3. How does Parker's triangle, "The Emotional Connection of Distinguishing Differences and Conflict," help to explain (a) why so many minority employees joined the class action lawsuit and (b) how Coca-Cola failed to "manage diversity"?

Integrative Writing Assignments

1. Research the details of other major discrimination cases such as: Texaco, CSX Transportation, Winn-Dixie, Denny's, Johnson & Johnson, Adams-Mark Hotels, or Bell South. How are these current or settled cases similar to or different from the Coca-Cola case? Apply Thomas & Ely's framework to each of these organizations. What can be learned about managing diversity by applying their model?
2. *At the time that the lawsuit was filed:*
   a. What were the internal and external pressures for and against diversity at the company? Were the priorities for managing diversity low, moderate, or high? Why?
   b. Repeat this analysis (step a above) for Coca-Cola at the *conclusion* of the case.

Bibliography

Bean, L. (2002a, September 30). *Coca-Cola to pay $8 million to resolve salary discrimination.* Retrieved September, 30, 2003, from http://www.diversityinc.com/members/3034print.cfm

Bean, L. (2002b, September 30). *Coca-Cola rebuked for missed opportunity to diversify board.* Retrieved October 20, 2003, from http:www.diversityinc.com/members/3597print.cfm.

Cole, Y. (2002, September 12). *Baloney meter measures Coca-Cola's claims of supplier-diversity progress* (electronic version). Retrieved September 30, 2003, from http:www.diversityinc.com/members/351printcfm

Coca Cola Corporation. (2003). *The Coca-Cola Company 2002 annual report.* Atlanta: Author.

Daft, D. (2000). Speech delivered to the Chief Executives Club of Boston, May 3, 2000. *Vital Speeches of the Day, 66*(19), 606–609.

Day, S. (2002, September 26). Anti-bias task force gives Coca-Cola good marks but says challenges remain. *The New York Times.* p. C3.

Derdak, T. (Ed). (1988). *International directory of company histories* (pp. 232–235). Chicago: St. James Press.

Europe shuns tainted Coke. (1999). *MacLean's, 112,* 26, p. 78.

Feldman, A. (2000). The real thing. *Money,* 29, 33–36.

Foust, D. (2000a). Coke: Say goodbye to the good ol' boy culture. *Business Week, 3683*(55), 58.

Foust, D. (2000b). Will Coke go better with Carl Ware? *Business Week, 3665* (55), 138.

Foust, D. (1999). A different cola war. *Business Week,* 3632(54), 38–39.

Harrington, A. (2000) Prevention is the best defense. *Fortune, 142*(2), 188.

Herman, A., Burns, A., Casellas, G. F., Cooke, E. D., Jr., Knowles, M. F., Lee, B. L.,

Holsendolph, E. (1999, June 1). Once again, Carl Ware takes on an assignment, a big one. *The Atlanta Journal and Constitution.*

Mokhiber, R. (2000). Coke settles race suit. *Multinational Monitor, 21*(12), 30.

Morris, B., and Sellers, P. (2000). What really happened at Coke. *Fortune, 141*(1), 14–17.

New Doug, old tricks. (1999, December 9). *Economist, 353*(8149), 55.

National Soft Drink Association (NSDA), (2003). Growing Up Together: The Soft Drink Industry and America

Retrieved from nsda.org/softdrinks/History/ growup.html

Pendergast, M. (2000). *For god, country and Coca-Cola the definitive history of the great American soft drink and the company that makes it.* New York: Basic Books.

Sivy, M. (2000). Why Coke still isn't it. *Money, 29*(2), 42.

Smith, V.E. (2000). Things are going better with Coke. *Newsweek, 135*(3), 52.

Unger, H. (1999a, May 12). Plaintiffs in suit against Coca-Cola to meet in court. *Knight Rider/Tribune Business News.*

White, B. (2002, April 12). Black Coca-Cola workers still angry: Despite 2000 legal settlement, protesters say little has changed. *The Washington Post,* p. E03.

Wiscombe, J. (2003). Corporate America's scariest opponent. *Workforce, 82*(4), 34–40.

Wyatt, K. (2002, September 25). Coke's diversity work gets approval. *Associated Press News Release.* Retrieved October 31, 2003, from http://www.ap.org

CULTURE AND GENDER IN FORD'S MEXICAN HIGH-PERFORMANCE PLANT

Helen Juliette Muller

University of New Mexico

Mexico and Brazil are the Latin American leaders in the automotive industry. Mexico is a unique model because of its close economic integration with the United States and its free trade agreements with the European Union. It generates about 2 million vehicles annually making it the world's ninth largest automotive producer (Intelamex Inc., 2001). Automotive products are Mexico's largest export, and the automotive sector is Mexico's largest employer. Ford Motor Company began investments in Mexico in the 1920s for assembly of car kits imported from the United States. In the 1980s, production sites in Mexico's northern states, such as Sonora and Chihuahua, became more attractive as integration with the U.S. industry occurred along with geographical decentralization of the industry. Moreover, the introduction of Japanese management practices in some plants fostered horizontal decision making, teamwork, and a reduction in top-down leadership. Previously, the organization of work had followed the Taylor-Fordist model with compartmentalized work, hierarchical decision patterns, and autocratic leadership.

The government of the state of Sonora, which lies just to the south and shares a common border with the U.S. state of Arizona, offered Ford executives an attractive series of financial and physical incentives to locate a new large-scale stamping and assembly plant (HSA) in its capital city of Hermosillo (a 3-hour drive south from the border city of Nogales, Arizona). Other incentives included Hermosillo's well-educated workforce (average schooling of 8 years), its extensive higher education infrastructure, and its proximity to land and sea transportation (at the port of Guayamas, a 11/2-hour drive south from Hermosillo) that could readily bring supplies from Japan and deliver cars to dealers in the United States. Moreover, other factors included workers' lower wages than in the United States coupled their lack of experience with industrial conflict because the Confederation of Mexican Workers union had close ties to government and a cooperative attitude toward management. It embraced lean production techniques such as rotation, multitasking, work teams, and the elimination of seniority-based and restrictive job classifications.

In 1985, Ford began its experiment in Sonora in partnership with Mazda of Japan to develop a high-tech strategy that became part of a highly integrated international production system with the purpose of achieving the most advanced global standards in auto quality and productivity (Shaiken, 1994). HSA was to be a learning laboratory for Ford's global operations while the partnership with Mazda was the avenue for learning about the lean production manufacturing system. In its formative years, the new plant helped to spur the regional economy that previously had been agriculturally focused. In a highly acclaimed study (Womack, Jones, & Roos, 1991), HSA

> had the best assembly-plant quality in the entire volume plant sample, better than that of the best Japanese plants and the best North American transplants . . . also surprisingly efficient, particularly given its modest level of automation. (p. 87)

Originally trained in both Mexico, Japan, and Spain by predominantly Japanese-Mazda experts in lean production to assemble Japanese-designed vehicles, HSA's carefully taught and highly skilled workers geared up at the turn of the century to learn, in-house, to continually improve the Ford Production System (FPS), an adapted lean system, under the direction of highly experienced Mexican managers who trained at Ford—U.S. Furthermore, European-designed vehicles (the Focus) began to be stamped and assembled at HSA. In 2000, auto analysts continued to highly regard HSA in a report: "Hermosillo Puts Together a First Class Performance Package" (Harbour and Associates, 2000). Such accolades are particularly impressive because Ford's overall productivity and quality was falling behind General Motors, DaimlerChrysler, and Toyota. Furthermore, by late 2002, following Ford's painstaking, internal audit of its plants, HSA ranked Number One in Ford Production System (FPS) ratings in Ford's North American plants (Olavarrieta, 2003).

CROSS-CULTURAL COLLABORATION

The creation of the plant's original, innovative organizational culture was a highly complex process that integrated the disparate influences of (a) Japanese managers and technicians and their lean sociotechnical production system incorporating both just-in-time (JIT) and total quality management (TQM), (b) U.S. managers and their traditional Fordist production legacy, and (c) a relatively young Mexican workforce inexperienced in automobile assembly and a unique human resource management system. Cultural innovation is difficult to achieve because managers have to figure out how to develop and inculcate distinctive sets of ideologies and cultural forms that fit their circumstances (Trice & Beyer, 1993). The mutual adaptation process of U.S. and Japanese managers and their production ideologies occurred simultaneously with in-depth socialization and skill building of the Mexican workforce. The confluence of these three factors resulted in a unique Ford-Mazda Mexican hybrid organizational culture and production system that has proven itself over time to be able to adapt to and deliver new auto designs while maintaining a high level of product quality.

One way in which the multinational alliance created the innovative, hybrid culture was to use cultural mediators who helped various parties learn and adapt. For example, a Cuban national who had worked for Ford-Detroit helped to instill modern business attitudes in Mexican workers. In an interview in Hermosillo, Mr. Fernandez, now retired, told a member of our study team: "My job was to help American and Japanese managers communicate and understand one another; I had to learn the JIT system first, then I had to try to teach this system to others who would really be using it." Mr. Fernandez cofacilitated cross-cultural management teams to establish plant guidelines. He would explain the point of view of Mexican workers to the Americans and Japanese as well as educate Mexican workers about U.S. and Japanese work habits. He felt that he was a cultural liaison because he explained cultural practices of each group to the other.

Plant workers have reported to our research team that they receive offers from other Mexican companies who know that HSA employees are highly productive and well rounded: many HSA employees eventually work for local companies as managers or trainers because they learned to cut costs, manage groups, and work efficiently, all of which are a big asset to developing a company that has little experience with a modern management system.

Mexicans, whose traditional managerial style is predominantly authoritarian and paternalistic, quickly adapted to the managerial values and systems of the multinational corporate hybrid culture. To work effectively with the lean production system, Mexican workers were able to draw on one work-related factor specific to their culture—cooperation, but at the same time, they had to adapt to another work-related cultural factor: power distance and its dimensions of control and authority. Power distance measures the extent to which less-powerful members of an organization accept the unequal distribution of power (Hofstede, 2001). In Mexico, power distance was found to be greater than in Japan and the United States. (United States has the least power distance). Mexican workers have great respect for authority; their upbringing has instilled in them an acceptance of parental absolute authority, and as a result, young executives do not question decisions of superiors (Kras, 1995). The much-heralded Japanese team-based lean system has inherent low power distance and is nonhierarchical. In a team situation, workers have to be in control of operations and are responsible for following through and resolving problems (through continuous improvement discussions) to achieve high-quality products. Mexicans traditionally do their jobs and wait to see results; they are unaccustomed to checking on their work because they feel that supervisors do not trust them if quality checks on performance are introduced (Kras, 1995).

Japanese lean system hybrids, such as HSA, concentrate their philosophy and practices on human moral values and collective behavior: trustworthiness, personal integrity, responsibility, initiative, personal development, loyalty, and honesty. Collective values and behaviors such as shared goals, mutual respect, interdependence and cooperation, group recognition, open communication, and perceived egalitarianism are key to building the culture of the lean system organization. Such values and behaviors represent a significant departure from those of the traditional Fordist system that is more individualistic, hierarchical, and centralized. These collectivist values are more similar to the orientation of Mexican workers than to individualistic-oriented Anglo-American (U.S.) workers who tend to complete with one another.

In order to institutionalize the high-performance manufacturing system, profitability, and ultimately customer satisfaction, continuous training enables HSA workers to be socialized into behavioral norms that ensure compliance with high quality standards: HSA workers take 8 weeks of thorough training following an intensive selection process and before starting work; only those with the highest motivation are selected to become vehicle-team members.

Team-based problem solving is integral to the Japanese lean system: workers are in control of operations and basically self-manage; they are responsible for resolving problems to achieve continuously evolving higher quality and productivity levels; they are multiskilled and rotate jobs (Phil & MacDuffie, 1999). Such lean system work processes are congruent with cultures that respect horizontal power relationships. Even though Mexican workers are known for their cooperative behavior, and, increasingly, corporate managers are learning to adopt nontraditional styles, the traditional Mexican managerial model does persist in which the boss retains a high degree of control and workers demonstrate deference to authority (Mosley, Valentine, & Godkin, 2002).

Because teams began to grow larger than originally formed in the early years, in 2000 HSA senior managers, who by now were all Mexican, placed renewed emphasis on fostering team-driven processes as a central underlying premise of corporate culture. Trusting the technician to develop competence to make the right decision was paramount. As Olavarrieta (2003) put it: "The human part of the business is key to our success." Job-related decisions had to be made at the lowest possible level, and at HSA, where there is only one job classification of production worker, this meant workers on the production line (the technicians). "Employee empowerment" was the phrase used by managers to describe this core principle. Moreover, as part of this core value, people's differences had to be respected—among employees, clients, support personnel, and the community—according to a senior human resources manager.

WORKFORCE DIVERSITY INITIATIVE AND GENDER DYNAMICS

In Mexico, women hold proportionally more managerial positions than in Japan (8%), but fewer than in the United States (44%). Women now make up about 22% of all managerial positions in Mexico, double the number from 10 years ago. Despite this trend, HSA only recently invited a woman to join its executive management level, but she has no line authority. She holds a black belt in the Six Sigma Quality program and by virtue of this status, she must belong to the executive level. Overall, women comprise about 10% of the administrative support category at HSA.

Workforce diversity programs in Mexico have been virtually unknown. Only recently, a few U.S.-based multinationals began to develop such programs in order to hire more women (Zabludovsky, 2001) or to train the workforce to accommodate and respect diverse people's behaviors. The lack of attention to factors such as culture and ethnicity in Mexican corporate programs may reflect the fact that almost all Mexicans are mestizo or people of mixed heritage. At HSA, the human resource manager explained that a new workforce diversity initiative came about for two reasons: "It is the right thing to do and it makes good business sense." There are two parts: (a) a training program for employees about appropriate skills and behavioral practices for a diverse workforce, and (b) a corporate policy on job quotas, set by the plant's operating committee (the executives) that targets 50% of new hires (technicians) to be women. Part of management's reasons for hiring women, as explained to me, is a belief that women assess quality differently and more effectively than men, and that such traits would be advantageous on the production line. Managers believe that women are more detail oriented than men, a characteristic much needed in production.

Plant personnel placed ads in local newspapers in an effort to recruit young women. A plant manager showed me an ad from the Hermosillo daily newspaper, *El Imparcial*, that read: "Planta De Estampado Y Ensambel De Hermosillo solicita PERSONAL FEMENINO para laborar en área de procuccion." Such gender-specific classifieds are not uncommon in Mexico. In the first half of 2001, the plant hired 16 women as technicians and, because one of them became pregnant, the production line technicians, for the first time, dealt with issues such as maternity leave and return-to-work procedures. HSA jobs are highly sought after, and it is not uncommon for 1,000 people to apply for 25 job openings.

The subject of workforce of workforce diversity is not easily talked about in Mexico; sexual orientation, for example, is a touchy subject. Therefore, diversity training focuses on valuing differences, customer diversity, diverse points of view, as well as consciously working with and valuing women and older people. Results of pre- and postfocus groups with technicians on work teams where women became participants indicated that employees needed to eliminate inappropriate jokes and demeaning language and to open up to those who differed from themselves. Moreover, language patterns had changed, and men needed to make more supportive statements to women.

Diversity training modules included both the plant's antiharassment training policy and procedures, and confidentiality and "zero-tolerance" rules. Ford-Michigan prepared diversity training material for use worldwide; at HSA, human resource personnel made adaptations to fit the local Sonoran environment. A senior manager, who holds the most significant production rank of all women employees and who was one of the first women engineers at HSA, explained to us that Mexican culture is chauvinistic but she thinks that it is changing now. She strongly believes that HSA "broke the paradigm" in the area by hiring women technicians and engineers. She believes that women have the competence to be part of the senior executive ranks at HSA.

CONCLUSION

In early 2002, HSA released 600 employees due to the shutdown of its Japanese-designed Escort model line. Such action is frowned on in Latin American countries, where strong bonds are forged between managers and employees and where safety nets are minimal. Firing a worker has enormous economic and social consequences in Latin America (Rohter, 2002). Given HSA's stellar performance data and its recent start-up of an on-site Lean Learning Academy for all of Ford's Latin American operations, it is highly unlikely that Ford's corporate executives would target HSA for closure. In fact, in 2003, there are rumors circulating in Hermosillo that because HSA is such a showcase plant that it will host the start-up of a new model vehicle for Ford.

The workforce diversity initiative at HSA was observed to be at the forefront of Mexican industry efforts to diversify employees; its diversity-training program is a new phenomenon in Mexican industry. HSA continues to be innovative with its ambitious human resources department managers. Changes in plant policy to adopt female hiring quotas illustrate that HSA is providing leadership—the fact that at least one woman was just made a member of the executive team is another example. When firm downsizing occurs, however, it is not unusual for the last people hired to be the first to go. Thus women are vulnerable because they encounter organizational culture resistance and because their jobs may be jeopardized if layoffs occur.

The departure of Japanese-trained personnel steeped in the lean production system, coupled with the replacement of Japanese-designed vehicles with European-designed vehicles, created intense challenges in the organization of work and proved the ability of the HSA sociotechnical system to adapt and continue with a very high performance work culture. Given that Mexican managers traditionally emphasized power over their subordinates, it is even more remarkable that the Mexican senior management team at HSA achieved such high FPS performance levels. HSA holds the distinction of being a model Ford plant at the beginning of Ford's second century.

Discussion Questions

1. What are features of Mexican culture and U.S. culture that could facilitate or hinder good interpersonal working relationships in a plant that employs workers/managers from both countries? Explain what skills and behaviors a manager (Mexican or U.S.) might need to use when people from both countries are working together.

2. Identify and discuss some common stereotypes and misperceptions about Mexico that are prevalent in your location. What needs to happen for people to begin to change those perceptions? What can be the consequence of such stereotypes for Mexican people who may work in your community?

3. What are the factors that positioned HSA to be such a high-performance workplace? Can these features be replicated in other plants—What would have to take place? Why do you think Ford U.S. plants are unable to achieve the high performance levels that are found at Hermosillo?

4. Workforce diversity programs are largely products of the U.S. corporate or government environment. What adaptations might need to be made by human resource managers and trainers in a multinational company that has offices or a plant in another cultural context such as Mexico?

Bibliography

Harbour & Associates Inc. (2000). *The Harbour report 2000: North America.* Troy, MI: Author.

Hofstede, G. (2001). *Culture's Consequences* (2nd ed.). Thousand Oaks, CA: Sage.

Intelamex Inc. (2001). *The Mexican intelligence report—auto industry.* Retrieved September 7, 2002, from http:// www.mex-i-co.com/Arc_Auto.html

Kras, E.S. (1995). *Management in two cultures* (Rev. ed.). Yarmouth, ME: Intercultural.

Mosley, G. G., Valentine, S., & Godkin, L. (2002). U.S. organizations' personnel management in Mexico: Staffing considerations and cultural challenges. *Latin American Business Review, 3*(1), 37–73.

Olavarrieta, G. (2003, May). Ford Hermosillo Manufacturing and Assembly Plant Lean Manufacturing Manager. Personal Interview. Hermosillo, Mexico.

Phil, F. K., & MacDuffie, J. P. (1999). What makes transplants thrive: Managing the transfer of "best practice" at Japanese auto plants in North America. *Journal of World Business, 34*(4), 372–91.

Rohter, L. (2002, August 11). Latin countries chafe at strings on I.M.F. help. *New York Times*, pp. 1 & 6.

Shaiken, H. (1994). Advanced manufacturing in Mexico: A new international division of labor? *Latin American Research Review, 29*(2), 39–71.

Trice, H. M., & Beyer, J. (1993). *The cultures of work organizations.* Englewood Cliffs, NJ: Prentice Hall.

Womack, J. P., Jones, D. T., & Roos, D. (1991). *The machine that changed the world: The story of lean production.* New York: Harper Collins.

Zabludovsky, G. (2001). Women managers and diversity programs in Mexico. *Journal of Management Development, 20*(4), 354–370.

BELIEVABILITY: A CASE OF DIVERSITY IN LAW ENFORCEMENT

Egidio A. Diodati
Assumption College

Here I sit, waiting to see the Chief. Waiting to see if any of those jerks are going to get what is coming to them and waiting to see just what is my fate. When this started, I was pretty much all I wanted to be—a uniformed patrol officer on a city police department. Now I am facing the possibility of disciplinary action.

My name is Janet Cruz and I am a 24-year-old Hispanic woman, who grew up like a lot of others in this city. My neighborhood was pretty diverse but I can't say that I ever felt any outright hostility to me personally. When I was in high school, my mom would say, "Stay with your own kind," when she did not like someone I was dating or hanging out with. You know, I dated just about anybody I wanted and it worked out or it didn't. To me most people are just people.

In my high school, they had this junior police cadet program, and I knew once I saw that being a cop was for me. Maybe it was the uniform, or the drilling, or taking care of each other—but as far as I was concerned, it was all good. After high school, I joined the National Guard to pay for college. There was no way mom could afford that. I made sure that it was a military police unit. The state university had a campus in the city with a major in Criminal Justice. So, I enrolled there. It was nearby and I could live with my Mom to save money.

All of these exposures to the "police" business left me with some valuable beliefs. First of all, this is a job about doing the right thing and helping people. Second, officers did not just work together; it was closer than that. It was a family that took care of each other—or at least I thought it was that way.

It really thrilled me that I had scored highly enough on the competitive entrance examination and got an appointment to the "Academy" the very first time I took the examination. When the academy started, the following weeks of training seemed to affirm much of what I had felt about police work with one exception. One of the sessions at the academy was given by someone who was not on the instructional staff, the Union Chief Steward.

Although he was in the uniform of a patrol officer, he was sterner, older, heavier, and generally less neatly dressed than the other instructors.

The class was told that the union represented the brotherhood of officers (collectively and individually) to the command staff made up of "superior officers." He said, "Our job is to represent all officers fairly, equally, and to the best of our ability." I think that unfortunately I may have placed too much faith in that statement.

After I finished my probationary period, I think I began to fit pretty well into the ranks. Sure, lots of guys came on to me, but I'm grown up and I dealt with it. I got to know Jack MacKenzie while working in Precinct Three, a tough section known as "the mile." He was a patrol officer and the steward of the precinct union local: everybody seemed to like him. We began to date. You know, I actually thought that he was a very funny guy and he told me that I was "cute." It worked for a while at least. It took me about three months to figure out that he was just too high maintenance. He wanted me to move in but when we spent too much time in his apartment, I noticed that it was all about him, his accomplishments, and his family. I never got much airtime. It must have been a power thing. Another thing that I noticed was that, after a few drinks, he began to make references to minorities that made me uncomfortable.

One night we went out for dinner and I broke up with him. I started with the, "It's me not you." thing, since I knew I had to leave room for his precious ego. I finished with the, "time apart" suggestion. It seemed to have gone fairly well. A bit later, a couple of guys on my shift mentioned that they had heard he broke up with me. I did not get into it. It was just not worth it.

When a couple of overtime details got canceled, I figured it was just bad luck. The overtime list was maintained by the union, and I could have filed a grievance, but it would have meant getting MacKenzie involved. When my backup was slower than usual, I chalked it up to a busy night. It occurred to me that Jack might just be behind this stuff, but I figured if I made anything out of it, things would just get worse

Well, here I sit 11 months later, at risk of losing my job, and I either see a pattern or am letting my imagination run away with me. Nevertheless, I see Jack MacKenzie as a major part of my recent twist of fate. About a month ago, a flyer was put in each officer's mail slot by the union and posted on the union bulletin board. It encouraged all officers to attend a political rally for one of the candidates for governor in the upcoming election. The union was going to rent a bus, and I could swear it said something about refreshments on the bus. I was going to be available and asked a couple of people if they were going and they said yes. So, I figured it might be fun.

On the day of the rally, my shift ended about 4 P.M. and I had just enough time to get home to shower, before getting back to get on the union bus going to the rally. As usual, I carried my badge and personal service weapon with me when I left the house. I spotted Paul Wilson, one of the guys from my precinct who had said he was going. We talked for a couple of minutes and walked to the bus. Paul is a great guy with a great family. He is always showing pictures of his wife and kids and is very easygoing. Paul is African

American, and he helped to found the minority officers association. As we walked toward the bus, I spotted MacKenzie and two other union shop stewards standing near some coolers at the back entrance to the bus. The other two guys were named Dalton and Taggert. I had seen them at a union meeting a couple of months earlier.

Paul and I sat near the front, about two seats behind the driver and began to talk with some of the people sitting up there. The noise level went up as MacKenzie and company entered through the back door. He yelled from the back to the driver to, "get going." I had seen him with a few drinks in him before, and he did seem like he had a few in him already. The rally was about a 45-minute drive, and although the noise level did go up, it was not bad. I could hear his voice in the back telling jokes and hear people laughing. Because one of the coolers was up near us in the front, I had a couple of beers.

After we got to where the rally was and went in, I heard that MacKenzie and couple of guys went across the street to a local pub. The rally went till about 10:30. After that, a group of us (Paul and a couple of other guys from my precinct) went over to the pub to get a sandwich and a beer. I could see MacKenzie gesturing in my direction, with the others around him laughing. About midnight, we all went back to the bus. I sat up near the front again because I was hoping to get some sleep on the way back and because I did not trust what MacKenzie or his crew might be up to doing.

It was getting loud in the back of the bus. They were still drinking. It was then that I began to hear his voice mentioning my name. Things like, "Yeh, Cruz was my Monica Lewinsky. It got worse but Paul Wilson said, "Just ignore them. They're drunk and they're just being jerks." The comments continued with things like (I'm not sure but I think it was MacKenzie who said it.) that he had a "cruz" missile. I kept my back to them but I'm sure I also heard Taggert and Dalton's voices with some comments.

You know what was really awful? Nobody spoke up to tell them to back off or that they were out of line. I really expected more. Then it got worse. First, one then another of the three would ask for oral sex saying, "Hey Monica, how about it?" Even though there were two other women on the bus, I just knew that they were talking to me.

After a bit, it quieted down for a while and I thought it was over. I was sitting in a seat on the aisle and I started to drift off when I felt a tap on my shoulder. I turned and saw MacKenzie standing over my right shoulder exposing himself with his pants open and I think he said something like, "You know that I am better than Wilson, how about it?" That's when I yelled for the driver to pull over and I got out. I heard a couple of voices tell the driver to, "Let the spic bitch go." The bus pulled away and I was left standing there.

Just when I thought that things could not get any worse, a guy jumped out of doorway and said, "How much baby?" I guess he thought I was a hooker. I tried to walk away and then he pushed me against the building. That's when I drew my personal service weapon, put him on the ground and started to scream for help. Pretty soon, the local police came. Would you believe that they drew their weapons, put me on the ground in cuffs, and then searched me?

As I told the local PD's watch commander the story, I could sense two things. First, he did not seem to believe me. Second, he was getting angrier by the minute. "So," he says," I guess it's not against procedure in your department to drink while carrying your personal service weapon." Obviously, it was. It was then that I said, "Look, that son of a bitch MacKenzie is lucky that I didn't shoot him.

About a half hour later, he came back to tell me, "O.K. honey, here is what we all have agreed to and you really don't have much say in it. So, listen up. We have agreed not looking at charges here in our jurisdiction. We are going to let your own department deal with you. You will be transported back to your department's headquarters building. There you will be turned over to your own Internal Affairs people, who are just waiting with baited breath to speak with you."

The ride back was not bad until it hit me that my riding in back made me look like a criminal. Lt. Bruce, head of IAB, met me and brought me directly to an interrogation room and left me alone. The wall opposite where I was sitting had a good-size mirror. I wondered who was on the other side. It wasn't feeling much like family now. God, I was tired, angry, and damn near tears.

Deputy Chief Miceli, a gruff and physically intimidating individual, entered the room and immediately began with some of his famous up close and personal straight talk—with none of the expletives deleted. He was clear that the Chief was going to end my career if I was not forthcoming with the IAB investigators. But, you know what, he just might do it anyway so the old boys in the department could cover their collective behinds. He then took my badge and gun and told me that I was suspended pending investigation. As he left, he wordlessly passed Lt. Bruce who was coming into the room.

Waiving his finger just inches from my face, he began, "Look Cruz, you're in some pretty deep trouble. Just because the other department is not filing criminal charges, it doesn't mean that this thing is over. Far from it, honey! Do you understand me? I want the whole story, right from the start. If I even think that you have left something out, you are going to be leaving this room in cuffs. Understand? You can ask for your union representative, but something tells me that they are probably not coming out from under the rock for you. You can ask for a lawyer, but we all know what that is going to look like, don't we?" He ceremoniously pushed the button on the tape recorder and said, "O.K. honey, take it from the top."

So, I went on to give Lt. Bruce chapter and verse on how it had happened. The interview was punctuated with a couple of questions that did not make me feel all that comfortable. "How much did you have to drink?" "Are you aware of the policy on off duty drinking while carrying personal firearms?" "Did you do anything to encourage this behavior?" I was ordered to have no contact with anyone on the bus until further notice and to go home until further notified. The next day, I did hear through the rumor mill that MacKenzie, Taggert, and Dalton had also been suspended but that the union was making real fuss about it, threatening a no confidence vote in the Chief.

About a week later I was summoned to a meeting in the Chief's office. At the head of the table was the Chief, with Lt. Bruce on his right, and

Miceli took the seat to his left. The Chief began, "Cruz, have a seat. MacKenzie claims that this is all made up by you because you are upset that he broke up with you. I'm not sure how much credibility to place in that statement. The results of the internal affairs investigation were severely hamstrung by the union. They would not provide a list of members on the bus and told all members not to give any information to us. They are telling the rank and file that we are just trying to break the union to put us in a good position for the upcoming contract negotiations. We are going to place a lot of weight on your statement. You are being returned to duty after a three-day loss of pay for conduct unbecoming an officer because you admitted to drinking when armed. MacKenzie is being terminated. Taggert and Dalton will be suspended without pay for three months. You should know that the union will probably grieve this and perhaps bring it to the state review board and they can act on it, if they see fit, including reversing it." Now that, I thought, was a fair result.

Now here I sit, waiting outside the Chief's office yet one more time. The union hired a law firm and brought the whole case to the state review board, and they have apparently made a ruling. After the door opens, again I find myself sitting opposite the Chief, Deputy Miceli, and Lt. Bruce. The Chief does not look happy but begins, "The state review board has come up with a finding after reviewing our reports and recommendations and looking at sworn statements provided by a number of officers who say that they were on the bus that night. The finding is that, although no one actually says MacKenzie exposed himself to you, he was abusive to you. They have upheld his termination. There was not enough evidence to support the suspensions of Taggert and Dalton, so their suspensions have been reversed with back pay. Several of the statements indicate that they saw you in several exchanges with one or more people in the back of the bus. That is in direct contradiction with your sworn statement. The review board finds that you have lied on a sworn statement and should be held responsible. As a result, you are being suspended for a month without pay. In addition, it might be a good idea if you were reassigned. We are sending you to be a school safety officer for a while."

Discussion Questions

1. Describe the corporate culture of this police department as you see it.
2. Was Janet Cruz treated fairly? Why or why not?
3. What role did the union play in this situation? What are the ramifications for other female officers?
4. Compare the earlier recommendation of the chief with the later recommendation of the state review board. Whose interests were served? Why do you think that the recommendations were so different?
5. Given the state of affairs at the end of the case, what recommendation would you make to Janet Cruz? Why?

NIGHTMARE ON WALL STREET

Melinda Ligos

In this unprecedented bull market, selling in the financial industry is more lucrative than ever. It's also hell for many women, who are blatantly harassed and discriminated against by their managers. When saleswomen head to Wall Street, they dream of big money, million-dollar deals, chauffeured limos, and a house in the Hamptons.

What many find instead is the stuff of nightmares—demeaning managers, crude jokes, physical assaults, and a glass ceiling so impenetrable it might as well be made of titanium steel. "The [financial industry] is the last bastion of testosterone gone wild," says Marybeth Cremin, the original plaintiff in one of two major class-action sexual discrimination/harassment lawsuits recently settled against two of the nation's largest securities firms. "This industry has been discriminating against women for years."

At the time this article went to press, both Merrill Lynch and Company and Salomon Smith Barney were reaching financial agreements with thousands of women who had filed discrimination suits against them. In the Smith Barney case, more than 22,500 former and current sales assistants and brokers throughout the country alleged widespread sexual harassment and discrimination. At Merrill Lynch, more than 900 current and former female brokers contend that the firm had discriminated against women in wages, promotions, account distributions, maternity leaves, and other areas. And as the result of the filing of a discrimination claim, the Equal Employment Opportunity Commission (EEOC) is currently investigating allegations of discriminatory practices alleged by a high-earning female broker at a third firm, Morgan Stanley Dean Witter [now Morgan Stanley].

While the very existence of these suits might seem disturbing, they seem to expose a much larger problem. Many financial industry insiders say sexual harassment and discrimination in the industry are not unique to the companies mentioned in these lawsuits. For many women who sell on Wall Street—especially in securities and investment banking businesses—harassment simply comes with the job. What's worse, sales managers not only tolerate this hostile environment, but actively promote it.

"Stereotypes about women's abilities run rampant in the financial industry," says Sheila McFinney, an organizational psychologist familiar with Wall Street. "A lot of men in management feel that women don't have the stomach for selling on Wall Street. They think they can't handle the adverse climate."

In addition, McFinney says, veteran Wall Street managers may not feel that women deserve to be in positions where they could potentially earn a lot of cash. "There's a lot of money coming into some of these firms," she says, "and there's this machismo culture that doesn't feel women should get a piece of the pie."

These stereotypes drive all kinds of business decisions, McFinney says, from who gets which accounts to who gets promoted to who gets which perks. And the problems are created by a group of predominately male managers who foster a culture in which women are, at best, made to feel uncomfortable and, at worst, driven to the point of personal and financial ruin. Of course, the financial industry isn't the only one in which sexual harassment and discrimination occur, but it does offer a particularly disturbing example of how things can go terribly wrong if managers allow these practices to fester.

A REAL TYRANT

Why do managers discriminate against women in the financial industry? Because they can. For years, most firms in the industry have required employees to sign mandatory arbitration agreements, which limit their ability to file claims in federal or state court. Instead, employees must submit complaints of discrimination to an arbitrator, who acts as judge and jury in determining the validity of an employee's claims. (Class-action suits—suits with multiple plaintiffs—traditionally have been exempt from mandatory arbitration.)

Industry insiders say the process is flawed, because the arbitrators tend to be older white males who often discount discrimination claims. "Managers have no fear of accountability," says Linda Friedman, a partner at Stowell and Friedman, the law firm representing the plaintiffs in both the Merrill Lynch and Smith Barney class-action suits. "There's no fear of repercussions, no fear of embarrassment or public scorn. Most managers believe they can get off scot-free." That's what one branch manager at Salomon Smith Barney may have believed—and apparently bragged about as he allegedly harassed and discriminated against female brokers and sales assistants in the company's Garden City, New York, branch for years.

When Roberta Thomann first came in contact with branch manager Nicholas Cuneo, she says, she tried to avoid him. Thomann, a successful sales assistant for the top broker at the branch in the early 1990s, says Cuneo was "a real tyrant. He treated women like garbage." Thomann says she tried to ignore it when Cuneo and other male brokers openly used crude language when referring to women in the office. According to court records, Cuneo once paraded a female sales assistant around the office who had worn culottes to work and told her to spread her legs at each male broker's desk so the broker could vote on whether the culottes violated Cuneo's dress code. (Note: Cuneo did not return repeated phone calls to discuss these allegations. In addition, Joan Walsh, director of employee relations at Smith Barney, said she could not comment on the specifics of the lawsuit.)

Thomann says she kept quiet at the beginning. "I would just think to myself, 'What an ass—,' and get back to work," Thomann says. Then, in 1994, Thomann, who was at that time a senior sales assistant, became pregnant and could no longer ignore Cuneo. She went on maternity leave for 8 weeks and was scheduled to return to work in mid-June. At four o'clock on the Friday before she was to come back, Thomann says she got a call from Cuneo. "He said that my position had been replaced, and I was going to be demoted," she says.

Thomann says she was offered a lowly sales assistant position in the bullpen, a notoriously rowdy area reserved for 11 broker trainees. "I was treated as if I had a disease," she says about her return to work. At one point, Thomann claims, the top broker she used to work for sent her and other sales assistants a memo promising that any charges of sexual harassment would be deliberated in the "Boom Boom Room," a room Cuneo had allegedly created in the basement of the office building, which was decorated in fraternity-house style, with a toilet bowl hanging from the ceiling.

Thomann says she wrote a letter to the branch's human resources department complaining of discriminatory treatment. "I thought, 'Now, they're really going to be in trouble,'" she says. But shortly after she filed the complaint, Thomann says, Cuneo began walking by her desk every 15 minutes, allegedly singing, "You're dead, you're dead, you're dead." Throughout the whole ordeal, according to court documents, Cuneo often openly displayed his lack of concern that Smith Barney would discipline him for violating its written antidiscrimination policies.

"I thought, 'Oh my God, nothing's going to happen,'" Thomann says. Two weeks later, her fears were confirmed when she got a letter from the human resources department stating that an investigation had revealed no discrimination. That was the last straw for Thomann. She quit her job in 1994 and gave up her Wall Street aspirations for good. She later became one of the original plaintiffs in the Smith Barney suit. "He thought he was invincible," Thomann says of her former boss.

As invincible as Cuneo may have felt, he allegedly tried to further safeguard himself from discrimination complaints by attempting to intimidate broker Pamela Martens and other female workers at the branch. Court records state that when Martens filed a discrimination complaint against Cuneo, he told at least one coworker that if he got into trouble because of the complaint, he would "f—[Martens] where she bleeds" and "snap [Martens'] neck." Martens was terminated by Smith Barney in October 1995, two days after Cuneo's retirement.

Wall Street insiders say Cuneo's reported air of invincibility is typical of managers in the financial industry. One successful female broker who works at a major Wall Street firm says her former manager used to call her and the only other female broker in the office "C—t One" and "C—t Two." "These guys are making big bucks, and they're real cocky," she says. "Their attitude is like, 'I'm not going to let some dumb bitch get in my way.'"

ANSWER YOUR OWN DAMN PHONE

Sexual harassment is only part of the story in the financial industry. Many female brokers who aren't harassed still face discrimination—sometimes in not-so-subtle ways. In both the Smith Barney and Merrill Lynch lawsuits, dozens of managers are accused of refusing to hire female brokers and managers, and of denying women the same pay and opportunities as their male counterparts, among other discriminatory acts.

When the Smith Barney case was filed, the plaintiffs claimed that less than 5 percent of Smith Barney's 11,000 brokers were female, and, although the company had 460 branch offices, fewer than 10 branch managers were women. "Indeed, the substantial majority of Smith Barney's employees are white males," the court filing alleged. The Merrill Lynch lawsuit tells a similar story. When that suit was filed, its plaintiffs complained that out of 76 sales managers, only seven were female, and only about 14 of its 125 brokers were women.

Why were the numbers so low? The plaintiffs in both cases allege that their managers purposely made it difficult for them to succeed. While Thomann and her female coworkers were struggling in Smith Barney's Garden City office, trouble was brewing in the Kansas City branch for broker Beverly Trice, who later became another of the lawsuit's original plaintiffs. Trice worked for Smith Barney from 1990 until 1996, and claims she was denied the same privileges enjoyed by the office's male brokers. For instance, when her sales assistant left the company, her sales manager allegedly refused to fill the position for 7 months, telling Trice that she could "answer her own damn phone." "I would be talking to a very important client, and I'd have to say, 'Hold on a minute,' and answer my other line, or I'd miss calls," Trice says. "It got so bad that after I interrupted a long-term client several times in one call, he told me that he couldn't handle it anymore."

In addition to being denied privileges of employment, Trice says her sales efforts were undermined by her male peers and supervisors. For example, on one occasion, she says her manager prevented her from mailing out her quarterly statement to clients in a timely fashion by falsely telling her that she couldn't send certain articles typically sent by brokers to their clients. Another time, a male broker in the office reportedly stole Trice's quarterly monitors from her desk and hid them for his own use.

After she filed several complaints with human resources, Trice claims that her boss fired her. His reason? "He said my desk was too messy," Trice says. "Then he started laughing raucously, and told me if I sued, I would never get a job in the business again." Sure enough, her manager was right. Trice says she had five major job offers withdrawn—some with salaries of more than a million dollars—after her former boss told the prospective employers that she was suing the firm. "This is a very small community," says Trice, who is still unemployed and spends her time working on a book about her experiences.

Managers at Smith Barney and Merrill Lynch might not be the only ones who allegedly have used such tactics to keep women in the industry's lower ranks. At least one woman, Allison Schieffelin, at a third brokerage firm, has filed a complaint with the EEOC against her current employer. For more than a dozen years, Schieffelin was on Wall Street's fast track, eventually taking home more than $1 million per year as a senior salesperson in the convertible bond department at Morgan Stanley Dean Witter.

But her progress began to stall a few years ago, when, she claims, she was denied many of the privileges that males in her position received. According to her lawyer, Wayne Outten, Schieffelin was excluded from male-only events, including trips to Manhattan strip clubs, and her division's annual 5-day golf outing to the Doral Resort and Spa in Florida. "The [golf trips] were very important opportunities to mingle with senior executives and clients, and Allison lost out," Outten says.

In 1996, although she was one of the company's superstars, her lawyer says, Schieffelin claims she was passed over when she became eligible to become a managing director. She was bypassed again the next 2 years. In the spring of 1998, her lawyer says, she was told that she would never become a managing director, even though men who seemed less qualified had received the title. "The only rationale [Morgan Stanley] has provided is extremely vague," Outten says. Outten alleges that Morgan Stanley has only one female managing director out of 40 in its North American division. Morgan Stanley refused to comment on the case, which is still in progress, and would not provide information about the number of females in top management.

Outten says super-successful saleswomen like Schieffelin—who is still working at the company—are often even more likely to experience some of these discriminatory actions than women who are less successful. "A lot of these guys have a sort of western gunslinger mentality," he says. "They don't care if women get jobs as clerks or secretaries. But when they think they could take away another guy's paycheck, they're going to fight nasty."

THE ANTI-MOMMY SENTIMENT

At one Wall Street firm, there's a cruel joke that goes like this: "There's only one thing worse than a female broker—a pregnant broker." "As soon as you're pregnant, they find some way to drum you out the door," says a male broker who works for the firm, which is among the most respected in the industry. Such appeared to be the case with Marybeth Cremin. For 13 years, Cremin, a broker at Merrill Lynch's branch office in Northbrook, Illinois, was managing more than $60 million in assets. A mother of three with an MBA, Cremin said she ignored remarks by her branch manager about how women couldn't balance work and family. She also claims that the manager refused to send her to financial planning seminars and other training opportunities "because he said I was too busy raising my children." "He pushed pregnant women out the door all the time," she says, "while telling male [brokers] that they should have more kids and a big mortgage so that they would be motivated to sell more. It was a big double standard."

When Cremin announced that she was pregnant with her fourth child, she says, the manager began pressuring her to transfer her book of customer accounts to other male brokers at Merrill Lynch. "He threatened to break up my partnership with a male colleague and reduce my support staff if I didn't give up my clients," she says. "But I told him I had worked very hard to get where I was, and I wanted to provide for my children."

Later in her pregnancy, Cremin had to go on total bed rest, and the manager turned up the heat, Cremin says. In June 1995, shortly after she gave birth, he reportedly told Cremin that he would give her a financial incentive—and a permanent part-time position as a financial planner—if she gave up her accounts. She took the offer. In August 1995, the week before Cremin was to start her new position, she says the manager's secretary called her to let her know the company was putting through her termination papers.

"I was dumbfounded," she says. "I said that there must be some kind of screw up." It turns out there was no mistake. The same secretary the following week confirmed the termination, Cremin says, and the manager "even had the nerve to call me on the phone and tell me why." Merrill Lynch maintains that Cremin resigned from her position. In addition, the company "is committed more than ever to improving the diversity of its workforce, particularly among [brokers]," says Joe Haldin, a Merrill Lynch spokesperson.

CHANGING THEIR WAYS?

To some victims of harassment and discrimination, Haldin's assertion may sound like corporate-speak aimed at deflecting criticism. But the fact is, executives at Wall Street firms are at least making efforts to address these problems. A recent study of Wall Street from the United States Commission on Civil Rights states that the industry deserves credit for having at least started to embrace diversity (though Mary Frances Berry, the Commission's chairwoman, laments a "dismal lack of progress").

As part of their respective settlement agreements, Merrill Lynch and Smith Barney have pledged to make sweeping changes in the way they treat women. Merrill Lynch is boosting its recruitment efforts, and between 1997 and 1998, Haldin says, the number of female brokers hired by the firm increased by about 7 percent. Merrill Lynch also has ended the practice of mandatory arbitration (a second Wall Street firm, Paine Webber, followed suit); and according to Haldin, the company is implementing a new policy this year governing the distribution of accounts, which ensures that female brokers "receive their fair share." In addition, the company is in the process of working out financial settlements with each plaintiff.

As part of its class-action settlement, Salomon Smith Barney has committed $15 million to diversity initiatives and last year hired a substantial number of female brokers. "Between 32 percent and 35 percent of all new brokers hired are females," says Walsh, Smith Barney's director of employee relations. In addition, she says, the company has conducted sexual harassment prevention training programs every year since 1995, and more than 8,000 managers have completed the workshop. Women are also encouraged to explore promotional opportunities with the company, she says.

These efforts may help some women—but they won't help many of the plaintiffs involved in the two class-action lawsuits. Some of those women left the financial industry after their experiences. Others remain with the companies they sued, or have gotten jobs at other firms. "Many of their lives are destroyed," says Friedman, the attorney representing both groups, "and their spirits are destroyed as well. Unlike women who are 20 years older than they are, most of these women grew up being told every day that there were no limits; that they could be anything they wanted to be. When they found out that wasn't true, it was a harsh reality that many won't recover from."

Managers who harass or discriminate also face harsh realities. Not only do they leave themselves open to lawsuits, but they also seriously jeopardize their companies' bottom lines. "Women are beginning to control a lot of money in this country," Cremin says. "As they become more sophisticated investors, they're going to want to buy from other women. And they're sure as hell not going to entrust their money to a firm that has a reputation for not being women-friendly."

MANAGING IN A MALE-DOMINATED INDUSTRY

Sexual harassment and discrimination happen in virtually every industry—but it's especially prevalent in industries that traditionally employ males. Here are some tips from Greg Rasin, a partner at Jackson Lewis, a New York–based law firm that specializes in labor and employment law, on what managers in male-dominated fields can do to make sure their sales force is female-friendly.

Create a Zero-Tolerance Policy
"Managers need to convince their male employees that discrimination and harassment won't be tolerated," Rasin says. Managers should create a policy prohibiting such behavior and distribute it to all employees.

Keep It Clean
"Seemingly innocuous jokes and sexual comments should be considered off limits," Rasin says. Employees who make lewd remarks should be disciplined immediately.

Rethink Social Outings
Taking clients to strip bars and similar outings isn't acceptable, Rasin says. "Women who work in an environment where this happens are put in an awful situation," he says. "They're either forced to go and potentially be embarrassed, or they're excluded. It's just wrong in today's world to entertain a client in this way—and it's discriminatory."

Distribute Accounts Fairly

That means, in part, working out a plan so that women who take maternity leave aren't unfairly penalized as a result. "Treat all medical leaves the same," he says. If a male salesperson is out for 3 months following a heart attack, you'd better treat him the same as you would a woman who's out on maternity leave."

AN OASIS FOR WOMEN

While most Wall Street firms are ruled by male managers, here's a big exception: Fiduciary Trust Company International, a global asset management firm, not only has a female CEO and president, it employs dozens of female vice presidents. In fact, 40 percent of the firm's professional staffers are women, and 26 percent of the senior staff is female. Many credit the large number of high-level females to the hiring practices of CEO Anne Tatlock, who says she strongly believes that "sex does not define your capability." But, she says, the company got its female-friendly reputation years before she came to Fiduciary in 1984. "Part of the reason was that the firm was founded to manage private wealth," she says, "and our clients wanted family-type relationships with our employees. Women are exceptional in this environment," Tatlock says.

A money manager for more than 37 years, Tatlock herself has had some struggles moving up the ranks. In the 1960s, she says, she was the first woman hired at Smith Barney "who was not a secretary." As she climbed the ladder in the financial world, Tatlock remembers "having to be smuggled in through the back door" of all-male clubs in order to give presentations to clients. She also remembers cases where she "did all the work" on an account, only to have a male colleague present her work to superiors as his own. Interestingly, though, Tatlock says she probably experienced less discrimination than women who entered the industry in the 1970s and later. "At first, I didn't have very high expectations for my career, so I probably didn't present myself as much of a threat," she says. Now, this high-ranking Wall Streeter is an inspiration to other women at the firm. Marilyn Fee White, Fiduciary's vice president of institutional new business, says Tatlock's presence at the helm sold her on the job. "It's wonderful to work in an organization that is attuned to the different strengths that both men and women bring to the business," she says.

Discussion Questions

1. From this article, what are the similarities and differences between the ways that women were treated at Fiduciary Trust Corporation International and how they were treated at Merrill Lynch & Co., Inc., Salomon Smith Barney, and Morgan Stanley Dean Whitter?
2. What potential advantages could women bring to this industry?
3. If you were a diversity consultant for Salomon Smith Barney, Merrill Lynch, or Morgan Stanley Dean Whitter, what policy changes would you recommend? Why?

FROM TAILHOOK TO TAILSPIN: A DISHONORABLE DECADE OF SEXUAL HARASSMENT IN THE U.S. MILITARY

Lori J. Dawson
Worcester State College

Michelle L. Chunis
Millbury, MA

> *Tailhook: 1. a hook-like device under Navy aircraft that latches onto cables on the deck of aircraft carriers to assist in their landing. 2. a private association of active duty reserve and retired Navy and Marine aviators and others, primarily known for the debauchery at its conventions. (CNN, 2000, August 25)*

In 1991, reports of misconduct at the thirty-fifth Annual Tailhook Convention received tremendous media attention, but this was neither the first nor the last of its conventions that drew criticism. In 1974, Senator William Proxmire gave the Navy his "Golden Fleece Award" for using its aircraft to transport conference attendees. Amid growing concerns regarding the 1985 convention, Vice Admiral Edward Martin, Deputy Chief of Naval Operations, sent a memo to the Commander of the Naval Air Force Pacific Fleet, stating:

> The general decorum and conduct last year was far less than that expected of mature naval officers. . . . a rambunctious drunken melee. . . . Heavy drinking and other excesses were not only condoned, they were encouraged. . . . We can ill afford this type of

behavior, and indeed must not tolerate it. (Department of Defense, Office of the Inspector General, 1992) (DOD, OIG)

After this, letters regarding proper conduct were routinely sent to attendees prior to the beginning of each convention. This was the case for the 1991 convention, where approximately 1,600 people arrived on naval aircraft; 2,000 people registered for the conference; and an additional 3,000 people attended the parties. According to official reports from the Naval Intelligence Service (NIS), these parties were centered around 26 hospitality suites on the third floor of the hotel. In the "Rhino Suite," a hole cut in a picture of a rhinoceros held a dildo. At other times, the dildo was removed and a partygoer's penis was inserted through the hole. Women entering the suite were forced to perform fellatio on whichever object happened to be protruding from it. The "gauntlet," a large group of men who groped, bit, and fondled women as they passed by, lined the third floor corridor outside the suites (DOD, OIG, 1992).

When the former president of the Tailhook Association failed to respond to her concerns about these behaviors, Lieutenant Paula Coughlin, a Navy helicopter pilot, wrote to the Assistant Chief of Naval Operations, who in turn notified his superior, Admiral Jerome Johnson. Recognizing the severity of the situation, Admiral Johnson immediately had the NIS begin an investigation. Approximixately 2,100 witnesses were interviewed as allegations of misconduct grew. The official victim assault summaries included reports of being bitten on the buttocks, grabbed in the crotch, groped on the breasts, pinched, called foul names, and shirts being pulled open. Although these acts clearly violated the Uniform Code of Military Justice (Article 93, cruelty and maltreatment; Article 128, assault; and Article 133, conduct unbecoming an officer), the Naval Inspector General stated that he faced a "What's the big deal?" attitude during the investigation. The fallout from the investigation led to the resignation of Navy Secretary Lawrence Garrett, Admiral Frank Kelso, and several other high-ranking officials, but not a single man stood trial (DOD, OIG, 1992).

The 1991 Tailhook scandal focused attention on sexual harassment in the military and resulted in sweeping policy changes. Based on the recommendations of the Defense Equal Opportunity Council Task Force on Discrimination and Sexual Harassment, the DOD revised its sexual harassment policy, incorporating 48 specific recommendations as department policy in August 1995. During confirmation hearings in 1997, Secretary of Defense William Cohen commented on the importance of upholding the "zero tolerance policy" for sexual harassment, yet sexual harassment and discrimination in the military continue to be pervasive.

TAILSPIN: THE SAGA OF SEXUAL HARASSMENT CONTINUES

In 1996, Maryland's Aberdeen Proving Ground became the focus of attention when a captain and four drill sergeants were brought up on a variety of charges including sexual harassment and rape of female trainees. Army reports alleged that some of the base's drill sergeants made a game of distributing a list of names of women who they believed would have sex with them. In one account, a female private was told to go to the home of Staff Sgt. Wayne Gamble to have sex with him (*New York Times*, 1997, May 14). According to sworn testimony, Gamble reportedly bragged of having sex with over 60 privates. Staff Sgt. Delmar Simpson, sentenced to 25 years in prison for his conviction on 18 counts of rape and 29 other offenses, was described by prosecutor Capt. Dave Thomas as a "sexual predator who was like an animal in the way he victimized the weaker soldiers under his command." After raping one woman for example, Simpson told her that "if you ever tell anyone about this, I'll slit your throat" (Ehrenreich, 1996). In defense of his client, Captain Ed Bradley argued:

> Simpson should be discharged from the Army, but not given a
> lengthy prison term, because he was never a threat to anyone except
> young soldiers. Sending Simpson to jail for the rest of his life will
> accomplish nothing. The first step toward rehabilitating a broken,
> humbled, defeated man is compassion. (McIntyre, 1997)

No mention was made by Bradley regarding rehabilitation of the broken victims whose lives were shattered by Simpson's abuse.

The controversy at Aberdeen overshadowed other cases of sexual harassment that year, including the retirement of Brig. Gen. Robert T. Newell, after his demotion to colonel for inappropriate conduct with a female subordinate (*New York Times*, 1996, December 27). 1996 also brought a class-action lawsuit by 23 women at Fort Bliss, Texas, alleging that they had been pressured to pose nude and/or perform sexual acts while working at the base (*New York Times*, 1996, August 29).

In the wake of the Aberdeen scandal, the Secretary of the Army set up a Senior Review Panel of high-ranking officers to investigate sexual harassment in the military. One of those appointed was the Army's then highest-ranking noncommissioned officer, Sgt. Maj. Gene McKinney. His tenure on the panel was short-lived, however, when he was accused of sexual harassment by retired Sgt. Maj. Brenda Hoster, who had once worked under him. Following her disclosure, five other women stepped forward, accusing McKinney of sexual harassment. McKinney was court-martialed and faced 19 charges ranging from indecent assault to adultery, including an accusation that he forced one woman to have sex with him while she was nearly 8 months pregnant. If convicted of all charges, McKinney faced up to $55^1/_2$; years in prison. In the end, he was found guilty of only one charge, obstruction of justice for encouraging a woman to lie to investigators. Why he would encourage someone to lie about an incident that didn't happen is left unexplained. Although demoted to master sergeant, he was allowed to retire and collect the significantly higher pension of a sergeant major (Bennet-Haigney, 1998; CNN, 1998, March 13).

The same week that McKinney was suspended pending the outcome of the investigation against him, three Army instructors in Darmstadt, Germany, were suspended for allegations of sexual misconduct made by 11 female soldiers. Charges included forcible sodomy and indecent assault (*USA Today*, 1997, February 13). Later in 1997, a two-star admiral was relieved of his duties pending investigation of sexual harassment charges; another admiral was dismissed from his post after allegations of inappropriate sexual conduct surfaced (Stout, 1997; *Washington Post*, 1997, August 6).

Deputy Inspector General for the Army, Maj. Gen. David Hale, was allowed to retire quietly while under investigation for sexual misconduct in 1998. Hale became the first retired general in the history of the U.S. Army to be court-martialed. He was ultimately convicted on seven counts of "conduct unbecoming an officer" for having inappropriate sexual relations with the wives of four subordinates, who claim Hale used his power over their husbands' careers to pressure them into sex (Plante, 1999a).

Late 1999 found a drill sergeant being demoted to private and sentenced to nearly 4 years in prison for sexual misconduct (Myers, 1999). Earlier that year, the army's top-ranking noncommissioned officer in Europe, Command Sgt. Maj. Riley Miller, was relieved of his duties pending the investigation of charges of sexual assault, sodomy, and kidnapping (Plante, 1999b; Stout, 1999).

This past year, the first woman ever to make three stars in the U.S. Army, Lt. Gen. Claudia Kennedy, had a less celebrated distinction. She became the highest-ranking officer ever to file a sexual harassment complaint against a former colleague. Kennedy made passing reference to having been sexually harassed in an interview in March, 1997:

> "When they investigated it, they found that the person who did a
> fairly benign thing to me had done very egregious things to two
> other women. . . . " (McIntyre, 2000).

At the time, Kennedy believed that her informal report of harassment was handled appropriately, and that some record had been added to the personnel file of her harasser, Maj. Gen. Larry Smith. She considered the matter closed and thought little of it, until hearing news that Smith was in line for a prestigious job in the Inspector General's Office, one that would include overseeing investigations of sexual harassment. Kennedy officially reported the incident only after Smith was being considered for the sensitive position in the Inspector General's Office. Kennedy has since retired, and it is expected that a "career-ending reprimand" for Smith is forthcoming (CNN, 2000, May 11). There is some hope that the publicity from a sexual harassment case involving officers at this level will prompt more serious action against sexually harassing behaviors by military personnel. This has yet to be determined.

We end the decade where we began—at the Tailhook convention. The Navy severed all ties with the Tailhook Association in October 1991. The conventions continued, but military personnel could attend only if they paid their own expenses and used their own leave time. In 1999, the Navy sent a contingency of officials to determine if it should restore ties with the Tailhook

Association. After the review was completed, Navy Secretary Richard Danzig decided the association had taken appropriate measures to ensure proper conduct at the conventions and hence renewed ties with the organization. This year marked the first convention where military aviators were officially allowed to attend the convention since 1991. An investigation is now underway to address allegations of what navy spokesperson Rear Adm. Steve Pietropaoli euphemistically referred to as "inappropriate physical contact" by conference attendess (CNN, 2000, August 25).

SEXUAL HARASSMENT: DEFINITION AND PREVALENCE

Reports of the prevalence of sexual harassment in the military are higher than those found in other employment settings (see Figure 1). In the largest study conducted to date in the United States, the Merit Systems Protection Board found that 42 percent of the more than 10,000 female federal employees surveyed reported some form of sexual harassment (USMSPB, 1981) and that harassment of women was more common in traditionally male occupations. Several recent studies have found similar results. In contrast, a survey of approximately 10,000 military women conducted by the DOD found that 64 percent of respondents reported some form of sexual harassment. The rate of harassment varied by military branch, with the lowest rate, 53 percent, found

---

The Equal Employment Opportunity Commission (EEOC) guidelines are the most frequently cited definition of sexual harassment. According to the EEOC:

Harassment on the basis of sex is a violation of Sec. 703 of Title VII of the Civil Rights Act. Unwelcome sexual advances, requests for sexual favors, and other verbal or physical conduct of a sexual nature constitute sexual harassment when:

1. Submission to such conduct is made either explicitly or implicitly a term or condition of an individual's employment,
2. Submission to or rejection of such conduct by an individual is used as the basis for employment decisions affecting such individual, or
3. Such conduct has the purpose or effect of unreasonably interfering with an individual's work performance or creating an intimidating, hostile, or offensive working environment.

The first two sections of this definition are referred to as "quid pro quo" harassment, and the third is referred to as "hostile working environment" harassment. The Department of Defense (DOD) uses this definition, with the replacement of "a person's job, pay, or career" for "employment" in the first section (Dorn, 1997).

FIGURE 1 EEOC Guidelines for Sexual Harassment

in the Air Force, and the highest rate, 72 percent, in the Marine Corps. Men in each branch of the service believed that military leaders were doing a better job of combating sexual harassment than did their female counterparts. Interestingly, there was a direct relationship between gender differences regarding perceptions of how effective military leaders were in trying to combat sexual harassment and the level of sexual harassment in that branch. Those branches with the least gender disparity in those perceptions had the lowest levels of sexual harassment; those branches where men and women showed the most disagreement about how well the leadership was handling harassment reported the highest levels of harassment (Niebuhr, 1997).

WHAT'S THE BIG DEAL?: MILITARY CULTURE AND CORRELATES OF SEXUAL HARASSMENT

Many sexual harassment theories focus on the role of organizational culture as it relates to sexual harassment in the institution. One such theory is the sex-role spillover theory. According to this theory, gender-based stereotypes and expectations dominate the workplace, especially in cases where there is a large gender skew (Gutek and Morasch, 1982). In predominately female occupations, such as teaching and nursing, the expectations of those roles are characterized by the traditionally feminine stereotypes of someone who is supportive, caring, gentle, helpful, and nurturing. In contrast, predominately male occupations, such as police work and military service, are associated with such traditionally masculine traits as assertiveness, strength, decisiveness, and competitiveness (Gutek and Dunwoody, 1987). In these male-dominated occupations, gender roles are more salient than work roles; thus, women are seen as women first and only secondarily as employees (Tangri and Hayes, 1997). When women's characteristics are perceived as incongruous with the needs of the job, they are subject to higher levels of harassment and discrimination (for example, the compassionate female soldier is looked down upon for being too soft). Conversely, women are also harassed and discriminated against when they engage in appropriate work role-related behaviors that are perceived as incongruous with stereotypical gender expectations (for example, the assertive female soldier is looked down upon for being unfeminine.)

Women who find themselves in this "damned if you do, damned if you don't" situation are often subject to sexualized work environments. The pages of one military woman's web site is replete with such stories, like this one from a female exMarine: "If I was forceful, I was a 'bitch.' If I was soft, I was not worthy of the uniform, and if I didn't put out, I was a 'bitch' and 'probably a lesbian'" (Anonymous, 1997). A former army recruiter describes a similar situation:

> It seems like every day in this job I run into some type of discrimina-
> tion or harassment. As a female recruiter, I have been asked to . . .
> flirt with [male recruits] to get them to enlist. I constantly hear
> remarks such as: I am a combat arms sergeant and do not know why

the Army needs women; I will never enlist a female; why did all of the females who deploy to Saudi have yeast infections; women's bodies look horrible in BDUs (it covers too much); women in the Army are sweaty; most women in the Army are either lesbian or easy, and all women really want is two men to have sex with them at the same time. I personally have been referred to as the bitch, or had statements said to me such as . . . she must be having PMS, and your ribbons must be uncomfortable the way they set upon your chest. When I try to make a complaint with my chain of command (naturally all males), I am coerced to agree that I have a problem or I am just taking these remarks out of context. . . . Bottom line: nothing works! (Anonymous, 1998)

The reaction of many of the 2,100 people interviewed regarding the Tailhook '91 incident provides a good example of the normative nature of sexual harassment in the military. Quoting directly from the official report:

A common thread running through the overwhelming majority of interviews concerning Tailhook 91 was—"what's the big deal?" Those interviewed had no understanding that the activities in the suites fostered an atmosphere of sexual harassment and that actions which occurred in the corridor constituted at minimum sexual assault and in many cases criminal sexual assault. That atmosphere condoned, if not encouraged, the gang mentality, which eventually led to the sexual assaults. (DOD, OIG, 1992)

In any organization, the attitudes of those in charge are directly related to the level of sexual harassment in the organization. When superiors take a proactive stance on education and prevention of sexual harassment, the level of harassment declines (Gruber, 1997). To say that top military personnel expressed dismissive attitudes toward both sexual harassment and women in the military is an understatement. More disturbing than the attitude of those interviewed during the Tailhook investigation was the attitude of top officials in charge of the investigation itself. The DOD report makes repeated references to improprieties by the Under Secretary of the Navy, the Naval Inspector General (IG), and the Commander of the Naval Investigative Service (NIS). These include an unwillingness to properly conduct the investigation, sexist attitudes, and victim-blaming statements.

The dismissive attitude of many top officers is reflected in this comment from the Naval IG, Rear Admiral George W. Davis, VI:

. . . Once we determined we had a cultural problem then it was our contention in that . . . the corporate "we" had allowed this to take place. And to interview squadron [commanding officers], to ask them why they allowed that to happen didn't make any difference because the whole system allowed it to happen. And frankly, I think a navy captain who had seen that over 4 or 5 years, had seen the

Rhino Room with a dildo hanging on the wall, is not going to walk in there in 1991 and change anything. (DOD, OIG, 1992)

The DOD report challenges the Admiral's comments by stating: While it is easy to be sympathetic to the attitude—that the Navy has allowed that kind of activity to go on for so many years the attendees that had become enculturated to it could not be expected to change it and therefore should not be held responsible for it—it must ultimately be rejected. For what the Naval IG failed to understand is that the time for attributing misconduct of that nature to a "cultural problem" had long since passed. . . . (DOD, OIG, 1992)

"Long since passed" would be a fitting way to describe the appropriateness of the attitudes expressed by Admiral Williams, the Commander NIS, as well. On several occasions, the commander expressed views that led others to question his suitability to lead the Tailhook investigation. He repeatedly tried to terminate the investigation prematurely, pressuring those individuals directly conducting the interviews to close their investigations. In one meeting, other high-ranking attendees were upset by the admiral's comment that the NIS "did not have a fart's chance in a whirlwind of solving the investigation" (DOD, OIG, 1992).

The admiral's attitudes toward women in the military, or women in general for that matter, were far from admirable. During the course of the investigation, not only did he state that men didn't want women in the military, but that he, himself, did not think women belonged in the military, stating that "a lot of female navy pilots are go-go dancers, topless dancers, or hookers" (DOD, OIG, 1992). A section of the report chronicling the commander's discussion of a sexual assault investigation is perhaps the most telling of all:

... the Commander met with a female NIS agent to review the statement of one of the assault victims. The Commander, NIS, commented on the victim's use of profanity in her statement. (According to the victim's statement, she described that she turned to two of her assailants as they were grabbing her and demanded of each of them "What the fuck do you think you're doing?" In her statement, the victim also stated that she told her commanding officer that she was "practically gang-banged by a group of fucking F-18 pilots"). The NIS agent related to us the Commander's reaction. . . . Then Adm. Williams—and I'll remember this quote forever. Then Adm. Williams made the quote to me "Any woman that would use the F word on a regular basis would welcome this type of activity. . . . " (DOD, OIG, 1992)

Have attitudes of top-ranking military personnel changed over this past decade? Most assuredly some have. Yet sexist attitudes and sexual harassment are still pervasive in every level of the military.

Discussion Questions

1. The Tailhook convention gave attendees informal networking opportunities outside the usual work realm.
   a. What informal networking opportunities exist in more traditional, non-military settings?
   b. How do these opportunities impact employment decisions, promotions, and corporate power?
   c. In what ways are these informal situations different from more formal networking within the confines of the office?
   d. Would some employees be less welcomed, less comfortable, or have less access to these informal networking opportunities?
   e. How would this impact their ability to do their job effectively?
2. How does the sex-role spillover theory apply to more traditional business settings? Cite examples from organizations familiar to you.
3. Discuss the effects of organizational and sociocultural power differentials in traditional work settings.
4. How might men and women perceive the severity of possible sexual harassment situations differently? Are there other group distinctions (race, class, sexual orientation, age) that might influence an individual's perceptions of sexual harassment?

References

Anonymous. (1997, February 7). "Why Women Leave the Military." Available: www.militarywoman.org/whyleave.htm

Anonymous. (1998, November 16). "Harassment Issues—File #3, 1998." Available: www.militarywoman.org/harass3.htm.

Bennet-Haigney, L. (1998). "Military Challenged to Punish Its Own in McKinney Trial." Available: www.now.org/nnt/05–98/mckinney.html

CNN. (2000, August 25). "Navy Investigating Alleged Misconduct at Latest Tailhook Convention." Available: www.cnn.com/2000/US/08/25/tailhook.allegations.02

CNN. (2000, May 11). "Sources: Army Substantiates General's Claim of Sexual Harassment." Available: www.cnn.com/2000/US/05/11/army.sex/index.html

CNN. (1998, March 13). "McKinney Not Guilty of 18 of 19 Counts in Sexual Misconduct Trial." Available: www.cnn.com/US/9803/13/mckinney.verdict/index.html

Department of Defense, Office of the Inspector General. (1992, September).

"Tailhook 91, Part 1—Review of the Navy Investigations." Available: www.inform.umd.edu/EdRes/Topic/WomensStudies/GovernmentPolitics/M . . . /4/tailhook-9.

DiTomaso, N. (1989). "Sexuality in the Workplace: Discrimination and Harassment." In J. Hearns, D. Sheppard, P. Tancred-Sheriff, and G. Burrell (eds.). *The Sexuality of Organizations.* Newbury Park, Calif.: Sage, pp. 71–90.

Dorn, E. (1997). "DOD Committed to Zero Tolerance of Sexual Harassment." *American Forces Information Service Defense Viewpoint, 12.* Available: www.defenselink.mil/speeches/1997/di1209.html.

Ehrenreich, B. (1996, December 2). "Wartime in the Barracks: Here's a Radical Solution to Ending the Harassment of Women in the Military." *Time, 148,* p. 25.

Gruber, J. (1997). "An Epidemiology of Sexual Harassment: Evidence from North America and Europe." In W. O'Donohue (ed.). *Sexual Harassment: Theory, Research, and Treatment.* Needham

Heights, Mass.: Allyn and Bacon, pp. 84–98.

Gutek, B., and V. Dunwoody. (1987). "Understanding Sex in the Workplace." In A. Stromberg, L. Larwood, and B. Gutek (eds.). *Women and Work: An Annual Review, Vol. 2*, Newbury Park, Calif.: Sage, pp.249–269.

Gutek, B., and B. Morasch. (1982). "Sex-Ratios, Sex-Role Spillover, and Sexual Harassment of Women at Work." *Journal of Social Issues, 38*, pp. 55–74.

Hill, M. (1980). "Authority at Work: How Men and Women Differ." In G. Duncan and J. Morgan (eds.). *Five Thousand American Families: Patterns of Economic Progress*. Ann Arbor, Mich.: Institute for Social Research, pp. 107–146.

Hotelling, K., and B. Zuber. (1997). "Feminist Issues in Sexual Harassment." In W. O'Donohue (ed.). *Sexual Harassment: Theory, Research, and Treatment*. Needham Heights, Mass.: Allyn and Bacon, pp. 99–111.

Kauppinen-Toropainen, K., and J. Gruber. (1993). "Sexual Harassment of Women in Nontraditional Jobs: Results from Five Countries." *Working Papers*. Ann Arbor, Mich.: Center for the Education of Women.

LaFountaine, E., and L. Tredeau. (1986). "The Frequency, Sources, and Correlates of Sexual Harassment Among Women in Traditional Male Occupations." *Sex Roles, 15*, pp. 433–442.

McIntyre, J. (1997, May 6). "Army Sergeant Sentenced to 25 Years for Rape." Available: www.cnn.com/US/9705/06/army.sex/index.html

McIntyre, J. (2000, March 31). "Pentagon Investigates Sexual Harassment Charge Filed by Top Female General." Available: www.cnn.com/2000/US/03/31/army.sex.charge.01

Myers, S. (1999, December, 3). "Prison Term for Drill Sergeant in Sex Case Involving Trainees." Available: www.nytimes.com

New York Times. (1997, May 14). "Allegations of Sexual Misconduct in the Military Persist." Available: www.feminist.org/911/sexharnews/_military.html

New York Times. (1996, December 27). "Air Force Demotes General." Available: www.nytimes.com

New York Times. (1996, August 29). "Women Complain of Harassment at Ft. Bliss." Available: www.nytimes.com

Niebuhr, R. (1997). "Sexual Harassment in the Military." In W. O'Donohue (ed.), *Sexual Harassment: Theory, Research, and Treatment*. Needham Heights, Mass.: Allyn and Bacon, pp. 250–262.

Plante, C. (1999a, July 14). "Retired General May Now Face Reduced Rank in Sex Case." Available: www.cnn.com/9907/14/army.general.sex/

Plante, C. (1999b, October 23). "Army's Top Enlisted Man in Europe Faces Kidnapping, Sodomy Charges." Available: www.cnn.com/US/9910/23/us.army.assault/index.html

Stewart, L., and W. Gundykunst. (1982). "Differential Factors Influencing the Hierarchical Level and Number of Promotions of Males and Females Within an Organization." *Academy of Management Journal, 25*, pp. 586–597.

Stout, D. (1997, May 31). "New Investigations of Harassment in the Military." Available: www.nytimes.com

Stout, D. (1999, October 23). "The Army's Top NCO in Europe Is Charged with Sexual Assault." Available: www.nytimes.com

Tangri, S., M. Burt, and L. Johnson. (1982). "Sexual Harassment at Work: Three Explanatory Models." *Journal of Social Issues, 38*, pp.33–54.

Tangri, S., and S. Hayes. (1997). "Theories of Sexual Harassment." In W. O'Donohue (ed.). *Sexual Harassment: Theory, Research, and Treatment*. Needham Heights, Mass.: Allyn and Bacon, pp. 112–128.

USA Today. (1997, February 13). "U.S. Military Sexual Harassment Charges Surface in Germany." Available: www.feminist.org/911/sexharnews/_military.html

Washington Post. (1997, August 6). "Admiral Relieved of Command After Harassment Complaints." Available: www.feminist.org/911/sexharnews/_military.html

Wolf, W., and N. Fligstein. (1979). "Sex and Authority in the Workplace. A Policy-Capturing Approach." *Academy of Management Journal, 32,* pp. 830–850.

THE CRACKER BARREL RESTAURANTS

John Howard
King's College London

Discrimination against lesbians and gays is common in the workplace. Sole proprietors, managing partners, and corporate personnel officers can and often do make hiring, promoting, and firing decisions based on an individual's real or perceived sexual orientation. Lesbian and gay job applicants are turned down and lesbian and gay employees are passed over for promotion or even fired by employers who view homosexuality as somehow detrimental to job performance or harmful to the company's public profile. Such discrimination frequently results from the personal biases of individual decision makers. It is rarely written into company policy and thus is difficult to trace. However, in January 1991, Cracker Barrel Old Country Store, Inc., a chain of family restaurants, became the first and only major American corporation in recent memory to expressly prohibit the employment of lesbians and gays in its operating units. A nationally publicized boycott followed, with demonstrations in dozens of cities and towns. The controversy would not be resolved until a decade later. In the interim, Cracker Barrel would also face several charges of racism from both its employees and customers—suggesting that corporate bias against one cultural group may prove a useful predictor of bias against others.

THE COMPANY: A BRIEF HISTORY OF CRACKER BARREL

Dan Evins founded Cracker Barrel in 1969 in his hometown of Lebanon, Tennessee, 40 miles east of Nashville. Evins, a 34-year-old ex-Marine sergeant and oil jobber, decided to take advantage of the traffic on the nearby interstate highway and open a gas station with a restaurant and gift shop. Specializing in down-home cooking at low prices, the restaurant was immediately profitable.

Evins began building Cracker Barrel stores throughout the region, gradually phasing out gasoline sales. By 1974, he owned a dozen restaurants. Within five years of going public in 1981, Cracker Barrel doubled its number of stores and quadrupled its revenues: In 1986, there were 47 Cracker Barrel restaurants with net sales of $81 million. Continuing to expand aggressively, the chain again grew to twice its size and nearly quadrupled its revenues during the next 5 years.

By the end of the fiscal year, August 2, 1991, Cracker Barrel operated over 100 stores, almost all located along the interstate highways of the Southeast and, increasingly, the Midwest. Revenues exceeded $300 million. Employing roughly 10,000 nonunionized workers, Cracker Barrel ranked well behind such mammoth family chains as Denny's and Big Boy in total sales, but led all U.S. family chains in sales per operating unit for both 1990 and 1991.

As of 1991, Cracker Barrel was a well-recognized corporate success story, known for its effective, centralized, but authoritarian leadership. From its headquarters, Cracker Barrel maintained uniformity in its store designs, menu offerings, and operating procedures. Travelers and local customers dining at any Cracker Barrel restaurant knew to expect a spacious, homey atmosphere; an inexpensive, country-style meal; and a friendly, efficient staff. All were guaranteed by Dan Evins, who remained as president, chief executive officer, and chairman of the board.

THE POLICY: NO LESBIAN OR GAY EMPLOYEES

In early January 1991, managers in the roughly 100 Cracker Barrel operating units received a communiqué from the home office in Lebanon. The personnel policy memorandum from William Bridges, vice president of human resources, declared that Cracker Barrel was "founded upon a concept of traditional American values." As such, it was deemed "inconsistent with our concept and values and . . . with those of our customer base, to continue to employ individuals . . . whose sexual preferences fail to demonstrate normal heterosexual values which have been the foundation of families in our society."

Throughout the chain, individual store managers, acting on orders of corporate officials, began conducting brief, one-on-one interviews with their employees to see if any were in violation of the new policy. Cheryl Summerville, a cook in the Douglasville, Georgia, store for 3 1/2 years, asked if she were a lesbian, knew she had to answer truthfully. She felt she owed that to her partner of 10 years. Despite a history of consistently high performance evaluations, Summerville was fired on the spot, without warning and without severance pay. Her official separation notice, filled out by the manager and filed with the state department of labor, clearly indicated the reason for her dismissal: "This employee is being terminated due to violation of company policy. The employee is gay."

Cracker Barrel fired as many as 16 other employees across several states in the following months. These workers, mostly waiters, were left without any legal recourse. Lesbian and gay antidiscrimination statutes were in effect in Massachusetts and Wisconsin and in roughly 80 U.S. cities and counties, but none of the firings occurred in those jurisdictions. Federal civil rights laws, the employees learned, did not cover discrimination based on sexual orientation.

Under pressure from a variety of groups, the company issued a statement in late February 1991. In it, Cracker Barrel management said, "We have re-visited our thinking on the subject and feel it only makes good business sense to continue to employ those folks who will provide the quality service our customers have come to expect." The recent personnel policy had been a "well-intentioned over-reaction." Cracker Barrel pledged to deal with any future disruptions in its units "on a store-by-store basis." Activists charged that the statement did not represent a retraction of the policy, as some company officials claimed. None of the fired employees had been rehired, activists noted, and none had been offered severance pay. Moreover, on February 27, just days after the statement, Dan Evins reiterated the company's antagonism toward nonheterosexual employees in a rare interview with a Nashville newspaper. Lesbians and gays, he said, would not be employed in more rural Cracker Barrel locations if their presence was viewed to cause problems in those communities.

THE BOYCOTT: QUEER NATIONALS VERSUS GOOD OL' BOYS

The next day, when news of Cracker Barrel employment policies appeared in *The Wall Street Journal, New York Times,* and *Los Angeles Times,* investment analysts expressed surprise. "I look on [Cracker Barrel executives] as pretty prudent business people," said one market watcher. "These guys are not fire-breathing good ol' boys." Unconvinced, lesbian and gay activists called for a nationwide boycott of Cracker Barrel restaurants and began a series of demonstrations that attracted extensive media coverage.

The protest movement was coordinated by the Atlanta chapter of Queer Nation, which Cheryl Summerville joined as co-chair with Lynn Cothren, an official with the Martin Luther King, Jr. Center for Non-Violent Social Change. Committed to nonviolent civil disobedience, lesbian and gay activists and supporters staged pickets and sit-ins at various Cracker Barrel locations, often occupying an entire restaurant during peak lunch hours, ordering only coffee.

Protesters were further angered and spurred on by news in June from Mobile, Alabama. A 16-year-old Cracker Barrel employee had been fired for effeminate mannerisms and subsequently was thrown out of his home by his father. Demonstrations continued throughout the summer of 1991, spreading from the Southeast to the Midwest stores. Arrests were made at demonstrations in the Detroit area; Cothren and Summerville were among several people arrested for criminal trespass at both the Lithonia and Union City, Georgia, stores. Reporters and politicians dubbed Summerville the "Rosa Parks of the movement," after the civil rights figure whose arrest sparked the Montgomery, Alabama Bus Boycott of 1955–1956.

Support for the Cracker Barrel boycott grew, as organizers further charged the company with racism and sexism. Restaurant gift shops, they pointed out, sold Confederate flags, black mammy dolls, and other offensive items. The Cracker Barrel board of directors, they said, was indeed a good ol' boy network, made up exclusively of middle-aged and older white men. In addition, there was only one female in the ranks of upper management. Among the numerous groups that joined in support of the protests were the National Organization for Women (NOW); Jobs with Justice, a coalition of labor unions; the National Rainbow Coalition, founded by Reverend Jesse Jackson; and the American Association of Public Health Workers. By early 1992, Summerville and Cothren had appeared on the television talk shows "Larry King Live" and "The Oprah Winfrey Show." The two were also featured in a segment on ABC's "20/20," after which Barbara Walters declared that she would refuse to eat at Cracker Barrel restaurants

THE RESOLUTION: NEW YORK ATTEMPTS TO FORCE CHANGE

Meanwhile, New York City comptroller, Elizabeth Holtzman, and finance commissioner, Carol O'Cleiracain, at the urging of the National Gay and Lesbian Task Force, wrote a letter to Dan Evins, dated March 12, 1991. As trustees of various city pension funds, which owned about $3 million in Cracker Barrel stock, they were "concerned about the potential negative impact on the company's sales and earnings which could result from adverse public reaction." They asked for a "clear statement" of the company's policy regarding employment and sexual orientation, as well as a description of "what remedial steps, if any, [had] been taken by the company respecting the employees dismissed."

Evins replied in a letter of March 19 that the policy had been rescinded and that there had been "no negative impact on the company's sales." Unsatisfied, the City of New York officials wrote back, again inquiring as to the status of the fired workers. They also asked that the company put forth a policy that "would provide unequivocally" that discrimination based on sexual orientation was prohibited. Evins never responded.

Shortly thereafter, Queer Nation launched a "buy one" campaign. Hoping to gain additional leverage in company decision making, activists became stockholders by purchasing single shares of Cracker Barrel common stock. At the least, they reasoned, the company would suffer from the relative expense of mailing and processing numerous one-cent quarterly dividend checks. More importantly, they could attend the annual stockholders meeting in Lebanon, Tennessee.

In November 1991, company officials successfully prevented the new shareholders from participating in the annual meeting, and they used a court injunction to block protests at the corporate complex. Nonetheless, demonstrators lined the street, while inside, a representative of the New York City comptroller's office announced the submission of a resolution "banning employment discrimination against gay and lesbian men and women," to be voted on at the next year's meeting. The resolution was endorsed by the Philadelphia Municipal Retirement System, another major stockholder. Cracker Barrel refused any further public comment on the issue.

THE EFFECT: NO DECLINE IN CORPORATE GROWTH

The impact of the boycott on the corporate bottom line was negligible. Trade magazines reiterated the company's claim that neither sales nor stock price had been negatively affected. Indeed, net sales remained strong, up 33% at fiscal year-end 1992 to $400 million, owing in good part to continued expansion: There were now 127 restaurants in the chain. Though the increase in same-store sales was not as great as the previous year, Cracker Barrel at least could boast growth, whereas other chains blamed flat sales on the recession. Cracker Barrel stock, trading on the NASDAQ exchange, appreciated 18% during the first month after news of the scandal broke, and the stock remained strong throughout the next fiscal year, splitting three-for-two in the third quarter.

Dan Evins had good reason to believe that the firings and the boycott had not adversely impacted profitability. One market analyst said that "the feedback they get from their customers might be in favor of not hiring homosexuals." Another even ventured that "it's plausible . . . the majority of Cracker Barrel's local users support an explicit discriminatory policy." Such speculation was bolstered by social science surveys indicating that respondents from the South and from rural areas in particular tended to be less tolerant of homosexuality than were other Americans.

Queer Nationals looked to other measures of success, claiming at least partial victory in the battle. Many customers they met at picket lines and inside restaurants vowed to eat elsewhere. Coalitions were formed with a variety of civil rights, women's, labor, and peace and justice organizations. Most importantly, the media attention greatly heightened national awareness of the lack of protections for lesbians and gays on the job. As the boycott continued, increasing numbers of states, counties, and municipalities passed legislation designed to prevent employment discrimination based on sexual orientation.

THE STANDOFF: OLD ANTAGONISMS, NEW ALLEGATIONS

As the November 1992 annual meeting approached, Cracker Barrel requested that the Securities and Exchange Commission make a ruling on the resolution offered by the New York pension fund administrators. The resolution, according to Cracker Barrel, amounted to shareholder intrusion into the company's ordinary business operations. As such, it should be excluded from consideration at the annual meeting and excluded from proxy ballots sent out before the meeting. The SEC agreed, despite previous rulings in which it had allowed stockholder resolutions regarding race- or gender-based employment bias.

Acknowledging that frivolous stockholder inquiries had to be curtailed, the dissenting SEC commissioner nonetheless expressed great dismay: "To claim that the shareholders, as owners of the corporation, do not have a legitimate interest in management-sanctioned discrimination against employees defies logic." A noted legal scholar warned of the dangerous precedent that had been set: "Ruling an entire area of corporate activity (here, employee relations) off limits to moral debate effectively disenfranchises shareholders."

Thus, the standoff continued. Queer Nation and its supporters persisted in the boycott. The Cracker Barrel board of directors and, with one exception, upper management remained all-white, all-male bastions. Lynn Cothren, Cheryl Summerville, and the other protesters arrested in Lithonia, Georgia, were acquitted on charges of criminal trespass. Jurors ruled that the protesters' legitimate reasons for peaceably demonstrating superseded the company's rights to deny access or refuse service. Charges stemming from the Union City, Georgia, demonstrations were subsequently dropped. Meanwhile, within weeks of the original policy against lesbian and gay employees, Cracker Barrel vice president for human resources, William Bridges, had left the company. Cracker Barrel declined comment on the reasons for his departure.

Lesbian and gay activists' charge of racism at Cracker Barrel seemed to be borne out over time. In the year 2000, a local human rights commission awarded $5,000 in damages to a black employee in Kentucky after she suffered racial and religious bias in the scheduling of shifts. Months later, the NAACP joined a group of employees and former employees in a class-action lawsuit against Cracker Barrel, alleging that the company repeatedly discriminated against African Americans in hiring, promotions, and firing practices. African-American workers further were said to have received less pay, to have been given inferior terms and conditions of employment, and to have been subjected to racial epithets and racist jokes, including one told by Dan Evins. In a second suit filed by the NAACP, along with 42 customers, and supported by over 400 witnesses, Cracker Barrel was accused of repeatedly offering better, faster, segregated seating to whites and inferior service to blacks. A similar case was filed by 23 African Americans in Little Rock a year later.

THE OUTCOME: POLICY REVERSALS

As of 2002, Cracker Barrel annual net sales surpassed two billion dollars. The company still had not issued a complete retraction of its employment policy with regard to sexual orientation, and those employees fired back in 1991 had never been offered their old jobs back. In contrast, for a year's work, Chairman Dan Evins regularly pulled in over a million dollars in salary, bonus, awards, and stock options.

A total of 14 states and the District of Columbia offered protections for lesbians and gays on the job, both in the public and private sectors. With over 400 restaurants in 41 states, Cracker Barrel now operated in 11 of those jurisdictions with protections: California, Connecticut, Maryland, Massachusetts, Minnesota, New Hampshire, New Jersey, New Mexico, New York, Rhode Island, and Wisconsin. (The other states with antidiscrimination statutes were Hawaii, Nevada, and Vermont.) Expansion had taken the company into areas even less receptive to employment discrimination. As one business editor had correctly predicted, "Cracker Barrel [wa]sn't going to be in the South and Midwest forever. Eventually they w[ould] have to face the issue—like it or not."

In 1998, the SEC reversed itself, allowing the New York City Employees' Retirement System to again offer a shareholder resolution, which was defeated yet again and again. By 2002, however, the tide was turning. In its proxy statement sent out in advance of the annual meeting, the Cracker Barrel board of directors still recommended that stockholders vote against the proposal. "[A]ny attempt to name all possible examples of prohibited discrimination other than those . . . specifically prohibited by federal law," it said, "would result in a long list" that was neither "appropriate" nor "necessary."

But shareholders were ready to defy the board. After 58 percent voted in support of the proposal in an informal vote, the board members unanimously agreed to add the category of sexual orientation to its equal employment opportunities policy.

THE PROPOSAL: FEDERAL LEGISLATION

In 36 states it is perfectly legal to fire workers because they are gay—or straight. For example, a Florida bar owner decided to newly target a lesbian and gay clientele and so fired the entire heterosexual staff. Queer activists boycotted, and the bar eventually was forced out of business. Still, in most American jurisdictions, employment discrimination based on sexual orientation remains a constant threat.

The vast majority of Americans, 80%, tell pollsters that lesbians and gays should have equal rights in terms of job opportunities. In every region including the South, among both Democrats and Republicans, solid majorities support federal legislation to remedy the situation. Nonetheless, despite several close votes in Congress, the Employment Non-Discrimination Act, or ENDA, has yet to be passed into law.

Although there are no federal laws to prevent discrimination based on sexual orientation, protections do exist for workers on the basis of religion, gender, national origin, age, disability, and race. Still, as the NAACP and other lawsuits against Cracker Barrel demonstrate, federal legislation does not ensure corporate compliance. Aggrieved parties and their supporters often must invest years of their lives in protest and litigation simply to achieve the equal treatment ostensibly guaranteed in the American marketplace. Even after the terms *race* and *sexual orientation* have been added to policy statements, broader cultural transformations will be required before these added burdens are removed from the shoulders of workers already greatly disadvantaged in our society.

Discussion Questions

1. Why is it difficult to trace workplace discrimination based on race and sexual orientation?
2. Do franchise operations, which prize uniformity—and thus reliability—in store design, products, and operating procedures, require uniformity of personnel policies? Were the regional variations that Dan Evins proposed on February 27, 1991, a viable corporate strategy? Why or why not?

3. How does the Cracker Barrel case support or challenge the notion that federal legislation is warranted to stop employment discrimination based on sexual orientation?

4. Why are particular retail products—inanimate objects such as mammy dolls—perceived to be racist?

5. Which areas of corporate activity should be open to broader scrutiny through shareholder resolutions? How much stake in the company should a shareholder have in order to present a resolution?

6. If a controversial corporate policy is reversed only after a decade of defiance, how should the company's public relations officers present the change to the media?

Bibliography

Atlanta Journal-Constitution, 6, 11 July 1993; 2, 3 April 1992; 29 March 1992; 4, 18, 20 January 1992; 9 June 1991; 3, 4, 5 March 1991.

Carlino, B. (1991, December 16). Cracker Barrel profits surge despite recession. *Nation's Restaurant News*, 14.

——. (1991, April 1). Cracker Barrel stocks, sales weather gay-rights dispute. *Nation's Restaurant News*, 14.

CBRL Group, Inc. Annual Reports, 2002, 2001.

——. Notice of Annual Meeting of Shareholders to be held on Tuesday, November 26, 2002. 30 October 2002.

Cracker Barrel Old Country Store, Inc. Annual Reports, 1999, 1996, 1992, 1991, 1990.

——. Notice of Annual Meeting of Shareholders to be held on Tuesday, November 26, 1996. 25 October 1996.

——. Third Quarter Report, 30 April 1993.

——. Second Quarter Report, 29 January 1993.

——. First Quarter Report, 30 October 1992.

——. Securities and Exchange Commission Form 10-K, 1992.

——. Securities and Exchange Commission Form 10-K, 1991.

Cheney, K. (1992, July 22). Old-fashioned ideas fuel Cracker Barrel's out-of-sight sales growth and profit increases. *Restaurants & Institutions*, 108.

Chicago Tribune, 5 April 1991.

Cracker Barrel Hit by Anti-Bias Protests. (1992, April 13). *Nation's Restaurant News*, 2.

Cracker Barrel sued for rampant racial discrimination in employment. (1999, October 5). NAACP press release.

Cracker Barrel's emphasis on quality a hit with travelers. (1991, April 3). *Restaurants & Institutions*, 24.

Dahir, M. S. (1992, June). Coming out at the Barrel. *The Progressive*, 14.

Documented cases of job discrimination based on sexual orientation. (1995). Washington, DC: Human Rights Campaign.

Farkas, D. Kings of the road. (1991, August). *Restaurant Hospitality*, 118–22.

Galst, L. (1992, May 19). Southern activists rise up. *The Advocate*, 54–57.

Greenberg, D. (1988). *The construction of homosexuality*. Chicago: University of Chicago Press.

Gutner, T. (1993, April 27). Nostalgia sells. *Forbes*, 102–3.

Harding, R. (1991, July 16). Nashville NAACP head stung by backlash from boycott support. *The Advocate*, 27.

——. (1991, April 9). Activists still press Tennessee eatery firm on anti-gay job bias. *The Advocate*, 17.

Hayes, J. (1991, August 26). Cracker Barrel protesters don't shake loyal patrons. *Nation's Restaurant News*, 3, 57.

——. (1991, March 4). Cracker Barrel comes under fire for ousting gays. *Nation's Restaurant News*, 1, 79.

Investors protest Cracker Barrel proxy plan. (1992, November). *Nation's Restaurant News*, 2, 14.

Larry King Live. CNN television, aired 2 December 1991.

Lexington-Fayette Urban County Human Rights Commission. (2000, August 2). Press Release: Lexington woman awarded $5,000 in discrimination case against Cracker Barrel. Retrieved from http://www.lfuchrc.org/News/2000/Press%20Release%20080200.htm

Los Angeles Times, 28 February 1991.

New York Times, 25 June 1999; 11 November 1992; 22 October 1992; 9 April 1992; 20 March 1991; 28 February 1991.

Oprah Winfrey Show. Syndicated television, aired January 1992.

Queer Nation. (n.d.) Documents on the Cracker Barrel Boycott. N.p.

San Diego Union-Tribune, 30 July 2003.

SEC upholds proxy ruling. (1993, February 8), *Pensions & Investments*, 28.

Star, M. G. (1992, October 26). SEC policy reversal riles activist groups. *Pensions & Investments*, 33.

The (Nashville) *Tennessean*, 27 February 1991.

20/20. ABC television, aired 29 November 1991.

Walkup, C. (1991, August 5). Family chains beat recession blues with value, service. *Nation's Restaurant News*, 100, 104.

Wall Street Journal, 9 March 1993; 2 February 1993; 26 January 1993; 28 February 1991.

Washington Lawyers' Committee for Civil Rights and Urban Affairs. (2003, July 30). Press Release: 23 African American patrons file lawsuit against Cracker Barrel Restaurants for civil rights violations. Retrieved from http://www.washlaw.org/news/releases/073003.htm

Wildmoon, K. C. (1992, December 10). QN members allowed to attend Cracker Barrel stockholder's meeting. *Southern Voice*, 3.

——. (1992, October 22). Securities and Exchange Commission side with Cracker Barrel on employment discrimination. *Southern Voice*, 1.

——. (1992, July 9). DeKalb drops most charges against Queer Nation. *Southern Voice*, 3.

EVALUATING ORGANIZATIONAL COMMITMENT TO DIVERSITY: AUDITING ORGANIZATIONAL WEBSITES

Carol P. Harvey

Assumption College

In the 21st century, Websites are an important channel of communication between organizations and their internal and external stakeholders. Although content varies by Website, employees, customers, job applicants, and suppliers can usually access information about an organization's mission, values, products, press releases, management staff, and sense of social responsibility through the use of technology.

Goals

- To learn how to evaluate an organization's Website in terms of its commitment to diversity
- To improve critical thinking skills by learning how to apply specific criteria (i.e., standards against which something is judged) and to measure the Website against those standards

INSTRUCTIONS

1. Form groups of 4–6 students.
2. Your instructor will assign each group one Website.
3. As a group, your task is to explore the Website and to evaluate it against the following criteria. Because Websites are so varied, the group may add additional criteria.

4. Once you have finished working with the Website and discussed it as a group, assign the company a letter grade ranging from A to F. Your grade should reflect a rating of how well the organization communicates a serious commitment to diversity.
5. Prepare a rationale for the letter grade selected by the group.
6. Objectively, present your findings (and if a computer is available in the classroom, demonstrate the strengths and weaknesses of the Website) to the class without revealing the grade that the group assigned to the organization.
7. Ask the class members for a show of hands for an "A," a "B," a "C," a "D," or an "F" grade.
8. Tell the class what grade your group assigned to the Website and explain your rationale according to the criteria listed and any additional ones that the group may have developed.

CRITERIA FOR EVALUATING WEBSITES IN TERMS OF DIVERSITY

1. **Evaluate how well the site communicates that diversity is important to this organization.** Is there a button that links to diversity on the home page? Is diversity mentioned in the organization's mission and/or value statements? How easy or difficult was it to access material related to diversity on this site?
2. **Evaluate the site in terms of its diverse visual images.** Are there pictures of diverse individuals throughout the site or are these only found in sections pertaining to diversity? If there are photographs of senior management and/or the board, do these indicate any dimensions of diversity?
3. **If the site has a "search" feature, evaluate the usefulness and currency of the diversity information that you obtain when this function is utilized. (Note: Whether or not there is a search feature, the group should thoroughly explore the site manually. There may be material about diversity that is not directly linked to diversity as a keyword.)** Material pertaining to diversity may be found on Websites under various headings such as: press releases, careers, job opportunities, community relations, EEO/AA, suppliers, awards, corporate reports, and others. You will need to explore the Website in depth.

Discussion Questions

1. Assume that you are a minority job applicant. You have an interview appointment set up with each of the companies whose Websites were presented in class. To prepare for the interview, you visited each of the Websites. What perceptions might you have of each company before you even walk in the door?
2. What internal issues can impact the importance or lack of importance that an organization gives to diversity on its Website?

EVALUTING DIVERSITY IN THE REAL WORLD: CONDUCTING A DIVERSITY AUDIT

Carol P. Harvey

Assumption College

Diversity audits are evaluations of an organization's diversity efforts based on qualitative and quantitative information about the status of diversity within the organization. Today, many organizations conduct these audits for various reasons such as determining the effectiveness of diversity recruiting and retention efforts, measuring the value of diversity training, surveying workers about the success of diversity initiatives, such as supplier programs and diversity councils. These audits reveal whether a gap exists between what is being done and what the organization should do in terms of diversity and are used as a basis for action planning.

Although this assignment is not as involved as a corporate internal diversity audit, it is designed to provide students with an opportunity to visit an organization and to gather enough information to evaluate its progress in terms of its diversity initiatives.

Goals

- To provide a capstone learning experience so that students are able to see how theory and cases studied during the semester apply in the real world
- To improve critical thinking skills by developing and applying criteria to the evaluation of an organization's diversity initiatives
- To give students an opportunity to conduct secondary and primary research
- To provide an opportunity to compare and assess the relative levels of commitment that organizations make in terms of implementing and managing diversity programs.
- To showcase the unique ways that some organizations are working to manage diversity and to illustrate that other organizations are limiting

their diversity initiatives to legal compliance rather than to making systemic changes

- To learn how to function productively in a team project environment

Dividing up the work equitably and preparing the criteria and questions for the interview are part of the assignment. Do not expect your instructor to do this for the group. It is important that the group follow these steps in order.

INSTRUCTIONS

After your instructor forms groups of 4 to 5 students

1. **Find an organization that is willing to work with your group** The group should meet early in the semester to brainstorm possible organizations that might be willing to participate in this project. As always, it may be easier to gain access if a group member already has an established relationship with an organization such as an internship placement, job, or family member who works there. Groups should always have two or three alternative organizations in mind just in case the first choice does not work out. Very early in the semester make contact with someone in the organization. Explain the assignment for what it is: an opportunity for students to learn firsthand how a real organization deals with diversity issues on a daily basis.

    The group needs to be realistic about a field assignment. Sometimes very small companies of less than 400 employees pose difficulties because of their limited financial and human resources. In contrast, in large *Fortune* 500 companies it may be difficult to find the right contacts. Some organizations may refuse to cooperate because they are afraid of what the team may learn. Even organizations that are willing to cooperate may find it difficult to schedule meeting times that work for students. So, it is imperative that the team line up both a first choice and at least one backup choice for this project and begin the process early in the semester in case the group encounters difficulties.

2. **Conduct secondary research** Secondary research resources are materials gathered for another reason. *Internal* examples include annual reports, press releases, employee handbooks, and any other materials that the organization can provide. Explain to your contact person that the group would like to be as knowledgeable as possible about the organization to maximize the time on the visit. So, any material that can be sent and read by the group *before* the visit will help the group to prepare. Remember that researching an organization's Website is a good way to begin and can offer useful information, but it is only the public face that the organization chooses to present.

    Students should also conduct thorough *external* secondary research on their organization for additional material. Utilizing various library databases, students may discover very useful information. For example, small local companies are often the subjects of newspaper articles that can be found in newspaper databases. Larger companies may have been involved in discrimination lawsuits that are detailed in legal databases, and students are not apt to be told about these on visits.

3. **Preparing to visit the organization** Make an appointment to interview *at least* two company representatives, managers or employees. If you can interview people from different functions and areas and levels (human resources, training, managers, and hourly employees), it will provide different perspectives and richer data. Although all team members do not need to go on the interview, at least two or three should participate to minimize bias. Because many organizations are reluctant to let students tape-record interviews, it is more realistic to be prepared to take notes. Of course, multiple visits would probably provide richer data, and some organizations will give students the time for this, but many will not.

   When making an appointment, it can be helpful to arrange for a tour of the organization. Student groups may discover interesting observations that contrast with the information that they will be given. For example, one student group visiting a medium-sized manufacturing plant, observed that the entire manufacturing workforce was composed of Asian women. They later learned that one of the top managers believed that Asian women had small hands that made assembling electrical components easier. So, he instructed his supervisors to hire only Asian women in the assembly area. Job applications from all others were immediately discarded.

   Before visiting the organization, the whole group should meet to work on three items: establishing criteria (i.e., standards) for a diverse organization, which your instructor will help you develop; preparing a list of thoughtful questions about diversity that the group will explore on the visit(s); and reviewing the semester's readings for ideas about how the theory may apply to this organization. If the team has gathered, read, and thoroughly discussed the secondary data, it will help the group to accomplish these tasks more effectively and efficiently.

4. **Visiting the organization/conducting primary research** Dress professionally, be on time, be polite, and be respectful of your contact's time constraints. If the group is thoroughly prepared and is knowledgeable about the organization, it will show. Occasionally, student teams are asked that the name of the company be kept confidential. If this issue comes up, it is important that you be honest. The teacher will have to know the true identity of the organization to assess the team's work. However, a fictitious name can be used for the paper and class presentation.

   Try to gather additional information through observation. Be sure to pay attention to "subtle" cues (i.e., Is there evidence that they really do what they say they do?). Sometimes teams discover interesting things on their visits about the racial, ethnic, gender, and age makeup of the various levels and divisions of the workforce. This is very helpful because some organizations may be reluctant to provide concrete numbers on the demographics of their workers. For example, is there signage in Braille or Spanish? Once a team was interviewing a manager who proudly pointed out that his nationwide retail chain made it a point to provide jobs to physically challenged workers. However, the team found that these workers were assigned to work *only* in the stockroom, unseen by the customers.

Sometimes student groups can obtain interesting material on the site visit(s) that will be helpful in writing their papers or as visual aids in class presentations. Teams have returned with both useful and sometimes comical examples of how an organization promotes diversity, such as written materials (copies of company newsletters, employee handbooks, and value statements) and artifacts (posters, coffee mugs, and even a beaded diversity key chain). It is part of the learning experience for the group to determine the value of these materials to managing diversity within their organization.

5. **Postvisit activity** Once the visit is completed, the real work begins. This is the most important part of the process and may require several team meetings. Groups that do well on this assignment, take ample time at this stage. The entire group should meet and debrief. In terms of diversity: What did they really see? What did they learn? How did the visit support or refute what they had learned through their secondary research? What seems contradictory? How can the theory learned during the semester, help to explain what they know about the organization?

After thoroughly discussing the data, the group should evaluate their organization *against their previously established criteria for a diverse organization.* At this point, the group may find that they omitted some factors and may want to add additional criteria.

6. **Written Report (NOTE: Your instructor may assign different length and content requirements)** Each team also will prepare a 10- to 12-page paper, which explains their findings in detail. The paper should be free from spelling and grammatical errors, cite all sources and interviews in a bibliography, and contain any additional helpful material in an exhibit section (copies of organizational value statements, relevant newspaper articles or press releases, company newsletters, etc.).

The report should detail the strengths and weaknesses of the organization's diversity initiatives. The paper should be organized with a one-paragraph executive summary; one page or less of company background (history, size, industry, organization, etc.); one to two pages explaining the group's criteria for a diverse organization; and one to two pages describing the visit(s). The remainder of the paper should focus on evaluating the organization's efforts in terms of diversity and conclude with the team's recommendations for improvement. The audit should conclude with the team assigning a letter grade (A, A-, B+, B, B-, etc.) and a rationale for the organization's diversity efforts.

7. **Presentation** The variety of student projects and the lessons about diversity management should be shared with the rest of the class. It is particularly interesting to see the different approaches and contrasts of the organizations. Each team of students should make a class presentation that details the results of their diversity audit. As a minimum, the presentation should include a short company background, a list of the group's criteria for a diverse organization, anything particularly interesting learned from the visit(s), and an explanation of the group's evaluation of their organization in terms of how it attempts to manage diversity.

It is expected that the group will use visual material (transparencies, PowerPoint slides, handouts, material supplied by the organization, etc.), rehearse their presentations so that individual speakers do not repeat each other's material, not exceed the time limits set by the instructor, and be prepared to answer questions from the class.

At the conclusion of the talk, the group, *without revealing the grade that they assigned to the organization*, should ask for a show of hands from the class members as to what letter grade from A–F should be assigned to this organization. Then, they can reveal what grade the group gave the company for their diversity efforts and the rationale behind the decision.

Contributors

Jeanne M. Aurelio, D.B.A., is a professor of management at Bridgewater State College in Bridgewater, Massachusetts. She has consulted with numerous corporations. Her areas of specialization include organizational culture and leadership.

Carlo M. Baldino taught inner-city high school. In 2001 he won two first-place journalism awards from the New England Press Association.

Michelle L. Chunis, B.S., L.C.S.W., graduated from Boston College School of Social Work. She is a clinician on the Victim's Services Team at Worcester Youth Guidance Center, working with children and adults who have experienced trauma.

Lori Dawson, Ph. D. is Associate Professor of Psychology and Co-Associate Director of Women's Studies at Worcester State College. Her research and volunteer work focuses on physical and sexual abuse, sexuality, and harassment.

Egidio A. Diodati is Associate Professor of management at Assumption College in Worcester, Massachusetts. Professor Diodati provides consulting services to corporations in the areas of network communications, market research, marketing, and management.

Steve Farough, Ph.D., is Assistant Professor of Sociology at Assumption College in Worcester, Massachusetts, where he teaches social theory, research methodology, and courses on race and gender. His current research is on white masculinities.

Paul Gorski is Assistant Professor in the Graduate School of Education at Hamline University. He created and continues to maintain the *Multicultural Pavilion* and the *McGraw-Hill Multicultural Supersite*, two Websites focused on multicultural education.

Diane Holtzman teaches Business Studies at The Richard Stockton College of New Jersey and public relations at Rowan University. Currently she is completing her doctorate in organizational leadership at Nova Southeastern University.

John Howard teaches in the Department of American Studies at King's College, University of London. He is the author of *Men Like That: A Southern Queer History* (University of Chicago Press, 1999) and the editor of three other volumes.

Gerald Hunt is Associate Professor of HR Management at Ryerson University in Toronto. He has published several articles and a book about sexuality issues in the workplace.

Donald Klein is a community and organizational psychologist at the Graduate School of The Unions Institute and a member of NTL Institute for Applied Behavioral Science. He has published books and articles on organizational diagnosis and transformative change.

Evonne Jonas Kruger, Ph.D., is Associate Professor of Business Studies at The Richard Stockton College of New Jersey. A graduate of Temple University, her areas of expertise are strategic management, managerial decision making, and community engagement.

Jeanne M. McNett, Ph.D., is Associate Professor at Assumption College in Worcester, Massachusetts. She served on the team that established the first public university for women in Saudi Arabia. She has worked with companies such as Mitsubishi, Nippon Express, and Sony.

Marc S. Mentzer, Ph.D., is Associate Professor of Industrial Relations & OB at the University of Saskatchewan and has published in *Canadian Journal of Administrative Sciences, Canadian Review of Sociology & Anthropology*, and *Organization Studies.*

Helen Juliette Muller, Ph.D., is Professor of Management at the Anderson Schools of Management, University of New Mexico. Her research focuses on organizational behavior, leadership, and gender in cross-cultural settings.

Michael A. Novak, Ph.D., is Professor of OB and Chair of the Management and Marketing department at the University of Massachusetts—Boston. His areas of specialization include leadership and creativity in organizations.

Carole G. Parker, Ph.D., is Associate Professor of management at Seton Hill University. She has served on the staff of the Gestalt Institute of Cleveland and is a member of NTL Institute for Applied Behavioral Science.

Asha Rao is Assistant Professor of Management at Rutgers University. Her research focuses on issues of cross-cultural conflict and its resolution in joint venture negotiations, multinational management, and domestic diversity situations.

Dale G. Ross, MSW, ACSW, CSW NCC, has been a therapist/educator. He has served on four professional speakers' bureaus addressing HIV/AIDS. He also presents programs on dysfunctional group dynamics/issues of the workplace, and men's issues.

Pamela D. Sherer, Ph.D., is Associate Professor of Management at Providence College, Providence, Rhode Island. Her research interests include diversity issues, faculty development practices, collaborative learning, and pedagogy and its technology.

Charles Dwaine Srock is an instructor of business studies at the Richard Stockton College of New Jersey, specializing in OB, management skills, and organizational development. He is completing his doctorate in management at Capella University.

Michael Whitty, Ph.D., is Professor of Labor Relations and Management, College of Business Administration, University of Detroit Mercy. He has published articles on AIDS in the workplace and on the ADA in the *Labor Law Journal*.

INDEX